Laurence Hutton

Literary Landmarks of London

Laurence Hutton

Literary Landmarks of London

ISBN/EAN: 9783743310711

Manufactured in Europe, USA, Canada, Australia, Japa

Cover: Foto ©ninafisch / pixelio.de

Manufactured and distributed by brebook publishing software (www.brebook.com)

Laurence Hutton

Literary Landmarks of London

LITERARY LANDMARKS

OF LONDON

By LAURENCE HUTTON

Fifth Edition

REVISED AND ENLARGED

LONDON

T. FISHER UNWIN

26, PATERNOSTER SQUARE

1889

[*All rights reserved*]

University Press:
JOHN WILSON AND SON, CAMBRIDGE, U.S.A.

PREFACE TO FOURTH EDITION.

THIS edition of THE LITERARY LANDMARKS OF LONDON, printed in cheaper and more popular form, has been thoroughly revised; a few supplementary Notes have been added by way of Appendix; and as far as possible it has been brought down to the present time.

L. H.

JANUARY, 1888.

INTRODUCTION.

LONDON has no associations so interesting as those connected with its literary men. To the cultivated reader the Temple owes its greatest charm to the fact that it was the birthplace of Lamb, the home of Fielding, and that it contains Goldsmith's grave. Addison and Steele have hallowed the now unholy precincts of Charter House Square and Covent Garden; the shade of Chatterton still haunts Shoe Lane; Fleet Street, to this day, echoes with the ponderous tread of Dr. Johnson; and the modest dwelling that was once Will's Coffee House is of far more interest now than all that is left of the royal palaces of Whitehall and St. James.

The Society of Arts, in marking with its tablets certain of the historic houses of London, is deserving of much praise; but only a few of the many famous old buildings which still exist in the metropolis are thus distinguished, and no definite clew to their position is given, even in the best of guide-books. When the houses themselves have disappeared, the ordinary searcher, in nearly all instances, has the utmost difficulty in finding anything more than a faint indication of their site. To remedy this in some measure is what is designed in the following pages. They are intended simply as a guide to a side of London which has never before received particular attention. The places of literary association in the metropolis and in the suburbs are noted with more or less accuracy in the ordinary hand-books and in the thousands of volumes — historical, traditional, local, and anecdotal — that have been published about the Great City; but in no single work has any attempt hitherto been made to follow the literary worthies of England to the spots they have known and loved in London as they have journeyed from the cradle to the grave.

The chief aims of this book have been completeness and exactness. It contains not only a great deal of matter which has never been printed before, but it verifies the statements and corrects the mistakes of the works that have gone before it. Innumerable volumes upon London have been consulted, from Stow and Strype to the younger Dickens; early insurance surveys, containing the number and position of every house in London since houses were first numbered, in 1767, have been compared with similar surveys of the present, by means of tracings and by actual measurements of the streets themselves; the first maps of London have been examined and compared in like manner with later and contemporary plans; directories for the last century and a half have been studied carefully; and it has been possible by these means to discover and note the exact sites of many interesting buildings, the position of which has hitherto been merely a matter of conjecture or entirely unknown.

The history of the London Directory has yet to be written. The oldest volume of that kind in the Library of the British Museum was "Published and sold by Henry Kent in Finch Lane, near the Royal Exchange," in 1736. It is a small pamphlet of fifty pages, and the original price was sixpence. It is prefaced by the following remarks: "The Difficulty which People are continually under, who have Business to transact, for Want of knowing where to find One Another, makes such a little PIECE as this very Useful, by saving a great deal of Trouble, Expense, and Loss of Time, in Dispatch of Affairs, especially to Merchants, Bankers and others who deal in Notes and Bills of Exchange."[1]

This directory was published at irregular intervals until 1827. In the earlier volumes, as the houses were not numbered, only the business streets and the names of residents who were business men were inserted. It was followed in 1772 by a rival Directory " Printed for T. Lowndes, No. 77 Fleet Street," the price of which was one shilling, and which contained, as the advertisement stated, " An Alphabetical List of the Names and Places of Abode of the Merchants and Principal Traders of the City of London, and Westminster, and the Borough of Southwark and their Environs, with the number of each House." This series lived only until 1799. The numbers of the houses were given first in Kent's Directory for 1768.

The official Post Office Directory was first published when Lowndes retired in 1799; and the separate Trades and Court departments first appeared in 1841. The initial number of " Boyle's Fashionable Court and Country Guide " is dated 1796, and it is continued to the present day. It contained from the outset an irregular court and street directory, both of the City and West ends of the town; but it was naturally less complete and thorough than the official Post Office Directory of the present day.

The difficulties met with in the preparation of the following pages have been many and great. Old houses have disappeared, streets have been renamed and renumbered, and in many instances entire streets have been swept away in the dreadful march of improvement. It is easier to-day to discover the house of a man who died two hundred years ago, before streets were numbered at all, than to identify the houses of men who have died within a few years, and since the mania for changing the names and numbers of streets began. Dryden, for instance, was living in 1686 in a house 'on the north side of Long Acre, over against Rose Street,' and easily traced now by the Dryden Press, which stands upon its site; while the house in which Carlyle lived for nearly half a century, and in which he died in 1881, when it was No. 5 Great Cheyne Row, Chelsea, was in 1885 No. 24 Great Cheyne Row, with nothing to distinguish it from the new No. 5 on the opposite side of the way.

The confusion caused by this renumbering and renaming can hardly be expressed in words, nor does there seem to the ordinary observer to be any good reason for these changes. Oxford Street, which Pennant described in 1790 as the longest street in Europe, was considered not long enough, and has been extended by the absorption of New Oxford Street, and renumbered; while the New Road, an equally important thoroughfare running nearly parallel with it from City Road to Edgeware Road, was deemed too long, and has been divided into Pentonville Road, Euston Road, and Marylebone Road, and of course renumbered. The following note, quoted in full from the London Post Office Directory for 1882, will give some faint idea of the confusion of numbers:—

That part of Oxford Street which lies to the west of Tottenham Court Road has been renumbered, the numbers beginning at Tottenham Court Road, and ending at the Marble Arch, — the even numbers being on the north, and the odd numbers on the south side; but the numbers of that part of the street which lies to the east of Tottenham Court Road not having been altered, many of the numbers in that part of the street are duplicates of new numbers which are near the Marble Arch: these duplicate numbers are distinguished here by being printed in black type, thus **(468)**. To avoid confusion, care should be taken, in addressing letters, to add the correct postal initials; and it may be desirable for the duplicated numbers to add either 'near Marble Arch,' or 'near Holborn,' as the case may be, as part of the address.

I rest this portion of my case here.

By some strange fatality the most interesting of the old buildings in London have been removed or — what is often worse — restored, while adjacent old buildings about which no tradition or association lingers are left intact. Drayton's house, in Fleet Street, has been altered and changed beyond recognition, but the two houses next door to it remain as in Drayton's day. The Bell Inn at Edmonton — Gilpin's Bell, and a favorite haunt of Charles Lamb during the last years of his life — has been taken down, in favor of a dull, commonplace public house, about which there is nothing attractive except its name, The Bell; while on all sides of it there exist, from the days of Lamb and Cowper and long before, and in all their old-fashioned picturesque beauty, the contemporary inns which neither of them chanced to make immortal.

It will be observed that no attempt has been made here to write a text-book or a biographical dictionary. Nothing has been preserved in these pages concerning the members of the guild of literature from Addison to Young excepting what may relate to their career in London; and the book appeals only to those who love and are familiar with Pepys and Johnson and Thackeray, and who wish to follow them to their homes and their haunts in the metropolis, — not to those who need to be told who Pepys and Johnson and Thackeray were, and what they have done. It will be observed, too, that the rank of these men in the world of letters is not to be inferred from the amount of space devoted to them here. Wordsworth and Herrick have assigned to them but a few lines, simply because they were not poets of brick and mortar, and knew almost nothing of town life; while whole pages are sometimes bestowed upon the half-forgotten authors of one immortal song, who spent all their days in London, and loved it well. A few writers will be missed, who, although British, — as Burns, Lever, and the Kingsleys, — have little or no association with London; while others have not been included, because, like Blake, they may be better known as painters, or, like Garrick, more famous as actors than as men of letters. These will find place, perhaps, in succeeding volumes, to be devoted to the artistic and dramatic memories of the metropolis. Living writers, of course, are not mentioned at all.

For the convenience of those interested in any particular writer, it has been thought best to arrange the work in the alphabetical sequence of the authors' names, and not topographically or chronologically, as is the ordinary plan; and to add to the interest, an attempt has been made to let the different subjects of the work speak for themselves, or to let their contemporaries speak for them, wherever it is possible so to do, giving in every instance in the margin the authorities quoted.

It is hoped that the full indices, local as well as personal, will enable the general reader to find, in any particular part of the town, what appeals to him most, and show him what is within his reach, no matter where he may be. By means of these, for example, it will be very easy, in walking with Johnson and Boswell from the club in Gerard Street through Long Acre and Bow Street, to Tom Davies's shop in Russell Street, Covent Garden, to call by the way on Dryden, Wycherley, Waller, Fielding, Charles Lamb, and Evelyn; to stop for refreshments at Will's or Button's or Tom's with Steele, Addison, Colley Cibber, Pepys, Davenant, and Pope; and going a step or two further to utter a silent prayer perhaps in the Church of St. Paul, Covent Garden, for the repose of the souls of Butler, Wycherley, Mrs. Centlivre, and 'Peter Pindar,' who sleep within its gates.

L. H.

April 7, 1885.

LITERARY LANDMARKS OF LONDON.

LITERARY LANDMARKS OF LONDON.

JOSEPH ADDISON.

1672–1719.

ALTHOUGH Addison wrote his name strongly and clearly in the literature and politics of England in the eighteenth century, and although he was closely identified with London, the traces he has left of his actual presence in the metropolis are few and slight.

Concerning his London homes, until his marriage in 1716 and settlement in Holland House, his biographers are strangely silent, and but little is to be gathered from the gossip of his contemporaries. It is only known that he lived in the Haymarket, in Kensington Square, in St. James's Place, St. James's Street, at Fulham, and at Chelsea.

His earliest associations with London were with the Charter House School, to which, after studying under his father's eye at Lichfield and Salisbury, he was sent as a private pupil. Here he was carefully drilled in the classics, and here too he first made the acquaintance of Steele, with whom in after years he was so intimately connected. The Charter House School stood, through many generations of boys, in Charter House Square, Smithfield. In 1872 those portions of the grounds which belonged to the school itself were transferred to the Merchant Taylors' Company, by whom new school-buildings were erected; but the Charter

House proper remained in 1885, as in Addison's day, with its chapel and cloisters, and its Pensioner's Hall, the home of the Poor Brethren, so familiar to all readers of 'The Newcomes.'

Addison left the Charter House in 1687 to enter Queen's College, Oxford; but he returned to London in 1703, and found lodgings in the Haymarket.

Pope was one day taking his usual walk with Harte in the Haymarket, when he desired him to enter a little shop, where, going up three pairs of stairs into a small room, Pope said, 'In this garret Addison wrote his "Campaign."'

<small>D'Israeli's Literary Characters.</small>

There is, unfortunately, no hint given by Pope, or by any of Addison's biographers, as to the position or number of Addison's Haymarket home.[2] His mode of life at this period, however, is thus described:—

We find it to have been the custom of Addison to be scarcely ever unprovided of some retreat in the immediate neighborhood of London, where he might employ his evenings and his leisure hours in study and the labor of composition; a satisfactory refutation of the injurious account given by Spence, on the authority of Pope, which represents him as habitually passing his evenings, often far into the night, in coffee-houses and taverns with a few convivial and obsequious companions. Sandy End, a hamlet of Fulham, was at this time [1707] his country retirement. He appears to have occupied apartments in a lodging or boarding house established at this place, whence several of the published letters of Steele are dated, written at times when he seems to have been the guest of Addison.

<small>Lucy Aikin's Life of Addison, chap. vii.</small>

When the time came to leave, Esmond marched homeward to his lodgings, and met Mr. Addison on the road, walking to a cottage which he had at Fulham, the moon shining on his handsome serene face. 'What cheer, brother?' says Addison, laughing. 'I thought it was

<small>Thackeray's Esmond, book iii. chap. ix.</small>

a footpad advancing in the dark, and behold, it is an old friend. We may shake hands, Colonel, in the dark; 't is better than fighting by daylight. Why should we quarrel because I am a Whig and thou art a Tory? Turn thy steps and walk with me to Fulham, where there is a nightingale still singing in the garden, and a cool bottle in a cave I know of. You shall drink to the Pretender, if you like. I will drink my liquor in my own way.'

Letters of Addison to the young Earl of Warwick, dated simply at Chelsea, are said to have been written — but this is merely traditional — in Sandford Manor House, at one time the residence of Nell Gwynne. This house, standing in 1885, was a little south of King's Road, towards the Thames.

That Addison was living in the village of Kensington in 1712, when Swift was his neighbor, there seems to be no question, although the site or the character of his house there is not now known.

The parish books do not give the name of Addison in either row (houses were not numbered in London till 1764), so that it is impossible to identify any particular dwelling now with the house of one of the kindest benefactors that society ever had. Still, it is pleasing to picture somewhere in the old square [Kensington Square] one of whom Thackeray, a hundred and forty years after, thus wrote from the same place: 'When this man looks from the world, whose weaknesses he describes so benevolently, up to Heaven, which shines on us all, I can hardly fancy a human face lighted up with more serene rapture, or a human intellect thrilling with a purer love and adoration, than that of Joseph Addison.'

Notes on Kensington Square.

Addison was married, in 1716, to the dowager Countess of Warwick; and their courtship Johnson likens to that of Sir Roger de Coverley with his disdainful widow. They do not seem to have been very happy in their union, which began and ended in the famous Holland House, Kensington Road, Kensington, one of the most interesting spots in all

England for the sake of its literary associations, and still standing in its noble grounds, in 1885.

Addison, according to the traditions of Holland House, used, when composing, to walk up and down the long gallery there, with a bottle of wine at each end of it, which he finished during the operation. There is a little white house, too, near the turnpike, to which he used to retire when the Countess was particularly troublesome.

<small>Thomas Moore's Diary, Oct. 23, 1818.</small>

This 'little white house' was the White Horse Inn, which stood on the corner of what have since been called Holland Lane and Kensington Road. It has disappeared; but on its site was built, in 1866, a public house called the Holland Arms Inn, where were preserved, in 1885, the fine old mahogany fittings of the original tavern, — benches upon which Addison and Steele have often sat, and tables which have held their bottles and their elbows, and heard their familiar talk.

It seems to have been in Holland House (for he died shortly afterwards) that Addison was visited by Milton's daughter, when he requested her to bring him some evidences of her birth. The moment he beheld her he exclaimed: 'Madam, you need no other voucher; your face is a sufficient testimonial whose daughter you are.' It must have been very pleasing to Addison to befriend Milton's daughter, for he had been the first to popularize the great poet by his critiques on 'Paradise Lost,' in the 'Spectator.'

<small>Leigh Hunt's Old Court Suburb, chap. xv.</small>

Addison died in Holland House, June 17, 1719.

The end of this useful life was now approaching. Addison had for some time been oppressed by shortness of breath, which was now aggravated by a dropsy, and, finding his danger pressing, he prepared to die conformably to his own precepts and professions. . . . Lord Warwick [his step-son] was a young man of very irregular life, and perhaps of loose opinions. Addison, for whom he did not

<small>Johnson's Lives of the Poets: Addison.</small>

want respect, had very diligently endeavored to reclaim him, but his arguments and expostulations had no effect. One experiment, however, remained to be tried. When he found his life near its end, he directed the young Lord to be called, and when he desired, with great tenderness, to hear his last injunction, told him : 'I have sent for you that you may see how a Christian can die.'

This account of Addison's last hours is not entirely credited by later writers. Hunt, in his 'Old Court Suburb' (chap. xv.), says: —

The story originated with Young, who said he had it from Tickell, adding that the Earl led an irregular life which Addison wished to reclaim. But, according to Malone, who was a scrupulous inquirer, there is no evidence of the Earl's having led any such life ; and Walpole, in one of his letters that were published not long ago, startled — we should rather say shocked — the world by telling them that Addison died of brandy. It is acknowledged by his best friends that the gentle moralist, whose bodily temperament was a sorry one as his mind was otherwise, had gradually been tempted to stimulate it with wine till he became intemperate in the indulgence. It is impossible to say what other stimulants might not gradually have crept in ; nor is it impossible that during the patient's last hours the physician himself might have ordered them.

It was but fitting that Addison, whose description of Westminster Abbey has been written in letters that cannot fade, should have found a resting-place within its walls, to await there, as he expresses it ('Spectator,' No. 26), 'that great day when we shall all of us be contemporaries, and make our appearance together.' He was buried in the north aisle of Henry the Seventh's Chapel; but his grave was unmarked for nearly a century, and the monument to his memory in the Poets' Corner was not erected until 1808.

Addison's body lay in state in the Jerusalem Chamber, and was borne thence to the Abbey at dead of night. The choir sang a funeral hymn. Bishop Atterbury, one of those Tories who had loved and honored the most accomplished of the Whigs, met the corpse, and led the procession by torch-light round the shrine of St. Edward, and the graves of the Plantagenets, to the Chapel of Henry VII.

Macaulay's Essays, vol. iii.

Addison, even after his marriage, as has been seen, was not one of the most domestic of men; and it is easier now to trace him to his clubs and his taverns than to his own firesides.

Addison's chief companions, before he married Lady Warwick, were Steele, Davenant, etc. He used to breakfast with one or other of them at his lodgings in St. James's Place, dine at taverns with them, then to Button's, and then to some tavern again for supper in the evening; and this was then the usual round of his life.

Spence's Anecdotes; Pope, section v., 1737-39.

Addison studied all morning, then dined at a tavern, and went afterwards to Button's. Button had been a servant in the Countess of Warwick's family, who [sic], under the patronage of Addison, kept a coffee-house on the south side of Russell Street, about two doors from Covent Garden. Here it was that the wits of that time used to assemble. It is said that when Addison had suffered any vexation from the Countess he withdrew the company from Button's house. From this coffee-house he went again to a tavern, where he often sat late and drank too much wine.

Johnson's Lives of the Poets: Addison.

It is reported to have been one of the most exquisite entertainments to the choice spirits, in the beginning of this [eighteenth] century, to get Addison and Steele together in company for the evening. Steele entertained them till he was tipsy, when the same wine that stupefied him only served to elevate Addison, who took up the ball just as Steele dropped it, and kept it up for the rest of the evening.

The Connoisseur, No. 92.

Addison frequented also the Devil Tavern in Fleet Street, opposite St. Dunstan's Church, the famous Devil Tavern of Ben Jonson (q. v.). Child's Bank, No. 1 Fleet Street, stands upon its site.

I dined to-day [October 12] with Dr. Garth and Mr. Addison at the Devil Tavern, near Temple Bar; and Garth treated. And it is well I dine every day, else I should be longer making out my letters. . . . Mr. Addison's election has passed easy and undisputed, and I believe if he had a mind to be chosen King he would not be refused. Swift's Journal to Stella, 1710.

Addison himself, in the 'Spectator,' tells of his familiarity with other well-known lounging-places of his day:—

Sometimes I am seen thrusting my head into a round of politicians at Will's, and listening with great attention to the narratives that are made in those little circular audiences. Sometimes I smoke a pipe at Child's, and while I seem attentive to nothing but the 'Postman,' overhear the conversation of every table in the room. I appear on Sunday nights at the St. James's Coffee House, and sometimes join the committee of politics in the inner room as one who comes there to hear and improve. My face is likewise very well known in the Grecian, the Cocoa Tree, and in the theatres. Spectator, No. 1.

Will's Coffee House, the father of the modern Club, played a very important part in the literature of the seventeenth and eighteenth centuries. It was on the northwest corner of Russell Street and Bow Street, Covent Garden, and included the two adjoining houses, one in each street. The old house, No. 21 Russell Street, still standing in 1885, is no doubt one of the original buildings.

Of Child's, in St. Paul's Churchyard, there is no trace left to-day, and even its exact site is unknown. The St. James's Coffee House was 'the last house but one on the southwest corner of St. James's Street, facing Pall Mall,' and was taken down in 1806. The Grecian stood on the site of a portion of Eldon Chambers, Devereux Court, Strand, between Essex Court and New Court in the Temple. It is marked by a tablet, and a bust of Essex, said to be the work of Caius Gabriel Cibber; and the Grecian Chambers at its back perpetuate its name. The Cocoa Tree Tavern stood at No. 64

St. James's Street, Piccadilly, where the Cocoa Tree Club afterwards was built.

Among his other places of resort were Squire's Coffee House in Fulwood's Rents, No. 34 High Holborn, where were, in 1885, old houses dating back to Addison's time; Serle's Coffee House, on the corner of Serle and Portugal Streets, Lincoln's Inn Fields, the old-fashioned door-posts of which were preserved in the stationer's shop on its site in 1885; "Dick's," No. 8 Fleet Street, a modernized French restaurant in 1885, the windows of whose square room at the back looked on the trees of Hare Court in the Temple; and the Bull and Bush, a quaint and picturesque old countrified inn, still standing in 1885, at the bottom of North End Road, Hammersmith.

Addison, after his return from the Continent in 1704, joined the famous Kit Kat Club, which was 'composed of thirty-nine noblemen and gentlemen, zealously attached to the Protestant succession of the House of Hanover.' It met originally in Shire Lane, at the Cat and Fiddle, which is said to have been called subsequently the Trumpet, and as such, is mentioned by Steele in the 'Tatler.' Still later it was known as the Duke of York's. With the street in which it stood, it has long since disappeared. Shire Lane itself, afterwards called Lower Serle's Place, was swept out of existence in 1868, with some thirty other disreputable lanes and alleys, to make way for the new Law Courts in Fleet Street and the Strand. It was on the east side of the present buildings, and had several outlets into the Strand at or near Temple Bar. Its reputation was always bad, and in the reign of the first James it was known as Rogue's Lane.

Spence's Anecdotes: Pope.   You have heard of the Kit Kat Club. . . . The master of the house where the club met was Christopher Kat. . . . Steele, Addison, Congreve, Garth, Vanbrugh, etc., were of it. . . . Jacob [Tonson] had his own and all their pictures by Sir Godfrey Kneller. Each member gave his; and he is going to build a room for them at Barn-Elms.

The forty-two pictures presented by the members of this club to Tonson the bookseller were removed by him in the beginning of the last century to Barn-Elms, and placed near his house, in a handsome room lately standing on the grounds of Henry Hoare, Esq. It was lined with red cloth, and measured forty feet in length, twenty in width, and eighteen in height. At the death of Mr. Tonson, in 1736, they became the property of his great-nephew, who died in 1767. They were then removed to Water Oakley, near Windsor, and afterwards to Mr. Baker's, in Hertingfordbury. _{Smith's Antiquarian Rambles in London, vol. i.}

Barn-Elms was at Barnes on the Thames, between Putney and Mortlake. Copies of the Kit Kat portrait of Addison are in the National Portrait Gallery, South Kensington, and in the Bodleian Library, Oxford. The club met later at the King's Arms Tavern, which stood on the north side of Pall Mall, near the Haymarket, and on the site of the Opera Colonnade. It went out of existence as a club early in the eighteenth century. Its place of summer resort was the Upper Flask, a tavern on the edge of Hampstead Heath, which has been for many years a private house. It was on the corner of East Heath Road in 1885; its old entrance-hall and low-ceilinged rooms still unchanged, although many additions and alterations had been made. And in its gardens, nearly opposite the Pool, stood, until destroyed in the great storm of Christmas, 1876, the famous mulberry-tree, showing every sign of its gray old age, under which had sat, through so many Arcadian afternoons, Addison, Pope, Steele, Congreve, and their compeers, when, because of their presence,

> 'Hampstead, towering in superior sky,
> Did with Parnassus in honor vie.'

MARK AKENSIDE.

1721-1770.

AKENSIDE came to London in 1747, when he took up his residence for a year or two in the house of his warm friend and patron, Jeremiah Dyson, on the top of Golder's Hill, near North End, Fulham. In 1749 or 1750, through Dyson's generosity, he was established as a practising physician in Bloomsbury Square.

Mr. Dyson parted with his villa at North End, and settled his friend [Akenside] in a sensible house in Blooms-bury Square, assigning him, with unexampled liberality, £300 a year, which enabled him to keep a chariot and make a proper appearance in the world.

Park's Hampstead (1818), p. 331.

Although Bucke, in his 'Life of Akenside,' says that the remainder of his life was passed in Bloomsbury Square, he is known to have been living in Craven Street, Strand, in 1759, before houses were numbered; and in 1762 he took a house in Old Burlington Street, Burlington Gardens, where, in 1770, he died. He was buried in an unmarked grave in St. James's Church, Piccadilly.

Akenside, in 1759, was appointed physician to St. Thomas's Hospital, then situated in Southwark, on the Borough High Street, between Thomas, Denman, and Joiner Streets. It was removed in 1871. Akenside's favorite resorts were Serle's Coffee House, on the corner of Serle and Portugal Streets (see ADDISON, p. 8); the Grecian, Devereux Court, Strand (see ADDISON, p. 7); and Tom's Coffee House, also in Devereux Court, which no longer exists, but which is not to be confounded with the Tom's of Russell Street, Covent Garden. He was also frequently to be found at the sign of The Tully's Head, the book-shop of Robert Dodsley, and a popular meeting-place of men of letters in London for several generations. It stood at the present No. 51 Pall Mall, 'the house with the archway leading into King's Place.' King's Place, running from King Street to Pall Mall, and subsequently called Pall Mall Place for some mysterious reason, was arched over, in 1885, by an old house; but no book-shop existed there, although there were book-dealers in plenty in its immediate neighborhood.

FRANCIS BACON.

1560-61-1626.

BACON was born at York House, on the Thames, in January, 1560-61, and christened in the old Church of St. Martin-in-the-Fields, standing on the site of the present structure.

He returned to York House in later years, and lived there for a time as Lord Chancellor of England, when it is recorded that in 1620 he kept his birthday in great splendor and magnificence, Ben Jonson celebrating the occasion by a 'short performance in verse.'

Lord Bacon, being in Yorke House garden looking on fishers throwing their nett, asked them what they would take for their draught. They answered *so much*. His lordship would offer them no more, but *so much*. They drew up their nett, and in it were only two or three little fishes. His lordship told them it had been better for them to have taken his offer. They replied they hoped to have

_{Aubrey's Lives of Eminent Persons: Bacon.}

had a better draught. But said his lordship: *Hope is a good breakfast, but an ill supper.*

York House, afterwards the property of the Dukes of Buckingham, when it was still called York House, stood on the site of George Court, and of Villiers, Duke, and Buckingham Streets, Strand; its later tenants perpetuating their names and their occupancy of the mansion in that way. Nothing is left of it now but the grand old watergate at the foot of Buckingham Street, the work of Inigo Jones; although portions of the old house, with the original highly decorated ceilings, were preserved until 1863, when the erection of the Charing Cross Railway Station and Hotel wiped them completely out of existence.

In 1592 Bacon entertained Queen Elizabeth at Twickenham Park, Twickenham, but his house has been taken down. The estate is covered with villas; and no trace of it, as it existed at that time, remains.

Bacon was married, in 1606, at the Chapel of St. Marylebone, described by Hepworth Dixon, in his 'Personal History of Bacon,' as standing then 'two miles from the Strand, among the lanes and suburbs wandering towards the foot of Hampstead Hill.' This church was on the site of the parish church built in 1741 on Marylebone Road, near Marylebone High Street.

Bacon was a member of Gray's Inn, and occupied chambers there for many years.

Lord Bacon, whom we have already mentioned as a member of Gray's Inn, lived at No. 1 Coney Court, which was unfortunately burnt down in 1678. The site is occupied by the present [1868] row of buildings at the west end of Gray's Inn Square, adjoining the gardens in which the great philosopher took such delight.

<small>Jesse's London, vol. iii.: Gray's Inn.</small>

He is said to have designed these gardens, and to have planted the old catalpa-tree still standing there in 1885.

Bacon is said to have found a temporary retreat at Parson's Green, Fulham; but the character of the Green has greatly changed of late years (see RICHARDSON), and neither the biographers of Bacon nor the local historians give any decided information as to the positive site of his Fulham home.

When the great Lord Bacon fell into disgrace, and was forbidden to appear at Court, he procured a license, dated September 13, 1621, to retire for six weeks to the house of his friend, Sir John Vaughan, at Parson's Green, who probably resided in the house now [1816] occupied by Mr. Maxwell as a boarding-school, a spacious mansion, built in that style of architecture which prevailed at the commencement of the reign of James I. _{Brayley's London and Middlesex, vol. v.}

Bacon died at the house of the Earl of Arundel, at Highgate, April 9, 1626, and was buried in St. Michael's Church, within the precincts of old Verulam.

The cause of his lordship's death was trying an experiment as he was taking aire in the coach of Dr. Witherborne, a Scotchman, physitian to the King. Towards Highgate _{Aubrey's Lives.}
snow lay on the ground, and it came into my lord's thoughts why flesh might not be preserved in snow as in salt. They were resolved they would try the experiment. Presently they alighted out of the coach, and went into a poore woman's house at the bottom of Highgate Hill, and bought a hen, and made her exenterate, and then stuffed the bodie with snow, and my lord did help to doe it himself. The snow so chilled him that he immediately fell so ill that he could not return to his lodgings (I suppose then at Gray's Inn), but went to the Earl of Arundel's house at Highgate, where they put him into a good bed, warmed with a panne; but it was a dampe bed that had not been layn in for about a year before, which gave him such a colde that in two or three days he died of suffocation.

Arundel House stood on the slope of Highgate Hill. It is known to have been occupied as a school in its later days, and according to Thorne, in his 'Hand-Book of the Environs of London,' it was pulled down in 1825; but neither Thorne nor any other writers upon the subject have been able to discover its exact position.

<small>Eliza Meteyard's Hallowed Spots of Ancient London, chap. iv.</small>
No account of the site of Lord Arundel's house at Highgate has been preserved. To clear up this point, Mr. Montague made many inquiries, though to no purpose. We have likewise sought in vain. It is supposed, however, to have been the most considerable house in the parish.

JOANNA BAILLIE.

1762–1851.

THE Baillies came to London in 1791, when they lived in Great Windmill Street, Piccadilly, in the house of their brother, Dr. Matthew Baillie, who took possession of it after the death of their uncle, the famous Dr. Hunter. It was a large, square, double house, on the east side, standing back from the street, and was numbered 16 in 1885.

In 1802 they went to Red Lion Hill, Hampstead, and on the death of their mother, in 1806, they took Bolton House, at Hampstead, where they spent the remainder of their uneventful lives, and where at the end of half a century they died. Bolton House, still standing in 1885, was a quiet, picturesque, old-fashioned mansion, on the top of Windmill Hill, built of red brick and three stories in height. It was the centre house of a row of three companion buildings, facing the Holly Bush Inn, and at the end of the street called Holly Hill.

Joanna Baillie lived many years at Hampstead, in Bolton House, on Windmill Hill, a little below the Clock House. Perhaps no person of literary distinction ever led a more secluded and unambitious life so near the metropolis. In the society of her sister, Miss Agnes Baillie, she seemed to care but little whether the world forgot her or not. But of this forgetfulness there was no danger. Every man of pre-eminent genius delighted to do her honor. The last time I saw the poet Rogers he was returning from a call on Joanna Baillie. William Howitt's Northern Heights of London: Hampstead.

Henry Crabb Robinson thus describes a visit to Joanna Baillie, in May, 1812 : —

We [Wordsworth and Robinson] met Miss Joanna Baillie and accompanied her home. She is small in figure, and her gait is mean and shuffling, but her manners are those of a well-bred lady. She has none of the unpleasant airs too common to literary ladies. Her conversation is sensible. . . . Wordsworth said of her with warmth : 'If I had to present to a foreigner any one as a model of an English gentlewoman, it would be Joanna Baillie.'

Joanna Baillie was buried in an altar tomb surrounded by iron railings, in Hampstead Churchyard, on the southeast side of the church, and near the gate and the churchyard wall. Within the church a mural tablet has been erected to her memory. Agnes Baillie, who survived her sister ten years, lived to the great age of an hundred and one. She lies in the same grave.

ANNA LETITIA BARBAULD.

1743-1825.

IN 1785 Mrs. Barbauld was living with her husband at Well Walk, Hampstead; and there the 'Correspondence of Richardson' was edited and given to the public. Later, she occupied a house on the west side of Rosslyn Hill, Hampstead, while Mr. Barbauld, a dissenting minister, preached in the Presbyterian chapel on the High Street there. This chapel was taken down in 1828. His next charge was at Newington Green; and his chapel on the north side of the Green, built in 1708, enlarged in 1860, was still standing in 1885. Mrs. Barbauld died in Church Street, Stoke Newington, in 1825, and was buried near the southern entrance of Stoke Newington Churchyard.

RICHARD BAXTER.

1615-1691.

THE domestic life of Baxter was very happy, but as unsettled as the times in which he lived. He was frequently in London, and had many temporary homes in and about the city. He was married, September 10, 1662, to Margaret Charlton, — 'A Breviate' of whose life he wrote, — in the Church of St. Bennet Fink, Broad Street Ward, near Finch Lane, Cornhill. This church was destroyed in the Great Fire, four years later.

For some years after the Restoration Baxter lived at Acton, a village on the Uxbridge Road, five miles beyond the Marble Arch, in a house no longer standing, and only described as being 'near the Church.' While here he was arrested and confined for a short time in the King's Bench Prison, then on the east side of the Borough High Street, Southwark, immediately adjoining the Marshalsea (see DICKENS). This building was taken down towards the close of the last century, and the new prison, built on the Borough Road, corner of Blackman Street, not very far distant, has itself since disappeared. Of his life here he wrote :—

My imprisonment was no great suffering to me, for I had an honest jailer who showed me all the kindness he could. I had a large room and liberty to walk in a fair garden, and my wife was never so cheerful a companion to me as in prison, and was very much against my seeking to be relieved, and she brought me so many necessaries that we kept house as contentedly and comfortably as at home, though in a narrower room ; and I had a sight of more friends in a day than I had at home in half a year.

His wife died in his 'most pleasant and convenient house' in Southampton Square, now Bloomsbury Square, in 1681.

He preached and lectured frequently in London: in the old church of St. Dunstan-in-the-West, Fleet Street, just inside Temple Bar; in St. Mary Magdalen's, Milk Street, Cheapside, destroyed in the Great Fire, and never rebuilt; in Park Street, Southwark, 'not far from the Brewery' (of Barclay and Perkins); in Swallow Street, Piccadilly; in Pinner's Hall, and in St. James's Market Place.

After the indulgence in 1672, he returned into the city, and was one of the Tuesday lecturers in Pinner's Hall, and had a Friday lecture in Fetter Lane [near Neville Court]; but on the Lord's days he for some time preached only occasionally, and afterwards more stately, in St.

Biographia Britannica: Baxter.

James's Market Place, where, in 1671, he had a wonderful delivery, by almost a miracle, from a crack in the floor.

Swallow Street ran from Piccadilly in a direct line to Oxford Street, a few yards west of what has since been called Oxford Circus. Its site is the present Regent Street, built in 1813 to connect Carlton House with Regent's Park. Strype described it as 'being very long . . . but of no great account for buildings or inhabitants.' Swallow Street, Piccadilly, and Swallow Place, Oxford Street, perpetuated its name as late as 1885. Of course no traces of Baxter's chapels remain, either here or in the neighborhood of Park Street, the enormous works of the great brewing firm having replaced whole blocks of houses in Southwark (see SHAKSPERE).

Pinner's Hall stood behind Pinner's Court, No. 54½ Old Broad Street. The modern Pinner's Hall, on the corner of Old Broad and Great Winchester Streets, and built partly on its site, was, in 1885, entirely devoted to business purposes.

St. James's Market, very much curtailed, stood, in 1885, in the block of buildings between Jermyn Street, Charles Street, the present Regent Street, and the Haymarket.

Another of his chapels was in Oxendon Street, on the west side, near Coventry Street. It backed upon the gardens of Mr. Secretary Coventry, who was not in sympathy with Baxter, or his form of worship, and who drove the congregation to other quarters by the disturbances he caused to be made under the chapel windows. This building stood until within a few years, and was latterly the home of a Scottish congregation.

Baxter spent the last years of his life in Charter House Lane, where he died December 8, 1691. He was buried, a few days later, in Christ Church, Newgate Street, by the side of his wife, 'next to the old altar, or table, in the chancel.' On his tomb was inscribed 'The Saint's Rest,' but no trace of it is now to be found.

Among the many houses demolished in 1864, for the purposes of the Metropolitan Meat Market and Metropolitan Railway Extensions, was that in which once resided, and where died, this eminent Non-conformist minister [Baxter], in 1691. The dwelling stood for many years; and although it was frequently repaired, the larger portion of it remained until 1864, on the eastern side of Charter House Lane, near to the Charter House. Pink's History of Clerkenwell, Appendix.

Charter House Lane was the eastern end of the present Charter House Street, running from St. John Street to the Square.

FRANCIS BEAUMONT.

1585–1615-16.

BEAUMONT was entered a member of the Inner Temple November 3, 1600; but of his life in London little is known, and that only during his association with Fletcher (see FLETCHER). Aubrey says:—

There was a wonderful consimilarity of phansy between him and Mr. Jo. Fletcher, which caused that dearnesse of friendship between them. I thinke they were both of Queene's Coll, in Cambridge. I have heard Dr. Jo. Earle say, who knew them, that his maine business was to correct the overflowing of Mr. Fletcher's witt. They lived together on the Bankside, not far from the Play House. . . . [They had] the same cloaths and cloaks &tc. between them.

The Play House was the Globe Theatre, the site of which is now covered by the Brewery of Barclay and Perkins, near Southwark Bridge Road (see SHAKSPERE). There remained in 1885 a number of quaint, plastered, two-storied houses on the Bankside, which were old enough to have harbored these twin spirits.

Tradition says that Beaumont and Fletcher were frequenters of the Mermaid Tavern in Cheapside, where Jonson and Shakspere were their companions (see JONSON). Beaumont was buried, according to the Register of Westminster Abbey, 'at the entrance of St. Benedict's Chapel, March 9, 1615-16.' He lies near Chaucer, in an unmarked grave.

ROBERT BLOOMFIELD.

1766-1823.

ROBERT BLOOMFIELD, the son of a tailor, came to London in 1781 to learn the shoemaker's trade. He lodged first, in a very humble way, at No. 7 Pitcher's Court, Great Bell Alley, Coleman Street, City; and later in Blue Hart Court, in the same alley. The character of the alley and its courts has entirely changed during the century that has passed, and no traces of any of his homes here are left.

After his marriage, in 1790, and while working at his cobbler's bench in Great Bell Yard, he wrote 'The Farmer's Boy.'

<small>Cunningham's Handbook of London: Coleman Street.</small> I saw in Mr. Upcott's hand the poet's shop card, neatly engraved and inscribed 'Bloomfield, Ladies' Shoe Maker, No. 14 Great Bell Yard, Coleman Street. The best real Spanish Leather at reasonable prices.'

Great Bell Yard was opposite Great Bell Alley; but its name has been changed to Telegraph Street, and it has been entirely rebuilt. No. 14 Telegraph Street was in 1885 a very new and glaring white glazed tile structure, let out as offices, and called 'The White House.'

JAMES BOSWELL.

1740–1795.

OF Boswell's life in London, so closely identified with that of the subject of his famous biography, but little is to be said, except in connection with Dr. Johnson (q. v.).

He came to the metropolis in 1760, and first met Johnson, in May, 1763, at the shop of Tom Davies, No. 8 Russell Street, Covent Garden (see JOHNSON). In July of the same year he removed from Downing Street to 'the bottom of Inner Temple Lane,' where Johnson was living, in order to be nearer to the object of his devotion. His chambers were in Farrar's Building, now rebuilt; Johnson's, at No. 1 Inner Temple Lane, opposite, are also rebuilt.

In 1768 Boswell was in Half Moon Street, Piccadilly; in 1769, in Old Bond Street, where on the 16th of October he entertained Johnson, Reynolds, Garrick, and Goldsmith; and in 1772 he was lodging in Conduit Street.

He died at No. 47 Great Portland Street, Oxford Street, in 1795. This street has been extended, renumbered and rebuilt. Boswell's house was on the east side, the seventh from the corner of Marylebone Street, towards Langham Street, then Queen Anne Street.

He was buried at his family seat in Scotland.

Johnson succeeded in electing Boswell a member of The Club (see GOLDSMITH and JOHNSON).

Life and Letters of Lord Macaulay, vol. ii. chap. viii.

I was well pleased to meet The Club for the first time. ... I was amused, in turning over the records of The Club, to come upon poor Bozzy's signature, evidently affixed when he was too drunk to guide his pen.

CHARLOTTE BRONTË.

1816–1855.

WHEN Charlotte and Anne Brontë came to London in 1848, without male escort, they stopped at the Chapter Coffee House, No. 50 Paternoster Row, the tavern frequented by their father, the only one of which they had any knowledge in the metropolis, and to which, as guests perhaps, no other women ever went. From here they sallied out to see their publisher, and astonish him with their identity as the authors of 'Jane Eyre' and 'The Tenant of Wildfell Hall.' Although Charlotte afterwards made short visits to London, and was entertained by Rogers and other noted men, she gives no hint in her letters as to where she lodged in later years. The Chapter Coffee House was in existence in 1885, as a place of refreshment, and but little changed (see CHATTERTON).[8]

Mrs. Gaskell's Life of Charlotte Brontë, vol. ii. chap. ii.

Half-way up, on the left-hand side [of Paternoster Row], is the Chapter Coffee House. I visited it last June [1856]. It was then unoccupied. It had the appearance of a dwelling-house two hundred years old or so, such as one sometimes sees in ancient country towns; the ceilings of the small rooms were low, and had heavy beams running across them; the walls were wainscoted, breast-high; the stairs were shallow, broad, and dark, taking up much space in the centre of the house. The gray-haired elderly man who officiated as waiter seems to have been touched from the very first by the quiet simplicity of the two ladies, and he tried to make them feel comfortable and at home in the long, low, dingy room upstairs. The high narrow windows looked into the gloomy Row; the sisters, clinging together in the most remote window-seat (as Mr. Smith tells me he found them when he came that Saturday evening to take them to the Opera), could see nothing of motion or of change in the grim dark houses opposite, so near and close, although the whole breadth of the Row was between.

BULWER LYTTON

1803–1873.

BULWER was born at No. 31 Baker Street, a three-storied plain brick house, standing in 1885, on the east side and next to the corner of Dorset Street; but in his youth his mother lived in Montague Square, in Nottingham Place, Marylebone, and at No. 5 Upper Seymour (now Seymour) Street, Portman Square, corner of Berkeley Mews, and numbered 10 in 1885. His first school was at Fulham, where he remained only a fortnight; his second at Sunbury, in Middlesex, fifteen miles from London, where, as he says in his Autobiography, he 'wasted two years.'

In 1829 he purchased and furnished the house No. 36 Hertford Street, Park Lane, to which he took his wife and infant daughter. It was unchanged in 1885. In 1837 a letter of Bulwer's was dated from 'The Albany' (see BYRON, p. 32).

In the year 1839 James Smith, in a letter, relates: 'I dined yesterday with E. L. Bulwer at his new residence in Charles Street, Berkeley Square, a splendidly and classically fitted up mansion. One of the drawing-rooms is a *fac-simile* of a chamber which our host visited at Pompeii. Vases, candelabra, chairs, tables to correspond. He lighted a perfumed pastille modelled from Vesuvius. As soon as the cone of the mountain began to blaze I found myself an inhabitant of the devoted city. . . .' There must be some mistake in this record ; the house in Charles Street on the north side is certainly not a mansion, but a dwelling of moderate size, and the Running Footman public house.'

<small>Timbs's Wits and Humorists, vol. ii.; James Smith.</small>

'At the time of the publication of 'Zanoni,' in 1841, Bulwer was living at No. 1 Park Lane, in a house since rebuilt.

Dr. Charles J. B. Williams, in his 'Recollections,' published in 1884, thus speaks of Bulwer, who was one of his patients : —

When I visited him at his residence in Park Lane, even on entrance at the outer door, I began to find myself in an atmosphere of perfume, or rather of perfume mixed with tobacco fume. On proceeding further through a long corridor and anteroom the fume waxed stronger, and on entrance to the presence chamber, on a divan at the further end, through a haze of smoke loomed his lordship's figure, wrapt in an Oriental dressing-robe, with a colored fez, and half reclined upon the ottoman.

In 1843 Bulwer occupied Craven Cottage at Fulham, on the banks of the Thames, just beyond the Bishop of London's Meadows. It stood in 1885, a complete but picturesque ruin, and must have been, in its day, a very remarkable specimen of fantastic architecture, embracing the Persian, Gothic, Moorish, and Egyptian styles. In the library Bulwer is said to have written more than one of his novels. He lived later in life at No. 12 Grosvenor Square, on the north side. He died at Torquay, and was buried from his own house, Grosvenor Square, in Westminster Abbey.

His favorite club was the Athenæum, on the southwest corner of Pall Mall and Waterloo Place.

JOHN BUNYAN.

1628-1688.

JOHN BUNYAN during his lifetime had few associations with London, although his bones lie not very far from those of the author of 'Robinson Crusoe' in the Cemetery of Bunhill Fields. He made occasional professional visits to town, however, when he usually preached in the meeting-house in Zoar Street, Southwark, 'near the sign of the Faulcon' (see SHAKSPERE). This Zoar Chapel was about one hundred feet from Gravel Lane, on the left hand of the street going towards that lane. It was used as a wheelwright's shop after Bunyan's time; and when it was destroyed, its pulpit was carried to the Methodist Chapel in Palace Yard, Lambeth. Bunyan gathered together congregations of three thousand persons on Sundays, and twelve or fifteen hundred on week days.

There is a tradition that he had lodgings at one time on London Bridge, but there seems to be but little foundation for the story. While he was on one of these visits to town, in 1688, he died at the house of his friend Mr. Strudwick, a grocer, 'at the Sign of the Star on Snow Hill.' Robert Philips, in his 'Life of Bunyan' (chap. xlv.), quotes, from a manuscript in the Library of the British Museum, the following account of his death:—

Taking a tedious journey in a slabby, rainy day, and returning late to London, he was entertained by one Mr. Strudwick, a grocer on Snow Hill, with all the kind endearments of a loving friend, but soon found himself indisposed with a kind of shaking, as it were an ague, which increasing to a kind of fever, he took to his bed, where, growing worse, he found that he had not long to last in this world, and therefore prepared himself for another, towards which he had been journeying as a PILGRIM and Stranger upon earth the prime of his days.

Snow Hill, in the seventeenth century, is described as having been a circuitous highway, between Holborn Bridge and Newgate, very narrow, very steep, and very dangerous. Pink, in his 'History of Clerkenwell,' believes that the house in which Bunyan died must have been removed when Skinner Street was formed, in 1802, if it existed so long as that. Skinner Street ran by the south side of St. Sepulchre's Church, but was itself wiped out of existence when the Holborn Viaduct was built. It would appear, therefore, that the Sign of the Star was directly under the eastern pier of the Viaduct.

An altar tomb with his recumbent figure upon it, on the southern side of Bunhill Fields Burial Ground, City Road, has been erected to Bunyan's memory, although there seems to be some doubt as to where he was actually buried there.

He was interred at first in the back part of that ground known as 'Baptists' Corner.' The tradition (and I think the probability) is, that his friend Mr. Strudwick 'had given commandment concerning his bones' that they should be transferred to the present vault whenever an interment took place. . . . It does not say, however, that Bunyan is underneath; and I know persons of respectability who affirm that he is not there. One gentleman assures me that the coffin was shown to him in another vault in quite another quarter of the ground. . . . On the other hand, the nephew of the late chaplain of Bunhill Fields informs me that his uncle invited him to see Bunyan's coffin in Strudwick's vault; and the son of the late Manager of the Graves always understood his father to mean, when he said 'that Bunyan was not **buried** there,' that it was not his original grave.

Phillips' Life of Bunyan, chap. xlvi.

EDMUND BURKE.

1730-1797.

BURKE arrived in London in 1750, and kept terms regularly in the Middle Temple. Of the details of his early life and struggles he rarely spoke; and almost nothing is known, except that he lived at 'The Pope's Head, over the shop of Jacob Robinson, bookseller and publisher, just within the Inner Temple Gateway,' and that shortly after his marriage, in 1756, he lived in Wimpole Street, Oxford Street.

The shop of Jacob Robinson has now disappeared, although just within the adjoining Middle Temple Gateway was, in 1885, a curious old house, occupied by a firm of law stationers, who were doing a business which their sign declared to have been 'established two hundred years.' Robinson's shop was on the west side of the Gateway, next the Rainbow Tavern, and was numbered afterwards 16 Fleet Street.

In 1764 Burke was living in Queen Anne Street, Oxford Street, and watching the debates in the House of Commons from the Strangers' Gallery.

In 1780 he occupied a house in Westminster, one side of which, according to Walcott in his 'Memorials of Westminster,' contained 'an arch of the eastern wall of the Old Gate leading into Dean's Yard.' This was a portion of the famous Gate House in which were confined so many illustrious state prisoners. It stood at the end of Tothill Street, covering considerable space on each side of that thoroughfare, and extending from Dean's Yard to the site of the

Westminster Hospital. Burke's house here was taken down some years ago.

In 1781 Burke had removed to the more fashionable neighborhood of St. James's Square.

From St. James's Square we pass eastward into Charles Street, interesting from its having been for a time the residence of Burke. It was here [in 1781] that Crabbe addressed to him that touching letter, and was admitted to that affectionate interview which happily so revolutionized the poet's fortunes.

<small>Jesse's London, vol. i.: St. James's Square.</small>

In 1787 Burke lived at No. 37 Gerard Street, Soho, in a house marked by the tablet of the Society of Arts. In 1793 he lodged at No. 6, and in 1794 at No. 25, Duke Street, St. James's, in houses greatly changed since his day.

He died at Beaconsfield in Buckinghamshire.

Burke's earliest flights of oratory were made in a debating-club held in the Robin Hood Tavern, Essex Street, Strand, of which no trace is now left. He was in after years a member of Brooks's Club, No. 60 St. James's Street, and an original member of The Club (see JOHNSON). He was also frequently to be found at The Tully's Head, Dodsley's Shop, No. 51 Pall Mall (see AKENSIDE).

SAMUEL BUTLER.

1612–1680.

BUTLER'S life in London was neither happy nor prosperous, and but few records are left of his existence here. He is believed to have had chambers at one time in Gray's Inn, although he was not a member of that Society. His later years were passed in poverty, and he died in Rose

Street, Covent Garden, which runs from No. 2 Garrick Street to No. 11 Long Acre (see DRYDEN), and was pronounced by Aubrey 'one of the meanest streets in that part of the city.'

Butler was buried in the yard of St. Paul's Church, Covent Garden; but contemporary authorities differ as to the exact position of his grave.

Butler was of a middle stature, strong sett, high coloured, with a heade of sorrell hair, a good fellowe and latterly much troubled with the gowt. . . . He dyed of a consumption September 25 (Anno D^{ni} 1680 *circiter*) and was buried 27, according to his owne appointment in the church yard of Covent Garden in the north part, next the church, at the east end. His feet touch the wall. His grave two yards distant from the pillaster of the dore (by his desire) 6 foot deepe. About 25 of his old acquaintances at his funerall, I, myself, being one. *Aubrey's Lives: Butler.*

This Samuel Butler, who was a boon and witty companion, especially among the company he knew well, died of a consumption, September 25th, 1680, and was, according to his desire, buried six feet deep in the yard belonging to the Church of St. Paul in Covent Garden, within the liberty of Westminster, viz. at the west end of the said yard, on the north side and under the wall of the church, and under that wall which parts the yard from the common highway. *Anthony Wood's Athenæ Oxonienses, vol. ii.*

A tablet to the memory of Butler was placed on the south side of the church 'by the inhabitants of the parish' in 1786, nine years before the old edifice was destroyed by fire. It was not renewed when the church was rebuilt; and the clerk of the vestry in 1885 had no knowledge of it, or of the position of Butler's grave. The churchyard has been levelled and covered with grass, where it is not paved with fragments of the old tombstones it used to contain, and few memorials to its illustrious dead are now to be found.

LORD BYRON.

1788–1824.

BYRON was born at No. 16⁴ Holles Street, Cavendish Square, in a house since numbered 24, and marked by the tablet of the Society of Arts. It is probably unchanged. He was christened in St. Marylebone Church, on the Marylebone Road near the High Street, when he was about six weeks old; but Mrs. Byron took her son to Scotland in his infancy, and he did not again see London until 1799, when he was brought to a house in Sloane Terrace, Sloane Street, while an eminent surgeon was preparing an instrument for the support of his ankle. He was then sent to a school which stood near the Saline Spring, on Wells Lane, Sydenham, but has now disappeared.

Moore, in his 'Life of Byron,' makes few allusions to his subject's different homes in London and elsewhere, or to his home life; and it is only by the occasional headings of his letters, and by their indirect personal allusions, that he can be traced to his various lodgings in town. In August, 1806, he wrote to a college friend from No. 16 Piccadilly; but he does not appear to have remained then long in London. No. 16 Piccadilly was on the site of Piccadilly Circus, and the house disappeared when Regent Street was formed, a few years later.

In the winter of the same year Byron was for a short time at Dorant's Hotel, which stood in Jermyn Street, nearly opposite Bury Street. Cox's Hotel, No. 56 Jermyn Street, was its direct successor in 1885; and here it was that he read the criticism of the 'Edinburgh Review' upon his 'Hours of Idleness,' which had such an effect upon him that the friend who found him in the first moments of excitement, fancied he had received a challenge to fight a duel, not being able in any other way to account for the hatred and defiance expressed in his face.

Byron occupied lodgings at No. 8 St. James's Street at various times, from early in the year 1808 to 1814. Here he published his 'Satire' in 1809, and from here, on the 30th March in the same year, he drove to take his seat for the first time in the House of Lords. Mr. Dallas writes:—

On that day, passing down St. James's Street, but with no intention of calling, I saw his chariot at his door, and went in. His countenance, paler than usual, showed that his mind was agitated. . . . He said to me, 'I am glad you happened to come in; I am going to take my seat, perhaps you will go with me.' I expressed my readiness to attend him; while at the same time I concealed the shock I felt on thinking that this young man, who by birth, fortune, and talents, stood high in life, should have lived so unconnected and neglected by persons of his own rank, that there was not a single member of the Senate to which he belonged, to whom he could or would apply to introduce him in a manner becoming his birth. I saw that he felt the situation, and I fully partook of his indignation. [Moore's Life of Byron, vol. i., 1809.]

While living in this house, No. 8 St. James's Street, in 1812, and shortly after the publication of 'Childe Harold,' he woke up on that historic morning to find himself famous. The house, still standing in 1885, had been altered, and a story added; but the adjoining house, No. 7, showed how it appeared in Byron's time.

A number of letters of his are addressed from No. 4 Bennet Street, St. James's Street, which he sometimes called 'Benedictine Street,' a house that was still used as a lodging-house half a century later. During these seven or eight years before his marriage he occasionally lived at Stevens's (afterwards Fischer's) Hotel, No. 18 New Bond Street, with an entrance on Clifford Street, opposite Long's; and at Gordon's Hotel, No. 1 Albemarle Street, corner of Piccadilly. According to Mr. Jesse, the greater part of 'The Corsair' was composed by Byron while he was walking up and down Albemarle Street, between Grafton Street and Piccadilly.

On the 9th of April, 1814, Byron wrote to Moore from A, No. 2, The Albany:—

Viscount Althorp is about to be married, and I have gotten his spacious bachelor apartments in the Albany, to which I hope you will address a speedy answer to this mine epistle.

The Albany is a long row of semi-detached buildings, extending from Piccadilly through to Burlington Gardens, just east of the Royal Academy of Arts. It is let out in chambers to single gentlemen, and has had many distinguished occupants. Here Byron wrote the 'Ode on the Fall of Napoleon,' and herefrom he set out to be married to Miss Milbanke, on January 2, 1815.

Lord and Lady Byron, in the spring of 1815, took possession of the mansion No. 13 Piccadilly Terrace, where in December of the same year the sole daughter of his house and heart was born; and this house, in January, 1816, Lady Byron quitted, never to see her lord again. It was still standing in 1885, near Park Lane, and numbered 139 Piccadilly.

Moore first met Byron at Samuel Rogers's, No. 22 St. James's Place, Piccadilly, in 1811 (see ROGERS).

Moore's Byron, vol. ii., 1811.

It was at first intended by Mr. Rogers that his company at dinner should not extend beyond Lord Byron and myself; but Mr. Thomas Campbell, having called upon our host that morning, was invited to join the party, and consented. Such a meeting could not be otherwise than interesting to us all. It was the first time that Lord Byron was ever seen by any of his three companions; while he, on his side, for the first time found himself in the society of persons whose names had been associated with his first literary dreams, and to two of whom he looked up with that tributary admiration which youthful genius is ever ready to pay its precursors. Among the impressions which this meeting left upon me, what I chiefly remember to have remarked, was the nobleness of his air, his beauty, the gentleness of his voice and manners, and — what was naturally not the least attraction — his marked kindness to myself. Being in mourning for his mother, the color as well of his dress as of his glossy, curling, and picturesque hair gave more effect to the pure, spiritual paleness of his features, in the expression of which, when he spoke, there was a perpetual play of lively thought, though melancholy was their habitual character when in repose. As we had none of us been apprised of his peculiarities with respect to food, the embarrassment of our host was not a little on discovering that there was nothing upon the table which his noble guest could eat or drink. Neither meat, fish, nor wine would Lord Byron touch, and of biscuits and soda-water, which he asked for, there had been unluckily no provision. He professed, however, to be equally well pleased with potatoes and vinegar, and of these meagre materials contrived to make rather a hearty dinner.

Some days after, meeting Hobhouse, I said to him, 'How long will Lord Byron persevere in his present diet?' He replied, 'Just as long as you continue to notice it.' I did not then know what I now know to be a fact, — that Byron, after leaving my house, had gone to a club in St. James's Street, and eaten a hearty meat supper. Rogers's Table Talk.

Byron's meeting with Sir Walter Scott, the latter thus describes in a letter to Moore, written after Byron's death : —

It was in the spring of 1815 that, chancing to be in London, I had the advantage of a personal introduction to Lord Byron. Report had prepared me to meet a man of peculiar habits and a quick temper; and I had some doubts whether we were likely to suit each other in society. I was most agreeably disappointed in this respect. I found Lord Byron in the highest degree courteous and even kind. We met for an hour or two almost daily in Mr. Murray's drawing-room [No. 50 A, Albemarle Street], and found a great deal to say Lockhart's Life of Scott, vol. i. chap. xxxiv.

to each other. . . . I saw Lord Byron for the last time in 1815, after I returned from France. He dined, or lunched, with me at Long's, in Bond Street. I never saw him so full of gayety or good-humor, to which the presence of Mr. Mathews, the comedian, added not a little. After one of the gayest parties I ever was present at, I set off for Scotland, and I never saw Lord Byron again.

Long's Hotel still stood, in 1885, at No. 16 New Bond Street,[5] and Murray's Publishing House was still in Albemarle Street, near Piccadilly, on the same spot as in the days of Scott and Byron.

Lord Byron died in Missolonghi, Greece, on the 19th of April, 1824. His remains were carried to England, lay in state in the house of Sir Edward Knatchbull, No. 25 Great George Street, Westminster (the Institution of Civil Engineers in 1885), on the 9th and 10th of July, and on the 16th of July were buried by the side of those of his mother in the family vault near Newstead Abbey.

Was with Rogers at half past eight; set off for George Street, Westminster, at half past nine. When I approached the house and saw the crowd assembled, felt a nervous trembling come over me which lasted till the whole ceremony was over. . . . The riotous curiosity of the mob, the bustle of the undertakers, etc., and all the other vulgar accompaniment of the ceremony mixing with my recollections of him who was gone, produced a combination of disgust and sadness that was deeply painful to me. . . . Saw a lady crying in a barouche as we turned out of George Street, and said to myself, 'Bless her heart, whoever she is!' There were, however, few respectable persons in the crowd, and the whole ceremony was anything but what it ought to have been. Left the hearse as soon as it was off the stones, and returned home to get rid of my black clothes and try to forget as much as possible the wretched feelings I had experienced in them.

[Moore's Diary, July 12, 1824.]

Byron's clubs were Watier's, a gambling-house, No. 81 Piccadilly, corner of Bolton Street, and the Alfred, No.

23 Albemarle Street, neither of which is now in existence. He was also a member of the Cocoa Tree Club, which still had the house No. 64 St. James's Street in 1885.

On the 9th of April, 1814, he wrote to Moore:—

I have also been drinking, and on one occasion, with three other friends of the Cocoa Tree, from six till four, yea, five in the matin. We clareted and champagned till two, then supped, and finished with a kind of Regency punch, composed of Madeira, brandy, and green tea, no real water being admitted therein. There was a night for you! without once quitting the table, excepting to ambulate home, which I did alone, and in utter contempt of a hackney coach, and my own *vis*, both of which were deemed necessary for our conveyance.

THOMAS. CAMPBELL.

1777–1844.

CAMPBELL saw almost nothing of London until his marriage, which took place in the Church of St. Margaret, Westminster, in 1803. He shortly afterwards hired a house at Sydenham, where he lived for seventeen years, and where the whole of 'Gertrude of Wyoming' was written.

In November, 1804, Campbell wrote from Sydenham to Constable:—

If you come to London and drink to the health of Auld Reekie over my new mahogany table, if you take a walk round my garden, and see my braw house, my court-yard, hens, geese and turkeys, or view the lovely country in my neighborhood, you will think this fixture and furniture money well bestowed. I shall indeed be nobly settled, and the devil is in it if I don't work as nobly for it.

<small>Constable and his Literary Correspondents.</small>

June 25, 1815. — Mr. Campbell asked me to come out and see him to-day, and make it a long day's visit. So after the morning service I drove out, and stayed with him until nearly nine o'clock this evening. He lives in a pleasant little box at Sydenham, nine miles from town, a beautiful village, which looks more like an American village than any I have seen in England. His wife is a bonny little Scotch woman, with a great deal of natural vivacity.

<small>George Ticknor's Life and Journal, vol. i. chap. iii.</small>

His mode of life at Sydenham was almost uniformly that which he afterwards followed in London, when he made it a constant residence. He rose not very early, breakfasted, studied for an hour or two, dined at two or three o'clock, and then made a call or two. . . . He would return home to tea, and then retire early to his study, remaining there till a late hour; sometimes even till an early one. His life was strictly domestic; he gave a dinner-party now and then, and at some of them Thomas Moore, Rogers, and other literary friends from town were present. His table was plain, hospitable, and cheered by a hearty welcome. •

<small>Cyrus Redding's Recollections of Fifty Years.</small>

Thorne, in his 'Hand-Book of the Environs of London,' described this house in 1876 as on Peak Hill, 'the third on the right before reaching Sydenham Station.' It still stood in 1885, unaltered since Campbell's occupancy of it, except that the gardens about it had been covered with modern villas, and that its rural character had disappeared. It was one of a row of tall red brick buildings near Peak Hill Road, with nothing to distinguish it from its neighbors, and was numbered 13 Peak Hill Avenue.

In 1820 Campbell settled in London, on his appointment as editor of the 'New Monthly Magazine.' He lodged for a time in Margaret Street, Cavendish Square, but soon took the house, then No. 10 Upper Seymour Street, since known as No. 18 Seymour Street, Portman Square, and unchanged in 1885, where he wrote 'Theodoric,' 'The Last Man,' etc., and where he remained until he lost his wife, in 1828. Greatly depressed in spirit after his bereavement, he resigned his

•

editorship and lived in loneliness and retirement at No. 61 Lincoln's Inn Fields. His chambers here were on the second floor, and the mansion was still standing in 1885.

In 1830 he was living at No. 1 Middle Scotland Yard, afterwards the Almonry Office. His other lodgings and homes in London were at 42 Eaton Street, Stockbridge Terrace, Pimlico, — a street since absorbed in Grosvenor Place, and of course numbered; No. 18 Old Cavendish Street, Oxford Street, on the west side; in York Chambers, St. James's Street, on the northeast corner of Piccadilly; and at No. 30 Foley Place, Regent Street, a few doors from Middleton Buildings. Foley Place was afterwards called Langham Street, and renumbered. In 1832, while devoting himself to the cause of Poland, he occupied an attic at the Polish Headquarters, in Sussex Chambers, No. 10 Duke Street, St. James's Street, still in existence in 1885. August 25, he writes : —

Here in the Polish Chambers I daily parade the main room, a superb hall, where all my books are ensconced, and where old Nol used to give audiences to his foreign ambassadors.   <small>Dr. Beattie's Memoir of Campbell, 1832.</small>

Again, September 28, he writes : —

I am not dissatisfied with my existence as it is now occupied. . . . I get up at seven, write letters for the Polish Association until half past nine, breakfast, go to the club and read the newspaper until twelve. Then I sit down to my own studies, and with many and also vexatious interruptions, do what I can till four. I then walk round the Park, and generally dine out at six. Between nine and ten I return to chambers, read a book or write a letter, and go to bed before twelve.   <small>Ibid.</small>

In 1840 Campbell leased the house No. 8 Victoria Square, Buckingham Palace Road, Pimlico. It still stood in 1885, on the south side and unaltered. He died at Boulogne, France, June 15, 1844, and on the 3d of July was buried in the Poets' Corner.

THOMAS CARLYLE.

1795-1881.

CARLYLE came first to London in 1824, and lodged with Charles Buller at Kew Green. Later, he was in the house of Edward Irving in Pentonville; and during the same year he took other rooms in Pentonville, not very far from his friend. He had various residences during his short visits to London; but it was not until 1834 that he finally went to the house at No. 5 Great Cheyne Row, Chelsea, which was his home until his death in 1881. Great Cheyne Row has been renumbered since Carlyle died; but his house, then No. 24, was standing in 1885. At the time of his taking possession he wrote to his wife:—

> The street runs down upon the river, which I suppose you might see by stretching out your head from the front window, at a distance of fifty yards on the left. We are called Cheyne Row (pronounced Chainie Row), and are a genteel neighborhood. The street is flag-paved, sunk-storied, iron-railed, all old-fashioned and tightly done up. The house itself is eminent, antique, wainscoted to the very ceiling, and has all been new painted and repaired; broadish stairs with massive balustrades (in the old style) corniced, and as thick as one's thigh; floors thick as a rock, wood of them here and there worm-eaten, yet capable of cleanness, and still with thrice the strength of a modern floor. And then as to rooms: Goody! Three stories besides the sunk story,—in every one of them three apartments, in depth something like forty feet in all, a front dining-room (marble chimney-piece, etc.), then a back dining-room or breakfast-room, a little narrower by reason of the kitchen stairs; then out of this, and narrower still (to allow a back window, you consider) a china room or pantry, or I know not

Froude's Carlyle, vol. ii. chap. xviii.

what, all shelved and fit to hold crockery for the whole street. Such is the ground area, which, of course, continues to the top, and furnishes every bedroom with a dressing-room, or second bedroom; on the whole, a most massive, roomy, sufficient old house, with places, for example, to hang, say, three dozen hats or cloaks on, and as many curious and queer old presses and shelved closets (all tight and new painted in their way) as would gratify the most covetous Goody: rent thirty-five pounds. . . . We lie safe at a bend of the river, away from all the great roads, have air and quiet hardly inferior to Craigenputtock, an outlook from the back windows into more leafy regions, with here and there a red high-peaked old roof looking through, and see nothing of London except by day the summits of St. Paul's Cathedral and Westminster Abbey, and by night the gleam of the great Babylon, affronting the peaceful skies. The house itself is probably the best we have ever lived in, — a right old strong, roomy brick house built nearly one hundred and fifty years ago [written in 1834], and likely to see three races of these modern fashionables fall before it comes down.

There he sat, aged, honored, famous, — the leading man of letters, perhaps, of his generation. An old dressing-gown wrapped around him, slippers on his feet, his face grim as granite, and his eyes with that sad prophetic gaze which is reproduced in all the photographs. On the book-shelves close around him were well-thumbed volumes, nearly all of them presentation copies, with the autographs of their mighty authors, chief among them a set of Goethe with notes in the poet's own handwriting. . . . Only the day before he had been sent for by the Queen of England as one of the two or three great men it behooved her to know and honor; and having spent several hours of conversation with her, he had pronounced her 'a nice homely body, just like scores of farmers' wives he had met in Allandale.' *Robert Buchanan's Sandie Macpherson.*

Froude, in his 'Carlyle' (vol. iv. chap. xxxv.), thus describes his last hours:—

His bed had been moved into the drawing-room, which still bore the stamp of his wife's hand upon it. Her work-box and other ladies' trifles lay about in their old places. He had forbidden them to be removed, and they stood within reach of his dying hand. He was wandering when I came to his side. He recognized me. 'I am very ill,' he said. 'Is it not strange that those people should have chosen the very oldest man in all Britain to make suffer this way?'... When I saw him next, his speech was gone. His eyes were as if they did not see, or were fixed on something far away.... This was on the 4th of February, 1881. The morning following he died. He had been gone an hour when I reached the house. He lay calm and still, an expression of exquisite tenderness subduing his rugged features into feminine beauty. I have seen something like it in Catholic pictures of dead saints, but never before or since on any human countenance.

ELIZABETH CARTER.

1717-1806.

FROM the age of nineteen until her death, Miss Carter — or Mrs. Carter, as she was called later in life — spent much of her time in London. As a young girl she visited her paternal uncle, who was a silk-mercer in the city, and other friends, until 1762, when the success of her 'Epictetus' made her comparatively independent, and she took apartments at No. 20 Clarges Street, Piccadilly, on the first floor. Here she lodged at intervals for many years. Upon the death of her landlord, and the breaking up of his establishment, she went for a season or two to a lodging-house in Chapel Street, May Fair; but she ultimately came back to the old neighborhood, and settled at No. 21 Clarges Street, where she died a very old woman in 1806. The numbers in Clarges Street have not been changed since her day.

There is a tradition that Miss Carter, while writing for the 'Gentleman's Magazine' under the name 'Eliza,' lodged for a time at St. John's Gate (see JOHNSON). She was buried in Grosvenor Chapel, an appendage to St. George's Church, Hanover Square. It is situated in South Audley Street, opposite Chapel Street.

SUSANNA CENTLIVRE.

1667(?)–1723.

THE history of the early part of Mrs. Centlivre's life is involved in obscurity. Even the place of her birth and the exact date are unknown; and until 1706, when she married Queen Anne's Yeoman of the Mouth, — or, as Pope more roughly expressed it, she became 'that Cook's wife of Buckingham Court,'— she never had permanent local habitation or a reputable name in the metropolis. She spent the last and happiest days of her life in Spring Gardens, Charing Cross. Her husband's house was on the corner of Buckingham Court. Spring Gardens — garden only in name — is a curiously crooked little street, immediately west of Trafalgar Square, connecting Whitehall with the east end of the Mall, and St. James's Park.

The place of Mrs. Centlivre's burial has been for many years undetermined, many of the older authorities — among others, the 'Biographia Dramatica' — placing it in the Church of St. Martin-in-the-Fields, in which parish she died. But search of the Register of St. Paul's, Covent Garden, shows that she was buried in that church, 'Decemb'r 4th, 1723.' The date of her birth or the position of her grave is not recorded.

THOMAS CHATTERTON.

1752–1770.

CHATTERTON'S career in London was crowded into four short melancholy months, and almost nothing is known of his life here. He found lodgings at first in a garret in the house of a Mr. Walmsley, a plasterer, in Shoreditch; he died by his own hands, in the house of a stay-maker in Brooke Street, Holborn; and he found rest in a pauper's grave in the burial-ground of the workhouse in Shoe Lane.

All that his biographers and admirers have been able to learn about his sad London experiences is given below: —

This boy [a nephew of Mr. Walmsley], who was the bedfellow of Chatterton, informed Mr. Croft that Chatterton used to sit up all night reading and writing; that he never came to bed till very late, often three or four o'clock, but that he was always awake when he waked, and got up at the same time. He lived chiefly upon a halfpenny roll, or a tart and some water. . . . He did not, however, wholly abstain from meat, for he was once or twice known to take a sheep's tongue out of his pocket. . . . Early in July Chatterton left his lodgings in Shoreditch, and went to lodge with Mrs. Angel, a sack-maker, in Brooke Street, Holborn. It were an injury not to mention historically the lodgings of Chatterton, for every spot he made his residence has become poetical ground. . . . Of his extreme indigence there is positive testimony. Mrs. Angel remembers that for two days, when he did not absent himself from his room, he went without food. . . . Mr. Cross, an apothecary in Brooke Street, bore evidence that while Chatterton lived with Mrs. Angel, he frequently called at the shop, and

John Davis's Life of Chatterton.

was repeatedly pressed by Mr. Cross to dine or sup with him, but always in vain. One evening, however, hunger so far prevailed over his pride as to tempt him to partake of a barrel of oysters, when he was observed to eat most voraciously. . . . Pressed hard by indigence and its companions, gloom and despondency, the mind of Chatterton became disordered, and on the night of the 24th of August, 1770, he swallowed a large dose of opium, which caused his death. . . . The inquest of the jury was brought in insanity, and the body of Chatterton was put into a shell, and carried unwept, unheeded, and unowned to the burying-ground of the workhouse in Shoe Lane.

We know, from the account of Sir Herbert Croft, that Chatterton occupied the garret, a room looking out into the street, as the only garret in this house does. . . . It was a square and rather large room for an attic. It had two windows in it, — lattice windows, or casements, built in a style which I think is called 'dormer.' Outside ran the gutter, with a low parapet wall, over which you could look into the street below. The roof was very low, so low that I, who am not a tall man, could hardly stand upright in it with my hat on; and it had a long slope, extending from the middle of the room down to the windows. Hotten's Adversaria.

No. 4 Brooke Street, Holborn, would be an interesting number if it remained; but as if everything connected with the history of this ill-fated youth, except his fame, should be condemned to the most singular fatality, there is no No. 4; it is swallowed up by an enormous furniture warehouse, fronting into Holborn, and occupying what used to be numbers one, two, three, and four Brooke Street. Thus the whole interior of these houses has been cleared away, and they have been converted into one long show-shop below. . . . Thus all memory of the particular spot which was the room of Chatterton, and where he committed suicide, is rooted out. What is still more strange, the very same fate has attended his place of sepulture. He was buried among the paupers in Shoe Lane; so little was known or cared about him and his fate, that it was some time, as stated, before his friends learned the sad story; in the mean time the exact site of William Howitt's Homes and Haunts of British Poets, vol. i.: Chatterton.

his grave was well-nigh become unknown. It appears, however, from inquiries which I have made, that the spot was recognized; and when the public became at length aware of the genius that had been suffered to perish in despair, a head stone was erected by subscription among some admirers of his productions. . . . The very resting-place of Chatterton could not escape the ungenial character of his fate. London, which seemed to refuse to know him when alive, refused a quiet repose to his ashes. . . . The burial-ground in Shoe Lane was sold to form Farringdon Market, and tombs and memorials of the deceased disappeared to make way for the shambles and cabbage stalls of the living.

On the 24th of August, 1770, at the age of seventeen years, nine months, and a few days, Chatterton put an end to his life by swallowing arsenic in water in the house of a Mrs. Angel, a sack-maker in this street [Brooke Street], then No. 4, now [1850] occupied by Steffenoni's furniture warehouse. His room, when broken open, was found covered with scraps of paper.

Cunningham's Hand-Book of London: Brooke Street, Holborn.

Contemporary directories show Steffenoni's to have been on the northeast corner of Holborn and Brooke Street. His number was 142 Holborn, occupied in 1885 by the establishment of the Universal Building Society. Mrs. Angel's was about two hundred feet from Holborn.

Chatterton, writing to his mother, May 6, 1770, says:—

I am quite familiar at the Chapter Coffee House, and know all the geniuses there. A character is now unnecessary; an author carries his genius in his pen.

And on the 30th May he wrote to his sister from 'Tom's Coffee House in Birchin Lane.'

The Chapter Coffee House stood at No. 50 Paternoster Row, on the south side of that street, on the corner of Chapter House Court and nearly opposite Ivy Lane. It ceased to exist as a coffee-house in 1854, but was opened as a tavern a few years later; and in 1885 the fine mahogany balustrades of the stairs, and the dining-rooms themselves, remained, comparatively unchanged since Chatterton's day (see BRONTË, p. 22).[3]

'Tom's' stood in Cowper's Court, Birchin Lane; but no trace of it remains.

GEOFFREY CHAUCER.

13—-1400.

NOTHING positive is known of the place of Chaucer's birth or education, although some of his commentators, upon the dubious authority of the following lines in the 'Testament of Love,' claim that he was a native of London.

Also in the Citie of London, that is to mee soe deare and sweete, in which I was foorth grown; and more kindely love have I to that place than to any other in yerth, as every kindely creature hath full appetite to that place of his kindely ingendure.

Richard Chawcer, the father of the poet, citizen and vintner, gave to the church of Aldermary, Bow Lane, his tenement and tavern, corner of Kerion Lane. It is not certain that the father of English poetry was born here; some claim the honor of his birthplace for Oxfordshire, and some for Berkshire. Camden says he was born in London; and if so, most probably at the corner of this lane, in the house just mentioned. *Smith's Antiquarian Rambles in London, vol. ii.*

The Church of St. Mary Aldermary, destroyed by the Great Fire, was rebuilt by Wren, and stands in Watling Street, near Bow Lane. Kerion Lane was never rebuilt after the Fire. It ran parallel with Upper Thames Street, north of St. James's Church, Garlickhithe. The present Maiden Lane is very near its site. It is by no means certain, however, that the poet was the son of the Richard Chawcer who is mentioned above.

The story of Chaucer being a member of the Temple, and while there beating the Friar in Fleet Street, is also thought now to be merely legendary. There is no absolute reason for supposing that he was the Chaucer whose name appeared upon the records.

<small>Chaucer's Life, by T. Speght; prefixed to the Black Letter Folio of 1598.</small> It seemeth that both of these learned men [Gower and Chaucer] were of the Inner Temple ; for not many years since Master Buckley did see a record in the same house where Geoffrey Chaucer was fined two shillings for beating a Franciscan Friar in Fleet Street.

Chaucer is believed to have been married in the chapel of the Savoy Palace, and to have written certain of his poems in the Palace itself. It stood on the north bank of the Thames, west of Somerset House ; and the last remnants of it were removed on the building of the approach to Waterloo Bridge. Its name is retained in Savoy Hill, Savoy Chapel, and Savoy Street, Strand. The present Savoy Chapel was built a century after Chaucer's death, the church in which he was married having stood on the site of the Admiralty Department of Somerset House.

Henry Thomas Riley, in his 'Memorials of London and London Life in the Thirteenth, Fourteenth, and Fifteenth Centuries,' published in 1868, and compiled from the 'Early Archives of the City of London,' quotes in full the 'Lease to Geoffrey Chaucer of the dwelling house at Aldgate 48 Edward III. A. D. 1374,' as follows : —

To all persons to whom this present writing indented shall come : Adam de Bevry, Mayor, the Aldermen and Commonalty of the City of London, Greeting : Know ye that we, with unanimous will and assent, have granted and released by these presents unto Geoffrey Chaucer, the whole of the dwelling house above the gate of Aldgate, with the rooms built over, and a certain cellar beneath the same Gate, on the south side of that Gate, and the appurtenances thereof ; to have and to hold the whole of the house aforesaid, with the rooms so built over and the said cellar and the appurtenances thereof, unto the aforesaid Geoffrey, for the whole life of him the same Geoffrey.

This gate was taken down in 1606; and another, built upon the same spot, was also removed entirely one hundred and fifty years later. Its site, by comparison with contemporary maps and plans, would seem to have been across the present Aldgate, about one hundred feet west of Houndsditch and the Minories, say half-way between Houndsditch and Duke Street on the north side, and between the Minories and Jewry Street on the south; probably at the junction of the parishes of St. Botolph Aldgate and St. Katherine Cree, marked on the house numbered 2 Aldgate in 1885.

Tradition also says that Chaucer wrote his 'Testament of Love' in the Tower, that he spent some of the later years of his life in Thames Street, and that he died in the immediate neighborhood of Westminster Abbey, where, in the Poets' Corner, all that is mortal of him lies.

Geoffrey Chaucer, 'the first illuminer of the English language,' had the lease for a tenement adjoining the White Rose Tavern, which abutted upon the Old Lady Chapel of the Abbey, at a yearly rent of 53s. 4d. from Christmas A. D. 1399, for fifty-three years. Here probably he died, on October 25, 1400. This house, the tavern, and St. Mary's Chapel were demolished in 1502, to give place to the gorgeous Mausoleum of King Henry VII. *M. E. C. Walcott's Memorials of Westminster, p. 219.*

There is still preserved a lease granted to him by the keeper of the Lady Chapel, which makes over to him a tenement in the garden attached to that building on the ground now covered by the enlarged Chapel of Henry VII. In this house he died, October 25th, in the last year of the fourteenth century. . . . Probably from the cir-*Dean Stanley's Westminster Abbey, chap. iv.* cumstances of his dying so close at hand, combined with the royal favor still continued by Henry IV., he was brought to the

Abbey, and buried, where the functionaries of the monastery were beginning to be interred, at the entrance of St. Benedict's Chapel. There was nothing to mark the grave except a plain slab, which was sawn up when Dryden's monument was erected. . . . It was not until the reign of Edward VI. [1551] that the present tomb, to which apparently the poet's ashes were removed, was raised near the grave by Nicholas Brigham, himself a poet, who was buried close beside, with his daughter Rachel. The inscription closes with the echo of the poet's own expiring counsel 'Ærumnarum requies mors.' Originally the back of the tomb contained a portrait of Chaucer.

Chaucer's association with the Tabard Inn is well known. In the 'Canterbury Tales' he says it

> 'Befel that in that season on a day,
> At Southwark at the Tabard as I lay
> Ready to wenden on my pilgrimage
> To Canterbury with devoute courage
> At night we came into that hostelry.'

The original Tabard, known to Chaucer, was taken down early in the seventeenth century. According to Stow (1598), it was amongst the most ancient of the many inns for receipt of travellers in Southwark. It was situated immediately opposite what was at that time known as St. Margaret's Hill. On its site was built a second Tabard, which stood until 1874, and was by many later-day pilgrims believed to be the original. 'The Talbot Inn' was painted above its gateway, and there was also a sign bearing the following inscription : 'This is the Inne where Sir Jeffry Chaucer and the nine and twenty pilgrims lay, in their journey to Canterbury, Anno 1383.' The latest Tabard, at No. 85 High Street, Borough, on the corner of Talbot Inn Yard, is of no interest in itself, except as marking the site and perpetuating the name of one of the most famous of old London hostelries.

THE EARL OF CHESTERFIELD.

1694-1773.

THE Earl of Chesterfield, born in London, was christened in St. James's Church, Piccadilly, and spent the greater part of his life in the metropolis. He lived at one time in St. James's Square, and later in Bedford Street, Covent Garden; but his most important London home was the mansion bearing his name in South Audley Street, May Fair. It was commenced in 1747, and was still standing in 1885, although its gardens have been built upon, and are shorn of their fair proportions.

But perhaps the most interesting apartment in the whole house [Chesterfield House] is the library; there, where Lord Chesterfield used to sit and write, still stand [1869] the books which it is only fair to suppose that he read, — books of wide-world and enduring interest, and which stand in goodly array, one row above another, by hundreds. High above them, in separate panels, are 'Kit Kat' sized portraits of all the great English poets and dramatists, down to the time of Chesterfield. . . . In another room not far from the library, one seems to gain an idea of the noble letter-writer's daily life; for it is a room which has not only its antechamber, in which the aspirants for his lordship's favor were sometimes kept waiting, but on its garden side a stone or marble terrace overlooking the large garden, stretching out in lawn and flower-beds, behind the house. Upon this terrace Chesterfield doubtless often walked, snuff-box in hand, and in company with some choice friend.

<small>Walford's Londoniana, vol. ii.: Chesterfield.</small>

This room is the subject of E. M. Ward's well-known picture, 'Dr. Johnson in the Anteroom of Lord Chesterfield,' —

an incident which is said to have occurred in 1749, although good authorities assert that the Earl did not occupy the house until three years later.

Chesterfield died in Chesterfield House in 1773, and was buried in Grosvenor Chapel, South Audley Street (see CARTER), according to the instructions contained in his will that he should be placed in the graveyard nearest to the spot where he might happen to die, and that the expenses of his funeral should not exceed one hundred pounds. His remains were afterwards removed to the family burial-place in Shelford Church, Nottinghamshire.

CHARLES CHURCHILL

1731-1764.

CHURCHILL was born in Vine Street, Westminster, in 1731, and was probably christened in the neighboring Church of St. John the Evangelist, Smith Square, of which his father was curate at the time of his birth.

Churchill was sent to Westminster School in 1739, where he remained ten years.

Shortly after [1746], having by some misdemeanor displeased his masters, he was compelled to compose and recite in the school-room a poetical declamation in Latin, by way of penance. This he accomplished in a masterly manner, to the astonishment of his masters and the delight of his schoolfellows, some of whom became afterwards distinguished men. We can fancy the scene at the day of recitation, — the grave and big-wigged schoolmasters looking grimly on, their aspect however, becoming softer and brighter, as one large hexameter rolls out after another; the strong, awkward, ugly boy un-

Gilfillan's Life of Churchill.

blushingly pouring forth his energetic lines, cheered by the sight of the relaxing gravity of his teachers' looks; while around you see the bashful, tremulous figure of poor Cowper, the small, thin shape and bright eye of Warren Hastings, and the waggish countenance of Colman [the elder], all eagerly watching the recital, and all at last distended and brightened with joy at his signal triumph.

St. Peter's College — or, as it is more familiarly called, Westminster School — in which have been educated so many famous Englishmen, is immediately adjoining the cloisters of the Abbey, the entrance being through the old gateway, said to have been designed by Inigo Jones, in Little Dean's Yard.

Churchill contracted a Fleet marriage at an early age, and lived unhappily with his wife. In 1758 he was appointed successor to his father in the Church of St. John, and is said to have preached his father's old sermons, and generally to have conducted himself in a manner unbecoming a clergyman. At the same time he was acting as tutor in a girls' seminary at Queen Square, Bloomsbury; but his habits were so irregular that he was compelled to resign both his church and his school.

One of Churchill's favorite places of resort was the Bedford, 'under the piazza in Covent Garden.' It was on the corner near the entrance to the theatre, and its name was perpetuated in 1885 in the Bedford Hotel.

He was a member of the Beefsteak Club, which met in a room at the top of Covent Garden Theatre in Churchill's time. Wilkes was his sponsor in the society; but his conduct was such as to shock and disgust even an assemblage of men not over particular; and to avoid expulsion, after the publication of his desertion of his wife, he resigned.

COLLEY CIBBER.

1671-1757.

COLLEY CIBBER, according to his own statement, 'was born in London on the 6th of November, 1671, in Southampton Street, facing Southampton House.'

Southampton House, afterwards Bedford House, taken down in the beginning of the present century, occupied the north side of Bloomsbury Square. Evelyn speaks of it in his Diary, October, 1664, as in course of construction. Another and an earlier Southampton House in Holborn, 'a little above Holborn Bars,' was removed some twenty years before Cibber's birth. He was, therefore, probably born at the upper or north end of Southampton Street, facing Bloomsbury Square, where now are comparatively modern buildings, and not in Southampton Street, Strand, as is generally supposed.

Cibber, in his 'Apology,' says nothing of his home life or of his social haunts, although he speaks frequently and freely of the scenes of his professional labors.

From 1711 until 1714 he lived in Spring Gardens, Whitehall (see Mrs. CENTLIVRE), 'near the Bull Head Tavern,' of which now there is no trace left.

Cunningham, in his 'Hand-Book,' quotes the following advertisement from the 'Daily Courant,' January 20, 1703 [*sic*, probably 1713]:—

In or near the old play house in Drury Lane on Monday last — the 19th of January — a watch was dropped having a Tortoise shell case inlaid with silver, a silver chain and a gold seal ring — the arms a cross wavy and cheque. Whoever brings it to

Mr. Cibber at his house near the Bull Head Tavern in Old Spring Gardens, at Charing Cross, shall have three guineas reward.

Walpole declared that Cibber wrote one of his plays in the little cottage which stood on the site of the afterwards famous Strawberry Hill (see WALPOLE).

He is known to have lived at Islington, and in Berkeley Square, in an old-fashioned town mansion, standing in 1885.

Colley Cibber lived in Berkeley Square at the north corner of Bruton Street, where my mother told me she saw him once standing at his parlor window, drumming with his hands on the frame. She said he appeared like a calm, grave, and reverend old gentleman. John Taylor's Records of my Life.

Among them all, Colley kept his own to the last. A short time before the last hour arrived, Horace Walpole hailed him on his birthday with a good-morrow, and ' I am glad, sir, to see you looking so well.' 'Egad, sir,' replied the old gentleman, all diamonded and powdered and dandified, 'at eighty-four it is well for a man that he can look at all.' ... And now he crosses Piccadilly and passes through Albemarle Street, slowly but cheerfully, with an eye and a salutation for any pretty woman of his acquaintance, and with a word for any 'good fellow' whose purse he has lightened, or who has lightened his, at dice or whist. And so he turns into the adjacent square; and as his servant closes the door, after admitting him, neither of them wots that the master has passed over the threshold for the last time a living man. In December, 1757, I read in contemporary publications that 'there died at his house in Berkeley Square, Colley Cibber, Esq., Poet Laureate.' ... Colley Cibber was carried to sleep with kings and heroes in Westminster Abbey. Doran's Annals of the Stage, vol. ii. chap. ii.

Dr. Doran is not to be relied upon here. Cibber certainly was not buried in the Abbey, and according to other authorities he died at Islington. A careful search through files of contemporary publications in the British Museum has failed to reveal any mention of the place of his death.

Samuel Lewis, in his 'History of Islington,' published in 1842, describes the 'Castle public house and tea gardens at the northern termination of Colebrooke (*sic*) Row, Islington' (see LAMB), and asserts that 'in the house next to this tavern, Colley Cibber lived and died' (chap. ix. pp. 351, 352). The Castle no longer exists.

Cibber was buried by the side of his father and mother, in a vault under the Danish Church, situated in Wellclose Square, Ratcliffe Highway (since named St. George Street). This church, according to an inscription placed over the doorway, was built in 1696 by Caius Gabriel Cibber himself, by order of the King of Denmark, for the use of such of his Majesty's subjects as might visit the port of London. The church was taken down some years ago (1868–70), and St. Paul's Schools were erected on its foundation, which was left intact. Rev. Dan. Greatorex, Vicar of the Parish of St. Paul, Dock Street, in a private note written in the summer of 1883, says:—

Colley Cibber and his father and mother were buried in the vault of the old Danish Church. When the church was removed, the coffins were all removed carefully into the crypt under the apse, and then bricked up. So the bodies are still there. The Danish Consul was with me when I moved the bodies. The coffins had perished except the bottoms. I carefully removed them myself personally, and laid them side by side at the back of the crypt, and covered them with earth.

Cibber was the only English actor ever elected a member of White's, which originally was situated at Nos. 69 and 70 St. James's Street, 'near the bottom on the west side.' In 1755, two years before Cibber's death, it was removed to the position it has so long held, Nos. 37 and 38 St. James's Street. He was also one of the original members of the 'Spiller's Head Club,' which met at the Inn of John Spiller, Clare Market, Lincoln's Inn Fields. The house, if standing, cannot now be identified, and Clare Market has changed greatly for the worse since Cibber's day.

He was frequently found at Tom's Coffee House, which stood at No. 17 Russell Street, Covent Garden. This building was taken down in 1865, and on its site was erected the National Deposit Bank.

Mr. Murphy told me also that he was once present at Tom's Coffee House, which was only open to subscribers, when Colley was engaged at whist, and an old general was his partner. As the cards were dealt to him, he took up every one in turn, and expressed his disappointment at every indifferent one. In the progress of the game he did not follow suit, and his partner said, 'What, have you not a spade, Mr. Cibber?' The latter, looking at his hand, answered, 'Oh, yes, a thousand!' which drew a very peevish comment from the General. On which, Cibber, who was shockingly addicted to swearing, said, 'Don't be angry; for, —— ——, I can play ten times worse if I like.' *John Taylor's Records of my Life.*

I cannot let slip the present opportunity in mentioning that the house in which I reside (No. 17 Russell Street, Covent Garden) was the famous Tom's Coffee House, memorable in the reign of Queen Anne, and for more than half a century afterwards; the room in which I conduct my business as a coin-dealer is that which in 1764, by a guinea subscription among nearly seven hundred of the nobility, foreign ministers, gentry, and geniuses of the age, became the card room and place of meeting for many of the now illustrious dead, till in 1768, when a voluntary subscription among its members induced Mr. Haines, the then proprietor, to take in the next room westward as a coffee room, and the whole floor *en suite* was constructed card and conversation rooms. *Till's Descriptive Particulars of the English Coronation Medals.*

SAMUEL TAYLOR COLERIDGE.

1772–1834.

COLERIDGE'S associations with London began when he was but ten years old. He entered the Blue Coat School on the 18th of July, 1782. Charles Lamb, in his Essay, 'Christ-Hospital Five and Thirty Years Ago,' describes Coleridge's experiences there; and Coleridge himself has frequently told the story of his school life.

"The discipline of Christ-Hospital in my day was extra Spartan. All domestic ties were to be put aside. 'Boy,' I remember Boyer saying to me once when I was crying, the first day of my return after the holidays, — 'boy, the school is your father; boy, the school is your mother; boy, the school is your brother; the school is your sister, boy; the school is your first cousin and your second cousin, and all the rest of your relations. Let us have no more crying.'

<small>Coleridge's Table Talk, 1832.</small>

Continuing an account of himself at school, Coleridge says: 'From eight to fourteen I was a playless day-dreamer, a *helluo librorum*, my appetite for which was indulged by a singular incident; a stranger who was struck by my conversation made me free of a circulating library in King Street, Cheapside.' The incident indeed was singular. Going down the Strand in one of his day-dreams, fancying himself swimming across the Hellespont, thrusting his hands before him as in the act of swimming, his hand came in contact with a gentleman's pocket; the gentleman seized his hand, and turning round . . . accused him of an attempt to pick his pocket; the frightened boy sobbed out his denial of the intention, and explained to him that he thought himself swimming the Hellespont.

<small>James Gilman's Life of Coleridge, vol. i. chap. I.</small>

Coleridge went to town [in 1782], and Buller placed him in the Blue Coat School. The family, being proud, thought themselves disgraced by this. His brothers would not let him visit them in the school dress, and he would not go in any other. The judge invited him to dine in his house every Sunday. One day, however, there was company, and the Blue Coat boy was sent to the second table. He was then only nine years old, but he would never go to the house again.

Henry Crabb Robinson's Diary, August 14, 1812

I heard this anecdote from a gentleman who was a schoolfellow of Coleridge's. Coleridge was wildly rushing through Newgate Street to be in time for school, when he upset an old woman's apple-stall. 'Oh, you little devil!' she exclaimed bitterly. But the boy, noting the mischief he had done, ran back and strove to make the best amends he could by gathering up the scattered fruit and lamenting the accident. The grateful woman changed her tone, patted the lad on the head, and said, 'Oh, you little angel!'

S. C. Hall's Retrospect of a Long Life : Coleridge.

Christ-Hospital, in Newgate Street, better known as the Blue Coat School, was built in 1553, on the site of the old Monastery of Grey Friars. The pupils in 1885 still wore the uncomfortable although picturesque dress originally designed for them in the reign of Edward, the Boy King, who was founder of the institution; and the 'Blue Coat Boys,' so frequently met with in the streets of London, are clad precisely as were Coleridge, Charles Lamb, Leigh Hunt, and many others who became afterwards distinguished men.

Coleridge was only occasionally in London in the early part of the century; the Continent or the Lake Country of England being more to his liking. In 1799 he lodged in King Street, Covent Garden; in 1801 he was found in Bridge Street, Westminster, the character of which street has entirely changed; and, according to Mr. Rogers, he lodged once in Pall Mall.

Coleridge was a marvellous talker. One morning he talked three hours without intermission about poetry, and so admirably that I wish every word he uttered had been written down. But sometimes his harangues were quite unintelligible, not only to myself but to others. Wordsworth and I called upon him one forenoon when he was lodging in Pall Mall. He talked uninterruptedly for about two hours, during which Wordsworth listened to him with profound attention, every now and then nodding his head as if in assent. On quitting the lodging I said to Wordsworth, 'Well, for my own part I could not make head or tail of Coleridge's oration ; pray, did you understand it ?' 'Not one syllable of it,' was Wordsworth's reply.

Rogers's Table Talk.

In 1810 Coleridge was living at No. 7 Portland Place, Hammersmith, a short street off Hammersmith Road ; and it is said that he once had lodgings in Edwardes Square, Kensington, although his biographers do not record it. In 1816 he went from No. 42 Norfolk Street, one of a row of old-fashioned houses still standing in 1885, next to the Strand end of the street, to the house of his friend and biographer, John Gilman at the Grove, Highgate, where he spent in comparative retirement the last years of life, and where in 1834 he died.

Coleridge's Highgate house was the third in the Grove, — counting from the top of Highgate Hill, — facing the Grove, and obliquely opposite St. Michael's Church, in which is a mural tablet to Coleridge's memory. The house — a roomy, respectable brick mansion, two stories high, with a fine outlook over Nightingale Lane and Lord Mansfield's Woods, towards Hampstead — was standing in 1885 as when Coleridge died in it fifty years before, except that a new brick gable had been lately added, blocking up the end window of Coleridge's bedroom, the room in which he breathed his last.

Dr. B. E. Martin, in a private letter from Highgate in 1884, writes : —

Recently an old laborer here, very old and fearing death, sent for the curate of the parish, who discovered that he was using laudanum for his rheumatism, and warned him of the risks he ran. The old man replied : 'Why, I know better, Parson; my brother was doctor's boy to Mr. Gilman fifty years or more ago, and there was an old chap there called Colingrigs, or some such name, as Mr. Gilman thought he was a-curing of drinking laudanum, and my brother he used to fill a bottle with that stuff from Mr. Gilman's own bottles, and hand it to me, and I used to put it under my jacket and give it to h'old Colingrigs, and we did that for years and it never hurted him.' . . . Mrs. Dutton, a charming old lady greatly respected in Highgate, lives in an ivy-covered cottage on the Grove, and remembers Coleridge well. She used to sit on his knee and prattle to him, and she tells how he was followed about the Grove by troops of children for the sake of the sweeties of which his pockets were always full.

Another old lady, as recorded by Hodder in his 'Memoirs of my Time' (chap. v.), gives another account of Coleridge's life in Highgate:—

Meadows, in these our pleasant perambulations, was wont to speak of an old lady who kept the Lion and Sun Hotel in that neighborhood [Highgate]. This was a favorite resort of Coleridge; and the communicative landlady used to remark that he was a great talker, and 'when he began there was no stopping him.' Whenever she returned to the room, she said, after leaving it for a short time, he would still 'be going on,' and sometimes he made such a noise that she wished him further.

The Red Lion and Sun Tavern, an old-fashioned two-storied red-tiled sloping-roofed little inn on the North Road, just beyond Hampstead Lane and the old Gate House, was standing in 1885.

Coleridge was buried in the yard of the old chapel in Highgate. His tomb was covered by a large slab. In 1866 the New Grammar School was built on these grounds, and the grave of Coleridge was enclosed in the crypt of its chapel. William Winter, in his 'English Rambles,' published in 1883, thus describes it as he saw it at that time:—

He should have been laid in some wild, free place, where the grass could grow, and the trees could wave their branches over his head. They placed him in a ponderous tomb, of gray stone, in Highgate Churchyard ; and in later times they reared a new building above it, — the Grammar School of the village, — so that now the tomb, fenced round with iron, is in a cold, barren, gloomy crypt, accessible, indeed, from the churchyard, through several arches, but dim and doleful in its surroundings, as if the evil and cruel fate that marred his life were still triumphant over his ashes.

Coleridge in his young days was fond of the Salutation and Cat, a public house at No. 17 Newgate Street, where his companions at times were Southey and Charles Lamb. This tavern, with an entrance on Rose Street, was known of late years simply as the Salutation. It was partly destroyed by fire in the year 1883. A much earlier Salutation Inn, which stood nearly opposite it, between the lodges of Christ-Hospital and a few yards back from Newgate Street, has long since disappeared.

WILLIAM COLLINS.

1720–1757.

WHEN Collins arrived in London in 1744, fresh from the University, he seems to have made himself very conspicuous by his fine clothes, empty pockets, and magnificent opinion of his own genius. He was to be found in the coffee-houses ; but no record is left of his lodging or home life, except that Dr. Johnson visited him once at Islington, in what part of that suburb is not known, and that he lived at one time near Soho Square.

Going from Oxford to London, he [Collins] commenced a man of the town, spending his time in all the dissipation of Ranelagh,

Vauxhall, and the Play houses; and was romantic enough to suppose that his superior abilities would draw the attention of the great world by means of whom he was to make his fortune. . . . I met him often, and remember he lodged in a little house with a Miss Bundy, at the corner of King's Square Court, Soho, now [1781] a warehouse. *Gilbert White, in the Gentleman's Magazine, 1781.*

King's Square Court is that part of the street since called Carlisle Street, which runs from Dean Street, Soho, to Great Chapel Street. In Collins's day Soho Square was King's Square.

Collins strutted about the Bedford Coffee House on the Piazza, Covent Garden (see CHURCHILL), and Slaughter's Coffee House, which stood on the west side of St. Martin's Lane, three doors from Newport Street, but which was taken down when Cranbourn Street was cut through the houses of that vicinity to make a new thoroughfare between Long Acre and Leicester Square.

GEORGE COLMAN, SR.

1732–1794.

GEORGE COLMAN, SR., 'the elder Colman,' was a pupil of Westminster School (see CHURCHILL, p. 50). In his youth he lived with his widowed mother near Rosamond's Pond in the southwest corner of St. James's Park. The pond was filled up in 1772, and the house taken down.

Colman was a member of the Society of Lincoln's Inn, and lived at one time in Great Queen Street, Lincoln's Inn Fields. He also lived in the left-hand corner of Bateman's Buildings, on the south side of Soho Square. It occupies the site of the gardens of the Duke of Monmouth, whose watchword on the night of Sedgemoor was 'Soho,' and was unchanged in 1885. Some years before his death, Colman lived in retirement in Richmond, a short distance west of Richmond Bridge, and he died in a retreat for the insane at Paddington. He was buried in the Church of St. Mary the Virgin, Kensington High Street. The old church has been removed, but a tablet to Colman's memory is to be found in the north transept of the new building erected on its site.

Kensington Church, as I remember it in my boyhood, was one of the few really picturesque buildings of the kind near London. It was, of course, by no means worthy of a parish which can boast of such aristocratic residents and neighbors as the Kensington of to-day, but it harmonized well with what is left of Old Kensington Square. . . . The old church, with its quaint curved gable to the street corner, and its well-weathered red brick, has also disappeared.

<small>Loftie's History of London, vol. ii. chap. xxi.</small>

Colman frequented Tom's Coffee House, No. 17 Russell Street, Covent Garden (see CIBBER). Among other clubs, he was a member of the Beefsteak Club, which met in Covent Garden Theatre (see CHURCHILL), and of the Dilettanti Society, which met, in Colman's day, at Parsloe's, St. James's Street, a tavern familiar to the literary men of more than one generation. It disappeared early in the nineteenth century.

GEORGE COLMAN, JR.

1762–1836.

'THE younger Colman,' like his father, was educated at Westminster School. He was a student of Lincoln's Inn, and occupied chambers in King's Bench Walk, Inner Temple.

He lived with his father for a time in Soho Square, and was a member of the Beefsteak Club.

He was married in St. Luke's, Chelsea (Chelsea Old Church), in 1788, and died at No. 22 Brompton Square, Knightsbridge, the numbers of which have not been changed.

He was buried by the side of his father in the vaults of Kensington Church.

WILLIAM CONGREVE.

1670–1729.

CONGREVE came to London in his twenty-first year, and entered the Middle Temple, where he remained for some time. He lived, successively, in Southampton Street, Howard Street, and Surrey Street, Strand, in houses that it is not possible to identify now, even if they still stand, which is not at all probable. Streets were not numbered until after Congreve's day. In Howard Street Mrs. Bracegirdle was his neighbor.

Congreve was very intimate for years with Mrs. Bracegirdle, and lived in the same street, his house very near hers, until his acquaintance with the young Duchess of Marlborough. He then quitted that house. The Duchess showed me [Dr. Young] a diamond necklace that cost seven thousand pounds, and was purchased with the money Congreve left her. How much better would it have been to have given it to poor Mrs. Bracegirdle ! *Spence's Anecdotes: Fourth Memorandum Book, 1757.*

It was while living in Surrey Street, in 1728, that Congreve received the memorable visit from Voltaire, in which he was so justly rebuked by the French philosopher.

Congreve spoke of his works as trifles that were beneath him, and hinted to me in our first conversation that I should visit him upon no other footing than upon that of a gentleman who led a life of plainness and simplicity. I answered that had he been so unfortunate as to be a mere gentleman, I should never have come to see him ; and I was very much disgusted at so unreasonable a piece of vanity.

<small>Voltaire's Letters on the English Nation.</small>

Congreve died in Surrey Street, and lies in the south aisle of the nave of Westminster Abbey, not far from the grave of Mrs. Oldfield.

Having lain in state in the Jerusalem Chamber, he was buried in Westminster Abbey, where a monument is erected to his memory by Henrietta, Duchess of Marlborough, to whom, for reasons either not known or not mentioned, he bequeathed a legacy of about ten thousand pounds.

<small>Johnson's Lives of the Poets : Congreve.</small>

One of Congreve's favorite taverns was the Half Moon, which has long since disappeared, but the site of which is believed to be marked by Half Moon Passage, No. 158 Aldersgate Street.

He was also a member of the Kit Kat Club (see ADDISON, p. 8).

ABRAHAM COWLEY.

1618–1667.

COWLEY, the son of a grocer, was born in Fleet Street, near Chancery Lane. His father's house is known to have 'abutted on Sargeant's Inn,' but no trace of it now remains. Izaak Walton must have been his near neighbor there.

He was a pupil of Westminster School (see CHURCHILL, p. 50), and went to Cambridge in 1636. In his Essays (XI., 'On Myself,') he says:—

When I was a very young lad at school, instead of running on holidays and playing with my fellows, I was wont to steal from them and walk in the fields, either alone with a book or with some one companion, if I could find any of the same temper.

Cowley had but little experience of London; and as his biographies show, he soon grew weary of city life, and sought rural quiet and retirement, first at Battersea, then at Barn-Elms, and finally at Chertsey, where he died. In his later years he is said to have shown a strange and marked aversion to female society, leaving a room the moment a woman entered it.

Cowley House ... in which Cowley spent his last days, is on the west side of Guildford Street [Chertsey], near the railway station. ... It was a little house, with ample gardens and pleasant meadows attached. Not of brick indeed, but half timber, with a fine old oak staircase and balusters, and one or two wainscoted chambers, which yet [1876] remain much as when Cowley dwelt there, as do also the poet's study, a small closet with a view meadow-ward to St. Anne's Hill, and the room, overlooking the road, in which he died. He lived here little more than two years in all. *Thorne's Hand-Book of London: Chertsey.*

The greater part of this house was taken down, and again rebuilt in 1878.

Cowley's allowance was at last not above three hundred a year. He died at Chertsey; and his death was occasioned by a mean accident, whilst his great friend, Dean Sprat, was with him on a visit there. They had been together to see a neighbor of Cowley's, who, according to the fashion of those times, made them too welcome. They did not set out for their walk home till it was too late, and had drank so deep that they lay in the fields all night. *Spence's Anecdotes, section i., 1728-30.*

This gave Cowley the fever that carried him off. The parish still talks of the drunken Dean.

It is but just to the memory of Cowley to say that other authorities assert that the cold which ended his life was contracted while he was 'staying too long in the fields to give directions to his laborers.' When Charles II. heard of his death he is said to have exclaimed, 'Mr. Cowley has not left behind him a better man in England.' Few men of Mr. Cowley's guild in England are more entirely forgotten in the Victorian age.

Cowley was buried in the Abbey, 'next to Chaucer's monument,' August 3, 1667.

Went to Mr. Cowley's funeral, whose corpse lay at Wallingford House [the site of which is occupied by the Admiralty Office on Whitehall], and was thence conveyed to Westminster Abbey, in a hearse with six horses, and all funeral decency; near a hundred coaches of noblemen and persons of quality following, among them all the wits of the town, divers bishops and clergymen.

Evelyn's Diary, August 3, 1667.

WILLIAM COWPER.

1731–1800.

COWPER was a pupil of Westminster School from his tenth to his eighteenth year, which were probably the happiest years of his life. Among his schoolfellows were Warren Hastings, Cumberland, and Churchill.

The time of William Cowper seems now, so far as Westminster is concerned, equally remote. It was in the churchyard of St. Margaret's, while he was a scholar at Westminster, that he received one of those impressions which had so strong an effect on his after life. Crossing the burial-ground one dark evening, towards his home in the school, he saw the glimmering lantern of a grave-digger at work. He approached to look on, with a boyish craving for horrors, and was struck by a skull heedlessly thrown out of the crowded earth. To the mind of William Cowper such an accident had an extraordinary significance. In after life he remembered it as the occasion of religious emotions not easily suppressed. On the south side of the church, until the recent restorations, there was a stone the inscription of which suggests the less gloomy view of Cowper's character. It marked the burial-place of Mr. John Gilpin; the date was not to be made out, but it must have been fresh when Cowper was at school, and it would be absurd to doubt that the future poet had seen it, and perhaps unconsciously adopted from it the name of his hero. Loftie's History of London, vol. ii. chap. xvi.

After leaving Westminster School, Cowper went into solitary lodgings in the Middle Temple; but in 1754 or 1755 he took chambers in the Inner Temple, where for a number of years he devoted much of his time to composition, and not a little of it to thoughts of love, — for it was here that he met his first great sorrow in life in the refusal of his family to permit his marriage with his cousin, and it was here that his mental derangement led to his attempt at suicide. After his removal in 1764 to the Asylum for the Insane, on St. Peter Street, St. Albans, he resolved to return no more to London, and probably never saw the metropolis again.[6] In none of the published Lives of Cowper, nor in the autobiographical fragment printed by Grimshaw, is any hint given as to the exact sites of Cowper's homes in the Temple, or elsewhere in London.

He completed the weary Task of his life in 1800.

When Cowper lived in the Temple he was frequently to be found at 'Dick's Coffee House,' No. 8 Fleet Street, near Temple Bar, then called 'Richard's' (see ADDISON, p. 8).

GEORGE CRABBE.

1754-1832.

CRABBE 'took lodgings near the Exchange' when he arrived in London, a literary adventurer, in 1780. In 1817 he lodged at No. 37 Bury Street, St. James's, rebuilt and a hotel in 1885. He was a welcome guest at Holland House (see ADDISON, p. 4), at the house of Mr. Murray the publisher, No. 50 A, Albemarle Street, Piccadilly (see BYRON, p. 33), and at the house of Edmund Burke, in Charles Street, St. James's Square (see BURKE, p. 28); but the greater part of his life was spent in the rural parishes of England, and London rarely saw him. He was a frequent guest at 'The Hill,' the house of his friend Lemuel Hoare, at North End, Hampstead Heath. It was, in 1885, a large yellow brick mansion that had been renewed, although its old gate-posts were retained. It faced the east, the last house on the Heath, and at the top of Hendon Road.

In one of his letters he says, 'I rhyme with a great deal of facility at Hampstead.'

In his Diary, July 15, 1817, he records the writing of 'some lines in the solitude of Somerset House, not fifty yards from the Thames on one side, and the Strand on the other, but quiet as the lands of Arabia.'

One of Crabbe's later resorts in London was the Hummums, on the southeast corner of the Market Place, Covent Garden, an old-fashioned hotel, still frequented in 1885 by the sons and grandsons of the men who knew and met Mr. Crabbe there. It boasts of its successive generations of patrons and guests, but is soon to be destroyed.

Crabbe, after his literary reputation had been established, was staying for a few days at the old Hummums; but he was known to the coffee-room and to the waiters merely as 'Mr. Crabbe.' One forenoon, when he had gone out, a gentleman called on him, and while expressing his regret at not finding him, happened to let drop the information that Mr. Crabbe was the celebrated poet. The next time that Crabbe entered the coffee-room he was perfectly astonished at the sensation which he caused; the company were all eagerness to look at him, the waiters all officiousness to serve him.

^{Rogers's Table Talk.}

ALEXANDER CRUDEN.

1701-1770.

CRUDEN settled in London in 1732, and opened a bookstall under the Royal Exchange. Here he prepared and published, in 1737, his 'Concordance,' the financial results of which were so disastrous as to ruin him in business and derange his mind. This Exchange, on the site of the present building, was destroyed by fire in 1838, and no trace of Cruden's shop remains.

Cruden was confined for a time in a private madhouse in Bethnal Green, from which he escaped.

His subsequent London homes were somewhere in the Savoy, in Upper Street, Islington, and later in Camden Passage, Islington Green.

After residing about a year at Aberdeen, he returned to London and resumed his lodgings at Islington [in Camden Passage], where he died on the morning of November 1, 1770, in the sixty-ninth year of his age. When the person of the house went to inform him that his

^{John Nelson's History of Islington, 1811, p. 39.}

breakfast was ready, he was found dead on his knees in the posture of prayer. He had complained for some days of an asthmatic affection, one of the paroxysms of which probably terminated his life.

Camden Passage, running from Camden Street, Islington, southerly, behind the High Street, and parallel with that thoroughfare, was in 1885 a short narrow crooked lane between rows of one- and two-storied brick houses, dingy, and some of them as old, probably, as Cruden's time; but his house, or the exact position of it, cannot now be discovered.

Cruden was buried in the ground of the Dissenters in Deadman's Place, Southwark, which was described as being 'the second turning in Park Street on the left from the Borough Market.' The cemetery is no longer in existence. The Brewery of Barclay and Perkins occupies a portion of its site.

RICHARD CUMBERLAND.

1732–1811.

CUMBERLAND entered Westminster School (see CHURCHILL, p. 50) in 1744, when he boarded in 'Peters Street, two doors from the turning out of College Street,'—a vague address, as Peters Street and Great College Street both run east and west.

Cumberland's Memoir of Himself, chap. i. I remained in Westminster School, as well as I can recollect, half a year in the shell, and one year in the sixth form. . . . When only in my fourteenth year, I was admitted to Trinity College, Cambridge.

At Westminster, with him, were the elder Colman, Cowper, Churchill, and Warren Hastings.

In his twentieth year, upon becoming Secretary to Lord Halifax, he found lodgings in Downing Street, and afterwards in Mount Street, Berkeley Square.

In my lodgings in Mount Street, I had stocked myself with my own books, some of my father's, and those which Dr. Richard Bentley had bestowed upon me. I sought no company, nor wished for any new connections. . . . About this time I made my first small offering to the press, following the steps of Gray with another 'Churchyard Elegy,' written on St. Mark's Eve. Cumberland's Memoir of Himself, chap. ii.

Cumberland, after his marriage, 'took a house for a short time in Luke Street, Westminster, and afterwards in Abingdon Buildings.' Abingdon Buildings ran from Abingdon Street to the Thames, opposite Great College Street. It disappeared on the erection of the new Houses of Parliament.

Later, Cumberland lived for many years in Queen Anne Street, at the corner of Wimpole Street. Here he wrote the 'West Indian,' and here, probably, he remained until he removed to Tunbridge Wells, in 1781.

Cumberland was again in London during the last few years of his life, and he died at the house of a friend in Bedford Place, Russell Square. He was buried close to Shakspere's statue, in the Poets' Corner.

ALLAN CUNNINGHAM.

1784–1842.

ALLAN CUNNINGHAM lived from 1824 until the time of his death, eighteen years later, at No. 27 Lower Belgrave Place, in a house unchanged in 1885, but then known as No. 98 Buckingham Palace Road. He was foreman for many years in the studio of Chantrey, on the corner of Lower Belgrave Place and Eccleston Street, still standing, half a century later, as Chantrey left it, and called Chantrey House.

Cunningham was buried in the northwest corner of the cemetery of Kensal Green.

Mrs. Thomson, in her 'Recollections of Literary Characters,' thus describes her first interview with Cunningham in Chantrey's studio:—

Covered with a sort of apron or pinafore, such as good old-fashioned cooks used to put on when cooking, a small chisel in his hand, his face wearing a puzzled look, and emerging from a half-finished monument, came forth Allan Cunningham. . . . 'There are some pretty things here,' he remarked, in his broad Scotch, — the broadest Scotch, — a Scotch never diluted by the slightest approach to English, — a Scotch just intelligible, and that is all.

MADAME D'ARBLAY.

1752-1840.

FANNY BURNEY was brought to London by her parents in 1760; and when her mother died, during the next year, she was at school near her father's house in Queen Square, Bloomsbury, perhaps under the tuition of Churchill (see CHURCHILL, p. 51). In 1774, when Dr. Burney was organist to Chelsea Hospital she lived in the grounds belonging to that institution.

Portions of 'Evelina' were written at No. 35 St. Martin's Street, Leicester Square.

Numerous were the friends who frequented Dr. Burney's hospitable residence in Poland Street [Oxford Street], and also that in Queen Square, which he afterwards occupied. The latter he subsequently exchanged for the house in St. Martin's Street, which had once been the abode of Sir Isaac Newton, and where still remained, above the attic, his observatory [see NEWTON], which, with due reverence, Dr. Burney caused to be repaired and preserved.

Mrs. Elwood's Literary Ladies of England, vol. ii.: Madame D'Arblay.

A letter of Miss Burney's, dated 1785, was written 'at Mrs. Delaney's, in St. James's Place,' St. James's Street. She became Madame D'Arblay in 1793; and after a long residence on the Continent, and at Bath and elsewhere in the provinces of England, she settled in London in 1818.

Thursday, October 18, 1818. — I came this evening to my new and probably last dwelling, No. 11 Bolton Street, Piccadilly. My kind James conducted me. Oh, how heavy is my forlorn heart! I have made myself very busy all day; so only could I have supported this first opening to my baleful desolation. No adored husband. No beloved son. But the latter is only at Cambridge. Ah! let me struggle to think more of the other, the first, the chief, as only one removed from my sight by a transitory journey.

Madame D'Arblay's Diary.

Sir Walter Scott was taken by Rogers to call on Madame D'Arblay in Bolton Street.

November 18. — I have been introduced to Madame D'Arblay, the celebrated authoress of 'Evelina' and 'Cecilia,' an elderly lady with no remains of personal beauty, but with a simple and gentle manner, and pleasing expression of countenance, and apparently quiet feelings.

Scott's Diary, 1826: Lockhart's Life of Scott.

Madame D'Arblay's house was standing in 1885, the numbers in Bolton Street being unchanged.

Afterwards she went to the corner of Piccadilly and Half Moon Street, on the east side of the latter thoroughfare; but the house no longer remains. She died in Lower Grosvenor Street, New Bond Street, in 1840.

WILLIAM DAVENANT.

1605–1668.

OF Davenant's private life in London little is known now, except that the first Lady Davenant died in Castle Yard (since called Castle Street), Holborn, — a short street opposite Furnival's Inn, the character of which has entirely changed during the last two centuries, — and that Davenant himself died in apartments over or immediately adjoining the Duke's Theatre, Portugal Row, the site of which was afterwards occupied by the College of Surgeons. The chief entrance to the theatre, which ran back to the south side of Lincoln's Inn Fields, was on Portugal Street, facing Carey Street.

The Tennis Court in Little Lincolnes Inne Fielde was turned into a play house for the Duke of Yorke's players, where Sʳ William had lodgings, and where he dyed April 166–

<small>Aubrey's Lives: Davenant.</small> [1668]. I was at his funerall; he had a coffin of walnutt-tree. Sir John Denham said 'twas the finest coffin that ever he sawe. His body was carried in a hearse from the play house to Westminster Abbey, where at the great west dore he was received by the singing men and choristers, who sang the service of the church to his grave, which is in the south crosse aisle, on which, on a paving stone of marble is writt in imitation of yᵗ on Ben Jonson, 'O rare Sʳ Wm. Davenant.'

I up and down to the Duke of York's play house to see, which

<small>Pepys's Diary, vol. iii., April 9, 1668.</small> I did, Sir W. Davenant's corpse carried out towards Westminster, there to be buried. Here were many coaches, and many hacknies, that made it look, methought, as if it were the buriall of a poor poet. He seemed to have many children, by five or six in the first mourning coach, all boys.

Davenant directed theatrical performances at Rutland House, which stood at the upper end of Aldersgate Street, near what has since been called Charter House Square; and at the Cock Pit Theatre, in Cock Pit Alley, afterwards called Pitt Place, Drury Lane. This theatre was long since taken down; and the street upon which it stood, and which ran from No. 20 Great Wild Street to No. 135 Drury Lane, entirely disappeared on the erection of the Peabody Buildings for Workingmen. Davenant's name is also associated with the Red Bull Theatre in Red Bull Yard, Clerkenwell; no trace of which, or even of the street that contained it now remains. Red Bull Yard is shown, by comparison with old maps, to be the present (1885) Woodbridge Street, or part of it; and the theatre probably stood behind the archway called Hayward's Place, St. John's Street, Clerkenwell, opposite Compton Street.

One of Davenant's haunts was the Brew House in Axe Yard, Westminster, afterwards Fluyder Street, on the west side of King Street, between Charles and Downing Streets. It is now covered by the public offices (see PEPYS).

THOMAS DAY.

1748–1789.

THE author of 'Sandford and Merton' was born in Wellclose Square, Shadwell. As a child he lived at Stoke Newington, where he received the first rudiments of his education. In 1757 he was sent to the Charter House (see ADDISON, p. 1), where he remained seven years. He was a student of the Middle Temple; but the greater part of his life was spent at Anningsley Park, Addlestone, Surrey.

DANIEL DE FOE.

1661-1731.

DANIEL DE FOE, son of James Foe, a butcher, was born in the parish of St. Giles, Cripplegate; and at the age of twelve was sent to the Dissenters' School, on the north side of Newington Green, near the Dissenting Chapel, where he remained four years, and received all the education his father was willing, or able, to give him. One of his schoolmates is said to have been named Crusoe.

In 1685 De Foe occupied a shop in Freeman's Court, Cornhill, at the east end of the Royal Exchange, a street no longer in existence. Here he remained in trade as a hosier and wool-dealer for ten years. He was afterwards engaged in the manufacture of tiles and bricks on the banks of the Thames at or near Tilbury, when he lived close to his place of business, and spent much of his leisure on the river.

In January, 1703, the House of Commons resolved that a book of his should be burned by the Common Hangman in Palace Yard, Westminster; and the Secretary of State issued the following interesting proclamation, still preserved in the Records:—

Whereas, Daniel De Foe, alias De Fooe, is charged with writing a scandalous and seditious pamphlet entitled 'The Shortest Way with the Dissenters.' He is a middle-sized spare man, about forty years old, of a brown complexion, and dark brown colored hair, but wears a wig; a hooked nose, a sharp chin, gray eyes, and a large mole near his mouth.

A reward of fifty pounds was offered for his discovery and arrest.

On the 29th inst. [July, 1703] Daniel Foe, alias De Foe, stood in the pillory before the Royal Exchange in Cornhill, as he did yesterday near the Conduit in Cheapside, and this day at Temple Bar. London Gazette, July 31, 1703.

Other missiles than were wont to greet a pillory reached De Foe ; and shouts of a different temper. His health was drunk with acclamations as he stood there, and nothing harder than a flower was flung at him. 'The people were expected to treat me very ill,' he said, 'but it was not so. On the contrary, they were with me, wished those who had set me there were placed in my room, and expressed their affection by loud shouts and acclamations when I was taken down.' John Forster's Biographical Essays: De Foe.

'The Great Conduit of sweet water' was at the Poultry end, the Little Conduit at the west end, of Cheapside. Both stood in the middle of the street.

Shortly after his release from prison De Foe took his family to Stoke Newington.

His house is still standing [1845]. It is on the south side of Church Street, a little to the east of Lordship's Lane or Road, and has about four acres of ground attached, bounded on the west by a narrow footway (once, if not still) called 'Cut-throat Lane.' Forster's Biographical Essays: De Foe.

'Robinson Crusoe,' published in 1719, is said to have been written in this house, which was destroyed in 1875, when De Foe Street was cut through its grounds.

Sophia De Foe was baptized, and Daniel De Foe, an infant, was buried, in Hackney Church. Both were children of Daniel De Foe. Old Hackney Church was taken down in 1806, and only the tower left standing.

De Foe died on the 24th of April, 1731, in the parish in which he was born, — that of St. Giles, Cripplegate. Forster says : —

The precise place of De Foe's death was in Rope Makers' Alley, Moorfields. Of this fact there can be no reasonable doubt, it being so stated in the 'Daily Courant' of the day following his death. Rope Makers' Alley no longer exists, but it stood opposite to where the London Institution now stands.

The London Institution, built in 1816, stood in 1885 at Nos. 11 and 12 Finsbury Circus. Rope Makers' Alley, as shown on an old map of that portion of London contained in Noorthbouck's 'History of London,' and published in 1772, ran from Finsbury Pavement to Grub Street, now Milton Street, and seems to be identical with the Rope Makers' Street of the present. Its character has greatly changed during the last hundred and fifty years.

De Foe was buried in the neighboring cemetery of Bunhill Fields; where stood, in 1885, a granite obelisk with an inscription stating that it was erected in 1870 'By the Boys and Girls of England to the Memory of the Author of Robinson Crusoe.'

THOMAS DE-QUINCEY.

1786–1859.

IT was late in November, 1802, when De Quincey, having run away from school, first arrived in London. He found miserable lodgings in Greek Street at the corner of Soho Square, and for some time lived the life of a vagrant in the streets and in the parks.

He bought his first dose of opium in 1804 at a chemist's shop in Oxford Street near the Pantheon, which was numbered 173 Oxford Street in 1885.

In 1808 and later, he lodged in Titchfield Street, Dean Street, Soho, and in Northumberland Street, Marylebone. About the same time he entered himself as a student in the Middle Temple.

The 'Confessions of an Opium Eater' were written in a little back-room at No. 4 York Street, Covent Garden, on the premises of Mr. Bohn, the book dealer and publisher, where De Quincey lived a comparatively secluded life for some time, seeing much, however, of Hood, Hogarth, and the Lambs. Mr. Bohn retired from business some years ago; but his house in York Street, occupied in 1885 by a publishing-firm, was quite unchanged.

CHARLES DICKENS.

1812–1870.

BORN at Portsea, Dickens was brought to London as a child, loved London as only London, it seems, can be loved, spent the greater part of his busy life in London, and rests now among London's cherished dead.

In Forster's biography we can follow Dickens from street to street in the metropolis, until we leave him in the Poets' Corner, on the banks of that Thames he knew so well. At the age of ten he was lodging in Bayham Street, Camden Town. 'A washerwoman lived next door, and a Bow Street officer lived over the way.' The life and the surroundings there were miserable enough.

The family then moved to No. 4 North Gower Street (now simply Gower Street), on the east side, a few doors from Francis Street, and between that thoroughfare and University Street. It has been renumbered. A large brass plate on the door told to the world that this was 'Mrs. Dickens's Establishment.' Here they remained until the elder Dickens was carried, like Mr. Dorrit, to the Marshalsea. The prisoner was lodged 'in the top story but one,' in chambers afterwards occupied by the Dorrits, and Charles for a time ran daily to visit him from Gower Street, across the town and the river.

That certain portions of the Marshalsea are still standing is not generally known. Indeed, the fact was not known to Dickens himself when he began 'Little Dorrit;' but in the Preface to that story he gives this account of a visit to it:—

I found the outer front court-yard metamorphosed into a butter shop; and I then almost gave up every brick of the jail for lost. Wandering, however [from the Borough High Street, a few doors from the Church of St. George], down a certain adjacent 'Angel Court leading to Bermondsey,' I came to 'Marshalsea Place;'... and whosoever goes here will find his feet on the very paving-stones of the extinct Marshalsea jail,—will see its narrow yard to the right and to the left, very little altered, if at all, except that the walls were lowered when the place got free,— will look upon the rooms in which the debtors lived, and will stand among the crowded ghosts of many miserable years.

The place still remained in 1885 as Dickens has described it;[7] and the associations of David Copperfield with the melancholy spot are those of the young Charles Dickens, who knew it as well as David knew it, and in much the same way.

Dr. B. E. Martin, in his admirable paper 'In London with Dickens' ('Scribner's Magazine,' March, 1881), tells how little is left of the early homes and haunts of the great novelist.

The blacking-warehouse at Old Hungerford Stairs, Strand, opposite Old Hungerford Market, in which he tied up the pots of blacking, has long since been torn down. That 'crazy old house with a wharf of its own, abutting on the water when the tide was in, and on the mud when the tide was out, and literally overrun with rats,' is now replaced by a row of stone buildings; the embankment has risen over the mud, and the vast Charing Cross Station stands opposite, on the site of the Old Hungerford Market, and of 'The Swan, or Swan and something else,' — the miserable old public where he used to get his bread and cheese and glass of beer. The very name of the street is gone, and Villiers Street has sponged out the memory of Hungerford Stairs. . . . Indeed, it is no longer possible to find any of the places he mentions in his narrative to Forster. . . . Bayham Street, where he lived, is entirely rebuilt.

During the residence of the elder Dickens in the Marshalsea his son found lodgings in a back attic in Lant Street Borough, where he afterwards placed Bob Sawyer. 'It's near Guy's, and handy for me, you know. Little distance after you 've passed St. George's Church, — turns out of the High Street on the right-hand side the way.' Mr. Sawyer does not give the number in asking Mr. Pickwick and 'the other chaps' to the famous party; but Lant Street undoubtedly still stands as Mr. Pickwick found it, and as the young Dickens knew it in 1822–24.

It is a by-street, and its dulness is soothing. A house in Lant Street would not come within the denomination of a first-rate residence, in the strict acceptance of the term, but it is Pickwick, a most desirable spot, nevertheless. If a man wished chap. xxx. to abstract himself from the world, to remove himself from within the reach of temptation, to place himself beyond the possibility of any inducement to look out of the window, he should by all means go to Lant Street.

It was during this period that Dickens ordered the 'glass of Genuine Stunning Ale,' and excited the sympathy and won the motherly kiss of the publican's wife, so pathetically told in 'Copperfield.' In a private letter, late in life, he declares this to have been an actual experience, and that the public house was the Red Lion, still standing in 1885 on the northeast corner of Derby and Parliament Streets, Westminster.

Of the many lodging-house homes of the Dickenses there is no particular reason to speak here. Little that is interesting is associated with them. The original Mrs. Pipchin was his landlady in Little College Street, Camden Town, now College Street, between Jeffreys Street and King's Road; and the original of the Marchioness waited on the family while they were in the Marshalsea.

Dickens's first school of any importance was described by one of his schoolfellows in 1871, as still standing on the corner of Granby Street and the Hampstead Road, in its original state, although the school playground in the rear was destroyed on the formation of the London and Northwestern Railway. It figures in one of his papers entitled 'Our School,' and its masters suggested Mr. Creakle and Mr. Mell of Salem House. In 1885 it remained comparatively unchanged.

Dickens was living in Furnival's Inn, Holborn, when 'Pickwick' was conceived and written; here was spent the first year or two of his married life, and here, in 1837, his eldest son was born. John Westlock, it will be remembered, lived in Furnival's Inn.

His rooms were the perfection of neatness and convenience,
<small>Chuzzlewit, chap. xlv.</small> at any rate; and if he were anything but comfortable, the fault was certainly not theirs.

Perhaps Dickens thought of his own young married life, when he painted sweet Ruth Pinch looking out upon the twilight into the shady quiet place, while her brother was absorbed in music, and her brother's friend stood silently but eloquently by her side.

In March, 1837, Dickens took his little family to No. 48 Doughty Street, Mecklenburgh Square, — a house still standing in 1885, — where he remained three years, and wrote 'Oliver Twist' and 'Nicholas Nickleby.'

Doughty Street runs from Mecklenburgh Square to John

Street, a quiet retired little street, cut off, at the John Street end, by iron gates, which are only opened for carts and carriages that have business in the street itself. The property belongs to the notorious Tichborne Estate, and by them is sacredly held as No Thoroughfare to the general public.

Late in the year 1839 Dickens removed to No. 1 Devonshire Terrace, Regent's Park. 'A house of great promise (and great premium), undeniable situation and excessive splendor, is in view.' Here he lived, while in London, until 1851, during which time he wrote, in the order named, 'The Curiosity Shop,' 'Barnaby Rudge,' 'American Notes,' 'Martin Chuzzlewit,' 'Christmas Carol,' 'The Chimes,' 'The Cricket on the Hearth,' 'Dombey and Son,' 'The Battle of Life,' 'The Haunted Man,' and 'David Copperfield.' A drawing of the Devonshire Terrace House, by Maclise, is reproduced in the third volume of Forster's 'Life of Dickens.' It was here that he lost by death, in 1841, the raven who figures in 'Barnaby Rudge' as 'Grip,' and whose last hours he so beautifully described in the letter now preserved in the Forster Collection at South Kensington.

Towards eleven o'clock he was so much worse that it was found necessary to muffle the stable knocker. . . . On the clock striking twelve he appeared slightly agitated ; but he soon recovered, walked twice or thrice along the coach-house, stopped to bark, staggered, exclaimed, 'Helloa, old girl!' (his favorite expression), and died. Kate is as well as can be expected, but terribly low, as you may suppose. The children seem rather glad of it. He bit their ankles ; but that was play.

Devonshire Terrace consists of three houses at the north end of High Street, Marylebone. No. 1, in 1885, was a large brick mansion, with a garden, on the corner of Marylebone Road.

Dickens moved to Tavistock House, Tavistock Square, in October, 1851.

In Tavistock Square stands Tavistock House. This and the strip of garden in front of it are shut out from the thoroughfare by an iron railing. A large garden with a grass plat and high trees stretches behind the house, and gives it a countrified look in the midst of this coal and gas steaming London. In the passage from street to garden hung pictures and engravings. Here stood a marble bust of Dickens, so like him, so youthful and handsome; and over a bedroom door and a dining-room door were inserted the bas-reliefs of Night and Day, after Thorwaldsen. On the first floor was a rich library with a fireplace and a writing-table, looking out on the garden; and here it was that in winter Dickens and his friends acted plays to the satisfaction of all parties. The kitchen was underground, and at the top of the house were the bedrooms. I had a snug room looking out on the garden; and over the tree-tops I saw the London towers and spires appear or disappear as the weather cleared or thickened.

<small>Hans Christian Andersen.</small>

In Tavistock House Dickens wrote portions of 'Bleak House,' 'Hard Times,' 'Little Dorrit,' and the 'Tale of Two Cities.' It was still standing in 1885, and occupied as a Jewish College. In 1860 Dickens removed to Gad's Hill; and he never afterwards had a permanent home in London, except the Chambers at No. 26 Wellington Street, corner of York Street, Strand, over the office of 'All the Year Round.'

Dickens's intimacy with his biographer naturally led him often to Forster's house, No. 58 Lincoln's Inn Fields, which, as Dr. Martin has shown us, was Tulkinghorn's house as well.

Here in a large house, formerly a house of State, lives Mr. Tulkinghorn. It is let off in sets of chambers now; and in those shrunken fragments of its greatness lawyers lie, like maggots in nuts. But its roomy staircases,

<small>Bleak House, chap. x.</small>

passages, and ante-chambers still remain; and even its painted ceiling, where Allegory in Roman helmet and Celestial linen sprawls among balustrades and pillars, flowers, clouds and big-legged boys, and makes the head ache, as would seem to be Allegory's object always, more or less.

This house was standing in 1885, little changed except that Allegory had been whitewashed out of sight by later tenants. It was in this house that on the 2d December, 1844, Dickens read 'The Chimes' to that brilliant company of his friends, as described by Mr. Forster.

An occasion rather memorable, in which was the germ of those readings to larger audiences, by which, as much as by his books, the world knew him in his later life, but of which no detail beyond the fact remains in my memory; and all are dead now who were present at it, excepting only Mr. Carlyle and myself. Among those, however, who have thus passed away, was one, our excellent Maclise, who, anticipating the advice of Captain Cuttle, had 'made a note' of it in pencil, which I am able here to reproduce. It will tell the reader all he could wish to know. He will see of whom the party consisted, and may be assured that in the grave attention of Carlyle, the eager interest of Stanfield and Maclise, the keen look of poor Laman Blanchard, Fox's rapt solemnity, Jerrold's skyward gaze, and the tears of Harness and Dyce, the characteristic points of the scene are sufficiently rendered. *Forster's Life of Dickens, vol. ii. chap. vii.*

The original of this drawing is in the Forster Collection in the Museum of South Kensington; and, as Dr. Martin says,—

In the left-hand corner of the room (as sketched by Maclise) you shall see the very frescos — weird figures with waving arms and pointing fingers — which Dickens placed with such ghostly effect on Tulkinghorn's ceiling. *Scribner's Magazine, March, 1881.*

The last home of Dickens in London was the house of Milner-Gibson, No. 5 Hyde Park Place, which he occupied for a few months. Writing herefrom to James T. Fields, January 14, 1870, he says:—

We live opposite the Marble Arch, in a charming house until the 1st of June, and then return to Gad's Hill. . . . I have a large room here with three fine windows overlooking the Park, unsurpassable for airiness and cheerfulness.

<small>Fields's Yesterdays with Authors: Dickens.</small>

Several numbers of 'Edwin Drood' were written in this house, which was unaltered in 1885.

Dickens died, June 9, 1870, at Gad's Hill, and was buried, June 14, in the Poets' Corner, Westminster Abbey.

Close under the bust of Thackeray lies Charles Dickens, not, it may be, his equal in humor, but more than his equal in his hold on the popular mind, as was shown in the intense and general enthusiasm shown at his grave. The funeral, according to Dickens's urgent and express desire in his will, was strictly private. It took place at an early hour in the summer morning, the grave having been dug in secret the night before; and the vast solitary space of the Abbey was occupied only by the small band of mourners, and the Abbey Clergy, who, without any music except the occasional peal of the organ, read the funeral service. For days the spot was visited by thousands; many were the flowers strewn upon it by unknown hands; many were the tears shed by the poorer visitors. He rests beside Sheridan, Garrick, and Henderson.

<small>Dean Stanley's Westminster Abbey.</small>

BENJAMIN DISRAELI.

1804–1881.

THE registry of the Spanish and Portuguese Jewish Synagogue, No. 10 Bevis Marks, proves the younger Disraeli to have been born December 21, 1804, although the residence of his father at that time is not given, and it is very difficult to determine now the place of his birth. It was, according to the various biographers, at Hackney, Islington,

St. Mary Axe, and Bloomsbury Square, and it is even said that Lord Beaconsfield himself once told a friend that he was born in a library in the Adelphi. It would seem, however, that Islington has the strongest claim to the distinction; and Dr. John B. Jeaffreson, in a letter to the London 'Standard,' in 1881, says that the D'Israelis were living in 1803 behind Canonbury Tower (see GOLDSMITH), that while this house was undergoing repairs they lived for a twelvemonth next door to Dr. Jeaffreson (grandfather of this writer), in Trinity Row, and that Benjamin Disraeli was unexpectedly born there, Dr. Jeaffreson being the medical attendant.

Dr. B. E. Martin, who has in many ways shown his interest in this work, and who has been of the greatest assistance in its production, has learned by personal inquiry that the members of the Jeaffreson family who were contemporaries of Benjamin Disraeli, and who were his playmates in infancy, always *believed* him to have been the child born in Trinity Row while his father was their immediate neighbor, although there is no absolute proof that such was the case. The name of D'Israeli does not appear in the London directories of 1804.

This Trinity Row house, still standing in 1885, but known as No. 215 Upper Street, Islington, and occupied on its lower floor by shops, is remembered as having been 'a well looking dwelling' in the early part of this century, its front windows commanding a view of Canonbury Fields, and its back windows overlooking its own moderately extensive grounds.

Benjamin Disraeli was baptized in the Church of St. Andrew, Holborn, July 13, 1817, and in the registry there is described as 'From King's Road, and said to be about twelve years of age.' The elder D'Israeli is known to have occupied, at that time, the house in King's Road, next to the corner of John Street, and left unchanged in 1885 except that it was then known as No. 22 Theobald's Road. King's Road ran from Gray's Inn Road to Bedford Row, north of Gray's Inn Gardens. Dr. Martin discovered from the ratebooks that Isaac D'Israeli paid rates from 1817 to 1829 on the house on the corner of Hart Street and Bloomsbury Square, numbered then 6 Bloomsbury Square, but since changed to No. 5. The house now No. 6 Bloomsbury Square, and generally supposed to have been the home of the D'Israelis, was then No. 6 A or 6½. All this is proved by the records of the Bedford Estate, in which Bloomsbury Square lies, as well as by statements of residents of the house for many years. Benjamin, therefore, was at least twelve years of age when his father went to Bloomsbury Square; and the following account of his 'visit to the room in which he was born' must be considered in the light of romance. The house was left unaltered in 1885.

Montagu Corry (Lord Rowton) told me that not long ago Lord Beaconsfield visited the house [in Bloomsbury Square] and asked leave to go over it, which was granted, although the attendant had no idea that the courtesy was extended to the Prime Minister. He sat for some time pondering and reflecting — a grand past and a great future opening before his mental vision — in the room in which he was born. Once I met the two, great father and greater son, at one of the receptions of Lady Blessington. It is certain that from the first to the last no parent ever received more grateful respect or more enduring affection from a child; and I well remember that on the evening to which I refer, the devotion of Benjamin Disraeli to Isaac D'Israeli, specially noticed by all who were present, was classed among the admirable traits of the after Prime Minister.

<small>S. C. Hall's Retrospect of a Long Life; Beaconsfield.</small>

A writer in 'Punch' shortly after the death of Lord Beaconsfield says that he went to a dame's school in Colebrook Row, Islington, kept by a Miss Palmer; and he is known to have been a pupil of an academy since called Essex Hall on Higham Hill, Walthamstow, Essex, six miles from town, where his desk and room were carefully preserved many years later. When a very young man, Disraeli spent a year or two as a clerk in a solicitor's office in the City, somewhere in the neighborhood of the Old Jewry; but his home was generally in his father's family, in town or in Buckinghamshire, until his marriage with Mrs. Lewis in 1839, when he took possession of her house, No. 1 Grosvenor Gate, corner of Park Lane and Upper Grosvenor Street. Here he lived until her death in 1872. This house was still standing in 1885.

In 1873 Disraeli moved to No. 2 Whitehall Gardens; and in 1881 he died at No. 19 Curzon Street, Mayfair, facing South Audley Street.

ISAAC D'ISRAELI.

1766-1848.

THE only home of Isaac D'Israeli's youth was his father's house at Enfield, where he was born, and where he remained until his marriage. The site of this house is unknown to the local historians; but Ford, in his 'Enfield,' believes it to have been on the ground since occupied by the terminus of the Great Eastern Railway.

As a young man D'Israeli came now and then to London to read the newspapers in the St. James's Coffee House in St. James's Street (see ADDISON, p. 7); and he spent many hours in the Reading Room of the British Museum. In the 'Memoirs of the Elder D'Israeli by his Son' the following story is told:—

My father, who had lost the timidity of his childhood, who by nature was very impulsive, and indeed endowed with a degree

of volubility which is only witnessed in the south of France, and
which never deserted him to his last hour, was no longer to be
controlled. His conduct was decisive. He enclosed his poem
to Dr. Johnson with an impassioned statement of his case, complaining, which he ever did, that he had never found a counsellor
or literary friend. He left his packet himself at Bolt Court [see
JOHNSON], where he was received by Mr. Francis Barber, the doctor's well-known black servant, and told to call in a week. Be
sure that he was very punctual; but the packet was returned
to him unopened, with a message that the illustrious doctor was
too ill to read anything. The unhappy and obscure aspirant
who received this disheartening message accepted it, in his utter
despondency, as a mechanical excuse. But, alas! the cause was
too true; and a few weeks after the great soul of Johnson quitted
earth.

The various homes of the elder D'Israeli are described in
the preceding paper (see the younger DISRAELI, pp. 86–89).

In Bloomsbury Square he wrote 'The Curiosities of
Literature,' and kindred works, and remained until he took
his family in 1825 to Bradenham House, Buckinghamshire,
where he died in 1848. A letter of his was written to the
Countess of Blessington, but without date, from No. 1 St.
James's Place, St. James's Street; and in 1835 both father
and son were at No. 31 A, Park Street, Grosvenor Square,
near the corner of King Street, and next door to the White
Bear public house. This street has been renumbered.

MICHAEL DRAYTON.

1563–1631.

IT is not now known when or under what circumstances
Drayton first saw London; and nothing is to be gathered
concerning his career here from the occasional personal

allusions scattered throughout his poems. According to Aubrey he 'lived at ye bay-windowe house next the east end of St. Dunstan's Church in Fleet Street.' This house, numbered 186 Fleet Street, was standing in 1885, altered and restored; but its next-door neighbor city-wards still showed what was its appearance when Drayton occupied it, and published in 1608 an edition of his 'Poems' 'at the Shop of John Smithwick, St. Dunstan's Church Yard under the Diall.' This churchyard, facing Fleet Street, was the Paternoster Row of that day, and much frequented by booksellers.

Drayton was buried in Westminster Abbey, according to Fuller 'in the south aisle near to Chaucer's grave and Spenser's, where his monument stands;' but Dean Stanley believes that he lies near the small north door of the nave. Mr. Marshall, the stonecutter in Fetter Lane, told Aubrey that the lines on his 'pious marble were writ by Francis Quarles, a very good man.' They declare that his name cannot fade; and yet when Goldsmith read them, a century later, he confessed that he had never heard the name before.

JOHN DRYDEN.

1631-1700.

DRYDEN was a pupil of Dr. Busby at Westminster School (see CHURCHILL, p. 51), where is still carefully preserved the old form upon which, in long sprawling schoolboyish letters, is the name I DRYDEN, carved by his own hands. He distinguished himself there as a juvenile poet, and won a scholarship to Trinity College, Cambridge.

According to Malone, he returned to London in 1657, when Scott believes that he lodged with Herringman the bookseller, in the then New Exchange, destroyed in 1737. Scott also throws doubt upon the stories of Dryden's dining at a 'threepenny ordinary' and being 'clad in homely drugget,' as asserted by Shadwell and others. His circumstances were certainly better than his earlier biographers would have us believe, when he married the daughter of the Earl of Berkshire a few years later.

The date of Dryden's marriage eluded inquiries of Malone and Scott. He was married by license in the Church of St. Swithin, by London Stone (as appears by the register of that Church), on the 1st December, 1663. The entry of the license, which is dated 'ultimo Novembis,' 1663, and is in the office of the Vicar-General of the Archbishop of Canterbury, describes him as a parishioner of St. Clement Danes of about the age of thirty, and the Lady Elizabeth [Howard] as twenty-five and of the parish of St. Martin-in-the-Fields. The poet's signature to the entry is written 'Driden.'

Note by Peter Cunningham, Johnson's Lives of the Poets; Dryden.

Scott gives the date of this marriage as 1665. The Church of St. Swithin, Cannon Street, was destroyed in the Great Fire of 1666, but rebuilt by Wren.

Peter Cunningham, with his usual care, in his 'Explanatory Notes to Johnson's Lives of the Poets,' traces Dryden to his different London homes, and shows that 'he lived from 1673 to 1682 in the Parish of St. Bride's, Fleet Street, on the water side of the street, in or near Salisbury Court (Rate Booke of St. Bride's, Fleet Street); and from 1682 to 1686 in a house on the north side of Long Acre facing Rose Street.'

The Dryden Press, founded a century and a half ago, stood in 1885 at No. 137 Long Acre, and marked the site of Dryden's house there.

There is a tradition that Dryden lived once in Fetter

Lane, where Otway was his neighbor; but the only authority for this is a mythical story of a combat of wit between him and Otway (see OTWAY), and the existence, as late as 1885, of a curious old tablet upon the quaint little house at No. 16 Fetter Lane, over Fleur-de-lys Court.[8] No record of his occupancy of this house is to be found in any of the biographies of Dryden, nor, it is said, in the parish books. By whom and when the stone was placed there is not now known. Its inscription reads: —

Here liv'd
John Dryden
Ye poet,
Born 1631 — Died 1700
Glorious John!

Dryden removed to his last London home, Gerard Street, Soho, in 1686.

Dryden's house . . . was the fifth on the left hand coming from Little Newport Street. The back windows looked upon the gardens of Leicester House, of which circumstance our poet availed himself to pay a handsome compliment to the noble owner.   Scott's Dryden, chap. xii.

This house, No. 43 Gerard Street, has been marked by the tablet of the Society of Arts. The gardens in its rear have long since disappeared.

One day, Mr. Rogers took Mr. Moore and my father [Sidney Smith] home in his carriage, and insisted on showing them by the way Dryden's house, in some obscure street. It was very wet; the house looked much like other old houses, and having thin shoes on they both remonstrated, but in vain. Rogers got out, and stood expecting them. 'Ah, you see why Rogers don't mind getting out,' exclaimed my father, laughing and leaning out of the carriage; 'he has got goloshes on · but, Rogers, lend us each a golosh, and we will then stand on one leg and admire as long as you please.   Lady Holland's Memoirs of Rev. Sidney Smith, chap. ix.

Dryden died at No. 43 Gerard Street, May 1, 1700.

His family were preparing to bury him with the decency becoming their limited circumstances, when Charles Montague, Lord Jeffries, and other men of quality made a subscription for a public funeral. The body of the poet was then removed to the Physicians' Hall [now destroyed; it stood on the west side of Warwick Lane, Paternoster Row], where it was embalmed, and lay in state till the 13th day of May, twelve days after his decease. On that day the celebrated Dr. Garth pronounced a Latin oration over the remains of his departed friend, which were then with considerable state, preceded by a band of music and attended by a numerous procession of carriages, transported to Westminster Abbey, and deposited between the graves of Chaucer and Cowley.

<small>Scott's Dryden, chap. vii.</small>

Johnson, in his 'Lives of the Poets,' quotes from a 'Life of Congreve,' printed in 1730, which on the titlepage is said to contain 'some very curious Memories of Mr. Dryden and His Family,' a remarkable account of Dryden's funeral and of a practical joke played by Lord Jeffries upon the mourning friends, which appears to have no foundation in fact, although it has been often repeated. From this statement it would seem that Dr. Garth —

finished his oration with a superior grace, to the loud acclamations of mirth which inspired the mixed, or rather *mob*, auditors. The procession began to move; a numerous train of coaches attended the hearse, but, good God! in what disorder can only be expressed by a sixpenny pamphlet soon after published, entitled 'Dryden's Funeral.' At last the corpse arrived at the Abbey, which was all unlighted. No organ played; no anthem sung; only two of the singing boys preceded the corpse, who sung an Ode of Horace, with each a small candle in his hand. The butchers and other mob broke in like a deluge, so that only about eight or ten gentlemen could get admission, and those forced to cut their way with their swords drawn. The coffin in this disorder was let down into Chaucer's grave, with as much confusion and as little ceremony as was possible, every one glad to save themselves from the gentlemen's swords or the clubs of the mob.

Dryden was a frequenter of Will's Coffee House in Bow Street (see ADDISON, p. 7), where, after his two-o'clock dinner, he was in the habit of going and occupying his established chair, his right to which no man was bold enough to dispute. It was placed by the window in summer, by the fire in winter; and from it he pronounced his opinions of men and books, surrounded by his crowd of admiring listeners, who pretended to agree with him, whether they did or not.

Dryden's mixture of simplicity, good-nature, and good opinion of himself is here seen in a very agreeable manner. It must not be omitted that it was to this house [Will's] Pope was taken when a boy, by his own desire, on purpose to get a sight of the great man, which he did. According to Pope, he was plump, with a fresh color, and a down look, and not very conversible. It appears, however, that what he did say was much to the purpose; and a contemporary mentions his conversation on that account as one of the few things for which the town was desirable. He was a temperate man, though he drank with Addison a great deal more than he used to do, probably so far as to hasten his end. Hunt's The Town, chap. viii.

In Covent Garden to-night, going to fetch home my wife, I stopped at the great Coffee House there [Will's], where I never was before, where were Dryden, the poet, I knew at Cambridge, and all the Wits of the town, and Harris the player [Joseph Harris], and Mr. Hoole of our College. And had I had time then or could at other times, it will be good coming thither, for there, I perceive, is very witty and pleasant discourse. But I could not tarry, and as it was late, they were all ready to go away. Pepys's Diary, vol. ii., February, 1663–64.

One of the most uncomfortable of Dryden's London experiences was the severe beating he received one night in 1679 in Rose Street, Covent Garden, after he had left Will's. Although a reward of fifty pounds was offered for 'the perpetrators of the outrage,' they were never legally punished. There seems to be no question, however, that Rochester instigated the deed, enraged by a satire which he attributed to Dryden, but which was written by another man. Rose Street, running from No. 11 Long Acre to No. 2 Garrick Street at its junction with King Street, has been greatly changed since Dryden's adventures there, although one or two old buildings still standing in the crooked, miserable little street in 1885 were no doubt witnesses of the memorable assault. A modern tavern bearing the old-fashioned name of The Lamb and Flag was built about 1880 in Rose Street, facing Garrick Street.

Dryden was fond of the mulberry tarts that were in his day a specialty of the Mulberry Gardens, upon the site of which Buckingham Palace was built.

TOM D'URFEY.

16— -1723.

OF Tom D'Urfey's career in London or elsewhere almost nothing is known except what is contained in No. 67 of the 'Guardian' (Thursday, May 28, 1713), when Mr. Addison, under a text from Horace, 'Blush not to patronize the Muse's skill,' makes a plea for help for D'Urfey in his impoverished old age, on the ground that he had 'enriched our language with a multitude of rhymes, and bringing words together, that without his good offices would never have been acquainted with one another, so long as it had been a tongue;' and adds that his old friend 'angles for a trout the best of any man in England:' surely reason enough for his meriting the charity of his fellow-men. From this paper it would seem that he was a most agreeable companion; that Charles II. had been seen leaning on his shoulder more than once, humming over a song with him; and that many an honest country gentleman had gained a reputation in his own county by pretending to have been in company with Tom D'Urfey in town. After having written more odes than Horace, and about four times as many comedies as Terence, he was, when Addison found him in 1713, in great difficulties. He lived, however, ten years longer, and continued to write until his death, in 1723. The time of his birth is unknown. He was buried in St. James's Church, Piccadilly, where is a tablet to his memory, said to have been erected by Sir Richard Steele. It contains simply his name and the date of his death, and is on the south wall of the church, on the outside, under the clock tower and nearly opposite the little door leading from Jermyn Street to the disused graveyard. Like so many objects of interest in London, it is entirely concealed from the public by an unsightly and unnecessary high brick wall.

D'Urfey is said to have found the suggestions for his 'Pills to Purge Melancholy' at a convivial meeting held at the Queen's Arms Tavern, Newgate Street. This inn was standing until within a few years at No. 70 Newgate Street. It had an entrance on St. Martin's-le-Grand. The New Post-Office buildings were erected on its site.

MARY ANN EVANS (GEORGE ELIOT).

1819–1880.

'GEORGE ELIOT' came to London in 1851, and for two years made her home with the Chapmans at No. 142 Strand, near Wellington Street,—a house rich in the literary associations of two centuries. A tourist's ticket-office in 1885, it was, in the days of Dr. Johnson, the famous Turk's Head Coffee House, frequented by so many distinguished men (see DR. JOHNSON).

While living here, Miss Evans wrote a number of essays for the 'Westminster Review,' besides doing editorial work; and here she first made the acquaintance of George Henry Lewes and many of the literary lights of her time.

Lewes and Miss Evans lived for a while at No. 16 Blandford Square, where she wrote, among other books, 'Romola' and 'Felix Holt,' in a quiet old-fashioned house not far from Regent's Park, and still standing in 1885, hardly changed since her occupation of it. The Priory, No. 21 North Bank, St. John's Wood, to which they removed in 1865, and where they remained until Lewes died, in 1878, was somewhat altered by a later tenant, who enlarged and beautified it. It was in 1885 one of the characteristic villas of that characteristic locality, plain, substantial, and in grounds of its own, shut out completely from the gaze of the passer-by.

Here, in the pleasant dwelling-rooms decorated by Owen Jones, might be met, at her Sunday afternoon receptions, some of the most eminent men in literature, art, and science. For the rest her life flowed on its even tenor, its routine being rigidly regular. The morning till lunch time was invariably devoted to writing; in the afternoon she either went out for a quiet drive of about two hours, or she took a walk with Lewes in Regent's Park. There the strange-looking couple — she with a certain sibylline air, he not unlike some unkempt Polish refugee of vivacious manners — might be seen swinging their arms, as they hurried along at a pace as rapid as their talk.

<small>Mathilde Blind's George Eliot: Famous Women Series.</small>

George Willis Cooke, in his 'George Eliot' (chap. v. p. 79), thus describes 'The Priory':—

Within, all was refinement and good taste ; there were flowers in the windows, the furniture was plain and substantial, while great simplicity reigned supreme. The house had two stories and a basement. On the first floor were two drawing-rooms, a small reception room, a dining-room, and Mr. Lewes's study. . . . The second floor contained the study of George Eliot, which was a plain room, not large. Its two front windows looked into the garden, and there were bookcases around the walls, and a writing-desk. All things about the house indicated simple tastes, moderate needs, and a plain method of life.

'George Eliot' was married to John Walter Cross at St. George's Church, Hanover Square, May 6, 1880, but died in her husband's house, No. 4 Cheyne Row, Chelsea, December 22 of the same year, and was buried in Highgate Cemetery.

The grave, in the new portion of the cemetery overlooking London, is covered by a plain gray granite shaft bearing the following simple inscription : —

> 'Of those immortal dead who still live on
> in minds made better by their presence.
> Here Lies The Body
> of
> 'George Eliot'
> Mary Ann Cross.
> Born 22nd November, 1819
> Died 22nd December, 1880.

JOHN EVELYN.

1620-1706.

EVELYN'S earliest recorded associations with London are of the Middle Temple.

> I repaired with my brother to the Tearme to goe into the new lodgings (that were formerly in Essex Court), being a very handsome apartment just over against the Hall Court, but four payre of stayres high, w'ch gave us the advantage of the fairer prospect.
>
> <small>Evelyn's Diary, 1640.</small>

Evelyn was married in 1647; and an entry in his Diary, the next year, shows him to have been then a resident of Sayes Court, Deptford, which came to him through his wife, and was his home for almost half a century.

> *Oct.* 7, 1665. — Then to Mr. Evelyn's . . . and here he showed me his gardens, which are, for variety of evergreens and hedged holly, the finest things I ever saw in my life. . . .
>
> *Nov.* 5, 1665. — By water to Deptford, and there made a visit to Mr. Evelyn, who, among other things, showed me some excellent paintings in little, in distemper, in Indian incke, water colours, graeving, and, above all, the whole secret of mezzo-tints, and the manner of it, which is very pretty, and good things done with it. . . . In fine, a most excellent person he is, and must be allowed a little for a little conceitedness; but he may well be so, being a man so much above others.
>
> <small>Pepys's Diary, 1665.</small>

Sayes Court was near the Government Docks at Deptford. It was taken down, according to Lysons, in 1728 or 1729, and the Workhouse built upon its site. This poor-house, looking much older than its actual age, and believed by many of the residents in Deptford to have been the original house occupied by Evelyn and by Peter the Great, was still standing in 1885, at the end of the modern Czar Street, Evelyn Street, and was the home of poor old men and women, — subjects of the private charity of W. J. Evelyn, Esq., the proprietor of the estate. A small patch of ground used as the garden of this house was all that was left, in anything like their natural state, of Evelyn's famous plantations, while a larger portion had been transformed into a public recreation ground, reached from Evelyn Street by Sayes Court Street. Evelyn's hedges, orangeries, and groves had all disappeared.

Evelyn, through his Diary, is easily traced to his various abiding-places in town.

Sept. 10, 1658. — I came with my wife and family to London; tooke lodgings at the 3 Feathers in Russell Street, Covent Garden, for all the winter, my sonne being very unwell.

No trace of the sign of the Three Feathers is to be found to-day.

March 24, 1662. — I returned home with my whole family, which had been most part of the winter since October at London in lodgings, neere the Abbey of Westminster.

Nov. 17, 1683. — I took a house in Villiers Street [Strand], York Buildings, for the winter, having many important concerns to despatch, and for the education of my daughters.

In 1686 he 'came to lodge at Whitehall in the Lord Privy Seales Loddgings.' He spent the winter of 1690 in Soho Square, then King's Square.

July 19, 1699. — Am now removing my family to a more convenient house here, in Dover Street, where I have the remainder of a lease.

Peter Cunningham, consulting the rate books of St. Martin's, discovers this house in Dover Street, Piccadilly, to have been about 'nine doors up, on the east side.'

Evelyn, in 1654, described the Mulberry Gardens in St. James's Park, on the site of which stands the northern portion of Buckingham Palace (see DRYDEN, p. 96), as 'ye only place of refreshment in ye towne for persons of ye best quality to be exceedingly cheated at.' The large number of places of refreshment in London to-day where persons of the best quality may be cheated at, is perhaps one of the most significant signs of the progress of civilization.

Evelyn also records his dining (Nov. 30, 1694) at Pontack's, in Abchurch Lane, with the Royal Society. No trace of Pontack's is now left.

MICHAEL FARADAY.

1791–1867.

FARADAY was born at Newington, but was taken as a child to Jacob's Wells Mews, Charles Street, Manchester Square, in 1796, where his family lived for some years. Charles Street, Manchester Square, is not to be confounded with Charles Street, Portman Square, its near neighbor. It was that part of the present George Street running from Spanish Place to Thayer Street; and Jacob's Wells Mews, little changed in appearance since that time, was still so called in 1885, and on the south side of George Street. From 1804 to 1812 the young Faraday was apprenticed to a bookseller, at No. 2 Blandford Street, Portman Square, where the same business was carried on seventy years later. The house was raised one story in the summer of 1884. It is marked by the tablet of the Society of Arts.

In 1813 Faraday was assigned apartments at the Royal Institution, No. 21 Albemarle Street, Piccadilly, still in the same place in 1885; and here he lived for nearly fifty years. After his retirement in 1858, he went to a house on Hampton

Court Green, where, nine years later, he died. He was buried in Highgate Cemetery; a plain stone against the east wall, about the centre of the old part of the cemetery, marking his grave.

He was an original member of the Athenæum Club.

GEORGE FARQUHAR.

1678-1707.

FARQUHAR settled in London in 1696, when he began his career as a writer for the stage. His first play, 'Love in a Bottle,' was produced at Drury Lane in 1698.

About 1700 Farquhar first met Mrs. Oldfield, as described by Dr. Doran in his 'Annals of the Stage' (vol. i. chap. xiv.).

The time is the close of the seventeenth century; the scene is the Mitre Tavern, St. James's Market, kept by one Mrs. Voss. . . . On the threshold of the open door stand a couple of guests. . . . The one is a gay, rollicking young fellow, smartly dressed, a semi-military look about him, good-humor rippling on his face, combined with an air of astonishment and delight. His sight and hearing are wholly concentrated on that enchanted and enchanting girl who, unmindful of aught but the 'Scornful Lady,' continues still reading aloud that rattling comedy by Beaumont and Fletcher. . . . Captain Farquhar, at whatever passage in the play, betrayed his presence by his involuntary applause. The girl looks towards him more pleased than abashed; and when the Captain pronounced that there was stuff in her for an exquisite actress, the flattered thing clasped her hands, glowed at the prophecy, and protested in her turn, that of all conditions it was the one she wished most ardently to fulfil.

St. James's Market, considerably reduced in size and importance, still exists between Jermyn Street, Charles Street, the present Regent Street, and the Haymarket; but the Mitre Tavern there is not mentioned by Stow, Strype, or in 'The New View of London' (1708), it does not appear on any of the old maps, and no trace of it is now to be found.

Farquhar, suffering in body, and on his death-bed, wrote his 'Beau's Stratagem' in six weeks, and lived only to hear of its brilliant success. He died in April, 1707, only a short time after its triumphant production at the Haymarket, and was buried in the Church of St. Martin-in-the-Fields.

The following touching letter to his friend Wilkes was his valedictory:—

<small>Cibber's Lives of the Poets: Farquhar.</small> DEAR BOB,—I have not anything to leave to perpetuate my memory but two helpless girls. Look upon them sometimes, and think of him who was to the last moment of his life thine, G. FARQUHAR.

HENRY FIELDING.

1707-1754.

FIELDING was little more than twenty years of age when he first settled in London, and began his literary career as a writer for the stage. In February, 1735, he was living in Buckingham Street, Strand. In 1737 he became a student of the Middle Temple, and was called to the Bar three years later, when 'chambers were assigned to him in Pump Court.'

Sir Roger de Coverley, walking in the Temple Garden and discoursing with Mr. Spectator about the beauties in hoops and patches who are sauntering over the grass, is just as lively a figure to me, as old Samuel Johnson rolling through the fog with the Scotch gentleman at his heels, on their way to Dr. Goldsmith's in Brick Court ; or Harry Fielding, with inked ruffles, and a wet towel round his head, dashing off articles for the Covent Garden Journal, while the printer's boy is asleep in the passage.   Pendennis, book ii. chap. viii.

It is an established fact that the 'Covent Garden Journal' had no existence until long after Fielding left the Temple; but Fielding might have dashed off 'copy' for some other publication at that period, as Thackeray, never very accurate about dates and details, describes; and the picture drawn of him with the wet towel, and the printer's devil snoring on the stairs, is too good to be destroyed.

It has now been ascertained that the marriage [Fielding's second marriage] took place at St. Benet's, Paul's Wharf, an obscure little church in the City, at present surrendered to a Welsh congregation, but at that time . . . much in request for unions of a private character. The date in the register is the 27th November, 1747.   Austin Dobson's Fielding, chap. iv.
. . . Either previously to this occasion or immediately after it, Fielding seems to have taken two rooms in a house in Back Lane, Twickenham, not far from the site of Copt Hall. In 1872 this house was still standing, a quaint old-fashioned wooden structure. . . . Now [1883] it no longer exists, and a row of cottages occupies the site.

St. Benet's still remained in 1885 on Upper Thames Street, corner of Bennet's Hill.

Mr. Dobson shows that Fielding must have entered upon his office of Justice of the Peace early in December, 1748, a document bearing date December 9 of that year describing him as 'Henry Fielding, Esq., of Bow Street, Covent Garden.' He then occupied the house upon the site of which the police station has been built. Cunningham and other writers assert that 'Tom Jones' was written in

Bow Street; but as it was published in February, 1749, only a month or two after his taking up his residence there, this can hardly be true. In Bow Street was Fielding's town home until he went to Lisbon, in 1754, to die. He spent the summer months in a cottage at Fordhook.

Henry Fielding, the Cervantes of England, resided occasionally, during the last mournful year of his life, at Fordhook, situated on the Uxbridge Road, at the distance of about a mile from the village of Acton, at the eastern extremity of Ealing. Fielding, whose pen had been the source of so much heartfelt mirth, was now oppressed by a complication of disorders, which threw a cloud over his fancy, and would have subjugated the whole powers of a mind less vivacious and elastic.

<small>Thomas Faulkner's Brentford, Ealing, and Cheswick, chap. iv.</small>

Wednesday, July 26, 1754.— On this day the most melancholy sun I ever beheld arose, and found me awake at my home at Fordhook. . . . At twelve precisely my coach was at the door, which I was no sooner told than I kissed my children all around, and went into it with some little resolution. My wife, who behaved more like a heroine and philosopher, though at the same time the tenderest mother in the world, and my eldest daughter, followed me; some friends with us, and others here took their leave, and I heard my behavior applauded, with many murmurs and praises, to which I well knew I had no title, as all other such philosophers may, if they have any modesty, confess on a like occasion.

<small>Fielding's Journal of a Voyage to Lisbon, 1754.</small>

Thorne, in his 'Hand-Book,' says that Fielding at one time occupied an old house on Barnes Common, known as Milbourne House; and there is a tradition that he lived for a short period in Beaufort Buildings, opposite Exeter Street, Strand.

He was a frequent visitor at the Bedford Coffee House, under the Piazza, Covent Garden (see CHURCHILL, p. 51).

JOHN FLETCHER.

1576-1625.

THE place of Fletcher's birth is not known to us, and almost nothing of his personal history in or out of London, except that he lived in the closest intimacy with Beaumont on the Bankside (see BEAUMONT), and that he was buried in the Church of St. Mary Overy (St. Saviour's), Southwark, at the end of London Bridge, one of the most ancient and interesting of London churches, although but little of the original building is now left.

Oldwit. — I knew Fletcher, my friend Fletcher, and his maid Joan; I shall never forget him; I have supped with him at his house on the Bankside; he loved a fat loin of pork of all things in the world; and Joan, his maid, had her beer-glass of sack, and we all kissed her; faith, and were as merry as passed. [Shadwell's Bury Fair, act I. scene 1.]

In the great plague 1625, a knight of Norfolk or Suffolk invited him [Fletcher] into the country. He stayed but to make himselfe a suit of cloathes, and while it was makeing, fell sick of the plague and dyed. This I had from his tayler who is now a very old man, and clarke of St. Mary Overy's. [Aubrey's Lives.]

In this church [St. Mary Overy's] was interred, without any memorial, that eminent Dramatick Poet, Mr. John Fletcher, son to Bishop Fletcher of London, who dyed of the Plague, the 19th of August, 1625. When I searched the Register of this Parish in 1670 for his obit for the use of Mr. Anthony à Wood, the Parish Clerk, aged above eighty, told me that he was his Tayler, and that Mr. Fletcher staying for a suit of cloaths before he retired into the country, Death stopped his journey and laid him low here. [Aubrey's History of Sussex, vol. v.]

A few years ago Fletcher's name and the date of his death were engraved upon a stone in the pavement of the choir of St. Saviour's, although the exact spot where his bones lie is not recorded.

JOHN FOX.

1517-1587.

FOX'S 'History of the Acts and Monuments of the Church,' more familiarly known as the 'Book of the Martyrs,' was published in 1553, the last year of the reign of Edward VI., and was written, it is said, while Fox was living in the famous Grub Street. Grub Street, in the parish of St. Giles, Cripplegate, was composed of mean low houses, old even in the sixteenth century, tenanted by compilers of pamphlets, penny and halfpenny papers, and 'criticks run to seed,' and gave its name, from the nature of its inhabitants, to a class of writing which was neither exalted nor pure. It lies between Fore Street and Chiswell Street, and has now been called Milton Street, in honor of the author, who emphatically had no connection or association with the original Grub Street or its literature. Its old houses have entirely disappeared.

After the accession of Mary, Fox left England, and did not return until the beginning of Elizabeth's reign. In 1565 he was an inmate of the household of his patron, the Duke of Norfolk, whose town mansion was then the Charter House, at the head of Aldersgate Street, which, taken from the Church by Henry VIII., did not become a school until 1611, when James was king (see ADDISON).

Fox preached at Paul's Cross, and is said to have held for a short time the living of St. Giles, Cripplegate, where he was buried in 1587. A mural tablet with a Latin inscription was erected to his memory in the church, and is still to be seen there. St. Giles's, one of the few remaining city churches which escaped the Great Fire of 1666, was built in 1545.

Paul's Cross stood on the north side of St. Paul's Churchyard, a few yards east of Canon Alley. The congregation worshipped in the open air.

SIR PHILIP FRANCIS.

1740–1818.

FRANCIS, in 1753, was sent to Paul's School, in St. Paul's Churchyard, on the east side of the Cathedral (see MILTON).

Much of his youth was spent out of England, but in 1761 he was appointed private secretary to William Pitt, Earl of Chatham; and Lady Francis thus describes his duties and position at that time:—

His manner of attending there was to come early in the morning to Lord C.'s house in St. James's Square, where he was shown into a library, and found his breakfast and the work of the day; and I have heard him say that he was so happy in having command of the books unmolested (for sometimes he had long intervals of leisure when his pen was not required), that he probably, from these agreeable remembrances, retained all his life a partiality for St. James's Square, in which, as soon as his circumstances permitted him, he bought a house. *Parkes' Life of Francis, vol. II.*

Francis lived subsequently in Harley Street, Cavendish Square; and from 1791 until the time of his death at No. 14 St. James's Square, in a house taken down some years ago. The East India Service Club was erected on its site. In 1791 he wrote:—

> I have removed into a very convenient house in St. James's Square, where I believe I am at anchor for life. The name of the situation sounds well, but you would be much mistaken in concluding that I live in a palace.

<small>Parkes' Life of Francis, vol. ii.</small>

He was a member, among other clubs, of Brooks's, No. 60 St. James's Street; but he withdrew on the publication of Taylor's 'The Identity of Junius,' which brought his name conspicuously before the club, and gave him a notoriety very distressing to him.

BENJAMIN FRANKLIN.

1706-1790.

FRANKLIN, at different periods of his life, spent a number of years in London. In his 'Autobiography' he thus relates his earliest experiences here, on his arrival in 1724:—

> Ralph [James Ralph] and I were inseparable companions. We took lodgings together at Little Britain, at three shillings and sixpence a week, which was all we could afford. . . . I then got into work at Palmer's, then a famous printing-house in Bartholomew Close, and here I continued near a year. . . . I now began to think of getting a little money beforehand, and, expecting better work, I left Palmer's to work at Watt's near Lincoln's Inn Fields, a still greater printing-house. Here I continued all the rest of my stay in London. . . . My lodgings in Little Britain being too remote, I found another in Duke Street, opposite the Romish Chapel. It was two pair of stairs backwards, at an Italian warehouse.

Little Britain a hundred and fifty years ago was a centre of the bookselling and printing trade. No trace is left of Palmer's in Bartholomew Close; but Watt's printing-house stood on the south side of Wild Court, a short street running from Great Wild Street, Drury Lane, to Sardinia Place. The greater part of the south side of this court had been taken down in 1885; but the opposite side, towards Great Queen Street, was still unchanged, — a row of wretched buildings, tenanted by the most miserable of the London poor.

Franklin's lodging-house in Duke Street, 'opposite the Romish Chapel,' was probably No. 6 Sardinia St., an ancient house facing the Sardinia Catholic Chapel in 1885.

In 1757 Franklin was again in London, as the agent of the American Colonies, to confer with the home Government.

At the invitation of his friend Collinson, he went in the first instance to the house of that gentleman, where he was hospitably entertained till he could procure suitable permanent lodgings; such lodgings he shortly after found at the house of Mrs. Stevenson, No. 7 Craven Street [Strand]; and they proved so convenient, comfortable, and every way pleasant, that he made his home there during all his long subsequent residence in London, embracing, in the two missions on which he was sent thither, about fifteen years. That house, says Dr. Sparks, is noted to this day, in the London guide-books, as the house in which Franklin resided. *Holley's Life of Franklin, chap. xii.*

Franklin's Craven Street house has been rebuilt. It bears a tablet of the Society of Arts. He was in London from 1757 to 1762, and again in 1764, when he remained in Craven Street for ten years.

Sparks has printed a number of Franklin's letters dated from Kensington; and no doubt written in an old house — standing in 1885, but doomed to destruction — in the grounds of the South Kensington Museum. It is a dingy two-storied brick building, some distance back from Cromwell Road, and facing it at its junction with Thurloe Place. It is barely visible from the thoroughfare, and is also marked by the Society of Arts.

Franklin was among the distinguished visitors at Don, Saltero's Museum and Coffee House, No. 18 Cheyne Walk, Chelsea (see SMOLLETT), and relates in his 'Autobiography,' with considerable pride, his long swim from Chelsea to Blackfriars.

JOHN GAY.

1688–1732.

GAY was but a lad when he began life in London, as a silk-mercer's apprentice, in the Strand; and settled home of his own he never seems to have had here. He was an inmate of the house of the Duchess of Monmouth; he had lodgings at one time at Whitehall; he lived for a time in retirement at Hampstead; and he finally became a member of the family of the Duke of Queensbury, either at Amesbury, Petersham, or in Queensbury House, which stood on the north side of Burlington Gardens, between Savile Row and Old Burlington Street. It was taken down at the end of the last century, when Uxbridge House, occupied in 1885 by the Western Branch of the Bank of England, was built upon its site. Gay died here in 1732.

His body was brought by the Company of Upholders from the Duke of Queensbury's to Exeter Change, and thence to the Abbey, at eight o'clock in the winter's evening [December 23]. Lord Chesterfield and Pope were present among the mourners. He had already, two months before his death, desired: 'My dear Mr. Pope, whom I

Dean Stanley's Westminster Abbey, chap. iv. pp. 287, 288.

love as my own soul : if you survive me, as you certainly will,
if a stone shall mark the place of my grave, see these words put
upon it : —
> "Life is a jest and all things show it :
> I thought so once, and now I know it,"

with what else you may think proper.' His wish was complied
with.

Exeter Change stood on the north side of the Strand,
between Wellington Street and Burleigh Street, and on the
site of the Lyceum Theatre. It was taken down in 1829.

Gay was a member of the Scriblerus Club, which met at
various taverns at the West End of London; and a frequenter
of Will's (see ADDISON, p. 7). The Rose Tavern, a favorite resort of Gay's, stood on the east side of Brydges Street, next
to Drury Lane Theatre, and was taken down to make room
for the extension of the theatre by Garrick in 1775 or 1776.

EDWARD GIBBON.

1737-1794.

GIBBON was born at Lime Grove, at the base of Putney
Hill, in a house no longer standing. He was baptized
in the parish church of Putney, St. Mary's, which was rebuilt
in 1836; and his early youth was spent in that then suburban town. In 1746 he was sent to the Free Grammar
School, London Street, Kingston-on-Thames, where he remained two years.

By the common methods of discipline, the expense of many
tears, and some blood, I purchased the knowledge *Gibbon's*
of the Latin syntax ; and not long since I was pos- *Memoir of*
sessed of the dirty volumes of Phædrus and Corne- *Himself.*
lius Nepos, which I painfully construed and darkly understood.

In 1749 Gibbon entered Westminster School (see CHURCH-ILL, p. 51), but his delicate health forced him to leave town after a short term there. During his school days and later, his London home was with an aunt who kept a boarding-house for Westminster boys in College Street, and afterwards in Dean's Yard.

Gibbon was sent to Oxford in 1752, and after his residence there spent five years in Switzerland before he returned permanently to London.

Gibbon, when young and fresh from Lausanne, saw little to enjoy in London, where he found 'crowds without company, and dissipation without pleasure.' In 1760 he lodged in this street [Bond Street], and studied in the midst of the fashionable world around him. He says, 'While coaches were rattling through Bond Street, I have passed many solitary evenings in my lodgings with my books.'

<small>Wheatley's Round about Piccadilly, chap. viii.</small>

Gibbon lived for a time in Pall Mall, but in 1772 he took the house No. 7 Bentinck Street, Manchester Square, where some of the happiest years of his life were spent, and where were written the first volumes of 'The Decline and Fall of the Roman Empire.'

<small>Gibbon's Correspondence, 1783.</small>

For my own part, my late journey has only convinced me that No. 7 Bentinck Street is the best house in the world.

Bentinck is a short, quiet street, running from Welbeck Street to Marylebone Lane. No. 7 has been renewed, and is almost the only house in the street that has undergone any change during the last century.

Gibbon died in 1794 at No. 76 St. James's Street, on the south corner of Little St. James's Street, in the house of Elmsley the publisher, who some years before had declined to take the risk of the printing of the history. Elmsley's house was taken down upon the erection of the Conservative Club.

Gibbon was a member of a number of fashionable clubs, including The Club (see JOHNSON); Boodle's, No. 28 St. James's Street; Brooks's, No. 60 St. James's Street; White's, Nos. 36 and 37 St. James's Street (see CIBBER, p. 54); and the Cocoa Tree Club, No. 64 St. James's Street (see ADDISON, p. 7).

I dined at the Cocoa Tree with Holt. We went thence to the play ('The Spanish Friar'), and when it was over returned to the Cocoa Tree. That respectable body, of which I have the honor of being a member, affords every evening a sight truly English. Twenty or thirty perhaps of the finest men in the kingdom, in point of fashion and fortune, supping at little tables covered with a napkin, in the middle of a coffee-room, upon a bit of cold meat or a sandwich, and drinking a glass of punch. At present [1762] we are full of King's counsellors and lords of the bed-chamber.

Gibbon's Diary, Nov. 24, 1762.

RICHARD GLOVER.

1712–1785.

'LEONIDAS' GLOVER was a Hamburg merchant on Poultney Hill (Cannon Street), but no trace of the site of his warehouse remains. He lived at No. 11 James Street, York Street, Buckingham Gate, and at No. 9 Bennet Street, on the northwest corner of St. James's Street; and he died in Albemarle Street, Piccadilly, in 1785. James Street has been lengthened, rebuilt, and renumbered since that time, and the site of Glover's house cannot positively be determined. It was opposite that portion of St. James's Park which has since been transformed into the Parade Ground of Wellington Barracks.

WILLIAM GODWIN.

1756–1836.

GODWIN'S earliest lodgings in London were 'near the new church in the Strand' (St. Mary-le-Strand), where he remained for a year, 1783–84, and where he published his first book. He occupied over a dozen different lodging-houses, always in the neighborhood of the Strand, between 1784 and 1792. Shortly after this he wrote: —

William Godwin, his Friends and Contemporaries, vol. i. chap. iv. In the beginning of the year 1793 I removed to a small house in Chalton Street [Euston Road], Somers Town, which I possess entirely to myself, with no other attendance than the daily resort of a bed-maker for about an hour each day.... In this year also I wrote the principal part of the novel of 'Caleb Williams.'

Godwin and Mary Wollstonecraft were married in Old St. Pancras Church, March 29, 1797, Godwin making no note of the fact in his diary. A few weeks later he wrote to a friend from No. 7 Eversham Buildings, Somers Town; and here, in September of the same year, Mary Wollstonecraft died.

Eversham Buildings was that part of the present Chalton Street which lies between Chapel Street (then Chapel Path) and Phœnix Street. It leads to the Polygon, where in 1800 and afterwards Godwin was living, and where he was wooed and won by his second wife.

The Polygon in 1885 was a block of plain, unassuming middle-class houses, irregular in shape, as its name implies, and occupying the centre of Clarendon Square.

In 1807 the Godwins removed to No. 41 Skinner Street, Holborn, which was on the south side of St. Sepulchre's

Church, Snow Hill. It connected Holborn with Newgate Street, and was entirely removed on the construction of the Holborn viaduct (see BUNYAN, p. 26).

I remember him when he kept a bookseller's shop on Snow Hill. He kept it under the name of Edward Baldwin; had it been carried on in his own name, he would have had few customers, for his published opinion had excited general hostility, to say the least. I was a schoolboy then, and can remember purchasing a book there, handed to me by himself. It was a poor shop, poorly furnished; its contents consisting chiefly of children's books with the old colored prints, that would contrast so strangely with the art illustrations of to-day. S. C. Hall's Retrospect of a Long Life: Godwin.

After his business failure in 1823 he was at No. 195 Strand, near Arundel Street, and opposite St. Clement's Church, and in Gower Place, Euston Square, working hard at his books, and seeing but little society except such as sought him in his retirement.

Godwin was living in New Palace Yard in 1832, when Douglas Jerrold took his son to call upon him.

I remember vividly accompanying my father to the dark rooms in the New Palace Yard, where I saw an old vivacious lady and old gentleman. My father was most anxious that I should remember them, and I do remember well that he appeared to bear a strong regard for them. . . . One morning he called on the Godwins, and was kept for some moments waiting in their drawing-room. It was irresistible, he never could think of these things. Whistle in a ladies' drawing-room! Still he did whistle, — not only *pianissimo*, but *fortissimo*, with variations enough to satisfy the most ambitious of thrushes. Suddenly good little Mrs. Godwin gently opened the door, paused still — not seen by the performer — to catch the dying notes of the air, and then, coming up to her visitor, startled him with the request, made in all seriousness, 'You couldn't whistle that again, could you?' Life of Douglas Jerrold by his Son, chap. vi.

The erection of the New Houses of Parliament has entirely changed the features of New Palace Yard. Godwin died here in 1836, and was buried by the side of Mary Wollstonecraft in the yard of Old St. Pancras Church, St. Pancras-in-the-Fields.

On the building of the Metropolitan and Midland Railways, and the destruction of portions of this graveyard, the bones of Godwin and of his two wives were removed, in 1851, to Bournemouth.

This cemetery on Old St. Pancras Road was known in 1885 as St. Pancras Gardens. Its character was still preserved, although no interments have been permitted there in many years. All the old tombs were still standing, except such as had been destroyed by the railway bridges.

Godwin was an active member of the Mulberry Club (see JERROLD). It held its meetings at the Wrekin Tavern, which stood until about 1870 at No. 22 Broad Court, Bow Street, on the corner of Cross Court.

OLIVER GOLDSMITH.

1728–1774.

WHEN Oliver Goldsmith, penniless, friendless, and forlorn, first arrived in London, in 1756, he found employment in the establishment of a chemist, at the corner of Monument Yard and Fish Street; but no houses dating back so far as the middle of the last century exist there now. In the same year, 1756, he is known to have attempted the practice of medicine on the Bankside, and also to have been reading proof for Samuel Richardson in Salisbury Court, Fleet Street (see RICHARDSON).

In the beginning of 1757 Goldsmith was usher in a school at Peckham; and Goldsmith House, as the school building was afterwards called, still stood, and was respected, for Goldsmith's sake, at Peckham, when John Forster wrote his 'Life of Goldsmith' in 1848. It was taken down in 1876.

In 1758 Goldsmith found lodgings at No. 12 Green Arbor Court, Old Bailey.

Irving, in his 'Life of Goldsmith,' quotes Bishop Percy, a warm friend of the author of 'She Stoops to Conquer,' as saying : —

I called on Goldsmith at his lodgings in March, 1759, and found him writing his 'Inquiry' in a miserable, dirty-looking room, in which there was but one chair ; and when, from civility, he resigned it to me, he himself was obliged to sit in the window.

In his 'Tales of a Traveller' ('The Club of Good Fellows'), Irving thus describes his own visit to Green Arbor Court, half a century after Goldsmith's death : —

At length we came upon Fleet Market, and, traversing it, turned up a narrow street to the bottom of a long, steep flight of stone steps, called Breakneck Stairs. These, he told me, led to Green Arbor Court, and that down them poor Goldsmith might many a time have risked his neck. When we entered the court I could not but smile to think in what out-of-the-way corners Genius produces her bantlings. . . . This Green Arbor Court I found to be a small square surrounded by tall and miserable houses, the very intestines of which seemed turned inside out, to judge from the old garments and frippery fluttering from every window. It appears to be a region of washerwomen, and lines were stretched about the little square, on which clothes were dangling to dry. . . . Poor Goldsmith ! what a time he must have had of it, with his quiet disposition and nervous habits, penned up in this den of noise and vulgarity !

Green Arbor Court in 1885 was little more than a patch of bare ground filled with carriers' carts and railway vans. The old houses had all disappeared, and brand-new brick buildings occupied their site. The court is open towards the Old Bailey; but the Holborn Viaduct Station stretches across its western end, where once were Breakneck Stairs, leading to Fleet Market and Seacoal Lane.

In 1760 Goldsmith removed to No. 6 Wine Office Court, Fleet Street, where he occupied more respectable lodgings than any to which he had before aspired. Here Dr. Johnson first visited him on the 31st of May, 1761. The house known as No. 6 Wine Office Court in 1885 was probably of later date than Goldsmith's time. It is nearly opposite the well-known Cheshire Cheese Tavern, where tradition says he frequently dined and supped with Dr. Johnson and other congenial friends (see JOHNSON).

Goldsmith wrote 'The Vicar of Wakefield' in Wine Office Court, and Dr. Johnson's description of a scene that occurred there after its completion will best show the character of the man and his mode of life at that time. Boswell reports his great friend as saying:—

> I received one morning a message from poor Goldsmith, that he was in great distress, and as it was not in his power to come to me, begging that I would come to him as soon as possible. I sent him a guinea, and promised to come to him directly. I accordingly went to him as soon as I was dressed, and found that his landlady had arrested him for his rent, at which he was in a violent passion. I perceived that he had already changed my guinea, and had a bottle of Madeira and a glass before him. I put the cork into the bottle, desired he would be calm, and began to talk to him of the means by which he might be extricated. He then told me that he had a novel ready for the press, which he produced to me. I looked into it, and saw its merit; told the landlady I should soon return, and, having gone to a bookseller, sold it for sixty pounds. I brought Goldsmith the money; and he discharged his rent, not without rating his landlady in a high tone for having used him so ill.

Boswell's Life of Johnson, 1763.

In 1764 Johnson found Goldsmith in a humble set of chambers at No. 2 Garden Court, Middle Temple, near the New Library and behind Fountain Court. The buildings have now disappeared. He went there from Gray's Inn, from whence he dated a letter on the 6th of March of the same year.

The five hundred pounds received for the 'Good Natured Man' gave Goldsmith a feeling of unlimited wealth; and he took chambers consisting of three rooms on the second floor of No. 2 Brick Court, Middle Temple, — on the right hand ascending the staircase, and overlooking the umbrageous walks of the Temple Garden. The lease he purchased for £400, and then went on to furnish the rooms with mahogany sofas, card-tables, and bookcases, with curtains, mirrors, and Wilton carpets. His awkward person was also furnished in a style befitting his apartment; for, in addition to his suit of Tyrian bloom satin grain, we find another charged about this time in the books of Mr. Filby, in no less gorgeous terms, being 'lined with silk and furnished with gold buttons.' Thus lodged and thus arrayed, he invited the visits of his most aristocratic acquaintances, and no longer quailed beneath the courtly eye of Beauclerc. He gave dinners to Johnson, Percy, Reynolds, Bickerstaff, and other friends of note, and supper-parties to young folks of both sexes. . . . Blackstone, whose chambers were immediately below, and who was studiously occupied on his 'Commentaries,' used to complain of the racket made by 'his revelling neighbor.'

Irving's Goldsmith, chap. xxiii.

In 1885 No. 2 Brick Court was precisely as Goldsmith left it when carried to his grave. His chambers have been changed as to furniture and equipments, of course, by the several generations who have followed him as their occupants; but the house (erected in 1704) and the little court are the house and court he knew so well.

Goldsmith's country home for a number of years was at

Canonbury House, in Islington, which then was a suburb of London. Nothing was left of the house, even in Goldsmith's day, but the old brick tower, still standing in 1885, in Canonbury Square, at the junction of Compton Road and Canonbury Place, and one of the most picturesque old structures in the metropolis. It was a favorite resort of publishers, authors, and literary men. Irving, in his 'Life of Goldsmith,' relates his visit to Canonbury Tower, and describes the painted wainscots and gothic windows of Goldsmith's sitting-room, where, no doubt, he gathered and entertained Johnson and his coterie. It is said that parts of 'The Deserted Village' and 'The Traveller' were written here.

Goldsmith also spent portions of the summers of 1771, 1772, and 1774 — in the last year only a few weeks before his death — in a farm-house on the west side of the Edgeware Road, 'near the six-mile stone' from London, where he wrote 'She Stoops to Conquer' and 'Animated Nature.'

Goldsmith died, and was buried, where the happiest and most peaceful years of his life had been spent, in the Temple. The end came on the 4th of April, 1774.

His death was a shock to the literary world, and a deep affliction to a wide circle of intimates and friends; for, with all his foibles and peculiarities, he was fully as much beloved as he was admired. Burke, on hearing the news, burst into tears. Sir Joshua Reynolds threw by his pencil for the day, and grieved more than he had done in times of great family distress. . . . Johnson felt the blow deeply and gloomily. In writing some time afterward to Boswell, he observed, 'Of poor Goldsmith there is little to be told more than the papers have made public. He died of a fever, made, I am afraid, more violent by uneasiness of mind. His debts began to be heavy, and all his resources were exhausted. Sir Joshua is of opinion that he owed no less than two thousand pounds. Was ever poet so trusted before?'

Irving's Goldsmith, chap. xliv.

Goldsmith's funeral took place at five in the afternoon of the 9th of April, when his staircase on Brick Court was crowded with mourners of all ranks and conditions of life, conspicuous among them being the outcasts of both sexes, who loved and wept for him because of the goodness he had done. The exact position of Goldsmith's grave is not known. The plain monument with the simple inscription, 'Here Lies Oliver Goldsmith,' was placed, in 1860, on the north side of the Temple Church, as near as possible to the spot where his remains are supposed to lie.

Goldsmith was a member of many clubs, notably, of The Club, afterwards called The Literary Club, which was founded by Dr. Johnson, Sir Joshua Reynolds, and others, in 1763. It originally met in the Turk's Head Tavern, which then stood on the corner of Greek and Compton Streets, Soho, but was subsequently removed to Gerard Street, hard by (see JOHNSON).

'I believe Mr. Fox will allow me to say,' remarked the Bishop of St. Asaph, 'that the honor of being elected into the Turk's Head Club is not inferior to that of being representative of Westminster and Surrey.' The Bishop had just been elected; but into such lusty independence had the club sprung up that bishops, even lord chancellors, were known to have knocked for admission unsuccessfully. *Forster's Goldsmith, book iii.*

He [Johnson] and Mr. Langton and I went together to The Club (1773), where we found Mr. Burke, Mr. Garrick, and some other members, and amongst them our friend Goldsmith, who sat brooding over Johnson's reprimand to him after dinner. Johnson perceived this, and said aside to some of us, 'I'll make Goldsmith forgive me,' and then called to him in a loud voice, 'Dr. Goldsmith, something passed to-day where you and I dined; I ask your pardon.' Goldsmith answered placidly, 'It must be much from you, sir, that I take ill;' and so at once the difference was over, and they were on as easy terms as ever, and Goldsmith rattled away as usual. *Boswell's Life of Johnson, 1773.*

A less important club of his met at the Globe Tavern, No. 134 Fleet Street, not far from Shoe Lane, and since destroyed.

Another of these free-and-easy clubs met on Wednesday evenings at the Globe. It was somewhat in the style of the Three Jolly Pigeons; songs, jokes, dramatic imitations, burlesque parodies, and broad sallies of humor formed a contrast to the sententious morality, pedantic casuistry, and polished sarcasm of the learned critic. . . . Johnson used to be severe upon Goldsmith for mingling in these motley circles, observing that having been originally poor he had contracted a love for low company. Goldsmith, however, was guided not by a taste for what was low, but what was comic and characteristic.

<small>Irving's Goldsmith, chap. xix.</small>

He belonged also to a card club at the Devil Tavern, No. 1 Fleet Street (see JONSON); to the Robin Hood Debating Club, held in the Robin Hood Tavern, Essex Street, Strand, afterwards removed to the Robin Hood Tavern in Butcher Row, behind St. Clement Danes, and taken down on the erection of the New Law Courts (see BURKE, p. 28); and also to 'a shilling rubber club,' which met at the Bedford, Covent Garden (see CHURCHILL, p. 51).

Goldsmith's taverns were more numerous even than his clubs. In 1757 his letters were addressed to the 'Temple Exchange Coffee House, near Temple Bar,' no sign of which is left.

He was frequently at the Mitre, No. 39 Fleet Street (see JOHNSON), at the Grecian, Devereux Court, Strand (see ADDISON, p. 7), at the Chapter Coffee House,³ No. 50 Paternoster Row (see BRONTË, p. 22, and CHATTERTON, p. 44), and at Jack's Coffee House, afterwards Walker's, at the corner of Dean and Queen Streets, Soho.

Walker's Hotel was —

in 1770 the oldest tavern in London, but three, and is now [1845] probably the oldest. Mr. Walker, the present landlord of this hotel, who has lived in it fifty years and has now reached the venerable age of ninety, is proud of the ancient honors of the house. On his card he duly informs his friends that it was here that Johnson, Garrick, Goldsmith, and other literary characters of eminence used to resort. The house is old, spacious, and quiet. Howitt's Homes and Haunts of the British Poets, vol. i.: Goldsmith.

Dr. Joseph Rogers, an old resident of Soho Square, in reply to inquiries about this ancient tavern, kindly furnishes the following information :—

Walker's Hotel consisted of five houses, two in Dean Street and three in Queen Street. The proprietor, when I first knew him, now [1883] nearly forty years ago, was a very old man. He had not the wit to adapt himself to modern notions, and continued to carry on his business in the old style until his business left him. At the time I made his acquaintance he was nearly insolvent. He was ultimately ejected from the premises, and died at the workhouse of the Strand Union, at the advanced age of ninety-five. When I took the premises, No. 33 Dean Street (corner of Queen Street), now thirty-four years ago, the poor old man led me over the place and showed me the different rooms. He pointed out that in my first-floor front room, Goldsmith, Johnson, and others used to meet. He also told me that in the four-post bed in the said room Nelson slept the night before he embarked from Portsmouth to fight the battle of Trafalgar. He took me into his cellars, and showed me some whiskey he had put down in 1800. There is no doubt of the truth of this, and you can make use of the information as you see fit. The present Queen's Hotel (No. 12 Queen Street) was the bar of the old hotel. The two houses beyond were simply used as lodging-houses.

Goldsmith wrote 'A Reverie' at the Boar's Head Tavern, Shakspere's Boar's Head, in Eastcheap (Cannon Street), which stood at the junction of that thoroughfare and Gracechurch Street, and was taken down when King William Street was formed, in 1831. Its site is occupied by the statue to William IV.

One of his favorite suburban taverns was the Old Red Lion, still standing in 1885, which, according to the inscription in curious old English letters along its renewed front, was 'established in 1415.' It is at No. 186 St. John's Street Road, Islington, near the junction of Pentonville Road, City Road, and High Street. It has been restored; but the old pointed gables and general antique style are retained.

He spent much of his leisure time, also, at the Old Baptist's Head, No. 30 St. John's Lane, Clerkenwell, on the site of which a new tavern bearing the same name was erected a few years ago; and at the White Conduit Tea Gardens, which stood on the east side of Penton Street, Pentonville, until 1849. A new White Conduit Tavern, in 1885, was at No. 14 Barnsbury Road, Penton Street.

JOHN GOWER.

Circa 1325–1408.

GOWER, who is said to have been a member of the Middle Temple (see CHAUCER, p. 46), seems to have seen but little of London, and no traces of his early life here are to be found. It is believed that he was married in the Church of St. Mary Overy, now St. Saviour's, Southwark, in 1397, by William of Wickham, then Bishop of Winchester; and he is known to have spent the last few years of his life in blindness in the priory of that church, which he enriched by his gifts and bequests, and where he died and was buried (see FLETCHER, p. 107).

And thus whan they hadde gone theyr journey, the one of them, that is to saye, John Gower, prepared for his bones a restynge place in the monastery of Saynt Mayre Overies, where, somewhat after the olde ffashion he lyeth ryght sumptuously buryed, with a garland on his head in token that he in his lyfe dayes flouryshed freshely in literature and science, and the same monument in remembraunce of hym erected, is on the north syde of the foresayde churche in the chapell of Saynte John, where he hath of his own foundation a masse dayly songe. Preface to Berthelet's Edition of Gower, 1532.

John Gower, Esquire, a famous poet, was then an especial benefactor to that work, and was there buried in the north side of that church, in the chapel of St. John, where he founded a chantry; he lieth under a tomb of stone, with his image also of stone over him; the hair of his head, auburn, long to his shoulders, but curling up and a small forked beard: on his head a chaplet like a coronet of four roses; a habit of purple damasked down to his feet; a collar of esses gold about his neck; under his head the likeness of three books which he compiled. Stow's Survey of London, Edition of 1603.

Gower's monument, for so many years in the Chapel of St. John, was repaired and recolored in 1832, and removed to the south transept of the church. The canons of the St. Mary Overy continued to perform 'a yearly obit to his memory' for a long time, and to attach to his tomb a notice saying that 'Whosoever prayeth for the soul of John Gower, he shall, so oft as he soe doth, have an M and a D of pardon.'

THOMAS GRAY.

1716-1771.

GRAY'S associations with London were slight and accidental. He was born on the 26th of November, 1716, in the house of his father, a money-scrivener, on the south side of Cornhill. This house, which stood on the site of

No. 41 Cornhill, between Birchin Lane and St. Michael's Church, was destroyed by fire in 1748. After he went to Eton he never had a permanent home in the metropolis, but lodged during his occasional visits, as his letters show, at a hosier's named Roberts, at the east end of Jermyn Street, near the Haymarket; or at 'Frisby the Oilman's,' on the opposite side of the way. The names of both Frisby and Roberts are to be found in the early directories, but before streets were numbered. Here he paid not more than half a guinea a week for his rooms, and dined at a neighboring coffee-house.

In 1759 Gray lodged in Southampton Row, Bloomsbury Square, near the then new British Museum, to the Reading Room of which he was a frequent visitor.

Gray, from his bedroom window, looked out on a southwest garden wall, covered with flowering jessamine through June and July. There had been roses, too, in this London garden. Gray must always have flowers about him, and he trudged down to Covent Garden every day for his sweet peas and pinks and scarlet Martogon lilies, double stocks and flowering marjoram. His drawing-room looked over Bedford Gardens, and a fine stretch of upland fields crowned at last against the sky by the villages of Highgate and Hampstead.

<small>Edmund Gosse's Gray: English Men of Letters, chap. vii.</small>

A letter of Gray to Walpole, written in 1737, shows him to have been at that time an inmate of his uncle's house at Burnham, and expresses his interest in 'the most venerable beeches and other very reverend vegetables who dream out their old stories to the winds' in the forest there. During his residence at Stoke, Burnham Beeches were his frequent resort.

West End, the house in which Gray's mother lived, and he wrote much poetry and many letters, now [1876] called Stoke Court, is about one mile north of the church. Gray described it as ' a compact neat box of red brick, with sash windows, a grotto made of flints, a walnut-tree with three mole-hills under it.' The house was rebuilt by Mr. Penn about 1845, on a larger scale, and is now a gentleman's villa. The room in which Gray wrote was, however, preserved, and forms a part of the present house. The walnut-tree and grotto were retained, and the basin of gold-fishes greatly enlarged. <small>Thorne's Hand-Book of the Environs of London: Stoke Pogis.</small>

The house in Gray's time was built of brick, and was three stories in height. It was afterwards covered with stucco, forming only a small wing to the right of the more pretentious mansion added to it by Mr. Penn. The present occupants have no knowledge of the walnut-tree or the grotto.

Gray's devotion to his mother and to her memory is well known. She was buried in Stoke Pogis Churchyard, which is without question the churchyard of the ' Elegy,' to the east of the church, and under a stone bearing his touching testimony that she was '.The careful tender mother of many children, one of whom alone had the misfortune to survive her.' Gray, at his own request, rests his head upon the lap of earth by her side.

GEORGE GROTE.

1794–1871.

GEORGE GROTE was born at Shortlands near Beckenham, in Kent, about ten miles from London. After four years in the Grammar School at Sevenoaks, he was sent to the Charter House School (see ADDISON, p. 1), where he remained until he was sixteen, and where it is recorded that at that age he was well flogged for giving a farewell supper, just before leaving school, to some of his classmates, at the Albion Tavern — still standing in 1885 — at No. 172 Aldersgate Street.

At the age of sixteen Grote entered the banking establishment of his father, No. 62 Threadneedle Street. He lived with his father in the banking-house until he was married, in 1820, when he took possession of a house 'in the court adjoining.' This was his town home for many years, and here the 'History of Greece' was designed and begun. He and his wife were often to be found in the Drapers' Garden hard by (see MACAULAY), which had been the breathing-place of his fellow historian.

Direct successors of the Grotes were still doing business in 1885 on the site of the original banking-house, on Threadneedle Street, corner of Bartholomew Lane. The 'adjoining court,' simply so described in the biography of Grote, was either Capel Court, by its side, in Bartholomew Lane, or New Court, or Shooter's Court, on Throgmorton Street, in its rear. The appearance of the entire block of buildings has been greatly changed of late years by the erection and extensions of the Stock Exchange and other business houses.

The Grotes had different suburban homes, — at Fortis Green, beyond Highgate; on the Green Lane, Stoke-Newington, near the New River; at Burnham; and at Dulwich, half a mile beyond Dulwich College. In 1836 Grote moved to No. 3 Eccleston Street, Belgrave Square, — an imposing mansion, numbered 3 Belgrave Place in 1885, — and in 1848 to No. 12 Savile Row, Burlington Gardens, where, in 1871, he died. This house was standing in 1885.

He was buried in Thirlwall's grave, in the Poets' Corner of Westminster Abbey.

HENRY HALLAM.

1777-78-1859.

HALLAM was a Bencher of the Middle Temple. In 1819, and later, he occupied an old-fashioned mansion at Fulham, called Arundel House, which in 1885 was still standing, although somewhat altered, on Fulham Road, opposite Parson's Green Lane.

He wrote his 'History of the Middle Ages' at No. 67 Wimpole Street, near Queen Anne Street, Cavendish Square, his home for many years.

He was a frequent partaker of the dinners of the Literary Club (see GOLDSMITH, p. 123).

WILLIAM HAZLITT.

1778-1830.

HAZLITT had no settled home of his own in London until after his marriage, in 1808; but during his occasional visits to town he lodged with his brother John, at No. 12 Rathbone Place, Oxford Street, in a house rebuilt in 1883, and later at No. 109 Great Russell Street, Bloomsbury Square, in a house which formed part of the old Tavistock House, but has now entirely disappeared.

Hazlitt was married to Miss Sarah Stoddard, on the 1st of May, 1808, at St. Andrew's, Holborn, now on the Viaduct.

The only persons present at the marriage, so far as I can recollect, were Dr. and Mrs. Stoddard, and Mr. and Miss Lamb; but I strongly suspect there were other guests of whom there is no remaining record. Lamb, in a letter to Southey, dated August 9, 1815, more than seven years after the event, thus alludes to his having been present: ' I was at Hazlitt's marriage, and had liked to have been turned out several times during the ceremony. Anything awful makes me laugh.' It was not an every-day kind of business this, with William Hazlitt for bridegroom, and Charles Lamb for best man, and Miss Lamb for bridesmaid; and all of a Sunday morning! I wonder whether Elia appeared at the altar in his snuff-colored smalls. I wonder whether Miss Lamb wore, after all, the sprig dress, or the China-Manning silk, or a real white gown? I wonder in what way Lamb misbehaved, so as to leave a strong impression on his mind — years after? To have been in St. Andrew's that day, and to have seen the whole thing from a good place, would have been a recollection worth cherishing.

Memoirs of William Hazlitt, part i. chap. xi.

In 1812 Hazlitt and his wife took possession of the house No. 19 York Street, Westminster, which had been occupied by John Milton; and here they lived until 1819. This house was taken down in 1877. It faced on York Street in Hazlitt's day, a few doors east of the spot where the Westminster Panorama was afterwards built; and the garden in its rear formed part of the lawn of Queen Anne Mansions in 1885 (see MILTON).

On knocking at the door [No. 19 York Street, Westminster], it was, after a long interval, opened by a sufficiently neat-handed domestic. The outer door led immediately from the street (down a step) into an empty apartment, indicating an uninhabited house, and I supposed I had mistaken the number; but on asking for the object of my search, I was shown to a door, which opened (a step from the ground) on to a ladder-like staircase, bare like the rest, which led to a dark, bare landing-place and thence to a large square wainscoted apartment. The great curtainless windows of this room looked upon some dingy trees; the whole of the wall over and about the chimney-piece was entirely covered, up to the ceiling, by names written in pencil, of all sizes and characters, and in all

C. G. Patmore's My Friends and Acquaintances, vol. ii.: Hazlitt.

directions, commemorative of visits of curiosity to the home of Pindarus (John Milton). There was near to the empty fireplace a table with breakfast things upon it (though it was two o'clock in the afternoon). Three chairs and a sofa were standing about the room, and one unbound book lay on the mantel-piece. At the table sat Hazlitt, and on the sofa a lady, whom I found to be his wife.

Once I dined with him [Hazlitt]. This (an unparalleled occurrence) was in York Street, when some friends had sent him a couple of Dorking fowls, of which he suddenly invited me to partake. I went expecting the usual sort of dinner, but it was limited solely to the fowls and bread. He drank nothing but water, and there was nothing but water to drink. He offered to send for some porter for me; but being out of health at the time I declined, and escaped after dinner to a coffee-house, where I strengthened myself with a few glasses of wine. Procter's Recollections of Men of Letters.

In 1820 Hazlitt was living in apartments at No. 9 Southampton Buildings, a short street running crookedly between Holborn and Chancery Lane. No. 9, on the west side of the street, and nine doors from Holborn, was taken down in 1883. He had in 1820 finally separated from his first wife. His changes of residence after the breaking up of his York Street home were many. Mr. Patmore found him in 1824 in Down Street, Piccadilly, and pleasantly describes his erratic life there, his late rising, his musing during the greater part of his days at the breakfast-table, and his stimulating himself to excess with very strong tea. About 1827 he lodged at No. 40 Half Moon Street, Piccadilly, in a house no longer standing; in 1829 he removed to No. 3 Bouverie Street, Fleet Street,—raised one story in 1885; and in 1830 he went to No. 6 Frith Street, Soho, where in the same year he died.

One Saturday afternoon in September [Sept. 18, 1830], when Charles Lamb was in the room, the scene closed. He [Hazlitt] died so quietly that his son, who Memoirs of William Hazlitt, part ii. chap. xix.

was sitting by his bedside, did not know that he was gone till the vital breath had been extinct a moment or two.

The house in which Hazlitt died was, in 1885, standing unchanged.

The grave of Hazlitt is in the yard of St. Anne's Church, Wardour and Dean Streets, Soho. Against the centre wall of the church on the Wardour Street side, and on the right hand as you enter the yard, is a flat stone standing under that of the King of Corsica. The inscription is so remarkable that it is given here in full:—

Near This Spot
Rests
William Hazlitt
Born April 10th, 1778. Died Sept. 18th, 1830.
He lived to see his deepest wishes gratified
As he expressed them in his Essay
'On The Fear of Death'
viz:
'To see the downfall of the Bourbons,
And some prospect of good in mankind.
(Charles X
Was driven from France 29th July, 1830)
'To leave some sterling work to the World'
He lived to complete his 'Life of Napoleon"
His desire
That some friendly hand should
consign him to the grave, was accomplished to a
limited but profound extent ; on these conditions
He was ready to depart, and to have inscribed
on his tomb,
Grateful and Contented.
He was
The first (unanswered) Metaphysician of the Age;
A despiser of the merely Rich and Great,
A lover of the People, Poor, or Oppressed ;
A hater of the Pride and Power of the Few
As opposed to the happiness of the Many.

> A man of true Moral Courage
> To Principles,
> And a Yearning for the good of Human Nature.
> Who was a burning wound to an Aristocracy
> That could not answer before men,
> And who may confront him before their Maker.
> He lived and died
> The unconquered Champion
> of
> Truth, Liberty and Humanity
> 'Dubitantes opera legite.'
> This Stone
> is raised by one whose heart
> is with him in the grave.

Hazlitt, while living a wild, unsettled life in Southampton Buildings, frequented the Southampton Coffee House in that street, which he has described in his chapter on 'Coffee House Politicians,' in his 'Table Talk,' published in 1823. This tavern, a door or two from Chancery Lane, was 'restored' in 1882 or 1883, and everything which belonged to it in Hazlitt's day destroyed by the demons of improvement and renovation.

Here [the Southampton] for several years he used to hold a sort of evening levee, where, after a certain hour at night (and till a very *uncertain* hour in the morning) he was always to be found, and always more or less ready to take part in that sort of desultory talk (the only thing really deserving the name of conversation), in which he excelled every man I have ever met with. Here, in that little bare and comfortless coffee-room have I scores of times seen the daylight peep through the crevices of the window-shutters, upon Table Talk that was worthy an intellectual feast of the gods.

<small>Patmore's My Friends and Acquaintances: Hazlitt.</small>

GEORGE HERBERT.

1593-1632.

GEORGE HERBERT was a pupil of Westminster School (see CHURCHILL, p. 51). In 1609 he left Westminster to enter Cambridge University, where, according to Izaak Walton, he consecrated the first fruits of his early age to virtue and a serious study of learning. He had but few associations with London.

ROBERT HERRICK.

1591-1674.

HERRICK was born in Wood Street, Cheapside, as he sings in his 'Tears to Thamasis,'—

> 'Golden Cheapside, where the earth
> Of Julia Herrick gave to me my birth,'—

and was baptized in the Church of St. Vedast, in Foster Lane, hard by. This church was destroyed in the Great Fire of the next century, but was rebuilt by Wren. Herrick's youth, it would seem, was spent in London; but he has left no record of his education, nor of his early life here, except that when he was about thirty years of age, he was adopted as one of the 'poeticale sonnes' of Ben Jonson. In 1615 he went to the University of Cambridge, and for twenty years lived a quiet and retired life in a country vicarage in Devonshire. When deprived of this by Cromwell, he lodged for some time in St. Anne's Lane (now St. Anne's Street), running from Orchard Street to Great Peter Street, Westminster, where he remained until the Restoration; but after that London saw him not again. His 'Hesperides' was published in 1648, 'to be sold at the Crown and Marygold, St. Paul's Church Yard,' a sign which was destroyed, of course, eighteen years later, with the cathedral and all its surroundings.

THOMAS HOLCROFT.

1744–1809.

HOLCROFT was born in Orange Court, Leicester Fields (since known as Orange Street, Leicester Square), and worked until he was fifteen years of age at the trade of his father, a shoemaker in South Audley Street. Few records of his London life have been left. He died in the parish of Marylebone.

THOMAS HOOD.

1799–1845.

THOMAS HOOD was born over the bookshop of Messrs. Vernon and Hood, in the Poultry, on the northwest corner of the little lane called Chapel Place, running between Grocers' Hall Court and St. Mildred's Court. The house has been taken down. The building upon its site was numbered 31 Poultry in 1885.

Hood's first school was in Tokenhouse Yard (No. 45 Lothbury), and was kept by the Misses Hogsflesh. The brother of these ladies was so painfully sensitive regarding the family name that he never answered to it, and the scholars were instructed to address him by his initial only. This story, told in later years by Hood to his friends, suggested to Lamb the subject of his unfortunate farce, 'Mr. H.'

Hood afterwards went to a school at Clapham, the site of which he once pointed out to his son, but which in his 'Memorials' of his father the younger Hood does not describe.

Hood was married in 1824; and a letter of Charles Lamb's 'To the Hoods, Robert Street, Adelphi,' is among the correspondence of Elia. This Robert Street house, No. 2, is no longer standing. The Hoods left London in 1829 to reside in the country, and did not return to town for a number of years.

Hood near the end of 1841 went to No. 17 Elm Tree Road, St. John's Wood, Regent Park, where he wrote, for the Christmas number of 'Punch,' 1843, 'The Song of the Shirt.' This house, a rigid, uncompromising three-story mansion, was standing in 1885 at the curve of the street, and was called 'The Cedars.'

After his removal to St. John's Wood, my father used to have little modest dinners now and then, to which his intimate friends were invited. Though the board did not groan, sides used to ache; and if the champagne did not flow in streams, the wit sparkled to make up for it. . . . On one occasion, to my mother's horror, the boy fell upstairs with the plum pudding. The accident formed a peg for many jokes; amongst others, a declaration that the pudding — which he said was a stair, not a cabinet, one — had disagreed with him, and that he felt the pattern of the stair-carpet breaking out all over him.

<small>Memorials of Thomas Hood, chap. ix.</small>

Early in the year 1844 the Hoods went to Finchley Road.

My new house is at Devonshire Lodge, New Finchley Road, St. John's Wood, where I shall be most happy to see you; it is just beyond the Eyre Arms, three doors short of the turnpike. The Magazine office [Hood's Magazine] is No. 1 Adam Street, Adelphi, and I am sometimes there of a morning. *Memorials of Thomas Hood, chap. xii.*

No. 1 Adam Street, Adelphi, is at the corner of Adelphi Terrace. There is no Devonshire Lodge in Finchley Road. The turnpike was afterwards called Queen's Road, and Hood's house was probably taken down to make room for the railway station.

Hood died at Devonshire Lodge, May 3, 1845, and on the 10th was buried in Kensal Green.

His funeral was quiet and private, though attended by many who had known and loved him. . . . Eighteen months afterwards his faithful wife was buried by his side. . . . I have a perfect recollection of my father's funeral, and of the unfeigned sorrow of those kind and beloved friends who attended it. It was a beautiful spring day; and I remember it was noticed that just as the service concluded, a lark rose up, mounting and singing over our heads. This was in the middle of the day. *Memorials of Thomas Hood, chap. xiii.*

The monument to Hood in Kensal Green was erected by public subscription, at the suggestion of Eliza Cook, and was unveiled by Lord Houghton, July 18, 1854. The simple epitaph was of his own selecting: 'He sang "The Song of the Shirt."'

THEODORE HOOK.

1788-1841.

HOOK was born in Charlotte Street, Bedford Square.

Met Hook in the Burlington Arcade ; walked with him to the British Museum. As we passed down Great Russell Street, Hook paused on arriving at Charlotte Street, Bedford Square, and, pointing to the northwest corner nearly opposite to the house (the second from the corner) in which he himself was born, observed, 'There by that lamp-post stood Martha the Gypsy.'

<small>Life and Letters of R. H. Barham, 1828.</small>

Bedford Square and its immediate neighborhood have seen but few changes during the last hundred years, although Charlotte Street in Hook's babyhood included the present Bloomsbury Street.

Hook went to school in Soho Square, at 'a green-doored, brass-plated establishment,' the number of which he does not give, but which might be any one of half a dozen similar houses answering to that description, and standing in 1885, as they had stood a century earlier, on different sides of the green. Here, according to his own story, he was a regular truant, walking about the neighboring streets during school hours, and inventing excuses for his unlawful absence.

Hook had no settled home in London when in 1810 he perpetrated his famous joke, known as the 'Berners Street Hoax.' Mrs. Tottingham, the unhappy victim, lived at No. 54 Berners Street (running from Oxford Street, northerly to Mortimer Street and the Middlesex Hospital), when there came to her door hundreds of tradespeople bearing goods of all sizes and descriptions, from a mahogany coffin to an ounce of snuff, ordered by Hook, in her name, to be delivered at the same hour; while at the same hour, at the invitation of Mrs. Tottingham (*per* T. H.), came as well bishops, ministers of State, doctors in haste to cure her bodily ailments, lawyers to make her will, barbers to shave her, mantua-makers to fit her, — men, women, and children on every conceivable errand. The damage done and the confusion created were very great; and Hook, who had spent six weeks in concocting and elaborating the scheme, witnessed the effects from a safe window over the way.

In 1820 Hook established the newspaper called 'John Bull.' Its office was in Gough Square, Fleet Street (see JOHNSON). At this time he was living in a small cottage at Somers Town.

In 1823 he was brought to England from the Mauritius in disgrace for the misconduct of a deputy for which he was held responsible, and was imprisoned in a sponging-house in Shire Lane (no longer in existence; see ADDISON, p. 8), where he remained nine months. To a consoling friend who congratulated him upon the comfort and brightness of his prison apartments, he replied, pointing to the arrangements made to prevent escape, 'Oh, yes, the room is cheerful enough barring the windows!' Subsequently he was removed to a lodging-house 'within the rule of King's Bench Prison,' in Southwark, where he spent a year. This house was in Temple Place, a row of buildings in the Blackfriars Road, not far from the Surrey Theatre.

After his final discharge from arrest, in 1825, Hook hired a cottage at Putney; but in 1827 he took a larger and more fashionable mansion, No. 5 Cleveland Row, directly opposite the Chapel Royal, St. James's, which was still standing in 1885.

In 1831 Hook settled at Egmont Villa, at Fulham, where the rest of his life was spent.

Here he engaged a comfortable but unpretending villa on the banks of the river, situated between the bridge [Putney Bridge] and the pleasure-grounds of the Bishop of London. . . . His library was the beau ideal of a literary workshop; of moderate dimensions, but light and cheerful, hung round with choice specimens of water-color drawings, and opening into a small garden.

<small>Barham's Life of Hook, vol. i. chap. xiii.</small>

This house was taken down in 1855. It stood on the site of the abutment of the Aqueduct of the Chelsea Water Works Company.

Hook died at Fulham on the 24th of August, 1841, and was buried very privately in the churchyard of All Saints there, immediately opposite the chancel window, and within a few steps of his own house. A simple stone, with his name and age, marks the spot; but no green mound was above him when his grave was visited in 1885, — not a blade of grass or a flower flourishing among the pebbles and rough, yellow, unsightly flints that surround his headstone.

Hook was a clubable man, and a frequenter of Crockford's, on the west side of St. James's Street, on the site of which the Devonshire Club, No. 50 St. James's Street, was afterwards erected, and of the Eccentrics, which met in his day in Chandos Street, Covent Garden (see SHERIDAN).

He was, however, more closely associated with the Athenæum Club, Waterloo Place and Pall Mall, than with any other.

At the Athenæum Theodore Hook was a great card; and in a note to a sketch of him in the 'Quarterly Review,' it is stated that the number of dinners at this club fell off by upwards of three hundred per annum after Hook disappeared from his favorite corner, next the door of the coffee-room.

<small>Timbs's Curiosities of London: Clubs.</small>

That is to say, there must have been some dozen of gentlemen who chose to dine there once or twice every week of the season, merely for the chance of Hook's being there, and permitting them to draw their chairs to his little table in the course of the evening. The corner alluded to will, we suppose, long retain the name which it derived from him, 'Temperance Corner.' Many grave and dignified personages being frequent guests, it would hardly have been seemly to be calling for repeated supplies of a certain description; but the waiters well understood what the oracle of the corner meant by 'Another glass of toast and water,' or 'A little more lemonade.'

He was also a member of 'The Honorable Society of Jackers,' which met as late as 1812 at the Black Jack Tavern, No. 12 Portsmouth Street, near Portugal Street, Lincoln's Inn Fields. This inn — called also the 'Jump,' from an exploit of Jack Sheppard, who was one of its frequenters — was still standing in 1885, although doomed to destruction, and was one of the oldest, most curious and interesting inns left in the metropolis. It had escaped the restorers, who have done so much to wipe out all that they have attempted to renew; and save the few slight repairs that had been necessary to keep it from tumbling to pieces, it was left as Joe Miller and the worthies of his and later days had known it. In the little dark back-parlor were the very benches and tables of a couple of centuries ago, carved with the now undecipherable initials of a thousand names, many of which, no doubt, were not born to die.

DAVID HUME.

1711-1776.

HUME spent but little time in London. In 1758 he was in lodgings in Lisle Street, Leicester Fields, and again in 1766, when Rousseau was his guest, and before their famous quarrel began. It was here that, as Rousseau asserted, Hume insulted him while talking in his sleep, — a grave charge, doubted by Hume's friends, who did not credit him with 'snoring in French.' While Hume was Under-Secretary of State, from 1767 to 1769, he occupied a house in Park Place, St. James's Street. The streets of London were not regularly numbered at that time, and the position of neither of these houses is known. He was a member of Brooks's, which was in his day at No. 52 Pall Mall. The British Institution, now no longer standing, afterwards occupied its site.

LEIGH HUNT.

1784–1859.

LEIGH HUNT was born in the village of Southgate, eight miles north of London, and in the parish of Edmonton, where lie the weary bones of Charles and Mary Lamb (see LAMB). He was educated at the Blue Coat School (see COLERIDGE, pp. 56–57), and in his Autobiography has given a graphic description of that establishment in his day, and of his own life there.

Christ-Hospital (for such is its proper name, and not Christ's Hospital) occupies a considerable portion of ground between Newgate Street, Giltspur Street, St. Bartholomew's, and Little Britain. There is a quadrangle with cloisters; and the Square inside the cloisters is called the Garden, and most likely was the monastery garden. Its only delicious crop for many years has been pavement. Another large area, presenting the Grammar and Navigation Schools, is also misnamed the Ditch; the town ditch having formerly run that way. In Newgate Street is seen the hall, or eating-room, — one of the noblest in England, adorned with enormously long paintings by Verrio and others, and with an organ. A portion of the old quadrangle once contained the library

Leigh Hunt's Autobiography, chap. iii.

of the monks, and was built or repaired by the famous Whittington, whose arms were to be seen outside; but alterations of late years have done it away. Our routine of life was this. We rose to the call of a bell at six in summer, and seven in winter; and after combing ourselves, and washing our hands and face, we went at the call of another bell to breakfast. All this took up about an hour. From breakfast we proceeded to school, where we remained till eleven, winter and summer, and then had an hour's play. Dinner took place at twelve. Afterwards was a little play till one, when we went again to school, and remained till five in summer and four in winter. At six was the supper. We used to play after it in summer till eight. On Sundays, the school time of other days was occupied in church, both morning and evening; and as the Bible was read to us every day before every meal, besides prayers and grace, we rivalled the monks in the religious part of our duties.

On the 13th of June, 1813, Byron and Moore dined with Hunt in Horsemonger Lane Gaol during his two years' imprisonment in that establishment for his libel upon the Prince Regent in the 'Examiner.'

Our day in the prison was, if not agreeable, at least novel and odd. I had, for Lord Byron's sake, stipulated with our host beforehand, that the party should be as much as possible confined to ourselves; and as far as regarded dinner my wishes had been attended to. . . . Soon after dinner, however, there dropped in some of our host's literary friends, who, being utter strangers to Lord Byron and myself, rather disturbed the ease in which we were all sitting. *Moore's Life of Byron, 1813.*

Hunt thus describes his prison surroundings:—

I papered the walls with a trellis of roses; I had the ceiling colored with clouds and sky; the barred windows were screened with Venetian blinds; and when my bookcases were set up, with their busts and flowers, and a pianoforte made its appearance, perhaps there was not a handsomer room on that side of the water. I took a pleasure, when a stranger knocked at the door, to see him come in *Hunt's Lord Byron and some of his Contemporaries, vol. ii.*

and stare about him. The surprise on issuing from the borough and passing through the avenue of a jail was dramatic. Charles Lamb declared there was no other such room except in a fairy tale.

Horsemonger Lane Gaol stood on the south side of Trinity Square, Newington Causeway. Its chief entrance — still standing in 1885, and occupied as an office for the stamping of weights and measures, — was on Union Road, formerly Horsemonger Lane. A public playground for children was opened on the site of the old prison in the spring of 1885.

When I first visited Leigh Hunt [1817], he lived at No. 8 York Buildings, in the New Road. His house was small and scantily furnished. It was in a tiny room, built out at the back of the drawing-room, or first floor, which he appropriated as a study, and over the door of this was a line from the 'Faery Queene.' ... He had very few books: an edition of the Italian Poets in many volumes, Spenser's works, and the minor poems of Milton being, however, amongst them. I don't think there was a Shakspere. There were always a few cut flowers in a glass of water on the table.

<small>Procter's Recollections of Men of Letters.</small>

New Road, which extended from City Road to Edgeware Road in Hunt's time, has been divided by the Metropolitan Board of Works, for some deeply mysterious reason, into Pentonville Road, Euston Road, and Marylebone Road. York Buildings, which no longer exists as such, was on the south side of the present Marylebone Road, between York Place and Gloucester Place, and not far from Marylebone Church.

There is, in the National Portrait Gallery at Kensington, a letter of Hunt's, dated 1830, from 'Cromwell Lane, Old Brompton.' This was that part of the street since called Harrington Road, which lies between Queen's Gate and Old Brompton Road. Hunt was living at No. 4 Upper Cheyne Row, Chelsea, in 1834, when Carlyle became his neighbor; and his surroundings at that time are thus described by the Chelsea Sage : —

Hunt's household. Nondescript! Unutterable! Mrs. Hunt asleep on cushions; four or five beautiful, strange, gypsy-looking children running about in undress, whom the lady ordered to get us tea. The eldest boy, Percy,— a sallow, black-haired youth of sixteen, with a kind of dark cotton nightgown on,— went whirling about like a familiar, pervading everything; an indescribable dream-like household. . . . Hunt's house excels all you have ever read of, — a poetical Tinkerdom, without parallel even in literature. In his family room, where are a sickly large wife and a whole school of well-conditioned wild children, you will find half a dozen old rickety chairs gathered from half a dozen different hucksters, and all seeming engaged, and just pausing, in a violent hornpipe. On these and around them and over the dusty table and ragged carpet lie all kinds of litter, — books, paper, egg-shells, scissors, and, last night when I was there, the torn heart of a half-quarter loaf. His own room above stairs, into which alone I strive to enter, he keeps cleaner. It has only two chairs, a bookcase, and a writing-table; yet the noble Hunt receives you in his Tinkerdom in the spirit of a king, apologizes for nothing, places you in the best seat, takes a window-sill himself if there is no other, and then, folding closer his loose flowing 'muslin cloud' of a printed nightgown, in which he always writes, commences the liveliest dialogue on philosophy and the prospects of man (who is to be beyond measure happy yet); which again he will courteously terminate the moment you are bound to go: a most interesting, pitiable, lovable man, to be used kindly but with discretion.

<small>Froude's Carlyle, vol. ii. chap. xviii.</small>

Upper Cheyne Row, which crosses Great Cheyne Row, not far from the house occupied so long by Carlyle, has been re-numbered; but Hunt's quiet old-fashioned little house, which in 1885 was No. 10, was pointed out by old residents of the street, who remembered Hunt's occupancy of it half a century before.

Hunt's homes and lodgings in London and its neighborhood were many and varied, and it is not possible to follow him to them all. He lived at one time at Paddington, where the windows of his study looked out on to Westbourne Grove; he lodged once near Coleridge, at Highgate; and when he wrote 'The Old Court Suburb,' he occupied the house No. 32 Edwardes Square, Kensington, which in 1885 was still standing as he left it.

<small>Leigh Hunt to Jerrold: Blanchard Jerrold's Life of Douglas Jerrold, chap. iv.</small> Furthermore, I want you to come up here [No. 32 Edwardes Square] and give me a look in. It will do your kindly eyes good to see the nice study into which I have escaped out of all the squalidities at Chelsea. Tea at all hours.

I did not know Leigh Hunt in his prime, but I knew him well when he lived at Edwardes Square, South Kensington. He was then yielding to the universal conqueror. His son tells <small>S. C. Hall's Retrospect of a Long Life.</small> us: 'He was usually seen in a dressing-gown, bending his head over a book or over a desk.' Tall and upright still; his hair white and straggling, scattered over a brow of manly intelligence; his eyes retaining much of their old brilliancy combined with gentleness; his conversation still sparkling, though by fits and starts,—he gave me the idea of a sturdy ruin that, in donning the vest of time had been recompensed for gradual decay of strength by gaining ever more and more of the picturesque.

Hunt lived early in this century in the Vale of Health, a little hamlet on Hampstead Heath. At one end is a monster caravansary of the common type, with merry-go-rounds and tea-gardens, called the Vale of Health Hotel; while at the other end is a smaller public house, called the Vale of Health Tavern; and between the two are a number of unassuming buildings of the 'villa' order, but none seemingly dating back to Hunt's time. Old inhabitants of the neighborhood say that its character has entirely changed during the last fifty years. Mr. Thorne believes that Hunt's house was on the site of the Vale of Health Hotel. During the last year of his life he is said to have lived at Hammersmith.[9]

June 30, 1859. — Drove to Hammersmith, where we found Leigh Hunt and his two daughters awaiting us. It was a very tiny cottage, with white curtains and flowers in the window; but his beautiful manner made it a rich abode. The dear old man talked delightfully about his flowers, calling them 'gentle household pets.

<small>Diary of James T Fields : Biographical Sketch.</small>

Hunt's name is not to be found in the 'London Directory' for 1859.

Hunt died, two months later, while visiting a friend in Chatfield House, — a modest two-storied brick dwelling on the west side of the High Street, Putney, and numbered 84 a quarter of a century afterwards. He was buried in Kensal Green.

MRS. INCHBALD.

1753–1821.

MRS. INCHBALD in 1784 was lodging in Leicester Court, Leicester Fields, afterwards Leicester Square, in very humble apartments, where she began the writing of the plays which have made her name known to-day.

In 1787 she lived in Russell Street, Covent Garden, in the house which had been Button's (see ADDISON, p. 6). Here she occupied herself in translating plays from the French, and here she sold for two hundred pounds her 'Simple Story,' written in Frith Street, Soho, years before.

In 1810 Mrs. Inchbald lived at No. 5, and afterwards at No. 11, George's Row, overlooking Hyde Park, and since called St. George's Place, not far from St. George's Hospital.

In 1812 she removed to No. 4 Earl's Terrace, a quaint, old-fashioned row of buildings with a strip of green before them, in Kensington Road opposite Holland Park. She lodged also in Sloane Street, Knightsbridge, and in Leonard Place, Kensington, near Earl's Court Road.

At all times Mrs. Inchbald seems to have determined to retain her perfect independence, and to have chosen to have her time and property at her own disposal. She had an enthusiastic love of home, although that home was often, indeed generally, only a single, or at most a couple of rooms up two or three pairs of stairs, occasionally in the attic, where she was waited on by the servant of the house, or sometimes not waited on at all, for she not unfrequently speaks of fetching her own water, and dressing her own dinner; and she once kept a coroneted carriage waiting whilst she finished scouring her apartment. . . . At one time she took up her abode in a boarding-house; but she could not, she said, when there, command her appetite and be hungry at stated periods, like the rest of the boarders; so she generally returned to her attic, her crust of bread, and liberty.

Mrs. Elwood's Literary Ladies of England, vol. i. : Mrs. Inchbald.

Mrs. Inchbald died at Kensington House, which stood at the entrance of Kensington High Street, almost opposite the Palace Gate. In Mrs. Inchbald's day it was a college of the Order of Jesuits. It was afterwards a private lunatic asylum, but was taken down in 1872 to make way for the grand mansion of Baron Grant, which also in its turn has disappeared.

Here [Kensington House] Mrs. Inchbald spent the last two years of her life; and here on the 1st of August, 1821, she died, we fear — how shall we say it of so excellent a woman, and in the sixty-eighth year of her age? — of tight lacing. But she had been very handsome, was still handsome, was growing fat, and had never liked to part with her beauty; who that is beautiful does?

Leigh Hunt's Old Court Suburb, chap. vi.

Mrs. Inchbald was buried in the yard of St. Mary's Church, Kensington (see COLMAN, p. 62). The gravestones were all removed on the destruction of the old church, and no tablet to her memory is to be found in the new

ANNA JAMESON.

1794-1860.

MRS. JAMESON came to London with her family in 1803, when they settled at Hanwell on the Uxbridge Road. In 1806 they were living 'in the busy region of Pall Mall.'

She began her married life in Chenies Street, which runs from Gower Street to Tottenham Court Road.

On her return to London after a continental tour in 1825 she lived for many years in the house of her sister, No. 7 Mortimer Street, Cavendish Square. The street has been lengthened, and of course renumbered. Mrs. Jameson's home was in the present Cavendish Street, a few doors from the Square.

Mrs. Jameson was visiting friends at No. 51 Wimpole Street in 1844, when she first met Mrs. Browning, then Miss Barrett, who lived next door.

From 1851 to 1854 she lived in Bruton Street, Berkeley Square.

Here she was able to collect her friends about her, and saw a good deal of what may fairly be termed brilliant society at the simple evening-parties which she held on Wednesday evenings, much after the fashion of the Roman *reunions*, in which the circle of her literary friends was diversified by a little admixture from the great world, and by

Memoirs of Anna Jameson: Later Life.

the occasional appearance of strangers of note, Americans and foreigners.

Mrs. Jameson, spending much time among the art treasures in the Print Room of the British Museum, was in lodgings in Conduit Street, Regent Street, in the spring of 1860; and here in March of that year she died.

She was buried by the side of her father and mother in Kensal Green.

DOUGLAS JERROLD.

1803-1857.

DOUGLAS JERROLD was born in Greek Street, Soho, January 3, 1803, during a visit of his mother to London; but his infancy and his youth were spent in the neighborhood of the various provincial theatres of which his father was manager.

After two years of life as a ship's boy, where he gathered, by hard experience, the knowledge afterwards displayed in his famous nautical drama, he settled in London in 1816, 'in humble enough lodgings in Broad Court,' a quaint little thoroughfare full of dingy old houses, running from Bow Street to Drury Lane. While living here he was apprenticed to a printer in Northumberland Street, Strand.

The young printer brought home joyfully enough his first earnings. Very dreary was his home, with his poor weak father sitting in the chimney-corner: but there was a fire in the boy that would light up that home; at any rate, they were very cheerful for one day.

Life of Douglas Jerrold by his Son, chap. iii.

In 1819 he was in the establishment of a printer in Lombard Street, his first employer having failed.

No record of Jerrold's home life in London for a number of years is preserved to us. In 1829 his address was No. 4

Augustus Square, Regent's Park, — a small two-storied, countrified cottage at the junction of Park Village and Augustus Street; left unaltered in 1885. In 1834 he was living in Thistle Grove, Fulham Road, Chelsea, since extended and renumbered; in 1835, in Michael's Grove, Brompton Road. In 1838 his address was Haverstock Hill. In 1844 he had a cottage in Park Village, East Regent's Park, near Augustus Square, which forty years later was as quiet and rural as a village street; and in 1845 he went to West Lodge, Lower Putney Common, where he remained eight or nine years.

This study [West Lodge] is a very snug room. All about it are books. Crowning the shelves are Milton and Shakspere. A bit of Shakspere's mulberry tree lies on the mantelpiece. Above the sofa are the 'Rent Day' and 'Distraining for Rent,' Wilkie's two pictures. Under the two prints laughs Sir Joshua's sly 'Puck,' perched upon a pulpy mushroom. . . . The furniture is simple solid oak. The desk has not a speck upon it. The marble shell upon which the inkstand rests has no litter in it. Various notes lie in a row between clips, on the table. The paper-basket stands near the arm-chair, prepared for answered letters and rejected contributions. The little dog follows his master into his study, and lies at his feet. Life of Douglas Jerrold by his Son, chap. xii.

That cottage at Putney, its garden, its mulberry tree, its grass-plot, its cheery library with Douglas Jerrold as the chief figure in the scene, remains as a bright and most pleasant picture in our memory. He had an almost reverential fondness for books, books themselves, and said he could not bear to treat them, or to see them treated, with disrespect. He told us it gave him pain to see them turned on their faces, stretched open, or dog's-eared, or carelessly flung down, or in any way misused. He told us this, holding a volume in his hand with a caressing gesture, as though he tendered it affectionately and gratefully for the pleasure it had given him. Recollections of Writers by Charles and Mary Cowden Clarke: Jerrold.

West Lodge, still standing in 1885, was one of two semi-attached houses (the other called Elm House) on the borders of Lower Putney Common, between the Lower Richmond Road and the River, and about a mile beyond Putney Bridge. It was a spacious irregular brick house, with red-tiled gabled roofs, surrounded by fine old trees, and with a wide stretch of common in front. It had more the appearance of a farm-house than a gentleman's villa. At West Lodge Mrs. Caudle was created.

In 1853 Jerrold was living in Circus Road, St. John's Wood, a street that has been renumbered within a few years.

Early in 1857 he removed to Kilburn Priory, St. John's Wood, a short street running northerly from Maida Vale to Upton Road; and here on the 8th of June of the same year he died. He was buried at Norwood, and on his tombstone are inscribed the lines by his son: 'Sacred to the memory of Douglas William Jerrold, born 1803, died 1857. An English writer whose works will keep his memory green better than any epitaph.'

Jerrold's clubs were very many. Thackeray worked hard, and successfully, to insure his election to the Reform, No. 104 Pall Mall; but he was more frequently to be found in humbler and more entertaining organizations.

Of the clubs he set afloat and gave names to within my own recollection, I particularly call to mind those which he christened, respectively, 'Hook and Eye' and 'Our Club;' the former holding its weekly meetings at the Albion in Russell Street, Covent Garden, and the latter at Clunn's, in the Piazza, Covent Garden. . . . Many years before this period Jerrold was an active member of a club called 'The Mulberries,' which was held in the Wrekin Tavern, in the neighborhood of Covent Garden, and in which a regulation was established that ' some paper or poem or conceit bearing upon Shakspere should be contributed by each member, the general title being " Mulberry Leaves." '

Hodder's Memorials of my Times, chap. i.

The Albion Tavern, No. 26 Russell Street, Covent Garden, was still in 1885 much frequented by theatrical people at all hours of the day and night. Clunn's (afterwards Richardson's) Hotel, No. 1, on the Piazza, Covent Garden, is no longer in existence. The site of the Wrekin Tavern was No. 22 Broad Court, Bow Street, on the corner of Cross Court. It was taken down about 1870 (see GODWIN, p. 118).

Jerrold was a member also of 'the Museum, a properly modest and literary club,' established in 1847, 'at the end of Northumberland Street,' Strand, of the Gratis and the Rational clubs; and he was first president of the Whittington Club, which met at the Crown and Anchor Tavern, Arundel Street, Strand (see JOHNSON and ROGERS). On its site the Whittington Club house, No. 37 Arundel Street, now closed, was afterwards built.

SAMUEL JOHNSON.

1709–1784.

THE story of Dr. Johnson's life, as he himself and as his friends have told it, has been so carefully and so minutely recorded that no attempt will be made here to tell it in any other way. His earliest experiences of London were in his extreme youth.

He says, in 'An Account of the Life of Dr. Samuel Johnson, from his Birth to his Eleventh Year, Written by Himself:'—

This year [1712] in Lent I was taken to London to be touched for the Evil by Queen Anne. My mother was at Nicholson's, the famous bookseller of Little Britain. I always retained some memory of this journey, although I was but thirty months old.

Boswell adds:—

Mrs. Piozzi has preserved his very picturesque description of the scene as it remained upon his fancy. Being asked if he could remember Queen Anne, 'He had,' he said, 'a confused but somehow a sort of solemn recollection of a lady in diamonds and a long black hood.' This touch, however, was without any effect.

Boswell's Life of Johnson, 1712, Æt. 3.

Johnson's next interview with royalty, when he met George III. in the library of Buckingham House in 1767, Boswell considers one of the most remarkable incidents of his life.

During the whole of this interview Johnson talked to his Majesty with profound respect, but still in his firm manly manner, with a sonorous voice, and never in that subdued tone which is commonly used at the levee and in the drawing-room.

Boswell's Johnson, 1767, Æt. 58.

Buckingham House was taken down in 1825, by order of George IV., and Buckingham Palace erected upon its site.

Johnson was a man of eight-and-twenty when he decided to try his fortunes in London; and he and Garrick arrived here together in March, 1737.

He had a little money when he came to town, and he knew how he could live in the cheapest manner. His first lodgings were at the house of Mr. Norris, a stay-maker, in Exeter Street, adjoining Catherine Street, in the Strand. 'I dined,' said he, 'very well for eightpence, with very good company at the Pine Apple in New Street, just by: several of them had travelled; they expected to meet every day, but did not know one another's names. It used to cost the rest a shilling, for they drank wine; but I had a cut of meat for sixpence, and bread for a penny, and gave the waiter a penny; so that I was quite well served, nay, better than the rest, for they gave the waiter nothing.'

Boswell's Johnson, 1737, Æt. 28.

New Street runs from St. Martin's Lane to the junction of King and Bedford Streets, but no Pine Apple exists there now.

About this period Johnson began his labors in the establishment of Edward Cave, editor of the 'Gentleman's Magazine,' at St. John's Gate, Clerkenwell, where he was engaged in 1737, and where he first met Savage.

St. John's Gate, Clerkenwell, one of the oldest and most interesting structures in London, had, as late as 1885, by rare good fortune, been spared by the demons of improvement. The Jerusalem Tavern still stood at the east side, and in its coffee-room was shown, among other interesting relics, what purports to be Johnson's armchair. A bench without a back or a three-legged stool was probably considered good enough for him when he worked for Cave. The editorial and printing rooms of the 'Gentleman's Magazine' were, it is said, over the street, in a room occupied in 1885 and for some years previously by the St. John's Ambulance Association. Here Johnson toiled, and here, as is recorded on the walls in large letters, 'Garrick made his essay as an actor in London, 1737, in the farce of the "Mock Doctor."'

In this same year Johnson was lodging at Greenwich; for Boswell quotes a letter from him to Cave, dated 'July 12, 1737, Greenwich, next door to the Golden Heart [no longer standing], Church Street.' Shortly afterwards he had lodgings in Woodstock Street, Oxford Street, and in Castle Street, near Cavendish Square, in houses which, if they remain, it is not possible to identify now. In Castle Street he wrote 'London.'

No detailed account of his places of residence for the next ten years is given by Boswell; but in 1748 he speaks of his temporary home at Hampstead.

For the gratification of posterity let it be recorded that the house so dignified [by the occupancy of Johnson] was the last in Frognal, Southward, now [1818] occupied by Benjamin Charles Stephenson, Esq. *Park's Hampstead, p. 334.*

No trace of this house now remains.

Johnson lived, from 1748 to 1758, at No. 17 Gough Square, Fleet Street. Here he began the publication of the 'Rambler,' in 1750; here his wife died, in 1752; and here he completed the Dictionary, published in 1755. It was in this house, no doubt, that he delivered himself of the famous definition of 'network' ('anything reticulated or decussated, at equal distances, with interstices between the intersections'), which has ever since made the meaning and use of the word so clear to the average mind. This house, still standing in 1885, has been marked by a tablet of the Society of Arts.

In Bolt Court he had a garden, and perhaps in Johnson's Court and Gough Square, which we mention to show how tranquil and removed these places were, and convenient for a student who wished, nevertheless, to have the bustle of London at hand; and Maitland describes Johnson's and Bolt Courts in 1739 as having 'good houses, well inhabited;' and Gough Square he calls fashionable.

<small>Leigh Hunt's The Town, chap. iii.</small>

Soon after this [in 1758], Mr. Burney, during a visit to the Capital, had an interview with him in Gough Square, where he dined and drank tea with him, and was introduced to the acquaintance of Mrs. Williams. After dinner Mr. Johnson proposed to Mr. Burney to go up with him into his garret, which, being accepted, he there found about five or six Greek folios, a deal writing-desk, and a chair and a half. Johnson gave to his guest the entire seat, and tottered himself on one with only three legs and one arm.

<small>Boswell's Johnson, 1758, Æt. 49.</small>

I went one day searching for Johnson's place of abode. Found with difficulty the house in Gough Square, where the Dictionary was composed. The landlord, whom Glen and I incidentally inquired of, was just scraping his feet at the door, invited us to walk in, showed us the garret room, etc. (of which he seemed to have the obscurest tradition, taking Johnson for a schoolmaster).

<small>Carlyle's Note Book, 1831: Froude's Carlyle, vol. ii. chap. x.</small>

On the 23d of March, 1759, Johnson wrote to Mrs. Lucy Porter:—

I have this day moved my things, and you are now to direct to me at Staple Inn [Holborn], London. I am going to publish a little story-book ['Rasselas'], which I will send you when it is out.

<small>Boswell's Johnson. 1759, Æt. 50.</small>

He retired to Gray's Inn, and soon removed to chambers in the Inner Temple Lane [No. 1], where he lived in poverty, total idleness, and the pride of literature. Mr. Fitzherbert ... used to say that he paid a morning visit to Johnson, intending from his chamber to send a letter to the City; but to his great surprise he found an author by profession without pen, ink, or paper. The present Bishop of Salisbury was also among those who endeavored, by constant attention, to soothe the cares of a mind which he knew to be afflicted with gloomy apprehensions.

<small>Arthur Murphy's Essay on the Life and Genius of Samuel Johnson.</small>

Johnson's house in Inner Temple Lane has since been removed, giving place to the more imposing but less interesting Johnson's Buildings, which stand upon its site.

Dr. Johnson's library was contained in two garrets over his chambers [Inner Temple Lane], where Lintot, son of the celebrated bookseller of that name, had formerly his warehouse. I found a number of good books, but very dusty and in great confusion. The floor was strewed with manuscript leaves in Johnson's own handwriting, which I beheld with a degree of veneration, supposing they might perhaps contain portions of the 'Rambler' or of 'Rasselas.' I observed an apparatus for chemical experiments, of which Johnson was all his life very fond. The place seemed to be very favorable for retirement and meditation.

<small>Boswell's Johnson, 1763, Æt. 54.</small>

Beauclerc gives the following account of a visit he made to Johnson in Inner Temple Lane with Madame de Boufflers, — a French lady of doubtful morality, who aspired to be considered a blue-stocking.

When Madame de Boufflers was first in England [1763], she was desirous to see Johnson. I accordingly went with her to his chambers in the Temple, where she was entertained with his conversation for some time. When

<small>Boswell's Johnson, 1765, Æt. 56.</small>

our visit was over, she and I left him, and were got into Inner
Temple Lane, when all at once I heard a noise like thunder.
This was occasioned by Johnson, who, it seems, on a little recollection had taken it into his head that he ought to have done
the honors of his literary residence to a foreign lady of quality,
and, eager to show himself a man of gallantry, was hurrying down
the stairs in violent agitation. He overtook us before we reached
the Temple Gate, and, brushing in between me and Madame de
Boufflers, seized her hand and conducted her to the coach.

Ozias Humphrey, R. A., an eminent painter, in a letter
to his brother dated September 19, 1764, and quoted by
Croker in his 'Johnsoniana,' gives the following picture of
Johnson's life in Inner Temple Lane:—

The day after I wrote my last letter to you, I was introduced
to Mr. Johnson by a friend. We passed through three very dirty
rooms to a little one that looked like an old counting-house,
where this great man was sat at breakfast. The furniture of this
room was a very large deal writing-desk, an old walnut-tree
table, and five ragged chairs of four different sets. I was very
much struck with Mr. Johnson's appearance, and could hardly
help thinking him a madman for some time, as he sat waving
over his breakfast like a lunatic. He is a very large man, and
was dressed in a dirty brown coat and waistcoat, with breeches
that were brown also (although they had been crimson), and an
old black wig; his shirt collar and sleeves were unbuttoned ; his
stockings were down about his feet, which had on them, by way
of slippers, an old pair of shoes. He had not been up long when
we called on him, which was near one o'clock. He seldom goes
to bed before two in the morning ; and Mr. Reynolds [Sir Joshua]
tells me he generally drinks tea about an hour after he has supped.
We had been some time with him before he began to talk, but
at length he began, and, faith, to some purpose : everything he
says is as *correct* as a *second edition* ; 'tis almost impossible to
argue with him, he is so sententious and so knowing.

Boswell had his first interview with Johnson in the house
of Mr. Thomas Davies the actor, No. 8 Russell Street,

Covent Garden; and he thus describes the momentous event: —

At last, on Monday the 16th of May [1763], when I was sitting in Mr. Davies's back-parlor, after having drunk tea with him and Mrs. Davies, Johnson unexpectedly came into the shop, and, Mr. Davies having perceived him through the glass door in the room in which we were sitting advancing towards us, he announced his awful approach to me somewhat in the manner of an actor in the part of *Horatio*, when he addresses *Hamlet* on the appearance of his father's ghost, 'Look, my lord, it comes!' I found that I had a very perfect idea of Johnson's figure, from a portrait of him painted by Sir Joshua Reynolds, soon after he had published his Dictionary, in the attitude of sitting in his easy-chair in deep meditation. *Boswell's Johnson, 1763, Æt. 54.*

Tom Davies's house still stood in 1885, but the ground floor had been turned into a green-grocer's shop.

One week later, May 24, Boswell for the first time called on Johnson, and 'found the Giant in his den.'

His chambers were on the first floor of No. 1 Inner Temple Lane. . . . He received me very courteously; but it must be confessed that his apartment and furniture and morning dress were sufficiently uncouth. His brown suit of clothes looked very rusty; he had on a little old shrivelled unpowdered wig, which was too small for his head; his shirt neck and knees of his breeches were loose, his black worsted stockings ill drawn up; and he had a pair of unbuckled shoes by way of slippers. But all these slovenly peculiarities were forgotten the moment he began to talk. . . . He told me that he generally went abroad at four in the afternoon, and seldom came home till two in the morning. I took the liberty to ask if he did not think it wrong to live thus, and not make more use of his great talents. He owned it was a bad habit. *Boswell's Johnson, 1763, Æt. 54.*

Concerning his personal appearance and carelessness of dress the following story may be told here: —

In general his wigs were very shabby, and their foreparts were burned away by the near approach of the candle, which his short-sightedness rendered necessary in reading. At Streatham Mr. Thrale's butler had always a better wig ready, and as Johnson passed from the drawing-room when dinner was announced, the servant would remove the ordinary wig and replace it with the newer one; and this ludicrous ceremony was performed every day.

Boswell's Johnson, 1778, Æt. 69: Note by Croker.

From 1765 to 1776 Johnson lived at No. 7 Johnson's Court, Fleet Street, in a house still standing in 1885, but miserable in its neglected old age. Here he wrote the Prologue to Goldsmith's 'Good Natured Man,' and published his 'Journey to the Hebrides,' his edition of Shakspere, and a new edition of the Dictionary. Johnson's Court was not so called, as has been generally supposed, because of his residence in it. The name was a mere coincidence; but it gave him the opportunity of referring to himself, while in Scotland with Boswell, as 'Johnson of that Ilk.'

I returned to London in February [1766], and found Dr. Johnson in a good house in Johnson's Court, Fleet Street (No. 7), in which he had accommodated Miss Williams with an apartment on the ground floor, while Mr. Levett occupied his post in the garret.

Boswell's Johnson, 1766, Æt. 57.

To my great surprise, he asked me to dine with him on Easter Day [1773]. I never supposed that he had a dinner at his house, for I never heard of his friends having been entertained at his table. He told me, 'I generally have a meat pie on Sunday; it is baked at a public oven, which is very properly allowed, because one man can attend to it; and thus the advantage is obtained of not keeping servants from church to dress dinner.' . . . I had gratified my curiosity much in dining with Jean Jacques Rousseau while he lived in the wilds of Neufchâtel. I had as great a curiosity to dine with Dr. Samuel Johnson in the dusty recess of a court in Fleet Street. I supposed we should scarcely have knives and forks, and only some strange, uncouth, ill-drest dish; but I found every-

Boswell's Johnson, 1773, Æt. 64.

thing in very good order. We had no other company but Mrs. Williams and a young woman whom I did not know. As a dinner here was considered as a singular phenomenon, and as I was frequently interrogated on the subject, my readers may perhaps be desirous to know our bill of fare. Foote, I remember, in allusion to Francis the *negro*, was willing to suppose that our repast was *black broth*. But the fact was that we had a very good soup, a boiled leg of lamb and spinach, a veal pie, and a rice pudding.

While living in Johnson's Court he first made the acquaintance of the Thrales (in 1765). He dined with them every Thursday during the winter, at Streatham, and gained in many ways by the association. Their house, Streatham Place, stood in Streatham Park, on the south side of the Lower Common at Streatham, Surrey, six miles from Westminster Bridge. It was taken down in 1863, and no trace of it remains.

Thrale's Brewery, afterwards Barclay and Perkins's, to which firm Johnson, as executor, sold the buildings and the business, stands in Park Street, west of the Borough High Street, Southwark, covering a large plot of ground (see SHAKSPERE).

We have often had occasion to sigh over the poverty of London in the article of genuine popular legends. One beerhouse is among the exceptions. The workmen at Barclay and Perkins's will show you [1842] a little apartment in which, according to the tradition of the place, Johnson wrote his Dictionary. Now, this story has one feature of a genuine legend; it sets chronology at defiance.
<small>Knight's London, vol. ii.: Beer.</small>

In 1776 Johnson took possession of the house No. 8 Bolt Court, Fleet Street, where the rest of his life was spent.

Having arrived in London late on Friday, the 15th March [1776], I hastened next morning to wait on Dr. Johnson at his house, but found he was removed from Johnson's Court to Bolt Court, No. 8, still keeping to
<small>Boswell's Johnson, 1776, Æt. 67.</small>

his favorite Fleet Street. My reflection at the time upon this change, as marked in my journal, is as follows: 'I felt a foolish regret that he had left a court which bore his name; but it was not foolish to be affected with some tenderness of regard for a place in which I had seen him a great deal, from whence I had often issued a better and a happier man than when I went in, and which had often appeared to me in my imagination, while I trod its pavement in the solemn darkness of the night, to be sacred to wisdom and piety.'

On Wednesday, April 3 [1776], in the morning I found him very busy [in Bolt Court] putting his books in order; and as they were generally very old ones, clouds of dust were flying around him. He had on a pair of large gloves such as hedgers use. His present appearance put me in mind of my uncle Dr. Boswell's description of him: 'A robust genius, born to grapple with whole libraries.'

Boswell's Johnson, 1776, Æt. 67.

On Monday, March 19th [1781], I arrived in London, and on Tuesday the 20th, met him in Fleet Street walking, or rather, indeed, moving along; for his peculiar march is thus described in a Short Life of him published [by Kearsley] very soon after his death: 'When he walked the streets, what with the constant roll of his head, and the concomitant motion of his body, he appeared to make his way by that motion, independent of his feet.' That he was often much stared at while he advanced in this manner may easily be believed; but it was not safe to make sport of one so robust as he was. Mr. Langton saw him one day, in a fit of absence, by a sudden start drive the load off a porter's back, and walk forward briskly without being conscious of what he had done. The porter was very angry, but stood still, and eyed the huge figure with much earnestness, till he was satisfied that his wisest course was to be quiet and take up his burthen again.

Boswell's Johnson, 1781, Æt. 72.

Dr. Johnson died at Bolt Court on the 13th of December, 1784, and was buried on the 20th of the same month, in Westminster Abbey. Charles Burney the younger, in a letter to Dr. Parr, dated December 21, gives the following account of his funeral:—

Yesterday I followed our ever-lamented friend Dr. Johnson to his last mansion. . . . He was followed to the Abbey by a large troop of friends. Ten mourning-coaches were ordered by the executors for those invited. Besides these, eight of his friends or admirers clubbed for two more carriages, in one of which I had a seat. But the executor, Sir John Hawkins, did not manage things well; for there was no anthem or choir service performed, no lesson, but merely what is read over every old woman that was buried by the parish. Surely, surely, my dear sir, this was wrong, very wrong. Dr. Taylor read the service, but so so. He lies nearly under Shakspere's monument, with Garrick at his right hand, just opposite the monument erected not long ago for Goldsmith by him and some of his friends.

Life and Works of Dr. Samuel Parr.

Dr. Johnson's house in Bolt Court was destroyed soon after his death, but its immediate neighbors have been little changed during the last hundred years.

It was to this house that the elder D'Israeli and Samuel Rogers (q. v.) as young men both brought their poems, in search of encouragement and advice.

Dr. Johnson for many years worshipped in the Church of St. Clement Danes, Strand; and on his pew, No. 18 in the North Gallery, is a brass plate bearing the following inscription : —

In this pew, and beside this pillar, for many years attended Divine Service, the celebrated Dr. Samuel Johnson, the Philosopher, the Poet, the great Lexicographer, the Profound Moralist, and Chief Writer of his time. Born 1709. Died 1784. In remembrance and honor of noble faculties, nobly employed, some inhabitants of the Parish of St. Clement Danes have placed this slight memorial A. D. 1851.

On the 9th of April [1773], being Good Friday, I breakfasted with Johnson on tea and cross-buns. He carried me to the Church of St. Clement Danes, where he had his seat ; and his behavior was, as I had imagined to myself, solemn and devout. I never shall forget the tremulous

Boswell's Johnson, 1773, Æt. 64.

earnestness with which he pronounced the awful petition of the Litany: 'In the hour of death and at the day of judgment, good Lord, deliver us.'

April 4, 1779, *Easter Day.* — I rose about half an hour after nine, transcribed the prayer written last night, and by neglecting to count time sat too long at breakfast, so that I came to church at the first lesson. I attended the Litany pretty well, but in the pew could not attend the Communion Service, and missed the prayer for the Church Militant. . . . I then received, I hope with earnestness; and while others received, sat down; but thinking that posture, though usual, improper, I rose and stood. . . . I gave two shillings to the plate.

<small>Johnson's Diary, Boswell's Johnson, 1779, Æt. 70.</small>

Johnson was a man of many clubs, and emphatically himself, as he describes Boswell, 'a clubable man.' In his Dictionary he defines a 'club' as 'an assembly of good fellows meeting under certain conditions;' and to a gentleman who expressed surprise at his frequent attendance at some of the humble city organizations of which he was so fond, he said, 'Sir, the great chair of a full and pleasant club is perhaps the throne of human felicity.'

One of Johnson's earliest clubs was founded in 1748, and was known as the Ivy Lane, or King's Head, Club. Sir John Hawkins, in his 'Life of Johnson,' says:—

The Club met weekly at the King's Head, a famous beefsteak house in Ivy Lane [Paternoster Row], every Tuesday evening. Thither Johnson constantly resorted, and with a disposition to please and be pleased, would pass those hours in a free and unrestrained interchange of sentiment which otherwise had been spent at home in painful reflection.

Hawkins has mentioned the cordiality with which (in after years) he insisted that such of the members of the Ivy Lane Club as survived should meet again and dine together, which they did twice at a tavern and once at his house.

<small>Boswell's Johnson, 1783, Æt. 74.</small>

Ivy Lane contains a few old houses, but the King's Head was destroyed by fire some years ago. There was in 1885, however, a public house of that name in Canon Alley, St. Paul's Churchyard, and still another and much older King's Head, dating back easily to Johnson's day, at No. 41 Newgate Street, which adjoins Queen's Head Alley, and is not one hundred yards east of Ivy Lane.

The most important and long-lived of Johnson's clubs was founded by him and Sir Joshua Reynolds in 1764. It had no name but The Club for some years, and first met in the Turk's Head Tavern, which stood then at the corner of Greek and Compton Streets, Soho, but was soon after removed to the neighboring Gerard Street (see GOLDSMITH, p. 123). Among the original members, besides Reynolds and Johnson, were Burke and Goldsmith. Later, when it was called the Literary Club, George Colman (the elder), Boswell, Sheridan, Garrick, and other distinguished men were elected.

They met at the Turk's Head in Gerard Street, Soho, one evening in every week at seven, and generally continued their conversation until a pretty late hour.

Boswell's Johnson, 1764, Æt. 55.

The Club met in different taverns, usually in St. James's Street after Johnson's death; and in 1864 it celebrated its centennial anniversary at the Clarendon Hotel, No. 169 New Bond Street, a few doors from Grafton Street.

To another of his clubs Boswell thus alludes: —

On Friday, April 6th [1781], he carried me to dine at a club which, at his desire, had been lately formed at the Queen's Arms in St. Paul's Churchyard. He told Mr. Hoole that he wished to have a City Club, and asked him to collect one; but, said he, 'Don't let them be *patriots.*' The company were to-day very sensible, well-behaved men.

Boswell's Johnson, 1781, Æt. 72.

There is no 'Queen's Arms' in St. Paul's Churchyard now, although there was an old tavern bearing that sign at the junction of Newgate Street and St. Martin's-le-Grand until within a few years (see D'URFEY, p. 97).

A short time before his death he organized a club in the Essex Head Tavern, which stood at No. 40 Essex Street, Strand, as late as 1885, on the corner of Devereux Court, and a few doors from the site of the famous Grecian (see ADDISON, p. 7). It was kept by an old servant of the Thrales. The club was unpretentious; and, as Johnson wrote to Reynolds, 'the terms are lax, and the expenses light. We meet thrice a week, and he who misses forfeits twopence.' Sir Joshua did not join.

Some of the rules of this club, as preserved to us, are worthy of perusal:—

The Club shall consist of four-and-twenty. ... Every member is at liberty to introduce a friend once a week, but not oftener. ... Every member present at the Club shall spend at least sixpence; and every member who stays away shall forfeit threepence. ... There shall be no general reckoning, but every man shall adjust his own expenses. ... One penny shall be left by each member for the waiter.

Leigh Hunt, in 'The Town,' declares that Dr. Johnson was probably in every tavern and coffee-house in Fleet Street; but the Mitre was unquestionably his favorite, and is now most familiarly associated with his name.

I had learned that his place of frequent resort was the Mitre Tavern in Fleet Street, where he loved to sit up late. ... I called on him, and we went thither at nine. We had a good supper and port-wine, of which he then sometimes drank a bottle. The orthodox high-church sound of the Mitre, the figure and manner of the celebrated Samuel Johnson, the extraordinary power and precision of his conversation, and the pride arising from finding myself admitted to his companionship, produced a variety of sensations and a

Boswell's Johnson, 1763, Æt. 54.

pleasing elevation of mind beyond what I had ever before experienced. . . . We finished a couple of bottles of port, and sat till between one and two o'clock in the morning.

At night [February, 1766] I supped with Johnson at the Mitre Tavern, that we might renew our social intimacy at the original place of meeting. But there was now a considerable difference in his way of living. Having had an illness in which he was advised to leave off wine, he had from that period continued to abstain from it, and drank only water or lemonade. Boswell's Johnson, 1766, Æt. 57.

The Mitre stood at No. 39 Fleet Street. The Mitre, in Mitre Court, No. 44 Fleet Street, is not the Mitre of Johnson and Goldsmith, although generally so considered, even by Peter Cunningham, the most careful and correct of guides to London.

A favorite tavern of Dr. Johnson was the famous Devil Tavern of Ben Jonson's day. It stood on the site of Child's Bank, No. 1 Fleet Street, between the Temple Gate and Temple Bar, — Hunt says, 'within a door or two of Temple Bar,' — and was taken down, according to Hare, in 1788 (see BEN JONSON, p. 175). Here in 1751 Dr. Johnson gave a supper to Mrs. Charlotte Lenox, in honor of the publication of her first novel, 'The Life of Harriet Stuart.'

The place appointed was the Devil Tavern; and there, about the hour of eight, Mrs. Lenox and her husband, as also the club [Ivy Lane Club] to the number of near twenty, assembled. The supper was elegant, and Johnson had directed that a magnificent hot apple-pie should make a part of it; and this he would have stuck with bay leaves, because, forsooth, Mrs. Lenox was an authoress. . . . About five [A. M.] Johnson's face shone with meridian splendor, though his drink had been only lemonade. The dawn of day began to put us in mind of our reckoning; but the waiters were all so overcome with sleep that it was two hours before a bill could be had, and it was not until near eight that the creaking of the street door gave the signal for our departure. Hawkins's Life of Johnson, 1751.

Another of Johnson's taverns was the Crown and Anchor, No. 37 Arundel Street, Strand, which extended in the rear to Mitford Lane. The Whittington Club met at this tavern many years later (see JERROLD, p. 155); as did Bobus Smith's 'King of Clubs' (see ROGERS).

He frequented also the Turk's Head, No. 142 Strand, near Somerset House, afterwards the house of Chapman the publisher, and the first London home of 'George Eliot' (see MARY ANN EVANS, p. 98). In 1885 it was a tourist's ticket-office.

At night [July 21, 1763] Mr. Johnson and I supped in a private room at the Turk's Head Coffee House, in the Strand. 'I encourage this house,' said he; 'for the mistress of it is a good civil woman, and has not much business.'

Boswell's Johnson, 1763, Æt. 54.

In 1763 Johnson is described as reading 'Irene' to Peter Garrick, at the Fountaine Tavern, No. 103 Strand, but no longer in existence. Strype describes it as 'a very fine tavern, very conveniently built,' and as fronting on the Strand 'close to the alley leading to Fountain Court.' Simpson's was erected on its site. The name of Fountain Court was changed to Savoy Buildings in the summer of 1884. He was often to be found at Clifton's, in Butcher Row, behind St. Clement Danes, and on the site of the front of the New Law Courts; at Tom's Coffee House, No. 17 Russell Street, Covent Garden, taken down in 1865 (see CIBBER, p. 55); at Will's, corner of Bow and Russell Streets (see ADDISON, p. 7); at the British Coffee House, Cockspur Street[10] (see SMOLLETT); at the Old Red Lion Tavern, St. John Street Road, Islington (see GOLDSMITH, p. 125); and at the Old Baptist Head Tavern, St. John's Lane, Clerkenwell (see GOLDSMITH, p. 126). There is a general impression that Johnson was a frequenter of the Cock, No. 201 Fleet Street[11] (see PEPYS), and of the Cheshire Cheese, No. 16 Wine Office Court, Fleet Street (see GOLD-

SMITH, p. 120); but although both of these existed before his day, a careful reading of his Life by Boswell has failed to discover any allusion to them.

BEN JONSON.

1573-74–1637.

MUCH of the story of Jonson's life rests upon mere tradition. Contemporary authorities differ in many respects in their meagre accounts of him; and the later biographers seem to agree only in doubting the statements made by his contemporaries.

All that is related of Jonson in the 'History of the Worthies of England, Endeavored by Thomas Fuller, D.D.,' and in 'The Lives of Eminent Persons, by John Aubrey,' is quoted here in full.

Fuller lived from 1608 to 1661; Aubrey, from 1626 to 1700. Fuller says ('Westminster,' vol. ii.): —

Benjamin Johnson [sic] was born in this City [Westminster]. Though I cannot, with all my industrious inquiry, find him in his cradle, I can fetch him from his long coats. When a little child he lived in Hartshorne Lane, near Charing Cross, where his mother married a bricklayer for her second husband. He was first bred in a private school in St. Martin's Church [in the Fields], then in Westminster School [see CHURCHILL, p. 51]. He was suitably admitted into St. John's College, in Cambridge, where he continued but a few weeks for want of further maintenance, being fain to return to the trade of his father-in-law. And let them blush not that have, but those who have not, a lawful calling. He helped in the structure of Lincoln's Inn, where, having a trowel in his hand, he had a book in his pocket.

Hartshorne Lane has since been called Northumberland Street (Strand), and entirely rebuilt.

Malone, in his 'Shakspere,' says that he 'found in the register of St. Martin's that a Mrs. Margaret Jonson was married in November, 1575, to Mr. Thomas Fowler,' and this Margaret Jonson he believes to have been the mother of Ben. The old Church of St. Martin-in-the-Fields was taken down in 1720.

His mother [Ben Jonson's] after his father's death, married a bricklayer, and 't is generally sayd, that he wrought some time with his father-in-lawe, and particularly on the garden wall of Lincoln's Inne, next to Chancery lane, and that . . . a bencher walking thro' and hearing him repeat some Greeke verses out of Homer, discoursing with him, and finding him to have a witt extraordinary, gave him some exhibition to maintaine him at Trinity College in Cambridge. . . . Then he came over into England, and acted and wrote, but both ill, at the Green Curtaine, a kind of nursery, or obscure play house, somewhere in ye suburbs (I think towards Shoreditch or Clerkenwell). . . . Long since, in King James's time, I have heard my Uncle Denver say (who knew him) that he lived without Temple Barre at a Combe-maker's shop about the Elephant and Castle. In his later time he lived in Westminster, in the house under wch you passe as you goe out of the Churchyard into the old palace, where he dyed. He lies buryed in the North aisle in the path of Square Stone (the rest is lozenge) opposite to the scutcheon of Robertus de Ros, with this inscription only on him, in a pavement square, blew marble, about 14 inches square, O, Rare Ben Jonson.

<small>Aubrey's Lives of Eminent Persons: Jonson.</small>

The Green Curtain was the Curtain Theatre, Shoreditch. Its exact site it is quite impossible to determine now, although Halliwell Phillipps, in his 'Illustrations of the Life of Shakspere' (London, 1874), places it 'on the south side of Holywell Lane, in or near the place called Curtain Court, which was afterwards called Gloucester Row and now Gloucester

Street.' It does not appear on any of the maps of London of its day, and Stow simply describes it as 'standing on the S. W. side [of Shoreditch] towards the Fields.'

Of the Elephant and Castle there is no trace left. It was on the south side of the Strand, between Temple Bar and Essex Street. The gateway to Lincoln's Inn was still standing in 1885 in Chancery Lane, nearly opposite Cursitor Street, and bore the date 1518.

This account I received from Mr. Isaac Walton (who wrote Dr. Jo Donne's Life, etc.) December 2, 1680, being then eighty-seven years of age; 'I only knew Ben Jonson, but my Lord of Winton knew him very well, and sayes he was in the 6th degree, that is the upermost fforme, in Westminster scole, at which time his father dyed, and his mother married a bricklayer, who made him (much against his will) to help in his trade. . . . My Lord of Winton told me he told him he was (in his long retyrement and sickness, when he saw him, which was often) much afflickted, that hee had profained the scripture in his playes, and lamented it with horror; yet at that time of his long retyrement his pentions, (so much as came in) was given to a woman that governed him, with whom he lievd and dyed nere the abie in Westminster; and that nether he nor she took much care for next weike, and wood be sure not to want wine, of which he vsually tooke too much before he went to bed if not oftner and soner. My Lord tells me he knows not, but thinks he was born in Westminster.' *Aubrey's Lives of Eminent Persons: Jonson, footnote.*

If Jonson was in the sixth form at Westminster School when his father died, his mother could not have been the Margaret Jonson the record of whose marriage in 1575 Mr. Malone saw in the register of St. Martin's, unless Jonson was born earlier than 1573-74, the generally accepted date.[12] The 'Biographia Britannica' and other authorities say that he was a posthumous child.

In 1598 Jonson killed 'Gabriel Spenser, the player' in a duel in Hoxton Fields, Shoreditch, now marked by Hoxton

Square; and he is said to have been living in 1607 in Blackfriars, where the scene of the 'Alchymist' is laid. He died in 1637.

Jonson's grave was 'dug not far from Drayton's.' According to the local tradition, he asked the king (Charles I.) to grant him a favor. 'What is it?' said the king. 'Give me eighteen inches of square ground.' 'Where?' asked the king. 'In Westminster Abbey.' This is one explanation given of the story that he was buried standing upright. Another that it was with a view to his readiness for the Resurrection. . . . This [original] stone was taken up when in 1821 the nave was repaved, and was brought back from the stoneyard of the clerk of the works, in the time of Dean Buckland, by whose order it was fitted into its present place in the north wall of the nave. Meanwhile the original spot had been marked by a small triangular lozenge, with a copy of the old inscription. When, in 1849, Sir Robert Wilson was buried close by, the loose sand of Jonson's grave (to use the expression of the clerk of the works, who superintended the operation) 'rippled in like a quicksand,' and the clerk 'saw the two leg-bones of Jonson fixed bolt upright in the sand, as though the body had been buried in the upright position; and the skull came rolling down among the sand, from a position above the leg-bones to the bottom of the newly made grave. There was still hair upon it, and it was of red color.' It was seen once more on the digging of John Hunter's grave, and it had still traces of red hair upon it.

Dean Stanley's Westminster Abbey, chap. iv.

The name is spelled 'Johnson' on the tombstone.

Jonson was also associated with the Globe Theatre, 'near the Bear Gardens,' Southwark, on the grounds afterwards occupied by the Brewery of Barclay and Perkins (see SHAKSPERE); and with its neighbor the Rose Theatre, the site of which was at the north end of the short alley called Rose Street in 1885. It ran from Park Street towards the Bankside, and lay between the Bear Gardens and the Southwark Bridge Crossing.

The most famous of Jonson's public resorts was the Devil Tavern, which stood at No. 1 Fleet Street, between the Temple Gate and Temple Bar. The banking-house of the Childs was built upon its site in 1788. Here he gathered together his 'boys,' and, as he himself says, 'drank bad wine at the Devil.'

The first speech in my 'Catiline' spoken to *Scylla's Ghost* was writ after I parted with my friends at the Devil Tavern. I had drunk well that night, and had brave notions. Bengemmens Jonson. MMS. Memoranda, Dulwich Collection.

The great room [in the Devil Tavern] was called 'The Apollo!' Thither came all who desired to be 'sealed of the tribe of Ben;' here Jonson lorded it with greater authority than Dryden did afterwards at Will's, or Addison at Button's. The rules of the club, drawn up in the pure and elegant Latin of Jonson and placed over the chimney, were, it is said, engraven in marble. In the 'Tatler' [No. 79] they are described as being in gold letters; and this account agrees with the rules themselves — in gold letters, upon board — still preserved in the banking-house of Messrs. Child, where I had the pleasure of seeing them in 1843. Cunningham's Handbook of London: Devil Tavern.

A bust of Apollo and a board containing the 'Welcome to the Oracle of Apollo,' taken from the Devil at the time of its destruction in 1788, are still to be seen in an upper hall of Child's Bank; but the 'Rules,' as described by Mr. Cunningham, are not to be found there.

Another tavern of Jonson's was the Mermaid in Cheapside, which was destroyed in the Fire of 1666.

Jonson is described as wearing a loose coachman's coat, frequenting the Mermaid Tavern, where he drank seas of Canary, then reeling home to bed, and after a profuse perspiration, arising to his dramatic studies. Scott's Dryden, chap. v.

Shakspere, according to tradition, was a frequenter of the Mermaid, and a companion there of Jonson.

Many were the wit combats betwixt Shakspere and Ben Jonson, which two I beheld like a Spanish galleon and an English man-of-war; Master Jonson, like the former, was built far higher in learning; solid but slow in his performances. Shakspere with the English man-of-war, lesser in bulk, but lighter in sailing, could turn with all tides, tack about, and take advantage of all winds, by the quickness of his wit and invention.

<small>Fuller's Worthies of England.</small>

As Fuller was but eight years old when Shakspere died, his accounts of what he saw and heard of Shakspere in the Mermaid are hardly to be relied upon.

The Mermaid in Bread Street, the Mermaid in Friday Street, and the Mermaid in Cheap, were all one and the same. The tavern situated behind had a way to it from these thoroughfares, but it was nearer to Bread Street than Friday Street. . . . The site of the Mermaid is clearly defined from the circumstance of R. W., a haberdasher of small wares 'twixt Wood Street and Milk Street, adopting the same sign, 'Over against the Mermaid Tavern in Cheapside.'

<small>Burns's Catalogue of the Beaufoy Tokens.</small>

Among the other public houses frequented by Jonson were the Half Moon in Aldersgate Street, marked by Half Moon Alley (see CONGREVE, p. 64); 'The Falcon near the Theatre, Bankside,' marked by Falcon Dock and Falcon Wharf, Nos. 79 and 80 Bankside (see SHAKSPERE); and the Three Cranes in the Vintry, described by Strype as being in New Queen Street, and marked now by Three Cranes Lane, Upper Thames Street, which runs parallel with Queen Street to the east of Southwark Bridge (see PEPYS). 'The Swan at Charing Cross,' of which Jonson speaks pleasantly, was probably the tavern called in 'The New View of London,' published in 1708, the 'Swan Inn on the N. W. side of the Strand, near St. Martin's Lane End.' It has long since disappeared.

A favorite suburban resort of Jonson was the Three Pigeons in the Market Place opposite the Town Hall, then the Market House, of Brentford. It was taken down some years ago, and a modern gin-palace built upon its site.

JOHN KEATS.

1795–1821.

KEATS was born in London on the 29th of October, 1795.

His maternal grandfather, Jennings, was proprietor of a large livery-stable called 'The Swan and Hoop' on the Pavement in Moorfields, opposite the entrance into Finsbury Circus. . . . Keats's father was the principal servant in 'The Swan and Hoop,' a man so remarkably fine in common sense and native respectability that I perfectly remember the warm terms in which his demeanor used to be canvassed by my parents after he had been to visit his boys. Recollections of Writers by Charles and Mary Cowden Clarke: Keats.

Keats is believed to have been born in the immediate neighborhood of these stables, the exact position of which cannot now positively be determined, although old maps and directories have been consulted, and the memories of old inhabitants of that portion of London have been severely taxed. Cunningham, in his 'Hand-Book,' places the 'Swan and Hoop Stables at No. 28, on the Pavement in Moorfields over against the riding-school, now [1850] a public house with that name.' But since Mr. Cunningham wrote, the Pavement has been extended and renumbered, and the sign 'Swan and Hoop' is no longer to be seen. 'No. 28 on the Pavement' in 1850 was a few doors from London

Wall. The riding-school on the corner of the Pavement and West Street, which leads to Finsbury Circus, standing in 1885, may perhaps be that to which Mr. Cunningham refers.

Keats was educated at Enfield, in the school of John Clarke, father of Charles Cowden Clarke, who describes it as still standing in 1878. It had already been converted into a railway-station; but the managers of the company had protected the buildings, and left almost intact one of the few remaining specimens of graceful English architecture of other days. In 1885, however, nothing remained of the old school but a drawing of it, preserved in the British Museum. Its bricks had been used in the construction of neighboring houses. The great Eastern Railway station stood upon its site.

Keats's mother died in 1810, while he was at this school; and the touching story of his grief there, of his hiding himself under his master's desk and refusing to be comforted, has been related by his biographers. He left Enfield soon after his first great sorrow, and studied for some time with a surgeon in Edmonton, living in Church Street in a house it is not possible to identify now. It was near the 'Bay Cottage' in which Charles Lamb thirty years later lived and died.

Charles Cowden Clarke follows Keats from one London home to another more completely than do any of his regular biographers.

Keats came to town in 1815, to enter as a student at St. Thomas's Hospital, then in Southwark (see AKENSIDE, p. 10); and he thus wrote to Clarke of his earliest London lodgings: —

Although the Borough is a beastly place in dirt, turnings and windings, yet No. 8 Dean Street is not difficult to find ; and if you would run the gauntlet over London Bridge, take the first turning to the right, and moreover knock at my door, which is nearly opposite a meeting, you would do me a charity, which, as St. Paul says, is the father of virtues.

It is difficult enough to find No. 8 Dean Street now. The railway viaduct has swept it completely away, and left only a house or two in Dean Street, which runs from No. 199 Tooley Street, near Hay's Lane, under the railway archway, towards Thomas Street.

In 1816 Mr. Clarke writes :—

Keats had left the neighborhood of the Borough, and was now living with his brother in apartments over the second floor of a house in the Poultry, over the passage leading to the Queen's Head Tavern, and opposite to one of the City Companies' Halls, — the Ironmongers', I believe.

The passage leading to the Queen's *Arms* Tavern, and called Bird in Hand Court, is under the archway numbered, in 1885, 76 Cheapside, near the Poultry. It is almost directly opposite Ironmonger Lane, where stands the Mercers' Hall, to which Mr. Clarke, confounding the name of the hall with the name of the street, probably alludes.[18]

In this lodging Keats wrote the greater part of his first volume of 'Poems,' published in 1817. He was shortly after the guest, for a time, of Leigh Hunt (q. v.), in Kentish Town; and letters of his to Fanny Brawne written in 1819 were dated from Great Smith Street, and 25 College Street, now Great College Street, Westminster. No. 25 was near the corner of the present Tufton Street. He also visited Hunt in the Vale of Health (see HUNT, p. 148), and took lodgings at Well Walk, Hampstead, 'in the first or second house on the right hand going up the Heath.' Here the greater part of 'Endymion' was written.

Winding south from the Lower Heath [Hampstead] there is a charming little grove in Well Walk, with a bench at the end whereon I last saw poor Keats, the poet of 'The Pot of Basil,' sitting and sobbing his dying breath into a handkerchief, glancing parting looks towards the quiet landscape he had delighted in so much, and musing as in his 'Ode to the Nightingale.'

<small>William Howitt's Northern Heights of London: Hampstead.</small>

His memory here is perpetuated by 'Keats Corner' and 'Keats Villa,'—two modern houses in Well Road, near its crossing with Well Walk.

It was on the same day, sitting on the bench in Well Walk (the one against the wall), that he [Keats] told me, with unaccustomed tears in his eyes, that his heart was breaking.

<small>Leigh Hunt's Lord Byron and his Contemporaries.</small>

Keats's Bench, so marked by a printed sign, stood at the end of Well Walk next the Heath in 1885; but the view of the quiet landscape has been spoiled by a villa opposite, built after Keats's death.

The various accounts of the search for Keats's last Hampstead home are so interesting that they are given here at length:—

Keats indeed took so great a liking to Hampstead, from his stay at Hunt's, that he became a resident here from 1817 till he left England in 1820. Here he wrote his 'Ode to a Nightingale,' 'St. Agnes,' 'Isabella,' 'Hyperion,' and began the 'Endymion,' which he finished at Burford Bridge. The house in which he lodged for the greater part of the time, then called Wentworth Place, is now [1876] named Lawn Bank, and is the end house but one on the west side of John Street, next Wentworth House. His walks were in his later months limited to the Lower, or the Middle, Heath Road, the seat at the top of Well Walk being his goal or resting-place.

<small>Thorne's Hand-Book of the Environs of London: Hampstead.</small>

From this time [1816] till 1820, when he left, in the last stage of consumption, for Italy, Keats resided principally at Hampstead. During most of this time he lived with his very dear friend Mr. Charles Brown, a Russian merchant, in Wentworth

Place, Downshire Hill, by Pond Street, Hampstead. Previous to this he and his brother Thomas had occupied apartments at the next house to Mr. Brown's. . . . By the aid of the statements of Leigh Hunt and Lord Houghton, we may trace most of the scenes in which the very finest poetry of Keats was written, for the noblest of his productions were all written at Hampstead. . . . It is to be regretted that Wentworth Place, where Keats lodged, and wrote some of his finest poetry, either no longer exists or no longer bears that name. At the bottom of John Street, on the left hand in descending the hill, is a villa called Wentworth House. . . . I made the most vigorous search in that quarter, inquiring of the tradesmen daily supplying the houses there, and of two residents of forty and fifty years. None of them had any knowledge or recollection of Wentworth Place.

<small>William Howitt's Northern Heights of London: The Vale of Health.</small>

H. Buxton Forman, in the Appendix to 'The Letters of John Keats to Fanny Brawne,' published in 1878, describes his thorough search for Wentworth Place, and this Hampstead home of Keats, and thus sums up the results: —

The gardener of Wentworth House, of whom, among many others, I have inquired for Wentworth Place, assures me very positively that some fifteen or twenty years ago, when Lawn Bank (then called Lawn Cottage) was in bad repair, and the rain had washed nearly all the color off the front, he used to read the words 'Wentworth Place' painted in large letters beside the top window at the extreme left of the old part of the house, as one faces it. . . . Not perfectly satisfied with this local evidence, I forwarded to Mr. Severn a sketch-plan of the immediate neighborhood, that he might identify the houses in which he visited Keats and Brown, and the Brawne family. He says that Wentworth House and Lawn Bank (and these two blocks only) constituted Wentworth Place, and that it was in Lawn Bank that Brown and Mrs. Brawne had their respective residences. . . . It will doubtless be admitted as proved that in Wentworth House and Lawn Bank we have the immortalized Wentworth Place of the period to which the present volume relates; and Mr. Howitt and Mr. Thorne both deserve our thanks for carrying the inquiry so nearly to a satisfactory conclusion as to land the investigator, one in one of the right houses and one in the other. It is true that Mr. Howitt transfers his house from one side of John Street to the other, and it must be noted that Mr. Thorne errs in two points. Lawn Bank *alone* was certainly not Wentworth Place ; and Keats cannot be said to have *lodged* there, for he was certainly Brown's guest.

Lawn Bank in 1885 was an irregular two-story house on the south side of John Street, Downshire Hill, nearly opposite St. John's Chapel, and next to Wentworth House. On the other side is a villa called 'Keats Cottage.' It seems in Keats's time to have been a semi-detached house, the Brawnes occupying the western, and Charles Brown, with whom Keats lived, the eastern and smaller half. It is hardly visible from the road, because of thick foliage and a high board fence. From this house Keats set out, in 1820, for Italy, never to return.

CHARLES LAMB.

1775–1834.

THERE is, in Lamb's familiar letters and in many of his essays, so much that is autobiographical, and his friends have so often and so fondly described him and his sister in their home life, that no attempt will be made here to tell Lamb's story except as he has told it himself, or as it has been told by those who knew and loved him well.

He first saw the light in Crown Office Row, in the Temple, in 1775.

I was born and passed the first seven years of my life in the Temple. Its church, its halls, its gardens, its fountain, its river,

I had almost said — for in those young years what was this king of rivers to me but a stream that watered our pleasant places ?— these are of my oldest recollections. . . . What a transition for a countryman visiting London for the first time, the passing from the crowded Strand or Fleet Street, by unexpected avenues, into its magnificent ample squares, its classic green recesses! What a cheerful liberal look hath that part of it which, from three sides, overlooks the greater garden ; that goodly pile of building strong, albeit of Paper height, confronting with mossy contrast the lighter, older, more fantastically shrouded one, named of Harcourt, with the cheerful Crown Office Row (place of my kindly engendure), right opposite the stately stream, which washes the garden-foot with her yet scarcely trade-polluted waters, and seems but just weaned from her Twickenham Naiades ! A man would give something to have been born in such places.

<small>Essays of Elia: The Old Benchers of the Inner Temple.</small>

The eastern half of the block, comprising Nos. 1, 2, and 3 Crown Office Row, still stood in 1885 as when built in 1737. The western end, Nos. 4, 5, and 6, becoming uninhabitable, was torn down and rebuilt in 1859–1861.

According to Fitzgerald's Memoir, Lamb went to a school overlookng 'a discolored, dingy garden in the passage leading into Fetter Lane from Bartlett's Buildings. This was close to Holborn.' It was afterward called Bartlett's Passage, but no trace of the school remains.

In 1782 'Charles Lamb son of John Lamb, Scrivener, and of Elizabeth, his wife,' entered the school of Christ-Hospital (see COLERIDGE, p. 57, and HUNT, p. 144), where he remained until he was fifteen. Talfourd, in his 'Life of Lamb' (chap. i.), says : —

Lamb was an amiable, gentle boy, very sensible and keenly observing, indulged by his schoolfellows and by his masters on account of his infirmity of speech. His countenance was mild, his complexion clear brown, with an expression which might lead you to think he was of Jewish descent. His eyes were not of the same color, — one was hazel, the other had specks of gray in the iris, mingled as one sees red spots in the bloodstone. His step was plantigrade, which made his walk slow and peculiar, adding to the staid appearance of his figure.

I remember L—— at school, and can well recollect that he had some peculiar advantages, which I and others of his schoolfellows had not. His friends lived in town, and were near at hand, and he had the privilege of going to see them almost as often as he wished. . . . L——'s governor (so we called the patron who presented him to the foundation) lived in a manner under his paternal roof. Any complaint he had to make was sure of being attended to. This was understood at Christ's, and was an effectual screen to him against the severity of masters, or, worse, the tyranny of the monitors.

<small>Essays of Elia: Christ-Hospital five-and-twenty Years ago.</small>

Leigh Hunt, in his 'Autobiography' (vol. i. chap. iv.), gives his recollections of Lamb when he came back to visit the old familiar school scenes, as he was so fond of doing: —

I have spoken of the distinguished individuals bred at Christ-Hospital, including Coleridge and Lamb, who left the school not long before I entered it. Coleridge I never saw until he was old. Lamb I recollect coming to see the boys, with a pensive, brown, handsome, and kingly face, and a gait advancing with a motion from side to side, between involuntary consciousness and attempted ease. His brown complexion may have been owing to a visit in the country, his air of uneasiness to a great burden of sorrow. He dressed with a Quaker-like plainness.

For a short time after quitting school (in November, 1789) Lamb was employed in the South Sea House with his brother John, who is described in 'My Relations' as James Elia, and who was some twelve years his senior.

Reader, in thy passage from the Bank, where thou hast been receiving thy half-yearly dividends (supposing thou art a lean annuitant like myself), to the Flower Pot, to secure a place for Dalston or Shacklewell, or some other thy suburban retreat northerly, didst thou never observe a melancholy-looking handsome brick and stone edifice to

<small>Essays of Elia: The South Sea House.</small>

the left, where Threadneedle Street abuts upon Bishopsgate? I dare say thou hast often admired its magnificent portals, ever gaping wide, and disclosing to view a grave court with cloisters and pillars, with few or no traces of goers-in or comers-out. . . . Such is the South Sea House; at least, such it was forty years ago, when I knew it, — a magnificent relic. . . . Peace to the Manes of the *Bubble*. Silence and destitution are upon thy walls, proud house, for a memorial. Situated as thou art, in the very heart of striving and living commerce, amid the fret and fever of speculation, with the Bank, and the 'Change, and the India House about thee, in the heyday of present prosperity, with their important faces, as it were, insulting thee, their *poor neighbor out of business*, to the idle and merely contemplative — to such as me; old house! there is a charm in thy quiet — a cessation — a coolness from business, an indolence almost cloistral, which is delightful.

The South Sea House was partly destroyed by fire in 1826. A modern South Sea House stands upon its site. It fronts on Threadneedle Street.

Lamb entered the service of the East India Company, as an accountant, on the 5th of April, 1792. The situation of the East India House is thus described in Brayley's 'London and Middlesex,' vol. iii.: 'From Nos. 12 to 21 Leadenhall Street, the East India House at the corner of No. 7 Leadenhall Market.' This building was taken down in 1862.

Lamb left the India House in 1825. On the 6th of April he wrote to Wordsworth:—

'Here I am then, after thirty-three years of slavery sitting in my own room at eleven o'clock this finest of April mornings, a freed man.' And to Barton he wrote later, 'Take in briefly, that for a few days I was painfully oppressed by so mighty a change, but it is becoming daily more natural to me. . . . I would not serve another seven years for seven hundred thousand pounds. I have got £441 net for life, sanctioned by act of Parliament, with a provision for Mary if she survives me.' <small>Talfourd's Life of Lamb, chap. xv.</small>

It is now six-and-thirty years since I took my seat at the desk. Melancholy was the transition at fourteen from the abundant play-time, and the frequent intervening vacations of school days, to the eight, nine, and sometimes ten hours a day at a counting-house. But time partially reconciles us to anything. I gradually became content, — doggedly contented, as wild animals in cages. To dissipate this awkward feeling, I have been fain to go among them once or twice since; to visit my old desk-fellows, my co-brethren of the quill, that I had left below me in the state militant. Not all the kindness with which they received me could quite restore to me that pleasant familiarity which I had heretofore enjoyed among them. We cracked some of our old jokes, but methought they went off but faintly. My old desk, the peg where I hung my hat, were appropriated to another. I knew it must be, but I could not take it kindly. D——l take me, if I did not feel some remorse — beast, if I had not — at quitting my old compeers, the faithful partners of my toil for six-and-thirty years, that smoothed for me, with their jokes and conundrums, the ruggedness of my professional road.

Essays of Elia: The Superannuated Man.

In 1795 and later, Lamb was lodging with his family at No. 7 Little Queen Street, Holborn; and here was enacted that awful tragedy, on the 22d of September, 1796, which clouded and saddened the life of Charles as well as Mary Lamb. On the 27th of September Lamb wrote to Coleridge: —

White, or some of my friends, or the public papers, by this time may have informed you of the terrible calamities that have fallen on our family. I will only give you the outlines: My poor, dear, dearest sister, in a fit of insanity, has been the death of our own mother. I was at hand only time enough to snatch the knife out of her grasp. She is at present in a madhouse, from whence I fear she must be moved to a hospital. God has preserved me to my senses, — I eat and drink and sleep, and have my judgment, I believe, very sound. My poor father was slightly wounded, and I am left to take care of him and my aunt.

On the 3d of October of the same year he wrote again to Coleridge: —

It will be a comfort to you, I know, to know that our prospects are somewhat brighter. My poor, dear, dearest sister, the unhappy and unconscious instrument of the Almighty's judgment on our house, is restored to her senses; to a dreadful sense and recollection of what has past. . . . On that first evening my aunt was lying insensible, to all appearance like one dying — my father with his poor forehead plastered over, from a wound he had received from a daughter dearly loved by him, and who loved him no less dearly — my mother, a dead and murdered corpse in the next room — yet was I wonderfully supported.

Holy Trinity Church, in Little Queen Street, facing Gate Street, was built upon the site of Lamb's house; and behind it, in the playground of the church school, was, in 1885, a tree standing in what had undoubtedly been Lamb's back garden.

Lamb, while living in Little Queen Street, frequented the Feathers, a public house in Hand Court, Holborn, the old sign of which was still, in 1885, over the archway that leads into the Court (No. 58 Holborn); and the tavern itself, one of the most curious of the old-fashioned inns to be found in that part of London, was as Lamb left it. The windows probably had not been washed since Lamb's time.

Another old inn with which he was familiar in those days was the Salutation and Cat, No. 17 Newgate Street, near Ivy Lane. Here Southey and Coleridge were often to be found with him (see COLERIDGE, p. 60). In later years he wrote to Coleridge : —

I imagine to myself the little smoky room at the Salutation and Cat, where we have sat together through the winter nights beguiling the cares of life with Poesy.

After the tragedy the Lambs went to Pentonville, living at No. 45 Chapel Street.

Also, in sifting the letters for facts and dates, I find that Lamb lived in Chapel Street, Pentonville, not as Talfourd and Procter thought a few months, but three years, removing thither almost immediately after the mother's death. It is a trifle, yet not without interest to the lovers of Lamb; for these were the years in which he met in his daily walks, and loved but never accosted, the beautiful Quakeress 'Hester,' whose memory is enshrined in the poem beginning, 'When maidens such as Hester die.'

<small>Anne Gilchrist's Mary Lamb, Preface.</small>

No. 45 Chapel Street in 1885 was the Agricultural Hotel, on the northwest corner of Liverpool Road, and almost the only house in the miserable, dull, uninteresting street, that seems to have been rebuilt during the present century. At the time the Lambs lived there, Chapel Street was out of town, and surrounded by gardens and green fields.

Lamb was back in his beloved Temple in 1800.

I live at No. 16 Mitre Court Buildings, a pistol-shot off Baron Maseres. . . . He lives on the ground floor for convenience of the gout; I prefer the attic story for the air! He keeps three footmen and two maids; I have neither maid nor laundress. . . . N. B. When you come to see me, mount up to the top of the stairs — I hope you are not asthmatical — and come in flannel, for it is pure airy up there. And bring your glass, and I will show you the Surrey Hills. My bed faces the river, so as by perking upon my haunches, and supporting my carcass with my elbows, without much wrying my neck, I can see the white sails glide by the bottom of King's Bench Walk, as I lie in my bed.

<small>Talfourd's Life of Lamb, chap. vi.</small>

The present Mitre Court Buildings bear date 1830.

In 1809 Lamb writes to Manning: —

While I think of it, let me tell you we are moved. Don't come any more to Mitre Court Buildings. We are at 34 Southampton Buildings [in a house still standing in 1885], Chancery Lane [see HAZLITT, p. 133], and shall be here until about the end of May, when we

<small>Talfourd's Life of Lamb, chap. ix.</small>

remove to No. 4 Inner Temple Lane, where I mean to live and die. . . . Our place of final destination — I don't mean the grave, but No. 4 Inner Temple Lane — looks out upon a gloomy churchyard-like court, called Hare Court, with three trees and a pump in it. Do you know it? I was born near it, and used to drink at that pump when I was a Rechabite of six years old.

In 1810, still writing to Manning, he describes these chambers: —

I have two sitting-rooms : I call them so *par excellence*, for you may stand, or loll, or lean, or try any posture in them, but they are best for sitting ; not squatting down Japanese fashion, but the more decorous mode which European usage has consecrated. I have two of these rooms on the third floor, and five sleeping, cooking, etc. rooms on the fourth floor. In my best room is a choice collection of the works of Hogarth, an English painter of some humor. In my next best are shelves containing a small but well-chosen library. My best room commands a court, in which there are trees and a pump, the water of which is excellent cold with brandy, and not very insipid without.

The house has been replaced by the modern Johnson's Buildings, but the trees and the court and the pump are still there.

The Lambs left the Temple in the autumn of 1817, and took lodgings, as he describes them in a letter to Haydon, dated in December of that year, 'at No. 20 Russell Court, Covent Garden East; half-way up, next the corner, left-hand side," and, as he writes to another friend, 'in the corner house delightfully situated between the two theatres.'

Russell Court, running from Drury Lane to Brydges Street, does not answer this description ; while No. 20 Russell *Street*, next to the corner of Bow Street, is ' on the left-hand side,' and 'between the two theatres.' This was classic ground, the site of Will's Coffee House (see ADDISON, p. 7); and it seems strange that Lamb should not have known this fact, or, if he did, should not have mentioned it in any of his letters. In November of 1817 Lamb wrote to Miss Wordsworth:—

Here we are, transplanted from our native soil. I thought we never could have been torn up from the Temple. Indeed, it was an ugly wrench, but like a tooth, now 'tis out, and I am easy! We never can strike root so deep in any other ground. . . . We are in the individual spot we like best, in all this great city. The theatres with all their noises; Covent Garden, dearer to me than any gardens of Alcinoüs, where we are morally sure of the earliest peas and 'sparagus; Bow Street, where the thieves are examined, within a few yards of us: Mary had not been here four-and-twenty hours before she saw a thief. She sits at the window working, and, casually throwing out her eyes, she sees a concourse of people coming this way, with a constable to conduct the solemnity. These little incidents agreeably diversify a female life.

<small>Talfourd's Life of Lamb, chap. x.</small>

Lamb, for the first time, lived in an entire house of his own in 1823, of which he wrote to Bernard Barton on the 2d of September:—

When you come Londonward you will find me no longer in Covent Garden; I have a cottage in Colebrook [properly Colnbrook] Row, Islington; a cottage, for it is detached; a white house with six good rooms; the New River (rather elderly by this time) runs (if a moderate walking-pace can be so termed) close to the foot of the house; and behind is a spacious garden with vines (I assure you), pears, strawberries, parsnips, leek, carrots, cabbages, to delight the heart of old Alcinoüs. You enter, without passage, into a cheerful dining-room, all studded over and rough, with old books; and above is a lightsome drawing-room, three windows full of choice prints. I feel like a great lord, never having had a house before.

<small>Talfourd's Life of Lamb, chap. xiii.</small>

'I am in Colebrook Cottage, Colebrook Row, Islington,' he wrote to Southey, 'close to the New River end of Colebrook Terrace, left hand from Sadlers Wells.'

This little three-storied house, numbered 19, was still standing in 1885. The sitting-room window had been altered, but nothing else. It is named Elia Cottage, and in its gardens a factory has been built. The New River still glides slowly by its door, but no longer is in sight, and no half-blind George Dyer could walk into it to-day. Enclosed within brick walls, and covered by a strip of green grass, it appears at intervals on its way to town, but not in this portion of Colebrook Row.

During the later years of Lamb's life, when he had occasion to spend a night in town, he lodged with Mrs. Buffam, at No. 24 Southampton Buildings, Chancery Lane, in a very curious stuccoed house, with a sloping tiled roof, unlike any other house in that vicinity. It stood unchanged in 1885. Hazlitt was his neighbor here.

In 1829 the Lambs removed to Enfield, to 'an odd-looking gambogish-colored house at the Chase side.'

The situation was far from picturesque; for the opposite side of the road only presented some middling tenements, two dissenting chapels, and a public house decorated with a swinging sign of a Rising Sun. Talfourd's Life of Lamb, chap. xvii.

In 1885 the odd-looking gambogish house on the Chase side had been completely transformed and enlarged. It stood on the east side of the road, and was 'The Manse' (so marked on its gate-posts) of Christ's Church opposite, which was built upon the site of one of the two dissenting chapels. The middling tenements were called Gloucester Place, and bore date 1823. They still faced the strip of green that separated them from the Lambs' cottage. Sargeant Talfourd has confounded the Rising Sun public house, which is some distance Londonwards, with the Crown and Horse-Shoes in Lamb's more immediate neighborhood. Both houses have swinging signs; and in both, probably,

Lamb passed many a pleasant hour. After leaving here, the Lambs lodged for a time at an ivy-covered house adjoining the Manse on the north. While Lamb is not personally remembered at Enfield, old inhabitants, in 1885, who knew his landlady, a Mrs. Westwood, still repeated the stories she told of her odd lodgers; and from some of them was derived the information which led to this identification of the houses.

In 1832 the Lambs took possession of a little cottage at Edmonton, where, on the 27th of December, 1834, Charles died. This house — Bay Cottage, but since called Lamb's Cottage — still stood, in 1885, next door to Lion House, on the north side of Church Street, Edmonton, about half-way between the church and the railway station, — a small and unpretending dwelling, lying back from the street, and but a few doors from the Jolly Farmer, an old tavern with which Charles was no doubt familiar. The Bell Tavern, at the other end of the hamlet, in Fore Street, corner of Gilpin Grove, no longer exists. On its site is a modern brick building called Gilpin's Bell, because of its association with John Gilpin's famous ride. To this corner Lamb, according to tradition, was wont to escort his friends on their way back to London. While the original Bell has disappeared, the old Horse and Groom and the Golden Fleece, almost adjoining it, still remain in all their ancient picturesque state; and it is hardly possible that Lamb and his companions invariably passed their doors without entering them, although no record is preserved of his frequenting any but the Bell. He was on his way to this tavern when he fell and received the slight injury to his face which hastened his death.

Lamb was buried in the quiet little churchyard at Edmonton. A tall flat stone, with an inscription by Cary, the translator of Dante, which is neither happy nor quite coherent, marks the spot, which is just beyond the path on the southwest of the church. Mary Lamb, who survived her brother a number of years, died in Alpha Road, St. John's Wood, and was buried in his grave on the 28th of May, 1847.

Talfourd, in writing to Henry Crabb Robinson, December 31, 1834, says:—

I doubt whether Mary Lamb will ever be quite herself again, so as to feel her loss with her natural sensibility. She went with Ryle yesterday to the churchyard, and pointed out a place where her brother had expressed a wish to be buried; and the wish will be fulfilled. *Diary of Henry Crabb Robinson, vol. ii. chap. xl.*

Robinson was one of the few friends of the Lambs who remembered Mary after the death of Charles. There are in his Diary accounts of repeated visits to her in her loneliness; and when her time came he saw her laid by her brother's side.

May 29, 1847.—Yesterday was a painfully interesting day. I attended the funeral of Mary Lamb. At nine a coach fetched me. We drove to her dwelling at St. John's Wood, from whence two coaches accompanied the body to Edmonton across a pretty country, but the heat of the day rendered the drive oppressive. We took refreshment at the house where dear Charles Lamb died, and were then driven towards our homes. . . . There was no sadness assumed by the attendants, but we all talked together with warm affection of dear Mary Lamb, and that most delightful of creatures, her brother Charles; of all the men of genius I ever knew, the one the most intensely and universally to be loved. *Diary of Henry Crabb Robinson, vol. ii. chap. xxi.*

LETITIA E. LANDON.

1802-1838.

'L. E. L.' was born at No. 25 Hans Place, Sloane Street, in a house destroyed some years ago; and received her early education at No. 22 Hans Place, a few doors beyond, in a house only taken down in the winter of 1884 (see Miss MITFORD).

In 1809 the family removed to Trevor Park, East Barnet, where the happy days of her childhood were spent. In 1815 the Landons were living in Lewis Place, Hammersmith Road, Fulham, and the next year at Brompton. Miss Landon was frequently an inmate of her grandmother's house in Sloane Street during her youth. In 1836 she went into lodgings at No. 28 Upper Berkeley Street, corner of Seymour Place, Connaught Square; and here she remained until her marriage in 1838 at St. Mary's Church, Wyndham Place, Bryanston Square, where Sir Edward Bulwer Lytton gave the bride away.

She died in Africa in the same year.

WALTER SAVAGE LANDOR.

1775-1864.

LANDOR was in no respects a Londoner. He made frequent visits to town, but was never here for any length of time. One of the earliest signs of his appearance in London is a letter of his, dated April 12, 1795, from

No. 38 Beaumont Street, Marylebone, on the west side, and written shortly after his rustication from Oxford. In 1801 his address was at ' R. Brown's, Esq., No. 10 Boswell Court, Carey Street.' Boswell Court ran from Carey Street to the back of St. Clement's Church. It disappeared on the construction of the New Law Courts.

Landor went to Italy in 1815, and London saw but little of him after that, except on his annual visits, during the later years of his life, to Gore House 'when the lilacs were in bloom.' Gore House, the residence of Lady Blessington, and so famous in its day, has disappeared. It stood very near, if not exactly on, the site of the Royal Albert Hall, Kensington Gore.

NATHANIEL LEE.

Circa 1650–1692.

NAT LEE was at Westminster School (see CHURCHILL, p. 51) until 1668, when he entered Trinity College, Cambridge. He made his first appearance as an actor in 1672, as *Duncan* in 'Macbeth,' at the Duke's Theatre, Lincoln's Inn Fields (see DAVENANT, p. 74); but although, as Cibber says, he was so pathetic a reader of the scenes he had written himself that he moved old actors to tears, he failed ignominiously as a player, and quitted the stage in despair. In 1684 he was 'sent to Bedlam,' where he was confined for four years. Bedlam, which is a cockney contraction for Bethlehem Hospital, stood, according to Stow, ' in Bishop's Gate Ward without the City wall, between Bishopsgate Street and Moorfields . . . against London Wall on the south side of the Lower Quarters of Moorfields.' Its exact site was on the north side of London Wall, extending from the present Finsbury Pavement to the present Bloomfield Street, and it backed on the present Finsbury Circus. It remained until the beginning of the nineteenth century, when it was removed to Lambeth.

Dryden wrote as follows to Dennis : —

I remember poor Nat Lee, who was then upon the very verge of madness, yet made a sober and a witty answer to a bad poet who told him it was an easie thing to write like a madman. 'No,' said he, 'it is very difficult to write like a madman, but it is a very easie matter to write like a fool.'

<small>Malone's Dryden, vol. ii.</small>

Lee died in 1692; and his death, and the cause of it, is thus described in the manuscript notes of William Oldys, the antiquary quoted by Baker in his 'Biographia Dramatica :' —

Returning one night from the Bear and Harrow in Butcher Row, through Clare Market to his lodgings in Duke Street [Lincoln's Inn Fields], overladen with wine, Lee fell down on the ground as some say, according to others on a bulk, and was killed or stifled in the snow. He was buried in the parish church of St. Clement Danes; aged about thirty-five years.

As he is known to have entered college in 1668, he must have been older than thirty-five when he died twenty-four years later. No trace of his grave remains in St. Clement Danes; and Butcher Row, afterwards called Pickett Street, in which stood the Bear and Harrow, was wiped out of existence some years ago, and the New Law Courts stand on its site. It was a very narrow street, running from Ship Yard to Holywell Street, by the side of St. Clement's Church.

JOHN LOCKE.

1632–1704.

LOCKE was sent in 1646 to Westminster School (see Churchill, p. 51), where he was a pupil, with Dryden, under Dr. Busby, and where he remained five or six years. He spent much time in Oxford and on the Continent; but in 1667 he took up his residence in London in the family of Lord Shaftesbury, then Lord Ashley, who lived in Essex House, formerly Exeter House, on the Strand. Its site is now marked by Essex Street; and the gate with the staircase to the water, at the end of the street, is the only portion of the old building that remains. In 1683 Locke requested that letters for him be 'left with Mr. Percivall at the Black Boy in Lombard Street, or with Mr. S. Cox at the Iron Key in Thames Street.'

Both of these signs had disappeared before houses in London were numbered, and it is not possible to identify their site.

Locke wrote portions of his 'Essay on the Human Understanding' at Shaftesbury's country house at Chelsea, on the site of which the Workhouse belonging to St. George's, Hanover Square, was built. In the gardens of this institution, on the south side of Fulham Road, near the upper boundary of Chelsea Parish, an old yew-tree, said to have been a favorite of Locke's, stood until 1883, when it was taken down. The dedication to the Essay was dated from Dorset Court, on the east side of Cannon Row, or Channel Row, Westminster, which has since disappeared, although Cunningham in his 'Hand-Book' believes the Dorset Court to have been that in Fleet Street; and it was first 'printed by Eliz. Holt for Thomas Basset, at the George in Fleet Street, near St. Dunstan's Church,' in 1690. He received thirty pounds for the copyright. Dorset Court, Fleet Street, was once the name of the present Salisbury Square.

A letter of Locke's was dated in 1694 'Over against the Plow in Lincoln's Inn Fields.' A Plough Tavern stood in Plough Court, Carey Street, opposite Serle Street, until the New Law Buildings wiped it out, with many other old passages and courts, and was the only tavern of that name in the immediate neighborhood of Lincoln's Inn Fields in Locke's time.

Locke died in retirement, ten years later, in Otis Manor House, — no longer standing, — at High Laver, Essex, and was buried in a vault near the south porch of High Laver Church, where there are an altar tomb and a tablet to his memory.

RICHARD LOVELACE.

1618–1658.

LOVELACE, who was, according to Wood, 'the most amiable and beautiful person that eye ever beheld,' and who in his prime was 'much admired and adored by the female sex,' received the rudiments of his education at the Charter House (see ADDISON, p. 1), and left it for Oxford in 1634. He saw but little of London until his later years. In 1648 he was confined in the Gate House at Westminster (see BURKE, p. 27), where he wrote the poem 'To Althea from Prison,' containing the well-known lines upon which much of his fame now rests, —

> 'Stone walls do not a prison make,
> Nor iron bars a cage.'

After his release he dragged out a miserable existence in London, and died in 1658.

Having consumed all his estate, he grew very melancholy (which at length brought him into a consumption), became very poor in body and purse, was the object of charity, went in ragged cloaths (whereas when he was in his glory he wore cloth of gold and silver), and mostly lodged in obscure and dirty places more befitting the worst of beggars and poorest of servants. Anthony Wood's Athenæ Oxonienses.

He is believed to have died in Gunpowder Alley, near Shoe Lane, which has been entirely rebuilt.

Aubrey says that Lovelace's death took place in a cellar in Long Acre, and adds: 'Mr. Edm. Wylde, etc., had made a collection for him and given him money.' But Aubrey's authority is not valued against Wood's. He is to be read like a proper gossip, whose accounts we may pretty safely reject or believe as it suits other testimony. Leigh Hunt's The Town, chap. iii.

Lovelace was buried in St. Bride's Church, Fleet Street, 'at the west end of the church;' but the building was destroyed in the Great Fire of 1666. The present St. Bride's was built by Wren, and contains no memorial to the poet.

SAMUEL LOVER.

1797–1868.

LOVER came first to London in 1834, when he lived in the neighborhood of Regent's Park, and later in Charles Street, Berners Street, which was then that part of the street afterwards called Mortimer Street, which fronts the Middlesex Hospital.

After his long American tour (1846-1848) and return to England, he settled in the more remote suburbs of Ealing, Barnes, and Sevenoaks; but he died in St. Heliers, and was buried in Kensal Green.

He was a member of the Garrick Club (see THACKERAY).

THOMAS BABINGTON MACAULAY.

1800-1859.

MACAULAY was carried to London in his infancy, and spent two years with his parents in Birchin Lane, Cornhill, where still remained in 1885 a few old houses, no doubt standing there in the beginning of the century, and as familiar to the future historian as to the merchants and merchants' clerks who occupy them and pass by them at the present day. In one of these — which one is not now known — Macaulay's infancy was spent. He was carried daily along Cornhill and Threadneedle Street to get the air and sunshine in the Drapers' Garden, which, greatly reduced in size, lies at the back of Drapers' Hall, and is approached by Throgmorton Avenue, a private passage from Throgmorton Street to London Wall. In 1885 it was a bright oasis in the desert of brick and mortar; and as long as Macaulay lived, it was one of his favorite haunts (see GROTE, p. 130). When Macaulay was a lad his father moved to Clapham, High Street, and took a house which was described 'as roomy and comfortable, with a very small garden behind, and in front a very small one indeed.' Here his happy childhood was spent. This house, No. 5, The Pavement, High Street, Clapham, was still standing in 1885. It faced the Common, and was the seventh house towards the Common from the Plough Inn (No. 156 High Street). The very small garden indeed, about twenty feet square, had been built upon, and contained a one-storied shop, occupied by a fishmonger. The larger garden in the rear and the unpretending house itself remained unchanged.

February 9.—I was talking to Stephen yesterday about Brougham and Macaulay. He said he had known Brougham above thirty years, and well remembers walking with him down to Clapham, to dine with old Zachary Macaulay, and telling him he would find a prodigy of a boy there, of whom he must take notice. This was Tom Macaulay. — The Greville Memoirs, 1886.

Macaulay went to school at Clapham for a time; but when, in 1818, the family left Clapham for London, he lived with his father in Cadogan Place, Sloane Street, and later, in 1823, in Great Ormond Street.

It was a large, rambling house at the corner of Lewis Place [and Great Ormond Street], and was said to have been the residence of Lord Chancellor Thurlow, at the time when the great seal was stolen from his custody. It now [1876] forms the east wing of a homœopathic hospital. — Macaulay's Life and Letters, vol. i. chap. iii.

Here he wrote the Essay on Milton, etc. It was still a hospital in 1885.

In August, 1857, he [Macaulay] writes: 'I sent the carriage home, and walked to the Museum; passing through Great Ormond Street, I saw a bill on No. 50. I knocked, was let in, and went over the house with a strange mixture of feelings. It is more than twenty-six years since I was in it. The dining-room and the adjoining room in which I once slept are scarcely changed; the same coloring on the wall, but more dingy. My father's study much the same; the drawing-rooms too, except the papering; my bedroom just what it was. My mother's bedroom — I had never been in it since her death. I went away sad,' — Loftie's History of London, vol. ii. chap. xx.

Between 1829 and 1834 Macaulay occupied chambers at No. 8 South Square, Gray's Inn, in a building that has since been torn down to make way for the extension of the Library.

Macaulay went to India in 1834, but returned to England in 1838, when he lodged for a time at No. 3 Clarges Street, Piccadilly, in a house still standing in 1885, and where he wrote, among other things, the paper on Clive. He was for a time in Great George Street, Westminster, and in 1840 —

<small>Life and Letters, vol. ii. chap. ix.</small> quartered himself in a commodious set of rooms on the second floor in the Albany [see BYRON, p. 32]. . . . His chambers, every corner of which was a library, were comfortably, though not very brightly, furnished. The ornaments were few, but choice.

In one of his letters he describes his surroundings as follows : —

<small>Life and Letters, vol. ii. chap. viii.</small> I have taken a comfortable suite of chambers in the Albany, and I hope to lead during some years a sort of life peculiar to my taste, — college life at the West End of London. I have an entrance hall, two sitting-rooms, a bedroom, a kitchen, cellars, and two rooms for servants, all for ninety guineas a year.

His chambers in the Albany were numbered E. 1. Here he wrote the Essays on Bacon, Hastings, and Addison, the 'History of England,' and published the 'Lays,' some of which had been written before.

In 1856 he left the Albany for Kensington, and hired the house in which the rest of his life was spent.

<small>Life and Letters, vol. ii. chap. xiv.</small> Holly Lodge, now [1876] called Airlie Lodge, occupies the most secluded corner of the little labyrinth of by-roads, which, bounded to the east by Palace Gardens and to the west by Holland House, constitutes the district known as Campden Hill. The villa — for a villa it is —

stands in a long and winding lane, which, with its high back paling, concealing from the passer-by everything except the mass of dense and varied foliage, presents an appearance as rural as Streatham presented twenty years ago. The only entrance for carriages was at the end of the lane farthest from Holly Lodge; and Macaulay had no one living beyond him except the Duke of Argyll.

During his residence in Kensington Macaulay was a regular attendant at the old Church of St. Mary there (see the elder COLMAN, p. 62).

He died at Holly Lodge on the 28th of December, 1859. His attending physician, Dr. Thomas Joyce, of No. 2 Pembridge Villas, Bayswater, in a private note dated September 27, 1883, says : —

I have much pleasure in giving you any information in my power respecting Lord Macaulay. He died in his library at Holly Lodge. For some time before he had been in ill health from weak heart. His servant, who had left him feeling rather better, found on his return his master fainting in his chair. I was quickly sent for, got him removed to his couch, where he expired in a few moments. None of his family were with him. His sister, Mrs. Trevelyan, arrived soon after his death, accompanied by her son, then a very young man, but now, I believe, the Irish Secretary. At the time of his seizure Lord Macaulay was reading a number of the 'Cornhill Magazine,' then a new publication; and, as far as my memory serves me, he was reading Thackeray's 'Adventures of Philip.'

Holly Lodge is still standing [1883], and is, I believe, unaltered.[14] You will find it on the top of Campden Hill, next the Duke of Argyll's [Argyll Lodge].

He was buried, January 9, 1860, in the Abbey.

We return to the western aisle of the south transept. There lies the brilliant poet and historian, who perhaps of all who have trod the floor of the Abbey, or lie buried within its precincts, most deeply knew and felt its manifold interests, and most unceasingly

Dean Stanley's Westminster Abbey, chap. iv.

commemorated them. Lord Macaulay rests at the foot of the statue of Addison, whose character and genius none has painted as he.

Macaulay was a member of the Athenæum Club, No. 107 Pall Mall, and of the Literary Club, founded by Johnson (see GOLDSMITH, p. 123, and JOHNSON, p. 167), to which he was elected in 1839. It met then in the Thatched House Tavern, No. 74 St. James's Street, on the site of the Conservative Club.

Macaulay was devoted to The Club, and rarely absent from it.

<small>Sir Henry Holland's Recollections of a Past Life, chap. viii.</small> If redundant at times in speech and argument, this could hardly be deemed a usurpation, seeing how they were employed. . . . I well remember the blank that was felt by us all at the first meeting of The Club after his death.

CHRISTOPHER MARLOWE.

1563–1593.

THERE are no records of Marlowe's life in London except that he was a player at the Curtain Theatre in Holywell Lane, Shoreditch (see JONSON, p. 172), and that he was killed in a disreputable brawl.

The story of Marlowe's death has been differently related, but

<small>Payne Collier's History of Dramatic Poetry, vol. iii.: Marlowe.</small> it seems now that he was killed by his rival in love. Marlowe found his rival with the lady to whom he was attached, and rushed upon him; but his antagonist, being the stronger, thrust the point of Marlowe's own dagger into his head. The event probably occurred at Deptford, where, according to the register of St. Nicholas Church, Marlowe was buried in June, 1593. And it is also recorded that he was 'slaine by Francis Archer,'

The present St. Nicholas Church was erected on the site of the old one, taken down in 1697. It stands on Deptford Green, west of the Dockyard, and contains no monument or tablet to Marlowe.

We read of one Marlowe a Cambridge Scholler, who was a poet and a filthy play-maker; this wretch accounted that meeke servant of God, Moses, to be but a conjuror, and our Sweet Saviour to be but a seducer and deceiver of the people. But harken, ye brain-sicke and prophane poets and players, that bewitch idle eares with foolish vanities, what fell upon this prophane wretch; having a quarrell against one whom he met in the street in London, and would have stab'd him; but the partie perceiving his villany prevented him with catching his hand, and turning his own dagger into his braines; and so blaspheming and cursing he yeelded up his stinking breath. Marke this, ye players that live by making fools laugh at sinne and wickedness. *The Thunderbolt of God's Wrath Against Hard-hearted and Stiff-necked Sinners. London, 1618, 4to.*

FREDERICK MARRYAT.

1792–1848.

MARRYAT was born in Westminster, and educated at a private school 'in the red brick house at the upper end of Baker Street, Enfield' (Ford's Enfield). From this school, after repeated truant exploits, he was taken in 1806, and sent to sea; and he did not settle finally on shore until 1830.

In 1832 his address was No. 38 St. James's Place, St. James's Street, which half a century later remained unchanged; and in 1837, and again in 1839, he lodged at No. 8 Duke Street, St. James's, in a house which was still a lodging-house in 1885. There he wrote and published 'Perçival Keene,'

In 1841 and in after years while on his periodical visits to London during the season, his letters were addressed to No. 120 Pall Mall, between Trafalgar Square and Waterloo Place, subsequently the site of the French Gallery. In 1842, however, he had a house — unaltered in 1885 — at No. 3 Spanish Place, Manchester Square, and here he wrote 'Masterman Ready.'

Among Marryat's suburban homes was Sussex House, Hammersmith, which still stood in 1885 opposite Brandenburg House, a little back from the river on the Fulham Road, and facing Alma Terrace. Marryat was also a frequent inmate of the house of his mother, at Wimbledon Common.

On the borders of the Common [Wimbledon Common] are several good houses. The most remarkable is Wimbledon House. ... In 1815 it was purchased by Joseph Marryat, Esq., M. P. (father of the novelist), and after his death, in 1824, was for several years the residence of his widow, who made the grounds famous for rare plants and flowers.

Thorne's Hand-Book of the Environs of London: Wimbledon.

Wimbledon House, at the southern extremity of Wimbledon Park, was left intact in 1885, but shut out from the town and the Common by high walls.

The apartment he [Marryat] occupied whilst on his visits to Wimbledon House, and in which he wrote, was one upon the second story overlooking the Park; and in this room, at a table covered with an African lion's skin, and on a little old black leather blotting-book, worn with use and replete to bursting with ruled foolscap, several of his books were composed. His handwriting was so minute that, the compositor having given up the task of deciphering it in despair, the copyist had to stick a pin in at the place where he left off to insure his finding it again when he resumed his task,

Life and Letters of Captain Marryat, vol. ii. chap. iii.

Marryat is also said to have lived in a white cottage called Gothic House, at the foot of the hill south of Wimbledon Common, and on the road to Kingston. It was standing in 1885.

Marryat died, and was buried, at Langham in Norfolk, where the later years of his life were spent.

His club was the United Service, Nos. 116 and 117 Pall Mall.

ANDREW MARVELL.

1620-1678.

MARVELL does not seem to have known much of London until 1657, when he was appointed Latin Secretary, under Milton, to Oliver Cromwell, and had lodgings in Scotland Yard, Whitehall; and the accounts preserved to us, of his life in London, then and later, are very vague. While he was sitting in the House of Commons as member for Hull, he occupied poor apartments on the second floor of a house in Maiden Lane, Covent Garden. Here he refused, with scorn, the bribes of Charles, while he had not a guinea in his pocket to pay for his daily bread. Marvell's Maiden Lane house has been taken down. It was next to the Bedford Head, on the site of which a modern Bedford Tavern (No. 41 Maiden Lane) has been built. For a number of years he occupied a small and unpretentious cottage on Highgate Hill, north of the then Lauderdale House, later the Convalescent House of St. Bartholomew's Hospital, and opposite Cromwell House. This cottage, in its old-fashioned garden, was in existence until 1869. Part of its front garden-wall still remained in 1885, with the stone steps leading from the street, upon which tradition says the poet was fond of sitting to watch the passer-by, perhaps to moralize upon the actions of Nell Gwynne, his uncongenial neighbor of Lauderdale House.

Marvell died at Kingston-upon-Hull, and was buried in the vault of the old Church of St. Giles-in-the-Field. The present church is of the eighteenth century.

Edward Thompson, the editor of Marvell's Works, gives the following account of his resting-place:—

In the year 1774 I visited the grand mausoleum under the Church of St. Giles, for the coffin in which Mr. Marvell was placed. In this vault were deposited upwards of a thousand bodies, but I could find no plate of an earlier date than 1772. I do therefore suppose that the new church is built upon the former burial-place. The epitaph placed on the north side of the church by his grand-nephew, Mr. Robert Nettleton, is supposed to be over his remains, and near to the monument of Sir Roger L'Estrange.

This epitaph upon a black marble mural tablet is on the north aisle of the church, opposite pews 13 and 14. The gilt lettering was almost obliterated in 1885.

Marvell was a frequenter of Haycock's Ordinary, which stood on the south side of the Strand, between Temple Bar and the present Palsgrave Restaurant (see PRIOR), and of the Rota, or Coffee Club, held 'at one Miller's' at the Turk's Head in New Palace Yard. No sign of the Turk's Head or of the New Palace Yard of Marvell's time now remains.

PHILIP MASSINGER.

1584–1638.

LITTLE is known of the personal history of Massinger, either in London or out of it, and his early biographers vary greatly in the dates they give of his birth and his death. The author of the 'British Theatre' says he was born in 1578, and died in 1659; but the dates attached hereto, taken from Anthony Wood, and the registry of the church in which he was buried, are probably correct. He was found dead in his bed 'in his own house, near the play-house on the bank side, Southwark' (see SHAKSPERE), and he was buried in the churchyard of St. Mary Overy, afterwards St. Saviour's, Southwark, at the end of London Bridge (see FLETCHER, p. 107, and GOWER, p. 126). His grave is now unknown; and the parochial register simply records the interment of 'Philip Massinger, a Stranger.'

His bodie being accompanied by comedians, was buried in the middle of the church yard there, commonly called the Bull Heade Church yard — for there are in all four church yards belonging to that church — on the 18th of March. _{Wood's Athenæ Oxonienses, vol. i. col. 525.}

A stone in the floor of the choir of the old church has had, within a few years, engraven upon it his name and the date of his death, although it is an established fact that he does not lie beneath it.

JOHN MILTON.

1608-1674.

ALTHOUGH the 'Prince of Poets' was born and died in London, received part of his education in London, was married frequently in London, and lived in many houses in the metropolis, there is left to-day hardly a trace of anything that he has touched, or that is in any way associated with him. Even his grave was desecrated, and the precise spot in which his bones lie cannot now be discovered.

He was born in Bread Street, Cheapside, at the sign of the Spread Eagle (his family crest), on the 9th of December, 1608, and was baptized in the neighboring Church of All Hallows. Both the house and the church were destroyed in the Great Fire of 1666. Black Spread Eagle Court was in 1885 covered by modern buildings; Nos. 58 to 63 Bread Street being occupied by one firm, who have on the top floor a bust of Milton, with an inscription stating that it stands on the site of the house of his birth.

All Hallows Church, on the corner of Bread and Watling Streets, was rebuilt by Wren after the Fire, but was taken down in 1878, and a large warehouse erected on its grounds. On this is placed a tablet containing a bust of Milton, and an inscription explaining its connection with the bard. The tablet with the lines of Dryden so often quoted, 'Three poets in three distant ages born,' etc., that adorned this church, has now been placed on the outside west wall of Bow Church, hard by.

Milton's christening is recorded in the register of All Hallows, still extant: 'The XXth daye of December, 1608, was baptized John, the sonne of John Milton, Scrivener.'

The young Milton was sent to Paul's School at an early age.

When he [Milton] went to schoole, when he was very young he studied very hard, and sate up very late, commonly till twelve or one o'clock at night, and his father ordered the mayde to sitt up for him, and in those yeares (10) composed many copies of verses which might well become a riper age. *Aubrey's Lives of Eminent Persons: Milton.*

Paul's School was destroyed in the Great Fire also. It was rebuilt soon after on the same site, on the east side of St. Paul's Churchyard, between Watling Street and Cheapside; but it was removed in the summer of 1884 to Hammersmith Road, West Kensington. The building known to the present generation as Paul's School, in St. Paul's Churchyard, was not erected until 1823.

Saw all the towne burned, and a miserable sight of Paul's Church, with all the roofs fallen, and the body of the quire fallen into St. Fayth's; Paul's school also. *Pepys's Diary, vol. ii., Sept. 7, 1666.*

London saw but little of Milton from his sixteenth year, when he was sent to Cambridge, until 1639; when, after a Continental tour, he lodged in the house of one Russell, a tailor in St. Bride's Churchyard.

The house, as I learned from an old and most respectable inhabitant of St. Bride's Parish, was on the left hand as you proceed towards Fleet Street through the avenue. It was a very small tenement, very old, and was burned down on the 24th of November, 1824, at which time it was occupied by a hair-dresser. It was — in proof of its age — without party walls and much decayed. *Howitt's Houses and Haunts of British Poets, vol. i.: Milton.*

The back part of the 'Punch' office now occupies its site. These lodgings were too small, and he took a garden house in Aldersgate Street, situated at the end of an entry, that he might avoid the noise and disturbance of the street.. . . . This house was large and commodious, affording room for his library and furniture. Here he commenced his career of pure authorship.

Masson, in his interesting and valuable sketch of Milton's life, prefixed to an edition of Milton's Poems published by Macmillan in 1874, says:—

Aldersgate Street is very different now, and not a vestige of Milton's house remains; it stood at the back of the part of the street on the right hand as you go from St. Martin's-le-Grand to where is now Maidenhead Court.

It seems to have been while they were living in the St. Bride's Churchyard house, although the authorities differ, that Milton's first wife, Mary Powell, who was the mother of his daughters, and to whom he was married in 1643, left her husband, on a visit to her family, and refused to return. Mrs. Milton, however, met her lord again at the house of a friend, 'in the lane of St. Martin's-le-Grand,' besought his forgiveness on her knees, and was taken back to his home, if not to his heart.

His first wife was brought up and lived where there was a great deal of company and merriment, dancing, etc., and when she came to live with her husband at Mr. Russell's in St. Bride's Churchyard, she found it very solitary; no company came to her, oftentimes heard his nephews beaten and cry; this life was irksome to her, and so she went to her parents.

<small>Aubrey's Lives of Eminent Persons: Milton.</small>

About 1644 Milton removed to the Barbican, Aldersgate Street, where he still taught school, and gave refuge to his wife's relations, who were royalists, and who felt more kindly towards him when they found that his was the winning side. His father-in-law died in his house at Holborn in 1647.

When it is considered that Milton cheerfully opened his doors to those who had treated him with indignity and breach of faith, — to a father who, according to the poet's nuncupative will, never paid him the promised marriage portion of a thousand pounds; and to a mother who, according to Wood, had encouraged the daughter in her perverseness, — we cannot but

<small>Todd's Milton, 1647.</small>

concede to Mr. Hayley's conclusions, that the records of private life contain not a more magnanimous example of forgiveness and beneficence.

Milton's house, No. 17 Barbican, was not taken down until 1864. A modern warehouse occupies its site.

The house to which Milton removed was in the street called Barbican, going from Aldersgate Street at right angles, and within a walk of two or three minutes from the former house. As you went from Aldersgate Street it was on the right side of the Barbican. It existed entire until only the other day, when one of the new city railways was cut through that neighborhood. Masson's Memoir of Milton.

Milton remained but a short time in the Barbican, for in 1646–47 he was to be found in a small house on Holborn, 'opening backwards into Lincoln's Inn Fields,' probably between Great and Little Turnstiles. While Latin Secretary to Cromwell he was lodged in Scotland Yard, Whitehall, and also at 'one Thompson's, next door to the Bull Head Tavern at Charing Cross, opening into Spring Gardens' (see CIBBER, p. 52), a short and quiet street connecting Whitehall and the present Trafalgar Square with the east end of the Mall and St. James's Park. He soon after took a 'pretty garden house' in Petty France, Westminster. Here he lived for eight years, and here losing his first wife he took to himself a second. William Howitt, in his 'Homes and Haunts of British Poets,' thus describes the house in Petty France as he saw it in 1868:—

It no longer opens into St. James's Park. The ancient front is now its back, and overlooks the fine old, but house-surrounded, garden of Jeremy Bentham. Near the top of this ancient front is a stone, bearing this inscription, 'Sacred to Milton, the Prince of Poets.' This was placed there by no less distinguished a man than William Hazlitt, who rented the house for some years, purely because it was Milton's. Bentham, when he was conducting people round his garden, used to make them sometimes go down on their knees to this house. The house is tall and narrow, and has nothing striking about it. No doubt, when it opened into St. James's Park, it was pleasant; now it fronts into York Street, which runs in a direct line from the west end of Westminster Abbey. It is No. 19.

Milton completely lost the use of his eyes in Petty France. This house, afterwards No. 19 York Street, Westminster, was taken down in 1877 (see HAZLITT, p. 132). Its gardens form part of the lawn of Queen Anne Mansions, where was still shown in 1885 an old tree said to have been planted by Milton himself.

Tradition says that Milton, after the return of the Stuarts in 1660, took refuge in Bartholomew Close (Duke Street, Aldersgate), which is still full of old houses spared by the Great Fire. Near the yard of the Church of St. Bartholomew the Great were a row of old buildings in 1885, facing on Cloth Fair, from the back windows of which the poet was no doubt often seen going in and out of the Close.

Milton, after the Restoration, withdrew for a time to a friend's house in Bartholomew Close. By this precaution he probably escaped the particular prosecution which was at first directed against him. Mr. Warton was told by Mr. Tyers, from good authority, that when Milton was under prosecution with Goodwin, his friends, to gain time, made a mock funeral for him, and that when matters were settled in his favor and the affair was known, the king laughed heartily at the trick.

Todd's Milton, section iv.

After Milton's pardon by Charles, he took a house in Holborn, 'near Red Lion Fields,' afterwards known as Red Lion Square; and later he went to Jewin Street, Aldersgate, where in 1662 he married his third and last wife, who survived him. Jewin Street has been entirely rebuilt.

The last years of Milton's life were spent in a house in Artillery Walk, Bunhill Fields, where he composed and dictated to his daughters his 'Paradise Lost,' 'Paradise Regained,' and 'Samson Agonistes,' and where he died in 1674.

Artillery Walk, Bunhill Fields, has entirely disappeared; and the nearest approach to it, in name, is Artillery Place, Bunhill Row. Milton's house, —

as has been ascertained with some trouble, was in that part of the present Bunhill Row, where there is now a clump of new houses to the left of the passenger, which turns northward from Chiswell Street towards St. Luke's Hospital and Peerless Pool. Masson's Memoirs of Milton.

It was on the west side of Bunhill Row, not very far from Chiswell Street.

An ancient clergyman of Dorsetshire, Dr. Wright, found John Milton in a small chamber hung with rusty green, sitting in an elbow-chair, and dressed neatly in black; pale but not cadaverous; his hands and fingers gouty and with chalk-stones. He used also to sit in a gray, coarse cloth coat, at the door of his house in Bunhill Fields, in warm sunny weather, to enjoy the fresh air; and so, as well as in his room, received the visits of people of distinguished parts as well as quality. Richardson's Explanatory Notes, etc., 8vo, 1734, p. iv.

Milton died of the gowte struck in, the 9th or 10th of November, 1674, as appears by his apothecaryes booke. ... He lies buried in St. Giles's, Cripplegate, upper end of the chancell, at the right hand. Mem. his stone is now removed; about two yeares since [1681] the two steppes to the communion table were raysed. I ghesse Jo. Speed and he lie together. Aubrey's Lives of Eminent Persons: Milton.

There was long credited a story to the effect that Milton's body was disturbed and desecrated on the occasion of the raising of the chancel of St. Giles's Church towards the end of the eighteenth century, and that fragments of his skeleton were carried off by relic-hunters; but Mr. C. M.

Ingleby, in his 'Shakspere's Bones' (London, 1883), thus discredits the report:—

On the 4th of August, 1790, according to a small volume written by Philip Neve,. Esq. (of which two editions were published in the same year), Milton's coffin was removed and his remains exhibited to the public on the 4th and 5th of that month. Mr. George Stevens, the great editor of Shakspere, who justly denounced the indignity intended, not offered, to the great Puritan poet's remains by Royalist Landsharks, satisfied himself that the corpse was that of a woman of fewer years than Milton. . . . Mr. Stevens's assurance gives us good reason for believing that Mr. Philip Neve's indignant protest is only good in general, and that Milton's hallowed reliques still rest undisturbed within their peaceful shrine.

The removing of the stone in 1679, alluded to by Aubrey, renders uncertain the exact place of his burial; and the inscription in the pavement of the middle aisle near the Lord Mayor's double pew, numbered 16 and 17, simply reads that he 'lies near this spot.'

An elaborate monument, containing his bust, was erected in the church, by public subscription, in 1862.

MARY RUSSELL MITFORD.

1787–1855.

MARY RUSSELL MITFORD'S earliest experiences of London, when she was eight or nine years old, were not of the most cheerful kind. The family lived on the Surrey side of Blackfriars Bridge while Dr. Mitford sought refuge from his creditors within the rules of King's Bench. In 1798 she was sent to a school at No. 22 Hans Place, Sloane Street (see MISS LANDON, p. 194), which is described, in her

'Life and Letters,' as being then a new house, bright, clean, freshly painted, and looking into a garden full of shrubs and flowers. The house had been rebuilt in 1885. The garden was still full of flowers, but the brightness and freshness of the buildings in the little square were things of the past. Here Miss Mitford remained as a scholar until 1803 ; and here, and to the later home of her teachers, — who were her warm friends as well, — at No. 33 Hans Place, she came, while in London, for a number of years. During her frequent excursions to town she lodged and visited in different places. In 1818 she was a guest at Tavistock House, Tavistock Square, afterwards the home of Dickens (see Dickens, p. 84). In 1826 she wrote from No. 45 Frith Street, Soho, — No. 49 in 1885. In 1828, when she came to London to see the first performance of 'Rienzi,' she lodged at No. 5 Great Queen Street, on the north side, near Lincoln's Inn Fields; and in 1834 she was at No. 35 Norfolk Street, Strand, in a house still standing and unchanged fifty years later, where she 'held a sort of drawing-room every morning,' and was lionized to her heart's content. Her friends were among the leading men and women in all professions and ranks. In 1836 she had apartments at No. 56 Russell Square, between Bedford Place and Southampton Row, where she writes : —

Mr. Wordsworth, Mr. Landor, and Mr. White dined here. I like Mr. Wordsworth, of all things. . . . Mr. Landor is a very striking-looking person, and exceedingly clever. Also we had a Mr. Browning, a young poet, and Mr. Procter and Mr. Morley, and quantities more of poets ; Stanfield and Lucas were also there.

In the later years of her life Miss Mitford rarely spent a night in town, coming up from Reading or Swallowfield only for the day, and to see Miss Barrett or some of her intimate friends. She died in 1855, and was buried in the churchyard of Swallowfield, — 'Our Village.'

MARY WORTLEY MONTAGU.

1690-1762.

LADY MARY WORTLEY MONTAGU, although born in Nottinghamshire, was christened in the Church of St. Paul, Covent Garden, since rebuilt (see BUTLER, p. 29).

Her London home during her youth was in Arlington Street, Piccadilly, at the house of her father, the Marquis of Dorchester, afterwards Duke of Kingston, who introduced her to the Kit Kat Club when it held its sittings at the Cat and Fiddle in Shire Lane (see ADDISON, p. 8). Lady Louisa Stuart, in Lord Wharncliffe's 'Life and Writings of Lady Montagu,' gives the following account of the scene:—

One day at a meeting to choose toasts for the year, a whim seized him [Lord Kingston] to nominate his daughter, then not eight years old, a candidate, alleging that she was far prettier than any lady on their list. The other members demurred, because the rules of the club forbade them to select a beauty whom they had never seen. 'Then you shall see her,' cried he; and in the gayety of the moment sent orders to have her finely dressed, and brought to him at the tavern, where she was received with acclamations, her claims unanimously allowed, her health drunk by every one present, and her name engraved, in due form, upon a drinking-glass. The company consisting of some of the most eminent men in England, she went from the lap of one poet or patriot or statesman to the arms of another, was feasted with sweetmeats, overwhelmed with caresses, and, what perhaps already pleased her better than either, heard her wit and beauty loudly extolled on every side. Pleasure, she said, was too poor a word to express her sensations,—they amounted to ecstasy. Never again, through her whole life, did she pass so happy a day.

Pope, in 1717, wrote to the Montagus at 'the Piazza, Covent Garden,' urging them to go to Twickenham, which they did. They lived at Savile House there for some time.

On the left of the Heath Road, east of the Railway bridge, is Savile House, a fine old red brick mansion with tall roofs, where for several years lived Lady Mary Wortley Montagu, who came here to be near Pope, — fast friends then, too soon to be bitter foes. Thorne's Hand-Book of the Environs of London: Twickenham.

This house remained in 1885 as Mr. Thorne has described it.

Occasionally during these years she lived in Cavendish Square.

After a long absence on the Continent, she returned to London in 1761.

Lady Mary Wortley is arrived. I have seen her. I think her avarice, her dirt, and her vivacity are all increased. Her dress, like her language, is a galimatias of several countries; the groundwork rags, and its embroidery nastiness. She needs no cap, no handkerchief, no gown, no petticoat, no shoes. An old black laced hood represents the first; the fur of a horseman's coat, which replaces the third, serves for the second; a dimity petticoat is deputy, and officiates for the fourth; and slippers act the part of the last. Correspondence of Horace Walpole, 1762.

In George Street, Hanover Square, Lady Mary Wortley Montagu passed some of the last months of her long life. From her long residence on the Continent she had imbibed foreign tastes and foreign habits; and consequently the change from the spacious magnificence of an Italian palace to a small three-storied house in the neighborhood of Hanover Square was as striking as it was disagreeable. 'I am most handsomely lodged,' she said, 'for I have two very decent closets and a cupboard on each floor.' Jesse's London, vol. i.: Hanover Square.

She removed to Berkeley Square in 1762, where she died the same year. She was buried in Grosvenor Chapel, in South Audley Street (see CHESTERFIELD, p. 50),

THOMAS MOORE.

1779–1852.

MOORE first came to London in 1799 to be entered as a student in the Middle Temple, and lodged for a time in a front room up two pairs of stairs, at No. 44 George Street, Portman Square, — numbered 106 in 1885, — paying six shillings a week for his accommodations. In 1801 he wrote to his mother from No. 46 Wigmore Street, Cavendish Square. This house, since rebuilt, was on the north side, and afterwards No. 40. In 1805 he was found at No. 27 Bury Street, St. James's, his London home for ten or twelve years. To this house he took his young wife in 1811; and he speaks of a visit to it when he was an old man, and of the associations recalled by the sight of the old familiar rooms. The house had even then been renumbered. It was 28 in 1835, and fifty years later a new building stood on its site.

A letter of Moore's dated from No. 15 Duke Street, St. James's, is preserved; and Byron in 1814 wrote to him at No. 33 Bury Street (this house is also gone); but while in town he was generally a guest at Holland House (see ADDISON, p. 3), at Gore House (see LANDOR, p. 195), at Lansdowne House, on the south side of Berkeley Square, or at other aristocratic mansions among the lords he so dearly loved.

Moore was married in the Church of St. Martin-in-the-Fields, March 25, 1811; and in 1812, and for about a year thereafter, lived at Brompton. A. J. Symington, in his 'Life of Moore' (chap. iv.), says: —

On Lady Day he [Moore] was so fortunate as to marry Miss Bessie Dyke, a native of Kilkenny, — a charming and amiable young actress of considerable ability. Their house was at York Place, Queen's Elms, Brompton. The terrace was isolated, and opposite nursery gardens. Mrs. Moore was very domestic in her tastes, and possessed much energy of character, tact, and a sound judgment.

York Place, since called York Mews, is south of the Fulham Road, between Church and Arthur Streets.

In 1817 Moore rented the cottage since known as Lalla Rookh Cottage, where he lost a daughter. He buried her in Hornsey Churchyard, not far from the spot where Rogers afterwards was laid (see ROGERS).

At the foot of the hill [Muswell Hill, Middlesex], lying back on the right, is a long, low brick cottage with a veranda in front and a lawn sloping down to a pond by the roadside, which was the residence of Abraham Newland, cashier of the Bank of England. . . . The poet Moore rented it in 1817, and his eldest daughter, Anne Barbara, died here, and lies in Hornsey Churchyard. From a mistaken tradition that the poem was written in it, the cottage is now [1876] named Lalla Rookh Cottage; the poem was written before, but published whilst Moore lived here. The cottage will be easily recognized; it lies next to the Victoria Inn (which nearly faces the entrance to the Alexandra Palace), and has 'Lalla Rookh' painted on the gate-posts. *Thorne's Hand-Book of the Environs of London: Muswell Hill.*

It remained, in 1885, back of Maynard Street and Muswell Hill Road.

Moore was a member of the Athenæum, corner of Pall Mall and Waterloo Place; Brooks's, No. 60 St. James's Street; and other clubs.

HANNAH MORE.

1745-1833.

HANNAH MORE never had a permanent home in London. She came first to town in 1774. In 1777 she was lodging in Henrietta Street, Covent Garden, and in Gerard Street, Soho; but she was generally the guest of David Garrick, or of his widow after his death in 1779, in the house No. 5 Adelphi Terrace, marked as the home of the great actor by the tablet of the Society of Arts. With the Garricks in London she is chiefly associated. Walpole writes of a visit he made to her at Adelphi Terrace in 1791; as long as Johnson lived, she was a welcome visitor at the house in Bolt Court; Sir Joshua Reynolds carried her to see his own and other pictures; and her popularity was great.

SIR THOMAS MORE.

1478-1535.

THOMAS MORE was born in Milk Street, Cheapside, 'the brightest star that ever shone in that *Via Lactea*' (Fuller's 'Worthies of England: More'). All traces of More's Milk Street were entirely destroyed in the Great Fire two centuries later.

More was educated at St. Anthony's Free School, which stood, as is shown in the old maps, on the site of the Consolidated Bank, No. 52 Threadneedle Street. He afterwards studied in New Inn, Wych Street, Drury Lane, adjoining Clement's Inn, and is said to have lived in the Charter

House (see ADDISON, p. 1) as a lay brother. In 1499 he became a student of Lincoln's Inn, and he was appointed law reader of Furnival's Inn after his admission to the bar.

From the period of More's marriage in 1507, he resided for some years in Bucklersbury; perhaps it was soon after 1514-15 that he purchased Crosby Place, for his advancement. then became rapid. ... It is far from impossible that this delightful work [Utopia] was written in Crosby Place. In the preface we have a complete picture of Sir Thomas's domestic habits about this period, and which, if it does not directly apply to Crosby Place, may certainly be applied to it by the mere substitution of the 'Life of Richard Third' for 'Utopia,' there being little or no doubt but the former work was written within its chambers, however it may be with the latter. Knight's London, vol. i.: Crosby Place.

Bucklersbury runs, as in More's day, from the Poultry to what is now Queen Victoria Street. It is very ancient, and is to be found in the maps of Saxon London. It was the quarter of traders in herbs and spices, even before the Norman Conquest, and until Shakspere's time; for he makes Falstaff say:—

Come, I cannot cry and say thou art this and that, like a many of these lisping hawthorn buds, that come like women in men's apparel and smell like Bucklersbury in simple time. Merry Wives of Windsor, act iii. scene 3.

Crosby Place, now Crosby Hall, has been 'restored' with elaborate care, and stands in Bishopsgate Street near its junction with Threadneedle Street (see SHAKSPERE).

Sir Thomas More's country house was at Chelsea in Middlesex, where Sr. John Danvers built his house. The chimney-piece of marble, in Sr. John's chamber, was the chimney-piece of Sr. Thomas More's chamber, as Sr. John himself told me. Where the gate is now, adorned with two noble pyramids, there stood anciently a gate house wch was flatt on the top, leaded, from whence is a most pleasant prospect of the Thames and the fields beyond; on this place Aubrey's Lives of Eminent Persons: More.

the Ld. Chancellor More was wont to recreate himself and contemplate.

It was at More's house in Chelsea that Holbein was first presented to Henry VIII.; and, according to tradition, Erasmus was also a visitor there. He says:—

<small>Sir James Mackintosh's Life of More.</small>

With him you might imagine yourself in the Academy of Plato. But I should do injustice to his house by comparing it to the Academy of Plato, where numbers and geometrical figures and sometimes moral virtues were the subject of discussion; it would be more just to call it a school and an exercise of the Christian religion. All its inhabitants, male and female, applied their leisure to liberal studies and profitable reading, although piety was their first care. No wrangling, no idle word, was heard in it; no one was idle; every one did his duty with alacrity, and not without a temperate cheerfulness.

This description of More's household by Erasmus may have referred to the Bucklersbury mansion, with which he was also undoubtedly familiar.

The old mansion [Sir Thomas More's] stood at the north end of Beaufort Row, extending westward at the distance of about one hundred yards from the water-side. Some fragments of the walls, doors, and windows, and parts of the foundation are still [1829] to be seen adjoining to the burying-ground belonging to the Moravian Society.

<small>Faulkner's Chelsea, vol. 1. chap. ii.</small>

Till within a very few years the ground remained in a state that might have admitted of ascertaining the site of the house [Sir Thomas More's]; but buildings have now shut it out from search, and nought remains but the name, Beaufort Row, to tell how it was once honored.

<small>Miss Hawkins's Anecdotes, vol. l. p. 42.</small>

The house was built in 1521. In the old chronicles of Chelsea it was known as Buckingham House in 1527, and was called Beaufort House in 1682. It was immediately facing the present Battersea Bridge, a little back from the river and about where Beaufort Street now runs. It was purchased by Sir Hans Sloane, and taken down in 1740,

More was imprisoned in the Tower for thirteen months, and arraigned at Westminster Hall, May 7, 1535. He was beheaded on Tower Hill.

The head of Sir Thomas More was putt upon London Bridge where, as trayter's heads are sett upon poles, and having remained some moneths there being to be cast into the Thames, because roome should be made for diverse others who in plentiful sorte suffered martyrdome for the same supremacie; shortly after it was brought by his daughter Margarett, least — as she stoutly affirmed before the Councill, being called before them for the same matter — it should be foode for fishes which she buried where she thought fittest. T. More's Life of Sir Thomas More, 1726.

After he [More] was beheaded, his trunke was interred in Chelsey Church, near the middle of the south wall, where was some slight monument erected, which being worn by time, about 1644, Sir —— Lawrence of Chelsey (no kinne to him) at his own proper costs and charges erected to his memorie a handsome inscription of marble. Aubrey's Lives of Eminent Persons: More.

This inscription was written by More himself, as Erasmus has shown. It has several times been renewed.

In the old parish church near the river More's monument still stands [1883]. The church is an interesting building of the most mixed character. So far, happily, not very much hurt by restorers. More made a chapel for his family tomb at the east end of the south aisle, and put up a black slab to record the fact. It has been twice 'improved,' and is said to have originally contained a reference to his persecution of heresy, for which a blank is now left in the renewed inscription, just the kind of evasion one can imagine the straightforward chancellor would himself have particularly disliked. The architectural ornaments of the monument are in what was then the new Italian style. It is uncertain where More is buried. Some say here; some say in the Tower Chapel. Loftie's History of London, vol. ii.: The Western Suburbs.

His head was carried by his daughter to Canterbury, and buried in the Roper Vault in St. Dunstan's Church there.

ARTHUR MURPHY.

1727–1805.

ARTHUR MURPHY, Walpole's 'writing actor,' who was nevertheless 'very good company,' was a clerk in a banking-house 'in the City,' and an unsuccessful player. On quitting the stage he determined to study law, was refused a call by the Benchers of Gray's Inn and the Temple because of his connection with the dramatic profession, but was admitted a barrister by the Society of Lincoln's Inn in 1757. He occupied chambers at No. 1 New Square, Lincoln's Inn, for upwards of a quarter of a century. The old house, in 1885, remained as in Murphy's time.

During the latter years of his life Murphy lived at Hammersmith, 'at the end of the Mall and on the Terrace overlooking the river.' This was afterwards called Hammersmith Terrace; and Murphy's house, the last one at the west end of the row, was standing in 1885. Its back windows look directly upon the Thames.

Murphy died at No. 14 Queen's Row, Knightsbridge, in a house little changed in 1885, when it was No. 59 Brompton Road, and was buried by the side of his mother in the parish Church of St. Paul, Queen Street, Hammersmith.

Murphy was a member of the Beefsteak Society, which met in his time in Covent Garden Theatre (see CHURCHILL, p. 51). He frequented Tom's Coffee House, No. 17 Russell Street, Covent Garden (see CIBBER, p. 55), 'the Bedford under the Piazza, Covent Garden.' (see CHURCHILL, p. 51), and 'George's in the Strand,' which stood at No. 213 Strand, near Essex Street and opposite the New Law Courts.

The George Tavern was erected on its site in 1868 (see SHENSTONE).

He was fond of going to The Doves (still a tavern in 1885), at the entrance to the Upper Mall, Hammersmith, near his own house, and at the end of Hammersmith Bridge (see THOMSON).

SIR ISAAC NEWTON.

1642–1727.

NEWTON seems to have seen little or nothing of London until he was sent to Parliament by the University of Cambridge in 1689, when he lodged 'at Mr. More's house in the Broad Sanctuary at the west end of Westminster Abbey.' Here he first met John Locke. In 1693, during a short stay in town, he wrote a letter from 'The Bull at Shoreditch,' an inn not mentioned by Stow, Nicholson, or in the 'History of Shoreditch,' and to be found on no old map.

In 1697, when appointed Warden of the Mint, he took a house in Jermyn Street, St. James's Street, where he remained until he went to Chelsea in 1709. In October, 1710, he removed to the house afterwards numbered 35 St. Martin Street, Leicester Square, where he lived for fifteen years and completed the second and third editions of his 'Principia.' The house was still standing in 1885, and was occupied by the Sunday school of the Orange Chapel, next door. It is marked by the tablet of the Society of Arts (see MME. D'ARBLAY, p. 73).

After Sir Isaac Newton took up his residence in London, he lived in a very handsome style, and kept his carriage, with an establishment of three male and three female servants. In his own house he was hospitable and *Brewster's Life of Newton, chap. xix.*

kind, and on proper occasions he gave splendid entertainments, though without ostentation or vanity. His own diet was frugal, and his dress was always simple.

It was here [St. Martin's Street] that the antiquary Dr. Stukely called one day by appointment. The servant who opened the door said that Sir Isaac was in his study. No one was permitted to disturb him there; but as it was near his dinner-time the visitor sat down to wait for him. In a short time a boiled chicken under cover was brought in for dinner. An hour passed, and Sir Isaac did not appear. The doctor then ate the fowl, and, covering up the empty dish, desired the servant to get another dressed for his master. Before that was ready, the great man came down. He apologized for his delay, and added: 'Give me but leave to take my short dinner, and I shall be at your service. I am fatigued and faint.' Saying this, he lifted up the cover, and without emotion turned about to Stukely with a smile. 'See,' he said, 'what we studious people are; I forgot that I had dined.'

<small>Walford's Old and New London, vol. iii. p. 172.</small>

Newton died in what was then known as Pitt's Buildings, Kensington, on the southeast side of Campden Hill. His house, afterwards called Orbell's Buildings, was for a time known as Newton House. In 1885 it was at the north end of Bullingham House, and formed a portion of Kensington College, the entrance to which was at No. 15 Pitt Street. The gardens and the house were intact. A rear entrance next to the old George Tavern, Church Street, near Campden Grove, and in the stable-yards to the inn, had but lately been closed.

He went into London and presided at the Royal Society for the last time on the 2d of March, 1727. The fatigue brought on a paroxysm of his complaint. He lingered in much pain, affectionately tended by his beloved niece . . . till the morning of Monday the 20th, when he died, in the eighty-fifth year of his age, — the highest of all human intelligence, till now.

<small>Tom Taylor's Leicester Square.</small>

The Royal Society, during Newton's presidency and for many years afterwards, met in a house in Crane Court, Fleet Street. On its site was a modern but picturesque turreted red brick building occupied by the Scottish Corporation in 1885.

On March 28, 1727, the body of Sir Isaac Newton, after lying in state in the Jerusalem Chamber, where it had been brought from his death-bed in Kensington, was attended by the leading members of the Royal Society, and buried at the public cost in the spot in front of the choir, which, being one of the most conspicuous in the Abbey, had been previously refused to various noblemen who had applied for it. <small>Dean Stanley's Westminster Abbey, chap. iv.</small>

Sir Isaac, after the meetings of the Royal Society, is known to have visited the Grecian, Devereux Court, Strand, on the site of the present Eldon Chambers (see ADDISON, p. 7).

THOMAS OTWAY.

1651-1685.

EXCEPT that Otway's life in London was generally disreputable, little is recorded of it. The low alehouse in which he perished miserably is the only spot mentioned as being in any way positively associated with him, and only the name of that is known now. His first and last appearance upon the stage as a player was made in the Dorset Garden Theatre, Salisbury Court, Fleet Street, in 1672. It stood behind the present Salisbury Square, and between Hutton Street, formerly Wilderness Lane, Dorset Street, and the Thames. Dorset Street and Dorset Buildings perpetuate its name.

In this play [The Jealous Bridegroom] Mr. Otway, the poet, having an inclination to turn actor, Mr. Behn gave him the *King* in the play for a probation part; but he, being not used to the stage, the full house put him to such a sweat and tremendous agony, that being dash't spoilt him for an actor.

<small>Downe's Roscius Anglicanus, p. 34.</small>

Dryden and Otway were contemporaries, and lived, it is said, for some time opposite each other in Fetter Lane. One morning the latter happened to call upon his brother bard about breakfast-time, but was told by his servant that his master was gone to breakfast with the Earl of Pembroke. 'Very well,' said Otway, 'tell your master that I will call to-morrow morning.' Accordingly he called about the same hour. 'Well, is your master at home now?' 'No, sir, he is just gone to breakfast with the Duke of Buckingham.' 'The d——l he is!' said Otway; and, actuated either by envy, pride, or disappointment, in a kind of involuntary manner he took up a piece of chalk which lay on a table and wrote over the door, —

<small>Walford's Old and New London, vol. i. chap. viii.</small>

'Here lives Dryden, a poet and a wit.'

The next morning Dryden recognized the handwriting, and told the servant to go to Otway and desire his company to breakfast with him; in the mean time to Otway's line of

'Here lives Dryden, a poet and a wit,'

he added, —

'This was written by Otway, opposit.'

When Otway arrived he saw this line linked with a rhyme, and, being a man of rather petulant disposition, he took it in dudgeon, and, turning upon his heel, told Dryden he was welcome to keep his wit and his breakfast to himself.

Otway's house, if he did live in Fetter Lane, — which is merely traditional, — must have been opposite the house said to have been occupied by Dryden, and in the grounds of the present Record Office (see DRYDEN, p. 93).

Otway died on the 14th of April, 1685.

Having been compelled by his necessities to contract debts, and hunted, as is supposed, by the terriers of the law, he retired to a public house on Tower Hill, where he is said to have died of want; or, as is related by one of his biographers, by swallowing, after a long fast, a piece of bread which charity had supplied. He went out, as is reported, almost naked, in a rage of hunger, and, finding a gentleman in a neighboring coffee-house, asked him for a shilling. The gentleman gave him a guinea; and Otway, going away, bought a roll and was choked by the first mouthful. All this, I hope, is not true. Johnson's Lives of the Poets: Otway.

If Lee died tipsy outside a public house, Otway died half-starved within one, at the Bull on Tower Hill. Doran's Annals of the Stage.

Otway had an intimate friend, who was shot; the murderer fled toward Dover, and Otway pursued him. On his return he drank water when violently heated, and so got a fever, which was the death of him. Spence's Anecdotes: John Dennis, section i. 1728–1730.

There is no sign of the Bull to be found on Tower Hill now, and the exact site of Otway's tavern is unknown.

He was buried in the churchyard of St. Clement Danes, April 16, 1685. No stone marks the spot.

WILLIAM PENN.

1644–1718.

WILLIAM PENN was born in his father's house 'upon Great Tower Hill, on the east side, with a court adjoining to London Wall.' Part of old London Wall was still to be found in 1885, back of the Tower Station of the Underground Railway, and in the identical court which once contained this house. According to Robert J. Burdette, in his Life of Penn, 'he was not born with his hat on, but this is the only time he was ever seen in his bare head.'

Penn received his early education at Chigwell Grammar School, about ten miles from London; and here, as he expresses it, the 'Lord first appeared to him,' when he was about twelve years of age. These visitations were repeated afterwards in his father's house, and at a private school he attended on Tower Hill. He went to Christ Church, Oxford, at the age of fifteen. After his suspension from college and a tour of two years on the Continent, he was entered as a student in Lincoln's Inn. During his stormy life in London, before and after he carried his colonization schemes into effect, he lived with his various Quaker friends when he was not confined in Newgate, the Tower, where he wrote 'No Cross, No Crown,' or 'within the rules of the Fleet,' composing the while innumerable pamphlets, and preaching in the various Friends' meeting-houses of the metropolis.

Penn is said to have occupied the house 'on the southwest corner of Norfolk Street, Strand, the last house in the street and overlooking the river,' on the site of which, No. 21 Norfolk Street, was the Arundel Hotel in 1885. And he is known to have lived at one time at Teddington, on the left bank of the Thames, near Twickenham.

He was buried at Chalfont, Bucks.

SAMUEL PEPYS.

1632-33-1703.

THE famous gossip was born on the 23d of February, 1632-33, but whether at Brompton, near Huntingdon, where his father had a small property, or in London, cannot now be determined. He was familiar with the metropolis in his childhood, but it is certain that he went to school at

Huntingdon before he entered Paul's School in London (see MILTON, p. 211).

To Paul's Schoole, it being opposition day there. I heard some of their speeches and they were just as school boys used to be, of the seven liberal sciences, but I think not so good as our's were in our time. Pepys's Diary, Feb. 4, 1662–63.

Pepys was married in the Church of St. Margaret, Westminster, on the 1st of December, 1655, and in the register is described as 'Samuel Peps of this parish, Gent.' This spelling of his name, together with that of the register of St. Olave's, Hart Street, recording his death, — 'Samuel Peyps, Esq.,' — may settle the point of its proper pronunciation.

Pepys, at the time of the opening of his Diary, 1659–60, was living in Axe Yard, on the west side of King Street, Westminster.

I lived in Axe Yard, having my wife, and servant Jane, and no other in the family than us three. Diary, 1659–60.

At Westminster by reason of rain and an easterly wind, the water was so high that there was boats rowed in King Street, and all our yard was drowned, that one could not get to my house, so as no man has seen the like almost, and most houses full of water. Diary, March 20, 1660.

Axe Yard, afterwards called Fludyer Street, is now covered by the Public Offices (see DAVENANT, p. 75). King Street at one time extended to Charing Cross, through the grounds of the Palace of Whitehall.

In June, 1660, Pepys took possession of a house belonging to, and adjoining, the Navy Office in Seething Lane.

Up early and with Commissioner Pett to view the houses in Seething Lane, belonging to the Navy, where I find the worst very good, and had great feares they will shuffle me out of them, which troubles me. Diary, June 4, 1660.

This morning we met at the office. I dined at my house in Seething Lane. Diary, June 18, 1660.

While Pepys was clerk in the Navy Office he made marks which are not yet effaced. To this day rules and regulations of his devising are in force at the Admiralty, and documents are issued to the fleet of Victoria, on plans formed by Pepys.

Seething Lane was spared by the Great Fire, but contains now no houses, seemingly, as old as the reign of James II. It runs from Crutched Friars to Great Tower Street; and the old Navy Office, which was removed in 1788, stood on the east side of the Lane, with its chief entrance on Crutched Friars.

From a 'Certificate' of the clergyman of the Church of St. Olave, Hart Street, preserved in the Bodleian Library, Oxford, and quoted in full by Lord Braybrooke in his 'Memoir' attached to the 'Diary and Correspondence of Samuel Pepys,' it seems that Pepys lived in this parish, probably in one house, for thirteen years (1660-1673), 'during which time the said Mr. Pepys and his whole family were constant attendants upon the public worship of God and his holy ordinances,' and that 'his Lady received the Holy Sacrament from my hands according to the rites of the Church of England upon her death-bed, few houres before her decease, in the year 1669.' It would also seem from the same document, dated May 22, 1681, that even after Pepys removed from the parish 'he continued to receive the Holy Communion with the inhabitants thereof.'

In 1684 Pepys lived in Buckingham Street, Strand. His house 'over against' Peter the Great's was on the west side of Buckingham Street, No. 14, at the end of the street and overlooking York Gate (see BACON, p. 12). It has been rebuilt.

In 1700 he removed to Clapham, under the advice of his physician, where, on the 26th of May, 1703, he died. No trace of his house remains. It was taken down in the middle of the eighteenth century.

Sept. 23. — I went to visit Mr. Pepys at Clapham where he has a very noble and wonderfully well furnished house, especially with Indian and Chinese curiosities; the Evelyn's Diary, 1700. offices and gardens well accommodated for retirement.

Pepys was buried by the side of his wife, 'in a vault by ye Communion Table,' in the Church of St. Olave, Hart Street, at the junction of Seething Lane and Crutched Friars. The building has been left comparatively untouched. Pepys erected an elaborate monument to his wife, with her bust and an inscription in elegant Latin, near the chancel. A memorial to Pepys himself in this church was unveiled in 1884 by James Russell Lowell. It is on the south wall, near the little door by which he was wont to enter the gallery, ascending from the churchyard by an outside staircase; but gallery, staircase, and door have all disappeared. On the bottom of this tablet are the words 'Erected by Public Subscription, 1883;' and Pepys in bas relief is now looking towards the monument to his wife. .

In 1677 Pepys was elected Master of the Clothworkers' Company, and left it a silver cup, which is carefully preserved. The new hall of the Clothworkers, built in 1860, stands upon the site of the old hall, on the east side of Mincing Lane, a few doors from Fenchurch Street. In 1684 he was elected President of the Royal Society, which met in his day in Arundel House, in the Strand, marked now by Arundel Street; and in Gresham College, which then stood on the east side of Old Broad Street, half-way between Wormwood and Threadneedle Streets, as shown in a map printed by Stow. It was taken down in the middle of last century. Gresham House, No. 22 Old Broad Street, stands upon its site. Gresham College, on the northeast corner of Gresham and Basinghall Streets, is of much later date.

In 1679-80 Pepys was confined in the Tower upon a charge of Popery and Treason, and in 1690 he was sent for a short time to the Gate House at Westminster (see BURKE, p. 27).

A list of the London taverns frequented by Pepys would simply be a list of all the taverns in London in Pepys's day.

Lord's Day. — Met with Purser Washington, with whom and a lady, a friend of his, .I dined at the Bell Tavern in King Street [Westminster] ; but the rogue had no more manners than to invite me and to let me pay my club.

<small>Diary, July 1, 1660.</small>

To the Mitre in Wood Street. Here some of us fell to handicap, a sport that I never knew before.

<small>Diary, Sept. 18, 1660.</small>

The Mitre in Wood Street was destroyed in the Great Fire of 1666. Mitre Court lies between Wood, Gresham, Milk Streets, and Cheapside. He frequented also the Mitre in Fenchurch Street, likewise a victim to the Great Fire, but soon after rebuilt. Its site is marked by Mitre Chambers, No. 157 Fenchurch Street.

Still another Mitre of Pepys's was that in Fleet Street near Temple Bar see (JOHNSON, p. 169).

A favorite tavern of his was the Leg, in King Street, Westminster, which at that time, as has been shown, extended through the precincts of Whitehall Palace to Charing Cross.

With Mr. Creed and More to the Leg in the Palace to dinner, which I gave them, and after dinner, I saw the girl of the house, being very pretty, go into a chamber, and I went in after her and kissed her.

<small>Diary, Apr. 6, 1661.</small>

This morning going to my father's I met him, and so he and I went and drank our morning draft at Samson's, in Paul's Church Yard.

<small>Diary, June 21, 1661.</small>

Of the Dolphin, 'near my house,' which was then in Seething Lane, no trace is left; and no hint is given as to its site.

At noon with my wife by appointment, to dinner at the Dolphin, with Sir W. Batten, and his lady and daughter Matt, and Captain Cook and his lady, a German lady but a very great beauty, and we dined together, at the spending of some wagers won and lost between him and I; and then we had the best musique and very good songs, and were very merry and danced. But, after all our mirth comes a reckoning of £4, besides 4s of the musicians which did trouble us, but it must be paid and so I took my leave and left them there about eight o'clock. *Diary, Nov. 22, 1661.*

We all went to the Three Cranes Tavern, and though the best room in the house is such a narrow dogg-hole that it made me loath my company and victuals, and a sorry poore dinner it was, too. *Diary, Jan. 23, 1661-62.*

This was probably the Three Cranes in the Vintry, in Queen Street, Upper Thames Street.

In Covent Garden to-night going to fetch home my wife, I stopped at the Great Coffee House there, where I never was before . . . and had I had time then, or could at other times, it will be good coming thither, for there I perceive is very witty and pleasant discourse. *Diary, Feb. 3, 1663-64.*

This was Will's Coffee House, in Russell Street, Covent Garden, corner of Bow Street (see ADDISON, p. 7).

He also frequented the Fleece Tavern in Covent Garden, where on one occasion he 'staid till late, very merry.' It stood on the corner of York Street and Brydges Street, afterwards Catherine Street.

To a little ordinary in Hercules' Pillars Alley, the Crowne, a poor sorry place and there dined and had a good dinner. *Diary, Jan. 30, 1666-67.*

At noon my wife came to me at my tailor's and I sent her home, and myself and Tom dined at Hercules' Pillars. *Diary, April 30, 1669.*

Hercules' Pillars Alley was on the south side of Fleet Street, near St. Dunstan's Church. In Strype's time, — beginning of the eighteenth century, — this street was almost entirely 'given up to such as keep publick houses.' It has been built over for many years.

To the Cock in Fleet Street, No. 201,[11] and to the Cock in Suffolk Street, Haymarket, of which latter now no trace is left, he often went with his wife, Mrs. Knipp, and other ladies of his acquaintance.

Diary, April 22, 1668. Thence by water to the Temple and there to the Cocke Alehouse and drank and eat a lobster and sang and were mighty merry.

Did walk to the Cock at the end of Suffolke Street, where I never was, a great ordinary mightily cried up, and *Diary, March 15, 1669.* there bespoke a pullet and while dressing he and I walked into St. James's Park, and thence back and dined very handsome, with a good soup and a pullet for 4s 6d, the whole.

On the 17th of January, 1659-60, he writes: 'I went to the Coffee Club and heard a very good discourse.' This was the Rota Club, which met at the Turk's Head, in New Palace Yard, — an inn that has long since disappeared.

Pepys's face was also well known at the 'Beare Inn, Southwark, at the foote of London Bridge.' It was 'opposite the end of St. Olave's Church in Tooley Street,' and was taken down in 1761. Other places of his resort were, — the Blue Bells, in Lincoln's Inn Fields; Carey House, in the Strand, near the Savoy; the Castle Tavern, 'by the Savoy near Exeter House,' which stood in Bell Inn Court, No. 407 Strand, as late as 1846; Chatelines, the French house, in Covent Garden; the Devil Tavern, near Temple Bar (see BEN JONSON, p. 76); the Goat Tavern, in Charing Cross; the Golden Eagle, in New Street, between Fetter Lane and Shoe Lane; the Golden Lion, near Charing Cross; the Heaven Tavern, in Lindsay Lane, Westminster, the site of the Committee Rooms of the House of Commons, — 'went to Heaven with Sudlin, and I dined' (Hell and Paradise were neighboring inns); the King's Head, Fleet Street, opposite Chancery Lane; the

King's Head in Tower Street; the King's Head opposite the church in Islington; the Pope's Head in Chancery Lane; the Pope's Head in Pope's Head Alley, running from No. 18 Cornhill to No. 73 Lombard Street (this was in existence as late as 1756); the Quaker, in the Great Sanctuary, Westminster, on the site of which the Sessions House was built; the Rhenish Wine House, on the south side of Cannon Row, Westminster (see LOCKE, p. 197); the Rhenish Wine House, in the Steel Yard, Upper Thames Street, on the site of which the Cannon Street Station has been built (the Steel Yard lay between All Hallows Lane and Cousin Lane); the Rose, in Russell Street, Covent Garden (portions of Drury Lane Theatre stand on its site); the Star, in Cheapside; the Sun in King Street, Westminster; the Sun 'behind the Exchange;' the Sun in New Fish Street (Fish Street Hill); the Sun in Chancery Lane; the Swan in Old Fish Street; the Swan in Fenchurch Street; the Three Tuns, 'in Charing Cross,' — probably the inn of that name which stood on the site of No. 66 Bedford Street, Strand, near the corner of Chandos Street; the White Horse Tavern, in Lombard Street; and the World's End, Knightsbridge, — 'a drinking place near the Park.'

None of these now remain, and the exact site of many of them it is not possible to discover. Besides the foregoing, he mentions scores of taverns by name, but gives no hint as to where they stood.

ALEXANDER POPE.

1688–1744.

THAT Pope was a native of London, there seems to be no question; but the exact spot of his birth has never been definitely settled. Johnson says his father was a linen-draper, who dwelt in the Strand. John Timbs believes that he was born in Old Broad Street, in the parish of St. Bennet Fink, where his father — a merchant, not a trades-man — had his abode; but, according to Spence, — and this is the generally accepted authority, — he was born in Plough Court, Lombard Street, and in 1688. Plough Court, opposite No. 37 Lombard Street, contains now none but the most modern of business houses; and in Old Broad Street is no building dating back to Pope's time.

Pope, a delicate child, was never thoroughly well, although he lived past middle age. He is said to have inherited his crookedness of person from his father, and his delicacy of constitution and fretfulness of temper from his mother, who was a victim to headaches. Johnson declares that his weakness of body continued through life, although the mildness of his mind — if it ever was mild — ended with his childhood.

Pope went to school at Marylebone, and afterwards at Hyde Park Corner, where he lisped in numbers. Later in life his address for a short time was 'at Mr. Digby's, next door to ye Golden Ball, on ye second terras in St. James's Street;' and a letter to him, extant, is addressed to 'Bridgewater House in Cleveland Court, St. James's.' A modern Bridgewater House was built upon its site in 1845. The pleasant old house No. 9 Berkeley Street, Piccadilly, opposite Devonshire House, is said to have been a home of Pope's.

We are glad to be able to point out the site of the London residence of the great poet Pope. He lived at one time at No. 9 Berkeley Street, close to his friend Lord Burlington; and it was here, possibly, in 1715, on the eve of his departure to his quiet retreat at Twickenham, that he composed his 'Farewell to London.' We are assured that in the lease of this house the name of Mr. Alexander Pope occurs as a former tenant. From the poet it passed into the hands of General Bulkley, who died at an extreme old age. A late occupant of the house well remembered that whenever the General visited it after it had ceased to be his own, it was his invariable habit to observe, with an air of respectful interest, 'This is the house Mr. Alexander Pope lived in.' Jesse's London, vol. I.: Piccadilly.

Pope is believed to have spent a year or two at Chiswick, and on good authority, although Faulkner in his 'Chiswick,' does not mention the fact. His father, dying in 1717, was buried in Chiswick Churchyard; and portions of the Iliad, it is said, were written on the backs of letters addressed to 'Mr. Pope at his house in ye New Buildings, Chiswick.' New Buildings, afterwards Mawson Row, a group of five three-storied red brick houses, on the west side of Chiswick Lane, at the corner of Mawson Lane, and half-way between the River and the Manor House, were unaltered in 1885.

Pope lived at the famous villa at Twickenham for a quarter of a century, and died there in 1744.

The villa — or villakin, as Swift called it — was much smaller when Pope took it than when he left it. In 1717 it comprised only a central hall with two small parlors on each side, and corresponding rooms above. He left it a brick centre of four floors with wings of three floors, each story with a single light towards the Thames. . . . After Pope's death his villa was sold to Sir William Stanhope, brother to the Earl of Chesterfield, who added wings to the house, and enlarged and improved the garden, greatly to the disgust of Walpole. Thorne's Hand-Book of the Environs of London: Twickenham.

This house was destroyed early in the nineteenth century. The present 'Pope's Villa' (1885) is entirely different in character, and does not even stand on the site of the original building. The Grotto, however, still remains.[15]

Pope was buried in a vault in the middle aisle of Twickenham Church, near the east end of the aisle.

The 'Essay on Man' is said to have been written at Bolingbroke House, Battersea. A portion of the west wing of this building was standing as late as 1885, on Mill Wharf, Church Road, Battersea, and was used as a residence by the foreman of the mill of Dives & Co., to whom the property belonged, the carved chimney-pieces and frescoed ceilings remaining intact. On the front of the wing overlooking the river was the famous cedar room in which Bolingbroke and Pope so often sat; the floor, walls, and ceiling of cedar still as redolent as a century and a half before.

Pope was also a frequent visitor of Bolingbroke at Dawley Court, in Harrington, Middlesex, not very far from Twickenham. Only one wing of the house remains. It stands between the Great Western Railway, on the south, and the Grand Junction Canal, on the north, and is about half a mile east of Hayes Station and twelve miles from Hyde Park Corner.

Pope's taverns were the Bedford, in the Piazza, Covent Garden (see CHURCHILL, p. 51); the Upper Flask, Hampstead Heath (see ADDISON, p. 9); and Slaughter's, which stood in St. Martin's Lane, three doors from Newport Street, but was taken down in 1843, when Cranbourne Street was cut through that section of the town to make a thoroughfare between Coventry Street and Piccadilly. H. R. Haweis, in his chapter on Handel in his 'Music and Morals,' associates Pope with another inn the identity of which is not very clear, as Regent Street did not exist until seventy-five years after Pope's death. He says:—

As Handel enters the 'Turk's Head,' at the corner of Regent Street, a noble coach and four drives up. It is the Duke of Chandos, who is inquiring for Mr. Pope. Presently a deformed little man in an iron-gray suit, and with a face as keen as a razor, hobbles out, makes a low bow to the burly Handel, who, helping him into a chariot, gets in after him, and they drive off together to Cannons, the Duke's mansion at Edgeware. There they meet Mr. Addison, the poet Gay, and the witty Arbuthnot, who have been asked to luncheon. The last number of the 'Spectator' lies on the table; and a brisk discussion arises between Pope and Addison, concerning the merits of the Italian Opera, in which Pope would have the better if he only knew a little more about music, and could keep his temper.

Among the traditions of Will's Coffee House, at the corner of Bow and Russell Streets, Covent Garden (see ADDISON, p. 7), is one to the effect that Pope was carried there in his youth to see and worship Dryden, whose works he even then greatly admired, and who was for some years the autocrat of that establishment. As Pope was born in 1688, and as Dryden died only twelve years later, Pope could have been little more than a child when this interview took place, if it took place at all.

Pope was a member of different clubs, of more or less renown.

Whilst deeply engaged in his translation of Homer, Pope frequently relaxed from his labors by a visit to town. . . . The dissensions which arose amongst the ministers before the death of Queen Anne, and which Swift strove in vain to reconcile, had interrupted the meetings of the political society called the October Club; but another association had been formed, which was known by the name of the Scriblerus Club, and of which Swift, Parnell, Arbuthnot, and Gay were members. At both these places Pope found himself a welcome guest; and as temperance and regularity were not the habits of the times, he was probably led into indulgences Roscoe's Life of Pope, 1715.

inconsistent no less with his infirm constitution than with his usual course of life.

Cunningham's Handbook of London: October Club. The October club was a club of country members of Parliament, of about the time of Queen Anne, about one hundred and fifty in number, Tories to the backbone. . . . They met at the Bell, afterwards the Crown, in King Street, Westminster.

King Street originally ran from Charing Cross to the Palace of Westminster, past or through the grounds of the Palace of Whitehall, and although very narrow and badly paved, was the chief thoroughfare between the two points. The formation of Parliament Street after the destruction of Whitehall in 1698 wiped out a large part of King Street, and the new Public Offices have left but a short portion of what remained. No Crown or Bell exists to-day. The Scriblerus Club had no proper home of its own, but met at some of the many taverns in St. James's Street or Pall Mall.

RICHARD PORSON.

1759–1808.

PORSON'S first home in London, when he arrived from Cambridge in 1791 or 1792, was at No. 5 Essex Court, Middle Temple, where he remained for some years, and where, putting out his candle in the midst of a prolonged debauch, he is described as staggering downstairs to relight it, and after many vain attempts uttering his famous curse against 'the nature of things.'

He had a temporary home, when he chose to avail himself of it, in the house of his friend Perry, in Lancaster Court, Strand. According to some authorities, Porson was married in 1795 in the Church of St. Martin-in-the-Fields, although no record of such marriage is to be found there.

In 1805 Porson was appointed principal Librarian to the London Institution, then at No. 8 Old Jewry. The building was destroyed by fire in 1863, and banks and business offices were built upon its site. He had apartments in the Instituiton, and died there in 1808. He was buried in Cambridge.

Among his places of bucolic resort were the African Coffee House, in St. Michael's Alley, — a short passage at the side of St. Michael's Church, Cornhill, where was, in 1885, a West Indian but no African Tavern; and the Turk's Head, No. 142 Strand (see JOHNSON, p. 170).

I afterwards used to meet Porson every night at the Turk's Head in the Strand, where he retained his devotion to brandy and water, and often tired the company with his recital of a burlesque parody of Pope's exquisite poem of 'Eloisa and Abelard.' *John Taylor's Records of my Life.*

The Cider Cellar, at No. 20 Maiden Lane, near Bedford Street, Covent Garden, which has now disappeared, was the spot to which his footsteps more frequently and more fondly turned. It was opposite the house (No. 26 Maiden Lane) in which Turner the painter was born; and the Adelphi Club, No. 21 A, Maiden Lane, stood on its site in 1885. It was what is called 'an all-night tavern,' and famous for its cider; hence its name. What Porson considered one of the greatest compliments ever paid to him was the remark of one of his boon companions of this place, that 'Dick can beat us all, — he can drink all night, and spout all day.'

MATTHEW PRIOR.

1664-1721.

THE first traces of Prior in London are at the Rummer Tavern, kept by his uncle, and described by Peter Cunningham as 'a famous tavern two doors from Lockitt's, between Whitehall and Charing Cross, removed to the water side of Charing Cross in 1710, and burnt down November 7, 1750.'

Lockitt's Ordinary stood on the site of Drummond's Banking House in Spring Gardens, and in an old map, dated 1734 and published in Smith's 'Antiquities of Westminster,' Rummer Court, unquestionably the site of the famous hostelry, is shown to have been situated between Buckingham Court and Cromwell Place. The Ship Tavern, at No. 35 Charing Cross, with an entrance into Spring Gardens, standing in 1885, is a direct descendant of the Rummer.

This uncle of Prior, into whose kindly hands he fell when his father's death left him a small boy without home, sent him to Westminster School (see CHURCHILL, p. 51), under Dr. Busby, and after giving him a moderate education there, received him into his own family at the Rummer Tavern. Here he attracted the attention of the Earl of Dorset, who was so much pleased with the lad and his proficiency in the classics that he defrayed the expenses of his University course.

Prior's London home was in 'Duke Street, Westminster, facing Charles Street.' Duke Street, afterwards called Delahay Street, has been greatly changed since Prior's day. Facing Charles Street is now a gate of St. James's Park, and

Charles Street itself forms the southern boundary of the new Government Buildings.

On July 30, 1717, Prior wrote to Swift:—

I have been made to believe that we may see your revered person this summer in England. If so, I shall be glad to meet you at any place; but when you come to London, do not go to the Cocoa Tree, but come immediately to Duke Street, where you shall find a bed, a book, and a candle; so pray think of sojourning nowhere else.

<small>Works of Swift: Correspondence, 1717.</small>

Prior's taverns were the Cocoa Tree, in St. James's Street (see ADDISON, p. 7); the Smyrna, in Pall Mall, the site of which cannot now be discovered; the Palsgrave Head, on Palsgrave Place, Strand, between Devereux Court and Shanet Place, since entirely removed and covered by the modern Palsgrave Restaurant, No. 222 Strand; and the Star and Garter, the meeting-place of the Brothers' Club, which stood at No. 44 Pall Mall on the north side, and upon the site of which a modern public house, bearing the same name, has been built.

Prior was also too often to be found in less creditable society and in less reputable neighborhoods. Johnson shows him to have deserted the company of Bolingbroke, Pope, and Swift in order to smoke a pipe and to drink with a common soldier and his wife in Long Acre. The woman is said to have been the original of the beautiful 'Chloe' of his poem; and, according to Pope, 'he used to bury himself, for whole days and nights together, with this poor, mean creature.'

BRYAN WALLER PROCTER

(BARRY CORNWALL).

1787-1874.

PROCTER knew nothing of London until 1807. In 1816 he was living in Brunswick Square. After his marriage in 1824 he occupied the upper part of a house in Southampton Row, not far from Red Lion Square, — the scene, at that time, of his daily labors; but in the next year he removed to the house of Mr. and Mrs. Basil Montague, No. 25 Bedford Square, on the north side, where in 1825 Adelaide Procter was born.

When Adelaide was a child the Procters lived 'in a little gothic cottage opposite Sir Edwin Landseer's, at No. 5 Grove End Road, St. John's Wood.' No little gothic cottage is standing there now which answers this description. No. 5 Grove End Road was called Salisbury House in 1885, but was not opposite Sir Edwin Landseer's. The numbers had not been changed since 1840.

Later, and for a number of years, their home was at No. 13 Upper Harley Street, Cavendish Square, where they entertained, in a modest but delightful way, many distinguished men and women. Upper Harley Street has since been called Harley Street, and renumbered. The Procters' house still stood on the east side, but was numbered 38 in 1885. In 1861 they went to No. 13 Weymouth Street, Cavendish Square, where, thirteen years later, 'Barry Cornwall' died. He was buried at Finchley. The Weymouth Street house has also been renumbered. It stood on the north side, near Beaumont Street.

SIR WALTER RALEIGH.

1552-1618.

RALEIGH is said to have been a member of the Middle Temple, but this is merely traditional; and as he declared at his trial that he had never read a word of law until he entered the Tower, it is believed that he had no connection with the Temple as a student, although he might have lived there before he took possession of Durham House, which was his town residence for twenty years. It stood between the Strand and the Thames; the Adelphi Terrace was built upon its river front, and Durham Street perpetuates its name. It was taken from him on the accession of James.

Durham House was a noble palace. After he [Raleigh] came to his greatness he lived there, or in some apartments of it. I well remember his study, which was on a little turret that looked into and over the Thames, and had the prospect which is as pleasant, perhaps, as any in the world, and which not only refreshes the eie-sight, but cheers the spirit (and to speak my mind) I believe enlarges an ingeniose man's thoughts. Aubrey's Lives of Eminent Persons: Raleigh.

Two old houses at Islington, which were standing at the beginning of the present century, had traditional associations with Raleigh. These were the Queen's Head Tavern, marked by Queen's Head Lane, Islington, and the Pied Bull.

The old Queen's Head has been coupled with the name of Sir Walter Raleigh, who is said, if not to have built, at least to have patronized and frequented, the house; and from the circumstance of his having in the thirtieth year of Elizabeth's reign [1588] obtained a patent 'to make lycenses for keeping of taverns and retailing of wynes Lewis's History of Islington, vol. iv. p. 150.

throughout Englande,' further conjecture has been hazarded that this was one of the houses so licensed by him, and that the sign of the Queen's head was adopted in compliment to his Royal Mistress.

A Queen's Head Tavern, built in 1830, stood in 1885 in Essex Road, on the corner of Queen's Head Street, Islington, on the site of Raleigh's house.

On the west side of Church Row, near Islington Green, at the corner of a footway (now closed up by new houses) leading into the Back Road, was recently standing [1829] the Pied Bull Inn. This was originally a country villa, erected probably a few years previous to the decease of Queen Elizabeth; and, according to a long-current tradition, it was once the residence of the brave Sir Walter Raleigh.

<small>Brayley's Londoniana, vol. iv.</small>

The present tenant [1740] of the Pied Bull Inn affirms that his landlord was possessed of some old account books, by which it appears, beyond all doubt, this house and fourteen acres of land now let at about £70 per annum, did belong to Sir Walter Raleigh, and that the oldest man in this parish would often declare that his father had told him Sir Walter proposed to wall in that ground with intention to keep some of his horses therein.

<small>Life of Raleigh, Anon. London, 1740.</small>

According to the parish records, 'a manservant of Sir Walter Raylie from Mile End' was buried in Stepney Church, August 25, 1596, from which it is inferred that Raleigh lived at that time in the parish.

Raleigh's first experiences of the Tower were in 1592, when he incurred the displeasure of Elizabeth by his devotion to one of her ladies of honor, Elizabeth Throgmorton, whom he afterwards married. After the death of the Virgin Queen in 1603 he was sent to the Tower by her successor, where he was confined for twelve years. Lady Raleigh was permitted to share her husband's imprisonment for some time; and here, in 1605, their son Carew was born. Raleigh is thought to have occupied the second and third stories of the Beauchamp Tower, and to have been confined in the Bloody Tower and the Garden House. Here he studied chemistry, and discovered the cordial to which his name was attached; wrote several works upon different subjects; and published, in 1614, his 'History of the World.'

Raleigh passed the night before his execution in the Gate House, Westminster (see BURKE).

A cousin of his coming to see him, Sir Walter, finding him sad, began to be very pleasant with him, whereupon Mr. Thynne counselled him: 'Sir, take heed you goe not too muche upon the brave hande, for your enemies will take exceptions at that.' 'Good Charles,' quoth he, 'give me leave to be merry for this is the last merriment that ever I shall have in this worlde, but when I come to the last parte, thou shalte see I will looke on it like a man,' and so he was as good as his worde.

<small>Edwardes's Life of Raleigh, vol. ii.</small>

He was beheaded in Old Palace Yard on the 29th of October (Old Style), 1618. Thomas Birch, in a sketch of Raleigh, prefixing an edition of his works, published by Dodsley at the Tully's Head in Pall Mall in 1751 (see AKENSIDE, p. 11), gives the following account of his execution:—

Then, having put off his Gown and Doublet, he called to the Executioner to shew him the Axe; which not being presently done, he said: '*I prythe let me see it. Dost thou think that I am afraid of it?*' And having it in his Hands he felt along the Edge of it, and smiling said to the Sheriff, '*This is a Sharp Medicine, but it is a Physician for all Diseases.*' Then going too and fro on every side of the Scaffold he desired the Company to pray to God to assist him, and strengthen him. The Executioner, kneeling down and asking his Forgiveness, Sir Walter, laying his Hand upon his Shoulder granted it; and being ask't which Way he would lay himself on the Block, he answer'd, '*So the Heart be right it is no matter which Way the Head lies.*' As he stoop'd to lay himself along, and reclin'd his Head, his Face being towards the East, the Executioner spread his own Cloak under him. After a little Pause he gave the Sign that he was ready for the

Stroke, by lifting up his Hand, and his Head was struck off by two Blows, his Body never shrinking nor moving. His Head was shewn on each Side of the Scaffold, and then put into a red Leather Bag, and with his Velvet Night Gown thrown over, was afterwards conveyed away in a Mourning Coach of his Lady's. His Body was interred in the Chancel of St. Margaret's Church in Westminster, but his Head was long preserv'd in a case by his Widow, who surviv'd him twenty-nine years, and after her Death by his Son Carew, with whom it is said to have been buried at West Horsley in Surrey.

Seeing a dim light in St. Margaret's Church near by, I entered the old temple, and found the boys of the choir at their rehearsal, and presently observed on the wall a brass plate which announces that Sir Walter Raleigh was buried here in the chancel after being decapitated for high-treason in the Palace Yard outside. Such things are the surprises of this historical capital, — the exceeding great reward of the wanderer's devotion. This inscription begs the reader to remember Raleigh's virtues as well as his faults, — a plea, surely, that every man might well wish should be made for him at last. . . . This church [St. Margaret's, Westminster] contains a window commemorative of Raleigh, presented by Americans, and inscribed with these lines by Lowell : —

<blockquote>
' The New World's Sons, from England's breast we drew
Such milk as bids remember whence we came ;
Proud of her past, wherefrom our future grew,
This window we inscribe with Raleigh's name.'
</blockquote>

<small>William Winter's English Rambles: Old Churches of London.</small>

SAMUEL RICHARDSON.

1689–1761.

ALTHOUGH it is not recorded in the earlier biographies of Richardson, and although, strangely enough, he does not mention the fact himself, in the autobiographical fragment contained in one of his published letters, Richardson was a pupil of Christ-Hospital (see COLERIDGE, p. 57). His name is to be found in the list of distinguished 'Blues' in Staunton's 'Great Schools of England.' He received here 'only common school learning;' and at the age of sixteen, by his own choice, he was apprenticed to Mr. John Wilde, of Stationers' Hall, a printer, with whom he served seven years. After the expiration of his time he worked as a compositor for five or six years, when he opened an establishment of his own in the centre, and later in the northwest corner, of Salisbury Court, afterwards Salisbury Square, Fleet Street, where he lived and transacted business for many years, keeping his office there even after he moved to more quiet homes in the suburbs of the West End of London.

The Square retains now none of the features familiar to the novelist, or to Johnson, Hogarth, and the worthies who were so often his guests there.

In town [1755] he took a range of old houses, eight in number, which he pulled down, and built an extensive and commodious range of warehouses and printing-offices. It was still in Salisbury Court, in the northwest corner, but it is at present [1802] concealed by other houses from common observation. The dwelling-house, it seems, was neither so large nor so airy as the one he quitted; and therefore the reader will not be so ready, probably, as Mr. Richardson seems to have been, in accusing his wife of perverseness in not liking the new habitation as well as the old. 'Everybody' (he says) 'is more pleased with what I have done than my wife.' Mrs. Barbauld's Life of Richardson.

Portions of 'Sir Charles Grandison' are believed to have been written in Lovell's Court, opening from No. 19 Paternoster Row, which in later years was devoted entirely to the printing, binding, and publishing of books.

While the celebrated Richardson, the author of 'Grandison,' 'Clarissa,' etc., was living, a Mr. Alderman Brydges had a dwelling-house and handsome garden in this court, which having the conveniency of an alcove, Richardson, as a friend to the alderman, is said to have written several of his works in this retired spot. The garden has been built up and considerably retrenched during some years past.

<small>Smith's Antiquarian Rambles in London.</small>

No trace of any garden in Lovell's Court remains.

Richardson's first country home was Selby House, afterwards called The Grange, at North End, Hammersmith. It had been divided into two mansions even in Richardson's time, one of which in 1885 was occupied by the artist Edward Burne-Jones; and it stood on the east side of what had lately been called West Kensington Road, opposite Grove Terrace, and between Hammersmith Road and Edith Villas. The house in 1885 was little changed, and much of Richardson's garden was left intact.

He lived in a kind of flower-garden of ladies.... He had generally a number of young ladies at his house, whom he used to engage in conversation on some subject of sentiment, and provoke, by artful opposition, to display the treasures of intellect they possessed.... He used to write in a little summer-house or grotto [at North End], as it was called, within his garden, before the family were up; and when they met at breakfast he communicated the progress of his story, which by that means had every day a fresh and lively interest.... In the middle of the garden, over against the house, we came to a kind of grotto, where we rested ourselves. It was on this seat, Mr. Le Fevre told me, that 'Pamela,' 'Clarissa,' and 'Grandison' received their birth; I kissed the inkhorn on the side of it.

<small>Mrs. Barbauld's Life of Richardson.</small>

In 1755 he removed to Parson's Green, Fulham.

On the site of the house which terminates Pitt's Place [Parson's Green], and which is now [1816] occupied as an academy by Dr. Taylor, stood an ancient mansion which formerly belonged to Sir Edward Saunders in 1682. The building, which was of a venerable character, and had in front a porch with seats on either side, was rendered interesting as having afforded a residence to Samuel Richardson, the celebrated novelist. Mr. Richardson removed hither from North End in 1755, and is said to have here written his novel of 'Clarissa Harlowe;' but that work was really published in 1748. Brayley's London and Middlesex, vol. v.

The house stood on the south side of, and directly facing, Parson's Green, between Peterborough House (on the east) and Cromwell Lodge (on the west). On the site of its garden stood, in 1885, Albyn House and the Duke's Head Tavern. No trace of it is left, and the character of the Green has entirely changed.

Richardson died of apoplexy, July 4, 1761, in this house in Parson's Green, and was buried, at his own request, by the side of his first wife, in the Church of St. Bride, in Fleet Street. A large stone in the pavement of the middle aisle, near the centre of the church, and by the side of the pews numbered 12 and 13 in 1885, records the fact that he lies beneath it. The parish, during the century or more that has elapsed since his death, has not had interest enough in the Father of the English Novel to erect a tablet to his memory; and the stone above him, placed there by the loving hands of his family, is concealed from the public by the coarse matting that generally covers it.

SAMUEL ROGERS.

1763-1855.

ALTHOUGH Rogers was a thorough Londoner, his homes in the metropolis were very few. He was born at Newington Green in 1763.

[Newington Green] is built round with houses evidently of a considerable age. There are trees and quietness about it still [1845]. In the centre of the south side is an old house, standing back, which is said to have been inhabited by Henry VIII. At the end next to Stoke Newington stands an old Presbyterian chapel, at which the celebrated Dr. Price preached, and of which afterwards the husband of Mrs. Barbauld was minister. Near this chapel De Foe was educated. In this Green lived, too, Mary Wollstonecraft, being engaged with another lady in keeping school. Samuel Rogers was born in the stuccoed house at the southwest corner, which is much older than it seems. Adjoining it is a large old garden.

William Howitt's Homes and Haunts of British Poets: Rogers.

Rogers was born in the first house that presents itself on the west side [of Newington Green], proceeding from Ball's Pond.

Lewis's Islington, chap. vii. p. 321, note.

This house is no longer standing; a row of new brick shops occupies its site, — almost the only modern innovation in 1885 in the old-fashioned, respectable, substantial square. The Green itself was still enclosed by an old wooden paling, and few of its surrounding houses bear date later than the early part of the present century.

In 1792, while living here, Rogers published his 'Pleasures of Memory.' He left this neighborhood about the year 1795, when he took chambers in the Temple, which he occupied for five years.

Rogers, like the elder D'Israeli, aspired to lay his youthful poems at the feet of Dr. Johnson, and went to Bolt Court, a few years before the old man's death, for that purpose; but he got no further than the door, the first blow of the knocker sending him and his companion out of the neighborhood of the Lion in a panic from which they did not recover until they were well up the Strand.

After leaving the Temple, Rogers lodged for a short time in Princes Street, Hanover Square; but he took possession of the famous house No. 22 St. James's Place, St. James's Street, in 1800, where he lived for more than half a century, and where he gathered about him the brightest intellects of his time.

What a delightful house it is! It looks out on the Green Park just at the most pleasant point. The furniture has been selected with a delicacy of taste quite unique. Its value does not depend on fashion, but must be the same while the fine arts are held in any esteem. In the drawing-room, for example, the chimney-pieces are carved by Flaxman into the most beautiful Grecian forms. The bookcase is painted by Stothard, in his very best manner, with groups from Chaucer, Shakspere, and Boccaccio. The pictures are not numerous, but every one is excellent. The most remarkable object in the dining-room is, I think, a cast of Pope, taken after death by Roubilliac. Life and Letters of Lord Macaulay, vol. i. chap. iv.

I forgot who introduced me to Mr. Rogers in the year 1820. He lived then, and until his death, in St. James's Place. It was not in a wide street, but it looked on to the Green Park. Upon the whole, I never saw any house so tastefully fitted up and decorated. Everything was good of its kind, and in good order. There was no plethora, no appearance of display, no sign of superfluous wealth. ... His breakfast-table was perfect in all respects. There was not too much of anything; not even too much welcome, yet no lack of it. Procter's Recollections of Men of Letters.

Rogers is silent, and, it is said, severe. When he does talk he talks well, and on all subjects of taste his delicacy of expression is pure as his poetry. If you enter his house, his drawing-room, his library, you of yourself say this is not the dwelling of a common mind. There is not a gem, a coin, a book thrown aside on the chimney-piece, his sofa, his table, that does not bespeak an almost fastidious elegance in the possessor. But this very delicacy must be the misery of his existence. Oh, the jarrings his disposition must have encountered through life! Byron's Diary, Nov. 22, 1813: Moore's Life of Byron.

Rogers died in St. James's Place, December 18, 1855. His house — No. 22, a charming residence — was unchanged in 1885, and unmarked by any tablet, although, with the exception of Holland House (see ADDISON, p. 3), it is perhaps the most interesting in London, on account of its literary associations.

The tomb of Rogers is in the northeast corner of Hornsey Churchyard.

Rógers was a member of Bobus Smith's 'King of Clubs,' which met at the Crown and Anchor Tavern, Strand, 'extending from Arundel Street eastward to Mitford Lane, in the rear of the south side of the Strand' (see JOHNSON, p. 170). The Whittington Club, No. 37 Arundel Street, was afterwards built upon its site (see JERROLD, p. 155). He was also one of the early members of the Athenæum, built on the site of the Courtyard of Carlton House, Waterloo Place, and Pall Mall.

NICHOLAS ROWE.

1673–1718.

ROWE is said to have received his early education at the Highgate Grammar School (see COLERIDGE, p. 59), and is known to have been a pupil of Dr. Busby at Westminster School (see CHURCHILL, p. 51), where he was chosen King's Scholar in 1685. In 1689 he was entered as a student in the Middle Temple. But little is recorded of his life in London, except that in his later years he lived in King Street, Covent Garden, where he died.

Rowe died the 16th of December, 1718, in the forty-fifth year of his age, and was buried the 19th of the same month in Westminster Abbey, in the aisle where many of our English poets are interred, over against Chaucer; his body being attended by a select number of his friends, and the Dean and choir officiating at his funeral.   *Dr. Welwood's Life of Rowe.*

Rowe frequented, among others, the Cocoa Tree Tavern, No. 64 St. James's Street.

The anecdotes connected with the Cocoa Tree when it was really the 'Wits' Coffee House' would fill a volume. One of them may be quoted here. Dr. Garth, who used often to appear there, was sitting one morning in the coffee-room, conversing with two persons of 'quality,' when the poet Rowe, who was seldom very attentive   *Old and New London, vol. iv. chap. xiii.*
to his dress and appearance, though fond of being noticed by great people, entered the door. Placing himself in a box nearly opposite to that in which the Doctor sat, Rowe looked constantly round with a view to catch his eye; but not succeeding, he desired the waiter to ask him for the loan of his snuff-box, which he knew to be a valuable one, set with diamonds, and the gift of royalty. After taking a pinch he returned it, but again asked for it so repeatedly that Garth, who knew him well, and saw through his purpose, took out a pencil and wrote on the lid two Greek characters, Φ and P, — 'Fie! Rowe!' The poet's vanity was mortified, and he left the house.

RICHARD SAVAGE.

1696-97–1743.

RICHARD SAVAGE was born in Fox Court, Holborn, January 16, 1696–97, and was baptized on the 18th of the same month by the rector of St. Andrew's Church, Holborn, as Richard Smith.

Such was the beginning of the life of Richard Savage. Born with a legal claim to honor and to affluence, he was in two months illegitimated by the parliament, and disowned by his mother, doomed to poverty and obscurity, and launched upon the ocean of life only that he might be swallowed by its quicksands or dashed upon its rocks.

<small>Johnson's Lives of the Poets: Savage.</small>

In 1885 the west end of Fox Court near Gray's Inn Road was torn down; but nearer Brooke Street were still standing many miserable, wretched tenements, two centuries old, in any one of which the cruel mother might have given life to her unhappy son.

The site of the shoemaker's stall in Holborn, where Savage worked as a youth, is unknown, nor is there any record as to where he lodged or lived.

Savage first met Johnson at Cave's, in St. John's Gate (see JOHNSON, p. 157); and a favorite tavern of his was the Cross Keys, in that neighborhood. It stood on the east side of St. John's Street, opposite the entrance of St. John's Lane, and facing the Gate. A modern Cross Keys Inn at Nos. 16 and 18 St. John's Street has been erected on its site. He frequented the Crown in King Street, Cheapside, which has disappeared, and in 1727 he went to Button's (see ADDISON, p. 6) to receive the seventy guineas which were subscribed by a number of gentlemen for his relief from distress. He is then believed to have been lodging somewhere in Westminster.

Of 'Robinson's Coffee House, near Charing Cross,' in which occurred the unfortunate broil which brought great subsequent trouble to Savage, there is no trace now. Johnson gives the following account of the affair:—

Merchant, with some rudeness, demanded a room, and was told that there was a good fire in the next parlor, which the company were about to leave, being then paying their reckoning. Merchant, not satisfied with this answer, rushed into the room and was followed by his companions. He then petulantly placed himself between the company and the fire, and soon afterwards kicked down the table. This produced a quarrel; swords were drawn on both sides, and one, Mr. James Sinclair, was killed. Savage, having likewise wounded a maid that held him, forced his way with Merchant out of the house.

They were committed to the Gate House at Westminster (see BURKE, p. 27), and afterwards to Newgate, and were tried at the Old Bailey. Savage was sentenced to death, but subsequently pardoned. What became of the petulant Mr. Merchant, who was convicted of manslaughter only, is not known.

Savage was familiar with all the disreputable taverns of his day, and was to be seen, too, in some of the more refined resorts. One of his experiences with Steele is thus described: —

Almost adjoining and to the east of Apsley House, formerly, stood a noted inn, the Pillars of Hercules.... The space between the Pillars of Hercules and Hamilton Place [Hyde Park Corner] was formerly occupied by a row of mean houses, one of which was a public house called the Triumphant Chariot. This was in all probability the 'petty tavern' to which the unfortunate Richard Savage was conducted by Sir Richard Steele, on the occasion of their being closeted together for a whole day composing a hurried pamphlet which they had to sell for two guineas before they could pay for their dinner.

Jesse's London, vol. i.: Piccadilly.

SIR WALTER SCOTT.

1771–1832.

SCOTT, on one of his earliest visits to London, in 1803, wrote to Ballantyne from '15 Piccadilly, West,' the house of Charles Dumergues, surgeon dentist to the Royal Family.

> *Lockhart's Life of Scott.* I should not omit to say that Scott was attended on this trip by a fine bull terrier named Camp.

Piccadilly has been renumbered. The Dumergues lived in the house afterwards No. 96 Piccadilly, corner of Whitehorse Street, which was unchanged in 1885;[16] and this was Scott's usual abiding-place in town until his daughter Mrs. Lockhart had a house of her own at No. 24 Sussex Place, fronting Regent's Park, between Hanover Gate and Clarence Gate, to which to invite him.

During the sojourn [in London] of 1809 the homage paid Scott would have turned the head of any less gifted man of eminence. It neither altered his opinions nor produced the affectation of despising it; on the contrary, he received it, cultivated it, and repaid it in his own coin. 'All this is very flattering,' he would say, 'and very civil; and if people are amused with hearing me tell a parcel of old stories, or recite a pack of ballads to lovely young girls and gaping matrons, they are easily pleased, and a man would be very ill-natured who would not give pleasure so cheaply conferred.'

Lockhart's Scott, vol. i. chap. xix.

In 1826 Scott was lodging at No. 25 Pall Mall, when he wrote in his Diary: —

> *Oct. 17.* — Here I am in this capital once more, after an April meeting with my daughter and Lockhart. Too much grief in our first meeting to be joyful, too much pleasure to be distressing; a giddy sensation between the painful and the pleasurable. . . . *Oct. 23.* — Sam Rogers and Moore breakfasted here, and we were very merry fellows.

Lockhart's Scott, vol. ii. chap. xxxvi.

This house, on the north side of Pall Mall, between John Street and Waterloo Place, has been rebuilt.

Scott, in his occasional visits to London, was to be found in all the best houses and in the most enjoyable society. He breakfasted with Rogers in St. James's Place (see ROGERS, p. 258), frequented the shop of Mr. Murray, No. 50

A, Albemarle Street, where he first met Byron, in 1815 (see BYRON, p. 34), and was welcome at the clubs.

During the later years of his life he stopped at the Waterloo Hotel, Nos. 85 and 86 Jermyn Street; at Long's, No. 16 New Bond Street, where he had his last meeting with Byron (see BYRON, p. 34), both unchanged in 1885;[5] and at the St. James Hotel, No. 76 Jermyn Street, on the south side between Bury and Duke Streets, since a Turkish Bath Establishment, from whence in 1832 he was taken to Abbotsford to die.

When I saw Sir Walter [Dr. Ferguson writes], he was lying in the second-floor back room of the St. James Hotel in Jermyn Street, in a state of stupor from which, however, he could be roused for a moment by being addressed.... I think I never saw anything more magnificent than the symmetry of his colossal bust, as he lay on the pillow with his chest and neck exposed.... At length his constant yearning to return to Abbotsford induced his physicians to consent to his removal; and the moment this was notified to him it seemed to infuse new vigor into his frame. *Lockhart's Scott, vol. ii. chap. xlvii.*

The St. James Hotel, No. 76 [Jermyn Street], on the south side, was the last London lodging of Sir Walter Scott. Here he lay for a period of three weeks after his return from the Continent, either in absolute stupor or in a waking dream. The room he occupied was the second-floor back room; and the author of this collection of London memoranda delights in remembering the universal feeling of sympathy exhibited by all (and there were many) who stood to see the great novelist and poet carried from the hotel to his carriage on the afternoon of the 7th of July, 1832. Many were eager to see so great a man; but all mere curiosity seemed to cease when they saw the vacant eye and prostrate figure of the illustrious poet. There was not a covered head, and the writer believes — from what he could see — hardly a dry eye, on the occasion. *Cunningham's Handbook of London: Jermyn Street.*

THOMAS SHADWELL

Circa 1640-1692.

LITTLE more is known of the London life of William the Third's Poet Laureate than that he was a member of the Middle Temple, lived at one time in Salisbury Court, now Salisbury Square, Fleet Street (see RICHARDSON, p. 253), and in Church Lane, afterwards Church Street, Chelsea, where he died. He was buried in St. Luke's Church, Chelsea; but no tablet records the fact, and his grave is unknown.

Mr. Shadwell died the 19th December, 1692, in the fifty-second year of his age, as we are informed by the inscription upon his monument at Westminster Abbey, although there may be some mistake in that date, for it is said in the titlepage of his funeral sermon, preached by Dr. Nicholas Bray, that he was interred in Chelsea on the 24th November of that year.

<small>Cibber's Lives of the Poets, vol. iii.; Shadwell.</small>

WILLIAM SHAKSPERE.

1564-1616.

SHAKSPERE left Stratford-on-Avon for London about 1585, when, according to tradition, he became connected in some way with one of the then existing theatres, *perhaps* holding the horses of the gentlemen who patronized the Red Bull, in Red Bull Yard, now Woodbridge Street, St. John's Street, Clerkenwell (see DAVENANT, p. 75). He was, however, more likely a player at the Blackfriars House, which was built in 1576, upon the ground now called Play House Yard, Ludgate Hill, and the site of which, according to Doran, 'is occupied by Apothecaries' Hall [No. 84 Water Lane, between Carter Lane and Play House Yard] and some adjacent buildings.' The theatre was restored twenty years later, when Shakspere and Burbage were interested in its management, but was destroyed during the Commonwealth and never rebuilt.

That Shakspere was afterwards a householder in the neighborhood of the Blackfriars Theatre, there is no question. In the Guildhall Library is preserved the original deed of conveyance of a house bought by him and described as ' abutting upon a streete leading down to Puddle Wharffe on the east part right against the King's Maiesty's Wardrobe.' This property in his will he bequeathed and devised unto his daughter Susannah Hall. Major James Walter, in his 'Shakspere's Home and Rural Life' (page 70), says: ' A house is [1874], or was till lately, pointed out near St. Andrew's Church as having been that which belonged to Shakspere; but this is only a matter of popular tradition.'

The Church of St. Andrew-by-the-Wardrobe, built by Wren after the Great Fire, and, of course, of later date than Shakspere's time, stood in 1885 in the modern Queen Victoria Street, between St. Andrew's Hill and Wardrobe Terrace.

Wardrobe Place, Church Entry, Ireland Yard, and Play House Yard still perpetuate the memory of this part of Blackfriars as it was in Shakspere's day; but everything else is changed. In 1885, around the wretched and forsaken burial-place, which is all that is left of St. Anne's Church, Carter Lane, — destroyed in the Great Fire, and never rebuilt, — was a fragment of stone wall, probably the only stones left standing in that parish which Shakspere may have seen.

Ireland Yard is believed to have been so called from the William Ireland mentioned in this deed of Shakspere's house as 'being now or later in the tenure or occupation of it.'

Shakspere, early in his London career, was associated with the Globe Theatre on the Bankside, which was built in 1594, and was under the management of the same company as the Blackfriars, but on the other side of the Thames and not far from the southern end of Old London Bridge. It was used as a sort of suburban or summer theatre until it was destroyed by fire in 1613. Maps and plans of Old London show it to have stood in the yard of the Globe Tavern, which was approached by Globe Alley, an offshoot of Maid Lane, afterwards New Park Street. Its exact site seems to have been in the establishment of the famous Brewery of Barclay and Perkins, and directly behind the houses which in 1885 were numbered 13, 15, and 17 Southwark Bridge Road, standing on the east side of that thoroughfare, nearly opposite Sumner Street. Globe Alley, Deadman's Place, and a number of other streets and lanes often trod by Shakspere have been entirely demolished in the frequent extensions of the premises of the great firm of brewers (see JOHNSON, p. 163).

Knight, in his 'London,' says that Shakspere lived as late as 1609 in the street since known as Clink Street, Southwark. In 1885 it extended from St. Mary Overy's Wharf to Bankend and the railway-crossing. Malone believes his Southwark abiding-place to have been 'near the Bear Gardens in the liberty of the Bishop of Winchester,' just west of Winchester Park, the site of which is now marked by Winchester Street and Winchester Yard. The Bear Gardens in 1885 was a short street running from No. 27 Bankside to No. 58 Park Street, between the Southwark Bridge Crossing and Emerson Street. This was on the exact site of the Bear Gardens existing during the reigns of the Tudors and the Stuarts, as is shown by comparison with old maps and plans of Southwark. It is composed of modern buildings, and its character is entirely changed. It contained in 1885 a White Bear Inn.

As for the baiting of bulls and bears, they are to this day much frequented, namely, in Bear Gardens on the Bankside, wherein be prepared scaffolds for beholders to stand upon. . . . Now to return to the west bank there be two bear gardens, the old and new places, wherein be kept bears, bulls and other beasts to be baited, as also mastiffs, in several kenels, nourished to bait them. These bears and other beasts are then baited in plots of ground, scaffolded about for the beholder to stand safe. Stow's Survey of London, Edition of 1603.

Slender. Why do your dogs bark so? Be there bears i' the town?
Anne. I think there are, sir; I heard them talked of.
Slender. I love the sport well, but I shall as soon quarrel at it as any man in England. You are afraid if you see the bear loose, are you not? Merry Wives of Windsor, act i. scene 1.
Anne. Ay, indeed, sir.
Slender. That's meat and drink to me now.

Clifford. Are these thy bears? We'll bait thy bears to death,
And manacle the bear-ward in their chains,
If thou dar'st bring them to the baiting-place. 2 Henry VI., act v. scene 1.
Richmond. Oft have I seen a hot o'erweening cur
Run back and bite because he was withheld,
Who, being suffer'd with the bear's fell paw,
Hath clapp'd his tail between his legs, and cried.

Edmond Shakspere, a brother of the bard, and an actor at the Globe, shared, perhaps, his Bankside home. The Parochial Monthly Accounts of St. Saviour's, Southwark (see FLETCHER, p. 107), still preserved, contain in the proper place the following entry: '1607. December 31st; Edmond Shakspere, a player, buried in the church, with a forenoone knell of the great bell.' His grave is unknown, although a few years ago, upon a stone in the pavement of the choir of the old church, were engraven his name and the date of his death.

The connection of William Shakspere with Southwark is one of the most unquestionable facts in his biography. His brother, as we have seen, was buried in the church. His theatre was the 'Gloabe upon Banckside.' Close to it, but rather more to the westward, was the Rose, another theatre. A little further in the same direction was two 'pitts' for bear-baiting and bull-baiting; and the locality is still [1883], or was very lately, known as the Bear Gardens, and is so marked on many maps. Another old name still extant is that of the Falcon Dock, close to which stood the Falcon Tavern, which is said to have been patronized by Shakspere and his company. Paris Garden was exactly on the spot now covered by the southern approaches of Blackfriars Bridge. If the modern visitor, therefore, wishes to identify the place where Shakspere played, he cannot do better than take the train from Charing Cross to Cannon Street, and when he has crossed the line of the Chatham and Dover Railway, he is in the classical region of Bankside. Looking towards the river he will see St. Peter's Church, immediately beyond which, a little to the right, were the bull and bear pits. The train then crosses the Southwark Bridge Road, on the right-hand side of which, looking from the railway, is Barclay and Perkins' Brewery. It covers the site not only of the Globe, but also of the Rose, the Hope, and various other places of a similar kind, which existed here from before Shakspere's time until all theatres were abolished by the Commonwealth.

Loftie's History of London, vol. i. chap. x.

In 1598 one William Shakspere was assessed five pounds on a house in the parish of St. Helen's, Bishopsgate Street, which he is believed to have occupied himself. There is no certainty that this was *the* Shakspere, although he was unquestionably familiar with that neighborhood, and with the adjacent Crosby Hall, the most important house in the parish, which has carefully been restored and is an interesting specimen of the domestic architecture of the fifteenth

century (see MORE, p. 223). It figures in Shakspere's
'Richard III.' as Crosby Place : ' At Crosby Place, then,
shall you find us both.' In Shakspere's day it was occupied by the mother of his friend Pembroke, who, as the
subject of all verse, is not unlikely to have entertained
there the applause, delight, the wonder of our stage, the
soul of the age in which she lived (see SYDNEY).

Then have you one great house called Crosby Place, because the same was built by Sir John Crosby, grocer and woolman. . . . The house he built of stone and timber, very large and beautiful and the highest at that time in London [1466]. . . . Richard, Duke of Gloucester, and Lord Protector, afterwards King, by the name of Richard III., was lodged in this house. . . . From this Crosby Place up to Leaden Hall Corner, and so down Grass Street, amongst other tenements are divers fair and large built houses for merchants and such like. <small>Stow's Survey of London, Edition of 1598.</small>

Crosby Place, or Hall, the Church of St. Saviour, where
it is to be supposed, naturally, that he was present at the
burial of his brother; and Middle Temple Hall, where
'Twelfth Night' is known to have been produced in 1601,
when Shakspere was probably an on-looker or director, —
are the only buildings still standing in London which are
in any way — and even these only by inference — associated with him.

Venerable Hall of the Middle Temple, thou art to our eyes more stately and more to be admired since we looked upon that entry upon the Table Book of John Manningham! The Globe has perished, and so has the Blackfriars. The works of the poet who made the names of these frail buildings immortal need no association to recommend them, but it is yet pleasant to know that there is one locality remaining where a play of Shakspere's was listened to by his contemporaries, and that play 'Twelfth Night.' <small>Preface to Knight's Pictorial Edition of Shakspere.</small>

Feb. 1601. — At our feast we had a play called 'Twelfth Night, or What you will,' much like the 'Comedy of Errors,' or 'Menechmi' in Plautus but most like and neere to that in Italian called 'Ingannii.' A good practise in it to make the steward believe his lady-widdowe was in love with him by counterfayting a letter as from his lady, in generall termes telling him what shee liked best in him and prescribing his gestures inscribing his apparaile, &c. and then when he came to practise, making him believe they tooke him to be mad.

<small>Templar's Diary, Harlein MS. British Museum.</small>

During his London life Shakspere is believed to have been a frequenter of the Mermaid Tavern, which stood on the south side of Cheapside, between Bread and Friday Streets, and where he is said to have had his conflicts of wit with Ben Jonson (see JONSON, p. 176); and tradition associates his name with the Falcon Tavern, taken down in 1808. Its site, until lately, was occupied by the Falcon Glass Works at the end of Holland Street, Southwark, opposite the Falcon Drawing Dock; and its name still lives in Falcon Docks and Falcon Wharf, Nos. 79 and 80 Bankside. Another tavern certainly known to Shakspere was the Boar's Head, in Eastcheap, the site of which is marked by the statue of William IV. (see GOLDSMITH, p. 125). It was a favorite tavern of Falstaff and Prince Hal. He also speaks of the White Hart Inn (White Hart Inn Yard, No. 61 Borough High Street in 1885): —

<small>2 Henry VI., act iv. scene 8.</small> Hath my sword therefore broke through London Gates, that you should leave me at the White Hart in Southwark?

The only letter in existence addressed to Shakspere is now preserved at Stratford-upon-Avon. It was directed by Richard Quyney 'To my loveing good Ffriend and Countryman, Mr. Wm Shackespere, deliver these,' and was written from the Bell Inn, Bell Inn Yard, Carter Lane, St.

Paul's Churchyard, — a hostelry without doubt well known to Shakspere himself. A comparatively modern Bell Inn, its direct descendant, stood upon its site in 1885.

PERCY BYSSHE SHELLEY.

1792-1822.

SHELLEY saw but little of London, which was the place neither of his birth nor of his death. He is known to have lived in a hotel in Dover Street, Piccadilly, where one of his children was born;[17] to have lodged at one time at No. 90 Great Russell Street (facing the present Bury Street, — the southeast wing of the British Museum was built on the site of this house); at one time on the corner of Hastings Street and Marbledown Place, Burton Crescent, Euston Road; and at No. 41 Hans Place, Sloane Street, in a house which has been raised two stories and renewed. Later he lived at No. 23 Chapel Street, South Audley Street, in a house also enlarged; and in 1817 he was an inmate of Hunt's Cottage at Hampstead (see HUNT, p. 148), when Keats was their neighbor.

Leigh Hunt was editing the 'Examiner,' and in spite of his two years' imprisonment was still liberal to the backbone. For Shelley was with him, talking wild radicalism at Hampstead, or discussing the destinies as the two friends rode into town on the stage. <small>Blanchard Jerrold's Life of Douglas Jerrold, chap. iii.</small>

Shelley was married to Mary Wollstonecraft Godwin, December 13, 1816, in St. Mildred's Church, Bread Street, corner of Cannon Street; and he wooed and won his bride in Old St. Pancras Churchyard, now St. Pancras Gardens, Old St. Pancras Road, Kentish Town, then a quiet peaceful spot, where by her mother's grave (see GODWIN, p. 118) Mary was fond of sitting with her book or her work. Of this marriage Godwin wrote:—

The piece of news, however, I have to tell you, is that I went to church with this same tall girl some little time ago to be married. Her husband is the eldest son of Sir Timothy Shelley, of Field Place, in the County of Sussex, Baronet ; so that, according to the vulgar ideas of the world, she is well married, and I have great hopes the young man will make her a good husband.

<small>William Godwin, his Friends and Contemporaries, vol. ii. chap. ix.</small>

WILLIAM SHENSTONE.

1714–1763.

SHENSTONE, at one time, lodged in Jermyn Street; and in 1740 dated his letters from 'the house of Mr. Wintle, Perfumer, near Temple Bar,' probably in Butcher Row (see LEE, p. 196).

The greater part of his life was spent in Shropshire; his occasional resting-place in town being the George Coffee House, afterwards numbered 213 Strand, near Essex Street, upon the site of which a modern tavern bearing the same name has been erected (see MURPHY, p. 227). It was at this inn that his 'warmest welcome' was found. In one of his letters he says:—

What do you think must be my expense, who love to pry into everything of the kind? Why, truly, one shilling. My company goes to George's Coffee House, where for that small subscription I read all pamphlets under a three-shilling dimension.

RICHARD BRINSLEY SHERIDAN.

1751-1816.

WHEN Sheridan and Miss Linley fled to London, they took refuge in the house of an oilman, at the Holborn end of Featherstone Buildings. The proprietor was the godfather of Charles Lamb, who relates in the Essay 'My First Play,' how his father and mother were playing quadrille when Sheridan arrived that evening 'with his harmonious charge.' Featherstone Buildings, little changed in 1885, was opposite the Great Turnstile.

Sheridan's first duel with Mathews, interrupted at Hyde Park, near the Hercules' Pillars, an inn just east of the present Apsley House (see SAVAGE, p. 261), was followed by a second at the Castle Tavern in Henrietta Street, Covent Garden, of which no trace remains now.

Sheridan was entered a student at the Middle Temple in 1772. In 1773 he and his wife were living in Orchard Street, Portman Square, where he wrote 'The Rivals,' produced in January, 1775, and 'The Duenna,' brought out in November of the same year. Of his home life almost nothing is known; and it is only from his own letters and from those addressed to him, that any hint is found as to his divers places of abode in London.

In 1778 his address was Great Queen Street, Lincoln's Inn Fields; in 1792, Lower Grosvenor Street, New Bond Street; in 1793, No. 10 Hertford Street, Mayfair; in 1804, Somerset Place, Portman Square; in 1810, Queen Street, Mayfair. He died in 1816 at No. 14 Savile Row, Burlington Gardens, in the house marked by the tablet of the Society of Arts; and he is supposed to have lived for a short time at No. 17 Saville Row, where half a century later was carefully kept a cast of his hand, with the inscription, —

'Good at a fight, better at a play,
Godlike in giving; but the Devil to pay.'

Sheridan's ghost is believed to haunt a certain upper back room in this house; and during its occupancy by the Saville Club, the scratching of his pen, it is said, was often heard in the silence of the early morning hours.

He was buried from the house of his friend Mr. Peter Moore, in Great George Street, Westminster, 'in the only spot that remained unoccupied in Poets' Corner.'

In 1815 Sheridan was arrested for debt and taken to a 'lock-up house' in Took's Court, Cursitor Street, Chancery Lane.

February 7.— Fox never wrote his speeches, was fond of preparing them in travelling, as he said a post-chaise was the best place to arrange his thoughts in. Sheridan wrote and prepared a great deal, and generally in bed, with his books, pen, and ink on the bed, where he would lie all day.

<small>Greville Memoirs, 1836.</small>

Sheridan's clubs were Brook's, — still at No. 60 St. James's Street in 1885, — and the Eccentric, which met first in a tavern in Chandos Street, Covent Garden, then at the Crown in Vinegar Yard, Drury Lane, — taken down some years ago, — and later at Tom Rees's, in May's Buildings, where it flourished as late as the middle of the nineteenth century. May's Buildings is a short street connecting St. Martin's Lane with Bedfordbury.

Immediately after the brilliant success of 'The Rivals,' Sheridan was proposed by Dr. Johnson himself, and elected, a member of The Club (see GOLDSMITH, p. 123).

He was a frequenter of the Bedford Coffee House, in the Piazza, Covent Garden (see CHURCHILL, p. 51); the One Tun Tavern, in St. James's Market, Jermyn Street, near the Haymarket, and long since taken down; and, according to

Moore's Diary, he was in the habit of stopping at the Adam and Eve, opposite Holland House, where he left his bills to be paid by Lord Holland.

The Adam and Eve has disappeared; but a very new structure in the same line of business, and bearing the old name, was erected on its site, in Kensington Road, near Shaftesbury House, and opposite Argyll Road.

Sheridan occasionally pledged his valuables at the shop of one Harrison, a pawnbroker at No. 95 Wardour Street, renumbered 143 Wardour Street, on the corner of Edward Street, where, in the same old house, the business was still carried on under the same name in 1885.

JAMES SHIRLEY.

1594-1666.

JAMES SHIRLEY, according to Anthony Wood, 'was born in, or near, the parish of St. Mary Woolchurch, where the stocks market now [1690] is.' This church, which stood on the site of the Mansion House, was destroyed in the Great Fire and never rebuilt. Shirley was educated at the Merchant Taylors' School, which stood on the east side of Suffolk Lane, Upper Thames Street, but was taken down when the school was removed to the Charter House in 1872.

He was a member of the Society of Gray's Inn, and lived for some time in Gray's Inn Lane, where he wrote the earliest of his dramatic works. During a portion of the Commonwealth he was a school-teacher somewhere in Whitefriars, and was living in Fleet Street near the Inner Temple Gate at the close of his life.

Shirley's house in Fleet Street having been burnt to the ground in the Great Fire of 1666, he was compelled to seek refuge in the neighboring village of St. Giles-in-the-Fields, whither, however, he retired only to die. As has been already mentioned, the loss of his property, added, probably, to the horrors of the terrible conflagration which he had witnessed, gave such a shock to his constitution that he survived the event scarcely twenty-four hours.

<small>Jesse's London, vol. iii.: Gray's Inn.</small>

Shirley and his wife, who died within a few hours of each other, were buried in one grave in the yard of the Church of St. Giles-in-the-Fields (see MARVELL, p. 208).

PHILIP SIDNEY.

1554–1587-8.

SIDNEY was not a native of London, although his father and grandfather lived in Threadneedle Street, where, no doubt, a portion of his own youth was spent. He has left but few traces of his life in town, except in court circles. He was a member of Gray's Inn, and is naturally believed to have been a frequent visitor at Crosby Place in Bishopsgate Street (see SHAKSPERE, p. 269); when it was the residence of 'Sidney's sister, Pembroke's mother,' to whom his 'Arcadia' was dedicated, and by whom, after his death, it was published.

Sidney was buried in Old St. Paul's Cathedral with no little pomp, his body having previously lain in state in the Minories after its arrival from the field of Zutphen, where his death-wound was received. The wooden monument erected to his memory was of course destroyed, with the cathedral, in the Great Fire.

The great Sir Philip Sidney, who was publicly buried at St. Paul's Cathedral in 1587, was a brother of the Grocers' Company, and was attended by that livery in all their formalities, who were preceded by the Lord Mayor, Aldermen, and Sheriffs 'rydinge in purple.'

<small>Nichols's Progress of Queen Elizabeth, vol. ii.</small>

The Grocers' Hall, damaged in the Great Fire, and afterwards restored, stood in 1885, as it stood in Sidney's day, at the end of Grocers' Hall Court, opposite No. 11 Poultry.

JAMES SMITH.

1775–1839.

HORACE SMITH.

1779–1849.

JAMES and Horace Smith were born at No. 36 Basinghall Street, London Wall, in one of the three or four old-fashioned houses still left in that old-fashioned street in 1885. It stood in a small court on the east side.

James Smith lived for some time at No. 18 Austin Friars, in a house at the end of the lane, also unaltered in 1885.

A second James Smith, coming to the place [Austin Friars] after he had been many years a resident there, produced so much confusion to both that the last comer waited on the author and suggested, to prevent further inconvenience, that one or other had better leave, hinting at the same time that he should like to stay. 'No,' said the wit, 'I am James the First! You are James the Second; you must abdicate.'

<small>Cunningham's Handbook of London: Austin Friars.</small>

He spent the last years of his life at No. 27 Craven Street, Strand, afterwards a private hotel, where he died. He was buried in the neighboring Church of St. Martin-in-the-Fields.

For some years before his death he [James Smith] suffered a good deal from gout; but while hobbling on his crutches, or being wheeled about in his bath-chair, he retained an almost youthful buoyancy of mind, referring with glee to the merry meetings of former times, indulging in his pleasant modes of jest and anecdotes, or singing with his nieces from morning to night. He died on the 24th of December, 1839, in his house in Craven Street, as he lived, a merry bachelor, 'with all the calmness of a philosopher,' we are told, but of what school we are left in ignorance. Peace, however, to the ashes of James Smith, which are deposited in the vault of St. Martin's Church.

Memoirs of the Countess of Blessington, vol. ii. chap. xiv.

James Smith was a member of the Athenæum Club on Pall Mall, the Union Club at the southwest corner of Trafalgar Square, and the Garrick, which, in his day, stood at No. 35 King Street, Covent Garden, but which in 1864 was removed to No. 15 Garrick Street, Long Acre (see THACKERAY).

Horace Smith was a member of the London Stock Exchange. Making a moderate fortune there, he retired to Tunbridge Wells, where he died, and was buried, in 1849.

SYDNEY SMITH.

1771-1845.

SYDNEY SMITH, who was born at Woodford in Essex, a few miles from London, established himself in 1804 at No. 8 Doughty Street, Mecklenburgh Square, a house unchanged eighty years later (see DICKENS, p. 82), and about the same time was appointed evening preacher to the Foundling Hospital, where his salary was fifty pounds a year. Two years afterwards he removed to No. 18 Orchard Street, Portman Square, — a two-storied red brick house, still standing in 1885.

In this house his means were slightly increased, yet he still remained poor. . . . But the pleasantest society at his house was to be found in the little suppers which he established once a week; giving a general invitation to about twenty or thirty persons, who used to come as they pleased. . . . At these suppers there was no attempt at display, nothing to tempt the palate; but they were most eagerly sought after, and were I to begin enumerating the guests usually to be found there, no one would wonder that they were so. Lady Holland's Memoirs of Rev. Sydney Smith, vol. iv.

Here he remained until he left London for Yorkshire in 1809.

In 1831 he was appointed to a prebendal stall in St. Paul's Cathedral, and writing to a friend he says: —

I have just taken possession of my preferment. The house is in Amen Corner, — an awkward name on a card, and an awkward annunciation to the coachman on leaving any fashionable mansion. I find too (sweet discovery!) that I give a dinner, every Sunday for three months in the year, to six clergymen and six singing-men, at one o'clock. Letters and Correspondence of Rev. Sydney Smith, 1831.

The residences of the Dean and Canons of St. Paul's are still in Amen Court, Amen Corner, Paternoster Row.

During Sydney Smith's many visits to London he stayed at Holland House (see ADDISON, p. 3); in Hertford Street, Mayfair; at No. 20 Savile Row, Burlington Gardens; at No. 18 Stratford Place, Oxford Street (unchanged in 1885); in Weymouth Street, Portland Place; etc. Between the years 1834 and 1839 he occupied the house No. 33 Charles Street, Berkeley Square, next to the corner of Queen Street, when he removed to No. 56 Green Street, Grosvenor Square (No. 59 in 1885), and to this house in 1845 he was brought from Combe-Florey to die.

He was buried by his own desire, as quietly as possible, in Kensal Green ; and his wife and son lie there by his side.

Those who wish to make a pilgrimage to the grave of Sydney Smith will be glad to know that they can easily find it by following the north walk until they are opposite the entrance to the Catacombs. Turning to the left at that point, they will discover, in the fifth row from the walk, a raised tomb of Portland stone. . . . With the solitary exception of a small painted window in the church at Combe-Florey, the grave in Kensal Green is the only memorial to Sydney Smith which England has to show.

<small>Stuart J. Reid's Life of Sydney Smith (1884), chap. xiv.</small>

Smith was a member of the King of Clubs, founded by his brother, which met at the Crown and Anchor in the Strand (see ROGERS, p. 258); and of The Club (see GOLDSMITH, p. 123, and JOHNSON, p. 167), to which he was elected in 1838.

TOBIAS SMOLLETT.

1721-1771.

SMOLLETT came first to London in 1739, and describes his journey hither in 'Roderick Random,' a novel which is believed to be in a great measure autobiographical. His first settled home was in Downing Street, where in 1744 he was practising, or seeking to practise, as a surgeon. In 1746 he was in humble lodgings in Curzon

Street, Mayfair; and in 1747 he married and took a more pretentious house, where he lived beyond his means, and wrote 'Roderick Random,' published by Osbourne in Gray's Inn Lane, in 1748. In 1750 he went to Chelsea, where he lived until he left England never to return.

His Chelsea home, called Monmouth House, stood at the end of Lawrence Street, at the junction of Upper Cheyne Row, — a large double house, still remembered in the parish, and taken down only a few years ago. His life here is described by himself in 'Humphrey Clinker,' in a letter of Jerry Mulford: —

Dick Ivy carried me to dine with S—— [Smollett], whom you and I have long known by his writings. He lives in the skirts of the town; and every Sunday his house is open to all unfortunate brothers of the quill, whom he treats with beef, pudding, and potatoes, port, punch, and Calvert's entire butt-beer. . . . I was civilly received in a plain yet decent habitation, which opened backwards into a very pleasant garden, kept in excellent order; and indeed I saw none of the outward signs of authorship, either in the house or the landlord, who is one of those few writers of the age that stand upon their own foundation, without patronage and above dependence. If there was nothing characteristic in the entertainer, the company made ample amends for his want of singularity. At two o'clock I found myself one of ten messmates at a table; and I question if the whole kingdom could produce such another assemblage of originals. . . . After dinner we adjourned into the garden, where I observed Mr. S—— gave a short, separate audience to every individual, in a small remote filbert walk, from whence most of them dropped off, one after another, without further ceremony; but they were replaced by other recruits of the same class, who came to make an afternoon's visit.

Monmouth House was the original Lawrence Manor House. Its gardens have entirely disappeared; the playgrounds of the new Board School covering their site.

From internal evidences, and from the dates of publication, 'Humphrey Clinker' and 'Sir Launcelot Greaves' were written in Chelsea. 'Peregrine Pickle' was 'Printed for the Author at Plato's Head, near Round Court, in the Strand, in 1751,' and was probably written in London.

Plato's Head was on the north side of the Strand, nearly opposite Buckingham Street. Round Court, which extended back to the present King William Street, disappeared in 1829, when the Strand Improvement Act was carried into effect.

Smollett frequented all the coffee-houses of his day, — Tom's, Will's, the Cocoa Tree, etc. (see ADDISON); but his favorite tavern was that to which his fellow-Scotchmen, in their clannish way, were wont to go, — the British Coffee House, in Cockspur Street (still standing in 1885), between Warwick Street and Spring Gardens.[10]

At Chelsea he was often to be found at Don Saltero's Coffee House, which stood at No. 18 Cheyne Walk, facing the river, and was kept as a public house as late as 1870. It is fully described by Steele in the 'Tatler' (see STEELE). In 1885 it was a private dwelling.

THOMAS SOUTHERNE.

1660–1746.

SOUTHERNE was a member of the Middle Temple in 1678, but he has left no traces of his life in London until his later years.

In William Oldys's Manuscript Notes to Langbaine is to be found the following description of Southerne: —

I remember him a grave and reserved old gentleman. He lived near Covent Garden, and used to frequent the evening prayers there [at St. Paul's Church], always neat and decently dressed, commonly in black, with his silver sword and silver locks; but latterly he seemed to reside in Westminster.

He [Southerne] was a perfect gentleman; he did not lounge away his days or nights in coffee-houses or taverns, but after labor cultivated friendship in home circles, where virtue and modest mirth sat at the hearth. .... He kept the even tenor of his way, owing no man anything; never allowing his nights to be the marrer of his mornings; and at six-and-eighty carrying a bright eye, a steady hand, a clear head, and a warm heart wherewith to calmly meet and make surrender of all to the Inevitable Angel.

<small>Doran's Annals of the Stage, vol. i. chap. x.</small>

Among the footnotes to an edition of Wood's 'Athenæ Oxonienses' published in the middle of the last century, is a letter from Southerne dated 'From Mr. Whyte's, Oylman in Tothil Fields, against Dartmouth Street, 1737.'

Southerne, the poet

'Tom sent down to raise
The price of prologues and of plays,'

lived for many years at Mr. Whyte's, an oilman's, in Tothill Street, against Dartmouth Street. The house is still [1850] an oilman's shop. On calling there in the year 1841, when the house was undergoing, as I thought, too effectual and radical a repair, Mr. Mucklow, the then tenant, informed me that his father had the business of a man named Girder, and Girder had the business of a man named Whyte. He knew nothing of Southerne, but had seen and admired Mrs. Siddons as Isabella in 'The Fatal Marriage.' The house had the date of 1671 upon it; and the balustraded balcony at the top was added when the repairs were made.

<small>Cunningham's Handbook of London: Tothill Street.</small>

Mr. Cunningham does not give the number of this house; but the address of Mr. Mucklow the oilman, in the London

Directory for 1840, was No. 4 Tothill Street. This building, by that strange fatality so frequently observed, has been taken down, while contemporary houses which have no literary associations remain. In 1885, No. 4, 'over against Dartmouth Street,' was the modern Cock Tavern, but in the front of it was still preserved the old stone, bearing date 1671.

Southerne died in Smith Street, Westminster, and was buried in the Church of St. Paul, Covent Garden, although at the present day the position of his grave is unknown (see BUTLER, p. 29). The old Church of St. Paul was destroyed by fire in 1795.

ROBERT SOUTHEY.

1774–1843.

SOUTHEY was sent to Westminster School (see CHURCHILL, p. 51) in March, 1788; but nothing of interest is recorded of his experiences there, except that he left in disgrace in 1792, because of an article he had written in a school magazine. In 1797 he entered Gray's Inn, his address being 'at Mr. Peacock's, at 20 Prospect Place, Newington Butts, near London.' Prospect Place has since been called Deacon Street, Walworth Road. The entire neighborhood has been renamed, renumbered, and rebuilt. He remained then, as in later years, but a short time in town, and he was rarely to be seen here. In November, 1823, he made a visit to the Lambs, at Colebrook Cottage, Islington (see LAMB, p. 191), and was always a welcome guest at the home of Murray the publisher, No. 50 A, Albemarle Street (see BYRON, p. 34), and at Rogers's house in No. 22 St.

James's Place, St. James's Street. He is also known to have enjoyed the society of Lamb and Coleridge in the humble rooms of the Salutation and Cat, No. 17 Newgate Street (see COLERIDGE, p. 60).

Southey's opinion of London, and of its effect upon him, is thus expressed in a letter written to a friend in 1806 :—.

London disorders me by over-stimulation. Company, to a certain extent, intoxicates me. I do not often commit the fault of talking too much, but very often say what would be better left unsaid, and that too in a manner not to be easily forgotten. . . . And so it is that the society of any except my friends, though it be sweet in the mouth, is bitter in the belly.

EDMUND SPENSER.
Circa 1553–1599.

VERY little can be gathered of Spenser's life in London, except the vague facts that he was born in East Smithfield, near Tower Hill; that he was educated at the Merchant Taylors' School, which then stood in Suffolk Lane, Upper Thames Street (see SHIRLEY, p. 275); that he was often at Essex House, formerly Exeter House, on the site of Devereux Court and Essex Street, Strand (see LOCKE, p. 197), and at Leicester House, which stood on the north side of Leicester Square, its gardens extending back to Lisle Street; and that, dying of a broken heart in King Street, Westminster (see PEPYS, p. 233), he was buried near Chaucer, in the Poets' Corner, receiving a monumental stone, when dead, from the men who are supposed to have neglected him living, and to have refused him the bread for which he asked.

It was distinctly in Spenser's poetical character that he received the honors of a funeral from Devereux, Earl of Essex. His hearse was attended by poets, and mournful elegies and poems, with the pens that wrote them, were thrown into his tomb. What a funeral was that at which Beaumont, Fletcher, Jonson, and in all probability Shakspere attended! what a grave, in which the pen of Shakspere may be mouldering away! In the original inscription, long ago effaced, the vicinity of Chaucer is expressly stated as the reason for the selection of the spot. . . . The inscription in pathos and simplicity is worthy of the author of the 'Faery Queen,' but curious as implying the unconsciousness of any greater than he at that very time to claim the title then given to him of the 'Prince of Poets.'

<small>Stanley's Westminster Abbey, chap. iv.</small>

Drummond, of Hawthornden, in his 'Conversations' with Ben Jonson, quotes the latter as giving the following account of Spenser's death:—

The Irish having robbed Spenser's goods and burnt his house and a little child new born, he and his wife escaped; and after he died for lack of bread in King Street, and refused twenty pieces sent him by the Earl of Essex, adding he had no time to spend them.

Drummond, the Father of Interviewers, is not always reliable in his reports of what his beloved, honored, and worthy friend said of Spenser or of others; and later historians are inclined to believe that Spenser's last days, although miserable enough, were not so utterly wretched as are here described. He certainly received immediate posthumous honors of no common kind.

RICHARD STEELE.

1671-1729.

STEELE, according to the baptismal register quoted by Henry R. Montgomery in his 'Memoir' (Edinburgh, 1865), was born in 1671, although nearly all earlier sketches of his career place the date as 1675 or 1676. He was sent to the Charter House in 1684, three years before Addison left that establishment for Oxford; and he himself did not enter the university until two years after his distinguished friend. The fact of this difference in their school course, and the strange fact that nowhere in the lives of either of them is any hint given of their association while in the university, would perhaps throw some doubts upon the truth of the picture so charmingly painted by Thackeray, of their devotion to each other while Charter House boys (see ADDISON, p. 1), particularly as Steele, though in a lower class, was Addison's senior in age by more than a year.

I am afraid no good report could be given by his masters and ushers of that thick-set, square-faced, black-eyed, soft-hearted little Irish boy. He was very idle. He was whipped deservedly a great number of times. . . . Besides being very kind, lazy, and good-natured, the boy went invariably into debt with the tart-woman; ran out of bounds, and entered into pecuniary or rather promissory engagements with the neighboring lollipop-venders and pie-men, exhibited an early fondness for drinking mum and sack, and borrowed from all his comrades who had money to lend. . . . Addison did his best themes. Addison wrote his exercises He ran on Addison's messages, fagged for him, and blacked his boots; to be in Joe's company was Dick's greatest pleasure, and he took a sermon or a caning from his monitor with the most boundless reverence, acquiescence, and affection. *Thackeray's English Humorists, Lecture the Third: Steele.*

Steele is said to have behaved to Addison in society with a marked deference, very uncommon and striking between old comrades, equal in age, and nearly so in all things excepting genius and conduct. In private, however, there can be little doubt that they associated together on terms of great familiarity and confidence, and were frequent depositaries of the literary projects of each other.

<small>Lucy Aikin's Life of Addison, chap. vii.</small>

Of Steele's life in London until the death of his first wife, and his marriage to the second in 1707, not much is known. To his dear Prue, however, he writes from Smith Street, Westminster, from Chelsea, and from many coffee-houses and taverns, of which more anon. In October, 1707, he took the house which was 'the last house but two on the left hand of Berry [or Bury] Street, St. James's,' or, as he addresses her later, 'at the third house, right hand turning out of Germain [Jermyn] Street.' Here they lived while in town until 1712, when they went to Bloomsbury Square. This Bury Street House, described by Peter Cunningham as standing 'over against No. 20,' was taken down in 1830.

They remained in Bloomsbury Square, 'in the prettiest house, to receive the prettiest woman, his own sweet Prue,' for three years. In 1715 he writes to her 'at her house over against Park Place, St. James's Street,' where three years later Lady Steele died. She was buried in the south transept of Westminster Abbey, near the Poets' Corner. It was while they were living in Park Place probably — for he was then described as Sir Richard Steele — that the execution for rent gave Steele the chance of displaying his coolness under difficulties as told by Johnson in his 'Life of Savage:' —

Sir Richard Steele one day having invited to his house a great number of persons of the first quality, they were surprised at the number of liveries which surrounded the table ; and after dinner, when wine and mirth had set them free from the observations of a rigid ceremony, one of them inquired of Sir Richard how such an expensive train of domestics could be consistent with his fortune. Sir Richard very frankly confessed that they were fellows of whom he would willingly be rid. And then, being asked why he did not discharge them, declared that they were bailiffs, who had introduced themselves with an execution, and whom, since he could not send them away, he had thought it convenient to embellish with liveries, that they might do him credit while they stayed.

Steele had numerous country-houses which he occupied for a shorter or longer period during the summer months. Soon after his second marriage he bought for his wife a pretty little cottage at Hampton Court, which he furnished handsomely, and which, by way of contrast to the Palace near by, he called the Hovel. In 1708 he wrote to his wife to join him 'at the house of Mrs. Hardresse, at the Square at Kensington, till all things be ready for your greater ease in town.' And in 1712 he retired to Haverstock Hill, it is supposed because of financial trouble. He is said to have composed many papers for the 'Spectator' here; and no doubt Pope and his other friends of the Kit Kat Club stopped for him here to carry him to the meetings of the society at the Upper Flask, in Hampstead (see ADDISON, p. 9).

Still descending Haverstock Hill, we arrive at the site of what was called Steele's Cottage. This cottage stood on the right-hand side of the road in a garden opposite to the public house called The Load of Hay, now [1869] modernized, and having much the air of a gin-palace. The cottage called Steele's Cottage, after Sir Richard Steele, was of late years divided into two dwellings, and had the name of Steele's Cottage painted on the front. . . . The long line of the new street called Adelaide Road bounded the open ground at the back, at no great distance. . . . The tenants informed me that they had notice to quit, and that in about another

<small>William Howitt's Northern Heights of London: Hampstead.</small>

year it would be swept away. This was verified in the spring of 1867, and Steele's Cottage now exists only in engravings.

The Load of Hay in 1885 was numbered 94 Haverstock Hill. 'Sir Richard Steele's Tavern,' No. 97 Haverstock Hill, and 'Steele's Studios,' in the same thoroughfare, perpetuate his name there.

Faulkner, in his 'Chelsea,' says: 'Steele appears from the parish books to have rented a house by the water-side at £14 per annum.' Its site is not known. In the register of Chelsea Church is recorded also the burial of one 'Margaret, daughter of Edward Seat, from Sir Richard Steele's, November 12, 1715.'

After Lady Steele's death he took a house 'in York Buildings,' Villiers Street, Strand; York Buildings being a general name for the streets and houses erected on the site of York House (see BACON, p. 12). Here he seems to have remained until he left London finally, in 1725. He died and was buried at Carmarthen, Wales, in 1729.

Not one of Steele's contemporaries was better acquainted than he with the coffee-houses and taverns of his day. Besides being a member of the Kit Kat Club, as has been shown, he frequented the Bull's Head Tavern, Clare Market, probably the tavern of that name at No. 40 Vere Street, on the east side, a few doors from Sheffield Street, and near Clare Market (it tumbled down from sheer old age in 1875 or 1876, and a Board School was built on its site); the King's Head, Pall Mall; the Devil Tavern, at Temple Bar (see JONSON, p. 175); the George, in Pall Mall, the site of which is now unknown; Dick's, No. 8 Fleet Street, in existence in 1885 (see COWPER, p. 67); the Fountaine, No. 103 Strand, marked by Fountain Court until the summer of 1884, when its name was changed to Savoy Buildings (see JOHNSON, p. 170); Lloyd's, at Abchurch Lane, corner of Lombard Street, and no longer standing; the

St. James's Coffee House (see ADDISON, p. 7) ; the Thatched House, St. James's Street (see MACAULAY, p. 204); Button's; and Will's, in Russell Street, Covent Garden (see ADDISON, pp. 6, 7) ; the Trumpet, in Shire Lane (see ADDISON, p. 8) ; the Grecian, in Devereux Court, Essex Street, Strand (see ADDISON, p. 7) ; the Hercules' Pillars and the Triumphant Chariot, both at Hyde Park Corner (see SAVAGE, p. 261) ; 'Don Saltero's,' at Chelsea (see SMOLLETT, p. 282); and the White Horse, at Chelsea.

Being of a very spare and hective constitution I am forced to make frequent journies of a mile or two for fresh Air. . . . When I came into the Coffee House I had no Time to salute the Company before my Eye was taken by ten thousand Gimcracks round the Room, and on the Ceiling. When my first astonishment was over comes to me a Sage of a thin and meagre Countenance ; which Aspect made me doubt whether Reading or Fretting made him so philosophick. But I very soon perceived him to be of that Sect which the Ancients called Ginquistæ ; in our Language Tooth-Drawers. I immediately had a Respect for the Man ; for these practical Philosophers go upon a very rational Hypothesis, not to cure but to take away the Part affected. My Love of Mankind made me very benevolent to Mr. Salter, for such is the Name of this Eminent Barber and Antiquary.

Steele in the 'Tatler,' No. 34.

Steele at Button's figures in the 'Original Jest Book' of Joe Miller, as one of the minor characters in a familiar tale localized many times since Steele's day : —

Two gentlemen disputing about religion in Button's Coffee House, said one of them, 'I wonder, sir, you should talk of religion when I 'll hold you five guineas you can't say the Lord's Prayer.' 'Done,' said the other ; 'and Sir Richard Steele shall hold the stakes.' The money being deposited, the gentleman began with 'I believe in God,' and so went cleverly through the Creed. 'Well,' said the other, 'I own I have lost. I did not think he could have done it.'

LAURENCE STERNE.

1713-1768.

STERNE saw but little of London, though he dearly loved the sensation he created, and the attention he received when he first arrived in town. In 1760 he lodged in Pall Mall, and, according to Dr. Johnson, had engagements for every day and night three months ahead. His stay on this occasion was of little more than the three months' duration, but he lived alone and in lodgings for some time during several subsequent seasons.

In the fragment of his life written by himself he gives no hint of his movements or mode of living here.

He died on the 18th of March, 1768, at No. 41 Old Bond Street, 'over the silk-bag shop.'

From the 'Travels in Various Parts of Europe, Asia, and Africa, by John Macdonald, 1790,' D'Israeli, in his 'Literary Miscellanies,' quotes the following story of Sterne's death. Macdonald was footman to a gentleman of quality.

'John,' said my master, 'go and inquire how Mr. Sterne is to-day.' . . . I went to Mr. Sterne's lodgings; the mistress opened the door. I inquired how he did; she told me to go up to the nurse. I went into the room, and he was just a dying. I waited ten minutes, and in five he said, 'Now it has come.' He put up his hands as if to stop a blow, and died in a minute.

The house No. 41 Old Bond Street, which was standing in 1885, was older than Sterne's day, and if not the actual house in which he died, it saw his body carried to the grave. Rev. W. J. Loftie, however, than whom there is no better authority in such matters, says — in his 'History of London' (1883), chap. xxi. note — that Sterne's house stood on the site of the shop of Agnew the picture-dealer, numbered, in 1885, 39 B, Old Bond Street.

Sterne was buried March 22.

And thus duly neglected by the whole crowd of boon companions, the remains of Yorick were consigned to the 'new burying ground near Tyburn,' of the parish of St. George's, Hanover Square. In that now squalid and long-decayed graveyard, within sight of the Marble Arch, and over against the broad expanse of Hyde Park, is still to be found a tombstone inscribed with some inferior lines to the memory of the departed humorist, and with a statement inaccurate by eight months of the date of his death, and a year as to his age. . . . But wherever the grave really was, the body interred in it, according to the strange story to which I have referred, is no longer there. That story goes that two days after the burial, on the night of the 24th March, the corpse was stolen by body-snatchers and by them disposed to a professor of anatomy at Cambridge; that the professor invited a few scientific friends to witness a demonstration, and that among them was one who had been acquainted with Sterne, and who fainted with horror on recognizing in the already partially dissected 'subject' the features of his friend. H. D. Traill's Sterne, chap. viii.: English Men of Letters.

This burial-ground of St. George's, Hanover Square, situated in Oxford Street, between Albion and Stanhope Streets, is not so wretched and deserted as Mr. Traill describes it. It is green and well cared for. Entirely shut out from the streets by high walls and houses, its very existence unknown to the thousands who pass by it daily, it is as quiet, secluded, and peaceful as a country churchyard, and in refreshing contrast with some of the modern garish cemeteries of the metropolis. Sterne's memorial, a high but plain flat stone, stands next to the centre of the west wall of the grounds, under a spreading flourishing old tree, whose lower branches and leaves almost touch it. The inscription is worth preserving, and is here given entire : —

Alas, Poor Yorick.
Near to this Place
Lies the body of
The Reverend Laurence Sterne
Dyed September 13 1768
Aged 53 Years.

Ah ! Molliter, ossa quiescant.
If a sound head, warm heart and breast humane,
Unsully'd worth, and soul without a stain,
If mental powers could ever justly claim
The well won tribute of immortal fame,
STERNE was the MAN who with gigantic stride
Mow'd down luxuriant follies far and wide,
Yet what though keenest knowledge of mankind
Unseal'd to him the Springs that move the mind.
What did it boot him, Ridicul'd, abus'd
By foes insulted and by prudes accus'd.
In his, mild reader view thy future fate,
Like him despise what t'were a sin to hate.

This monumental stone was erected to the memory of the deceased by two *Brother Masons*, for although he did not live to be a member of their *Society*, yet all his uncomparable. Performances evidently prove him to have acted by *Rule* and *Square ;* they rejoice in this opportunity of perpetuating his high and unapproachable character to after ages. W. & S.

JOHN SUCKLING.

1608—.——.

SUCKLING was born at Whitton, in the parish of Twickenham. He is described by Aubrey as an extraordinary accomplished gentleman who grew famous at Court for his readie sparkling witt, as being uncomparably readie at repartying, and as the greatest gallant of his time. In person, according to the same authority, he was of middle stature and slight strength, brisque eie, reddish fac't and red nose, (ill liver) his head not very big, his hayre a kind of sand colour. Cunningham says he lived in St. Martin's Lane in 1641. He died, a batchelor, in Paris, and of poyson, Aubrey believes, in 1646, and at the age of twenty-eight. Rev. Alfred Suckling, in his 'Biography' of the poet, written in 1836, says that the date of his death is unknown, although it was unquestionably earlier than 1642.

Suckling's favorite sister is known to have lived in Bishopsgate Street, and he was frequently in her house there, which contained the original portrait of Suckling, by Vandyke, engraved by Vertue, and well known to print-collectors.

He was a frequenter of the Bear-at-the-Bridge-Foot, a tavern which stood at the Southwark end of Old London Bridge until 1761, about a hundred feet east of the present structure (see PEPYS, p. 238); and Aubrey, in whose pages we get the fullest account of him, shows him to have been ' one of the best bowlers of his time in England. He play'd at Cards rarely well, and did use to practise by himself abed, and there studied the best way of managing the Cards. I remember his Sisters comeing to the Piccadillo, Bowling Green, crying for feare he should lose all their portions.'

'Piccadillo Hall, erected in the fields beyond the mewse, a faire House and two Bowling Greenes' was. on the corner of Windmill and Coventry Streets. It stood until the end of the seventeenth century; and the Argyll Rooms, No. 9 Great Windmill Street, east side, were built upon the site of its tennis court.

With all his graces and accomplishments, Suckling has left nothing behind him but his immortal description of the fair bride whose

> 'feet beneath her petticoat
> Like little mice stole in and out,
> As if they feared the light.'

EMANUEL SWEDENBORG.

1688-1772.

SWEDENBORG received his first spiritual manifestations 'at an inn in London' in 1744.[8] He had been here before as a student (1710 to 1713); and he made other and subsequent visits to town, lodging in later years at No. 26 Great Bath Street, Coldbath Fields, where he died in 1772. His house is no longer standing. No. 26 Great Bath Street, between Warner Street and Coldbath Square, on the west side of the way, was a rusty little house in 1885, but probably not more than half a century old. The street has not been renumbered.

Upon this Swedenborg raised himself up in bed, and placing his hand upon his breast, said with earnestness: 'Everything that I have written is as true as you now behold me; I might have said much more had it been permitted me. After death you will see all, and then we will have much to say to each other on this subject.' He told the people of the house what day he should die; and, as Shearsmith's maid reported, he was pleased with the anticipation; his pleasure was, according to the maid's comparison, like that which she would have felt if she had been going to have a holiday or some merry-making. His faculties were clear to the last. On Sunday, the 29th March, 1772, hearing the clock strike, he asked his landlady and her maid, who were both at his bedside, what o'clock it was, and upon being answered, he said, 'It is well. I thank you, God bless you,' and then in a moment after he gently gave up the ghost.

He is buried in the Swedish Church, Prince's Square, Ratcliffe Highway (since called St. George's Street), a mural tablet recording the fact.

Pink's History of Clerkenwell, chap. iv.

I give one more example of robbing the grave of an illustrious man, through the superstition of many and the cupidity of one. ... In 1790, in order to determine a question raised in debate, whether Swedenborg was really dead and buried, his wooden coffin was opened, and the leaden one was sawn across the breast. A few days after, a party of Swedenborgians visited the vault. 'Various relics' (says White, 'Life of Swedenborg,' 2d ed., 1868, p. 675) 'were carried off. Dr. Spurgin told me he possessed the cartilage of an ear. Exposed to the air, the flesh quickly fell to dust, and a skeleton was all that remained for subsequent visitors. ... At a funeral in 1817, Granholm, an officer in the Swedish Navy, seeing the lid of Swedenborg's coffin loose, abstracted the skull, and hawked it about amongst London Swedenborgians, but none would buy. Dr. Wahlin, pastor of the Swedish Church, recovered what he supposed to be the stolen skull, had a cast of it taken, and placed it in the coffin in 1819.'

<small>C. M. Ingleby's Shakspere's Bones, p. 21.</small>

JONATHAN SWIFT.

1667-1745.

SWIFT, in his 'Journals and Correspondence,' has given but few hints of his various London lodging-houses, and these are generally indistinct and vague. He was at one time in King Street, between St. James's Street and St. James's Square; he was the guest of Sir Andrew Fountaine 'at his house in Leicester Fields,' and he speaks of lodging 'over against the house in Little Ryder Street,'—afterwards Ryder Street,—St. James's. Within a few months, in 1710, he is known to have occupied three different sets of chambers.

September 20. — I change my lodgings in Pall Mall for one in Bury Street [St. James's], where I suppose I shall continue while in London. . . .

September 29. — I lodge in Bury Street, where I removed a week ago. I have the first floor, a dining and bed chamber, at eight shillings a week, — plaguy dear; but I spend nothing for eating, never go to a tavern, and very seldom in a coach; yet, after all, it will be expensive. . . .

<small>Swift's Journal to Stella, 1710.</small>

December 28. — I came home to my new lodgings in St. Alban's Street [Haymarket], where I pay the same rent for an apartment two pair of stairs; but I have the use of the parlor to receive persons of quality.

St. Alban's Street was completely demolished on the construction of Waterloo Place. It is not to be confounded with the present St. Albans Place, which was then Market Lane, and ran to Pall Mall as an outlet of St. James's Market (see BAXTER, p. 18).

In 1711 Swift was lodging in Chelsea, to which village he frequently walked from town.

I leave my best gown and periwig at Mrs. Van Homrigh's, then walk up Pall Mall, out at Buckingham House [afterwards Buckingham Palace], and so to Chelsea, a little beyond the church. I set out about sunset, and get there in something less than an hour. It is two good miles, and just 5,748 steps.

<small>Swift's Letters, 1711.</small>

His house was in 'Church Lane, half a mile beyond Chelsea Church.' Church Lane, afterwards Church Street, runs from the river to Fulham Road, near which Swift must have lived.

From Chelsea he removed to Suffolk Street, Haymarket, to be near the Van Homrighs.

It is not pleasant to have old places altered which are connected with interesting recollections, even if the place or recollection be none of the pleasantest. When the houses in Suffolk Street were pulled down, we could not help regretting that the abode was among them in which poor Miss Van Homrigh lived, who died for love of Swift. She resided there with her mother, the widow of a Dutch merchant,

<small>Leigh Hunt's The Town, chap. ix.</small>

and had a fortune. Swift, while in England upon the affairs of the Irish Church, was introduced to them, and became so intimate as to leave his bed-gown and cassock there for convenience. He found the coffee also very pleasant.

He next moved to St. Martin's Street, Leicester Fields, and a month later to Panton Street, Haymarket. In 1712 he lodged for a time 'in the Gravel Pits, Kensington,' — a name given generally, in his day and later, to the region north and northwest of Kensington, between Notting Hill, Bayswater, Kensington Palace, and Holland House, and since called Campden Hill.

In 1725, when Swift returned to London after a long absence, he lodged for a time with Gay in Whitehall.

Swift, lodging most probably, as we know was his habit, in later years in some of the suburban purlieus of St. James's, had already become a notable figure in this company, which met at Will's Coffee House, in Bow Street [see ADDISON, p. 7], or at the St. James's Coffee House [see ADDISON, p. 7], where the Whigs at that time most resorted. . . . Those who frequented the place had been astonished, day after day, by the entry of a clergyman, unknown to any there, who laid his hat on the table, and strode up and down the room with a rapid step, heeding no one and absorbed in his own thoughts. His strange manner earned him, unknown as he was to all, the name of the 'mad parson.'

Henry Craik's Life of Swift, chap. v.

He was equally familiar with the Smyrna at the West End, and with Pantock's at the City end of the town; and, like so many of his contemporaries, is more easily traced to his clubs and to his taverns than to his homes in London, if his various abiding-places here can be termed homes. In his 'Journal to Stella,' he writes : —

Pantock told us that although his wine was not so good, he sold it cheaper than others; he took but seven shillings a flask. Are not these pretty rates?

Pantock's was in Abchurch Lane, Lombard Street (see EVELYN, p. 102). The street is now composed of comparatively modern business houses, and no sign of Pantock's remains. The Smyrna was in Pall Mall, but its position is unknown.

Another of Swift's city taverns was Garraway's, which has long since disappeared. It stood in Change Alley, Cornhill; and its site is marked by a tablet recording this fact, on a building facing Birchin Lane. He frequented also the Devil Tavern, near Temple Bar (see JONSON, p. 175); the Fountaine, No. 103 Strand, which gave its name to Fountain Court, called Savoy Buildings in 1885 (see JOHNSON, p. 170); Button's, in Russell Street, Covent Garden (see ADDISON, p. 6); Ozinda's, 'just by St. James's;' The Globe, No. 134 Fleet Street; and the George, in Pall Mall (see STEELE, p. 290).

He was a member of the October Club, which met at the Bell Tavern in King Street, Westminster; the Scriblerus Club, which met at different West End taverns; and the Brothers' Club, which gathered generally at the Star and Garter in Pall Mall, opposite Schomberg House (see PRIOR, p. 247).

March 20. — I made our society change their house, and we met together at the Star and Garter, in the Pall Mall; Lord Arran was President. The other dog was so extravagant in his bills that for four dishes, first and second courses, without wine or dessert, he charged twenty-one pounds six shillings and eight pence to the Duke of Ormond.
Journal to Stella, 1712.

JOHN TAYLOR.
1580-1654.

TAYLOR was early apprenticed to a Thames waterman, and for a number of years he was employed in some capacity by the governors of the Tower of London. He was called the Water Poet, and is said by tradition to have 'chop'd verses' with Shakspere, whose contemporary he was. He relates, in his 'Pennyless Pilgrimage,' that he set out from London, July 14, 1618, from 'the Bell Inn that's Extra Aldersgate.' It was two doors from the Barbican, but no sign of it now remains. In 1647 he left the Rose Tavern on Holborn Hill, on a pilgrimage to the Isle of Wight, where Charles II. was then staying. The Rose disappeared some years ago. It was on the banks of the Fleet River, and its site is at the steps leading to the Viaduct on the southeast corner of Farringdon Street.

He died in Phœnix Alley, Long Acre, in 1654.

John Taylor, the Water Poet, kept a tavern in this alley. One of his last works (his 'Journey into Wales,' 1652) he describes as 'performed by John Taylor, dwelling at the sign of the Poet's Head, in Phœnix Alley, near the middle of Long Acre.' He supplied his own portrait and inscription:—

> 'There's many a head stands for a sign;
> Then, gentle reader, why not mine?'

His first sign was a mourning crown; but this was too marked to be allowed. He came here in 1652, and, dying here in 1654, was buried, December 5, in the churchyard of St. Martin-in-the-Fields. His widow, it appears from the rate-books of St. Martin's, continued in the house, under the name of the Widow Taylor, five years after his death. In 1658 'Wid(ow) Taylor' is scored out, and 'Mons. Lero' written at the side. The rate they paid was 2/2 a year. *Cunningham's Handbook of London: Phœnix Alley.*

Phœnix Alley, since called Hanover Court, runs from No. 55 Long Acre to Hart Street. Where his tavern stood cannot exactly be determined; but the old house, numbered 6 Hanover Court in 1885, at the junction of the parishes of St. Paul, Covent Garden, and St. Martin-in-the-Fields, which undoubtedly dates back as far as the middle of the seventeenth century, was probably familiar to Taylor and his friends.

WILLIAM MAKEPEACE THACKERAY.

1811-1863.

THACKERAY'S earliest experiences in London, like those of that kindest benefactor society ever had,— the Addison whose name he honored; the kind, just, sincere, impartial moralist and writer he so dearly loved, — were of the Charter House School (see ADDISON, p. 1). He was brought from Calcutta when very young, and is represented by one of his schoolmates (George Venables, in Trollope's 'Thackeray') as a pretty, gentle, rather timid boy, with no skill in games, and not much taste for them, popular among the boys he knew, but never very happy in his school associations or daily life. He was 'on the Foundation,' wore a gown, and lived in the school. In the cloisters is a tablet to his memory, next to that of John Leech. His last public appearance was at a Charter House dinner, only a few days before he died. He gave the time-honored Latin toast, asking the blessing of Providence upon the Foundation, and passed forever from the old school with a prayer upon his lips for its success and its perpetuity.

When Thackeray was called to the bar in 1834, and for some years afterwards, he occupied, with Tom Taylor, chambers at No. 10 Crown Office Row, in the Temple, where many of his working hours were spent. This building is no longer standing.

He also frequently stopped at the Bedford, in Covent Garden (see CHURCHILL, p. 51). In 1837 he took his young wife to a house in Albion Street, Hyde Park, not many yards from the grave of Sterne; and he lived there and in Great Coram Street, near the Foundling Hospital, until the failing health of Mrs. Thackeray forced him to give up housekeeping altogether.

For a time he lived at No. 88 St. James's Street, in the building afterwards known as Palace Chambers; but from 1847 to 1853 his home was at No. 13 (in 1885, No. 16) Young Street, Kensington, where he wrote 'Vanity Fair,' 'Pendennis,' 'Esmond,' and portions of 'The Newcomes.'

I once made a pilgrimage with Thackeray (at my request, of course, the visit was planned) to the various houses where his books had been written; and I remember, when we came to Young Street, Kensington, he said, with mock gravity, 'Down on your knees, you rogue, for here "Vanity Fair" was penned; and I will go down with you, for I have a high opinion of that little production myself.' He was always perfectly honest in his expressions about his own writings, and it was delightful to hear him praise them when he could depend upon his listeners. A friend congratulated him once on that touch in 'Vanity Fair' in which Becky *admires* her husband when he is giving Steyne the punishment which ruins *her* for life. 'Well,' he said, 'when I wrote that sentence, I slapped my fist on the table, and said, "*That* is a touch of genius."' [Fields's Yesterdays with Authors: Thackeray.]

In 1853 Thackeray took the house No. 36 Onslow Square, South Kensington, where he wrote 'The Virginians,' etc., and lived for eight or nine years. Onslow Square has been renumbered. Thackeray's was one of a row of uniform three-storied brick houses on the south side of the Square near Sumner Place. Mrs. Ritchie in a private note, dated 1884, says:—

Our old house was the fourth, counting the end house, from the corner by the church in Onslow Square, the church being on the left hand, and the avenue of old trees running in front of our drawing-room windows. I used to look up from the avenue and see my father's head bending over his work in the study window, which was over the drawing-room.

The following description of his daily life here is worth preserving: —

To Onslow Square I accordingly went on the morning fixed, and found Mr. Thackeray in his study to receive me; but instead of entering upon business in that part of the house, he took me upstairs to his bedroom, where every arrangement had been made for the convenience of writing. I then learned that he was busily occupied in preparing his lectures on 'The Four Georges,' and that he had need of an amanuensis to fill the place of one who was now otherwise occupied. . . . Often he would light a cigar, and after pacing the room for a few moments would put the unsmoked remnant on the mantelpiece, and resume his work with increased cheerfulness, as if he had gathered fresh inspiration from the gentle odors of the sublime tobacco. It was not a little amusing to observe the frequency with which Mr. Thackeray would change his position, and I could not but think that he seemed most at his ease when one would suppose he was most uncomfortable. . . . Mr. Thackeray was in his dressing-gown and slippers, and received us in his bedroom, where, as I have already stated, he generally passed his mornings and wrote his books. His study being a small back-room behind the dining-room, on the ground floor, and being exposed to the noises from the street, he had caused his writing-table and appliances to be carried upstairs to the second floor, where two rooms had been thrown into one, the back to be used as a sleeping-chamber, and the front, which was considerably larger than the other, as a sitting-room.

Hodder's Memoirs of my Time, chap. xi.

In 1862 Thackeray moved to a house he had built for himself at No. 2 Palace Green, Kensington, — an imposing double mansion of red brick, in bright gardens of its own.

It is the second house on the left as one enters the gate of Kensington Palace Gardens, from Kensington High Street, but has been enlarged and changed since his day. Here he died on Christmas eve, 1863.

The last words he corrected in print were: 'And my heart throbbed with an exquisite bliss.' God grant that on that Christmas eve when he laid his head back on his pillow, and threw up his arms as he had been wont to do when very weary, some consciousness of duty done, and Christian hope throughout life humbly cherished, may have caused his own heart so to throb when he passed away to his Redeemer's rest. . . . He was found peacefully lying as above described, composed, undisturbed, and to all appearance asleep on the 24th of December, 1863. He was only in his fifty-third year; so young a man that the mother who blessed him in his first sleep blessed him in his last! *Charles Dickens in the Cornhill Magazine, January, 1864.*

Thackeray was buried in Kensal Green Cemetery on the 30th of December, 1863. Charles Dickens, Mark Lemon, Dr. Russell of the 'Times,' John Everett Millais, John Leech (so soon to follow him and to lie by his side), Anthony Trollope, Robert Browning, George Cruikshank, Tom Taylor, Louis Blanc, Charles Mathews, Theodore Martin, and Shirley Brooks were among the old friends who carried him to his rest.

Thackeray's first lectures were prepared while he was living in Young Street, and were delivered in the summer of 1851 at Willis's Rooms (formerly Almack's), No. 26 King Street, St. James's Street, to great crowds of the intellectual and social lights of the kingdom.

Charlotte Brontë writes:—

London, June 2 [1851].—I came here on Wednesday, being summoned a day sooner than I expected, in order to be in time for Thackeray's second lecture, which was delivered on Thursday afternoon. This, as you may suppose, was a genuine treat to me, and I was glad not to miss it. It was given in Willis's Rooms, where the Almack *Mrs. Gaskell's Life of Charlotte Brontë, vol. ii. chap. ix.*

Balls are held; a great painted and gilded saloon, with long sofas for benches. I did not at all expect the great lecturer would know me or notice me under these circumstances, with admiring duchesses and countesses seated in rows before him; but he met me as I entered, shook hands, took me to his mother, whom I had not seen before, and introduced me.

Thackeray's clubs were the Athenæum, No. 107 Pall Mall, the Garrick, and the Reform, No. 104 Pall Mall.

Thackeray was standing at the top of the steps leading into the Reform Club, the thumb and forefinger of each hand in his waistcoat pockets, as was constantly his wont, when Jerrold, a fellow-member of the club, was about to enter the building. 'Have you heard the news?' inquired Thackeray, as Jerrold ascended the steps. 'No,' replied the latter. 'The Prince is dead; poor dear Gentlewoman!' A delicate piece of patronage bestowed by literature upon majesty itself.

<small>Hodder's Memoirs, chap. xvii.</small>

On the Tuesday he came to his favorite club, the Garrick, and asked for a seat at the table of two friends, who of course welcomed him, as all welcomed Thackeray. It will not be deemed too minute a record by any of the hundreds who personally loved him, to note where he sat for the last time at that club. There is in the dining-room on the first floor a nook near the reading-room. The principal picture hanging in that nook, and fronting you as you approach it, is the celebrated one from the 'Clandestine Marriage.' Opposite to this Thackeray took his seat and dined with his friends. He was afterwards in the smoke-room, a place in which he delighted.... On Wednesday he was out several times, and was seen in Palace Gardens reading a book. Before the dawn of Thursday he was where there is no night.

<small>Shirley Brooks, Illustrated London News, 1864.</small>

Dickens came rarely to the club; but Thackeray was dearly fond of it, and was always there. I remember a speech of his at an annual dinner, then always held on Shakspere's birthday, in which he said, 'We, the happy initiated, never speak of it as the Garrick; to us it is the G., the little G., the dearest place in the world.'

<small>Edmund Yates: Fifty Years of London Life, chap. ix.</small>

The Garrick Club, founded in 1831, was situated until 1864 at No. 35 King Street, Covent Garden, on the north side and near the present Garrick Street. This was the only Garrick Club that Thackeray knew. The modern building at No. 15 Garrick Street, Long Acre, was not occupied until the year after Thackeray's death.

JAMES THOMSON.

1700–1748.

WHEN Thomson first came to London in 1725, he lived in humble lodgings in the house afterwards numbered 30 Charing Cross, between Cragg's Court and Great Scotland Yard. Jesse and others believe it to have been the identical old round front house still standing there as late as 1885. Here on the first floor he spent some time in comparative poverty, and here he is said to have written part of his 'Summer.'

Other portions of 'Summer' were written while he was tutor in an academy in Little Tower Street, Eastcheap. This house, afterwards No. 12, has been taken down; but next to it, at No. 11 Little Tower Street, was, in 1885, the Ship Tavern, as old as Thomson's day, and well known to the poet.

Later in life, when his circumstances were better, Thomson lived in the West End of London.

So charming Thomson wrote from his lodgings, a milliner's in Bond Street, where he seldom rose early enough to see the sun do more than glisten on the opposite windows of the street. *Mrs. Piozzi's Journey through Italy.*

Thomson lodged for some time at Rosedale House in Kew Foot Lane, Richmond, not far from the Green. It has been greatly altered, and was in 1885 a plain red brick mansion near the street, with a little bit of lawn in front. 'Rosedale House' was painted upon its gateposts. The gardens and relics of the poet, which were for many years carefully preserved here, have gradually disappeared.

He died in this house in 1748; and a brass mural plate at the west end of the north aisle of Richmond Church has been placed above the spot where he lies.

Thomson received subscriptions for the 'Seasons' at the Smyrna Coffee House, Pall Mall (see SWIFT, p. 300), and was a frequent guest of the Old Red Lion Tavern, in St. John's Road, Islington (see GOLDSMITH, p. 126).

Another favorite suburban resort of his was 'The Doves,' at Hammersmith, an old-fashioned river-side public house, still in existence as late as 1885, at the lower end of the Upper Mall, and a little to the west of the Suspension Bridge. His name and memory are still held sacred here; and on the door of the adjoining cottage, which in his day was part of the inn, is a well-worn, highly polished brass plate, upon which is engraved 'The Seasons.' It is believed that his 'Winter' was conceived and written in a room in this house, overlooking the river, when the Thames was covered with ice and the neighboring country with snow, — an assertion which Faulkner, in his 'Fulham,' says is well authenticated.

JOHN HORNE TOOKE.

1736–1812.

HORNE TOOKE was born in the house of his father, John Horne, a poulterer, and the 'Turkey Merchant' from whom the son once claimed descent. His shop was in Newport Market, which stood between Great Newport, Grafton, and Litchfield Streets, Soho, but has now disappeared.

Tooke spent two years at Westminster School (see CHURCHILL, p. 51) before he went to Eton. In 1756 he entered the Inner Temple, and from 1760 to 1773 he was curate of St. Lawrence's, Brentford, six miles from Hyde Park Corner.

In 1777 he was imprisoned in the Tower for his violent and outspoken sympathy with the American colonists in their rebellion against the mother-country.

In 1802 Tooke retired to Wimbledon, where ten years later he died. His house was on the southwest corner of Wimbledon Common, — a two-storied brick cottage, still standing in 1885, facing the Green and backing on the Crooked Billet and Hand in Hand, two old inns.

I often dined with Tooke at Wimbledon, and always found him most pleasant and most witty. There his friends would drop in upon him without any invitation. . . . Tooke latterly used to expect two or three of his most intimate friends to dine with him every Sunday; and I once offended him a good deal by not joining his Sunday dinner-parties for several weeks. <small>Rogers's Table Talk.</small>

Tooke was buried in the yard of Ealing Old Church (St. Mary's) under an altar tomb.

A tomb had long been prepared for Mr. Tooke in his garden at Wimbledon, in which it was his firm purpose to have been buried; but after his decease, being opposed by his daughters and an aunt of theirs, his remains were transferred to this churchyard, where they were interred according to the rites and ceremonies of the Church of England, otherwise it was his desire that no funeral ceremonies should be read over his body, but six poor men should have a guinea each to bear him to the vault in his garden.

<small>Faulkner's Brentford, Ealing, and Chiswick, chap. ii.</small>

EDMUND WALLER.

1605-1687.

WALLER is said to have been a member of the House of Commons when he was sixteen or seventeen years of age, and to have been a resident of London for some time; but nothing is known of his personal career here except that he was married 'to his rich city heiress' in the Church of St. Margaret, Westminster, that he lived at one time in Bow Street, Covent Garden, on the site of the Police Station (see FIELDING, p. 105), and that between the years 1660 and 1687 he lived on the west side of St. James's Street, Piccadilly. In the latter year he went to Beaconsfield to die.

He was a frequent visitor at Berkeley House, on the site of which Devonshire House, Piccadilly, between Berkeley and Stratton Streets, was built; and Aubrey preserves the story of a catastrophe that befell him at the Water Gate of Somerset House, Strand:—

Waller had but a tender, weak bodie, but was always very temperate. — Made him damnable drunk at Somerset House, where at the water stayres he fell down and had a cruel fall. 'T was a pity to use such a sweet swan so inhumanly

The Somerset House of Waller's day, built by the Protector, whose name it bore, was taken down in 1775 to make way for the present buildings, which were completed in 1786.

HORACE WALPOLE.

1717-1797.

HORACE WALPOLE was born on the west side of Arlington Street, Piccadilly; but he afterwards occupied the opposite house, No. 5 Arlington Street, which is marked by the tablet of the Society of Arts as having been the residence of his father. While in town from 1745 to 1779 he lived here, and also in his father's house in Downing Street, — the official residence of the first Lord of the Treasury ever since Sir Robert Walpole's occupancy of it in 1735.

The greater part of Horace Walpole's youth, however, was spent in his father's house at Chelsea, afterwards the Infirmary of Chelsea Hospital, which was but little changed in 1885, except that one story had been added. The drawing-room was Ward No. 7.

Walpole is now particularly associated with Strawberry Hill, — the house where so many of his days were passed, and upon which so much of his thought was spent. It still stood in 1885, on the banks of the Thames, at Twickenham, ten miles from Arlington Street and Berkeley Square.

Strawberry Hill . . . stands on a gentle elevation about three hundred yards from, and overlooking, the Thames immediately above Twickenham. . . . When Walpole rented the house it was little more than a cottage, and the grounds were of narrow compass. As soon as he became its owner, he began to enlarge the house and extend the grounds. The cottage grew into a villa, the villa into a mansion. . . . Strawberry Hill, when completed, was a Gothic building, but Gothic of no particular period, class, or style. Windows, doorways, and mouldings of the thirteenth century stood side by side with others of the fifteenth and sixteenth. Ecclesiastical were co-mingled with secular features, collegiate with baronial or military. Next to an Abbey Entrance was the oriel of an Elizabethan Manor-house, or the keep of a Norman Castle, while battlements and machicolation frowned over the wide bay windows that opened on to the lawn. . . . Walpole was in his thirtieth year when he took Strawberry Hill; and he spent fifty summers in it, improving the house, adding to his collections, and enjoying the lilacs and nightingales in his grounds. . . . As it now stands [1876], Strawberry Hill is a renewal of Walpole's house, with modern sumptuousness superadded. All the old rooms are there, though the uses of many have been changed. . . . The grounds and gardens are as beautiful and attractive as of old, the trees as verdant, the rosary as bright, the lawn as green, and in their season Walpole's 'two passions, lilacs. and nightingales,' in as full bloom and abundance as ever.

[margin: Thorne's Hand-Book of the Environs of London; Strawberry Hill.]

From 1779, for eighteen years, Walpole's town house was No. 11 Berkeley Square; and here, in 1797, he died.

I came to town this morning [October, 1779] to take possession of Berkeley Square, and was as well pleased with my new habitation as I can be with anything at present.

[margin: Walpole's Letters, 1779.]

This mansion was on the southwest corner of Hill Street, and was numbered 42 Berkeley Square in 1885.

Walpole was a member of Brook's Club, No. 60 St. James's Street, among others, and of the Blue Stocking Club, which met 'at Mrs. Montague's, on the northwest corner of Portman Square.'

He frequented Dodsley's shop, at the sign of the Tully's Head, No. 51 Pall Mall (see AKENSIDE, p. 11); and the Bedford Coffee House, 'under the Piazza, in Covent Garden' (see CHURCHILL, p. 51).

IZAAK WALTON.

1593-1683.

OF Walton's youth and education nothing is known. Anthony Wood found him engaged as a 'sempster,' or linen-draper, in the Royal Burse, Cornhill (on the site of the Royal Exchange), where his shop was seven feet and a half long, and five feet wide. Later, he occupied half a shop in Fleet Street, between Chancery Lane and Temple Bar.

Walton dwelt on the north side of Fleet Street, in a house two doors west of the end of Chancery Lane, and abutting on a messuage known by the sign of The Harrow. . . . Now the old timber house at the Southwest corner of Chancery Lane, till within these few years [1760] was known by that sign; it is therefore beyond doubt that Walton lived at the very next door, and in this House he is, in the deed above referred to, which bears date 1624, said to have followed the trade of a *Linen Draper*. It further appears by that deed, that the house was in the joint occupation of Isaac Walton and John Mason, hosier, from whence we may conclude that half a shop was sufficient for the business of Walton. Sir John Hawkins's Life of Walton.

He subsequently removed into Chancery Lane.

Isaac Walton lived in what was then the seventh house on the left hand as you walk [in Chancery Lane] from Fleet Street to Holborn. Sir Harris Nicolas derived this information from the Parish Books. Cunningham's Handbook of London: Chancery Lane.

This house is believed to have stood next to Crown Court, on the site of the house numbered 120 Chancery Lane in 1885.

Walton quitted London in 1643.

Finding it dangerous for honest men to be there, he left the city, and lived some time at Stafford and elsewhere, but mostly in the families of eminent clergymen of England, by whom he was much beloved.

<small>Wood's Athenæ Oxonienses.</small>

Walton lived in the parish of Clerkenwell after his retirement from business; and here, according to the parish registers, were baptized, in St. James's Church, February 10, 1650, his son Izaak Walton, and again, on September 7, 1651, another son Izaak Walton. Both of these children died in early infancy. In 1653, while still living in Clerkenwell, 'There is published a book of eighteen pence price called the Compleat Angler; or contemplative man's recreations, being a discourse of Fish and Fishing, not unworthy of perusal. Sold by Richard Marriot in St. Dunstan's Church Yard, Fleet Street.'

The antiquarians of Clerkenwell, unfortunately, have been able to find no trace of the site of Walton's house, either from tradition or the rate-books.

Walton bought his fish-hooks at the shop of one Charles Kerbye, in Harp Alley, Shoe Lane, a street entirely changed since Walton's day; and he was fond of fishing the Lea from Ware to Tottenham.

The Swan Inn at Tottenham High Cross was the place of resort of Izaak Walton, the angler; he used to tarry here awhile before he went to the river Lea to fish, and again on his return. In the front of this house in the year 1643, there was an harbour, the favorite resting place of Walton, of which mention is made in the 'Complete Angler.'

<small>William Robinson's History of Tottenham, vol. i. p. 91.</small>

The White Swan Inn was left intact in 1885, on the northwest corner of Tottenham High Cross, between the Cross itself, on the opposite side of the High Road, and the old well. It stood a little back from the street, — a white stuccoed house of one story and an attic, with a quaint old gable. There was a skittle alley in its rear, and a little bit of bright garden at its side, — all that was left of the gentle angler's sweet shady arbor, woven by Nature herself, with her own fine fingers, of woodbine, sweet-brier, jessamine, and myrtle. While a drink like nectar was still brewed in the interesting old inn, no fishermen went there to sup it in the last quarter of the nineteenth century, and Izaak Walton was absolutely unknown to those who served or quaffed it. The river Lea is about five minutes' walk from the doors of the Swan.

One of the most interesting memorials of Walton left us is the monogram 'I. W.' and the date '1658' scratched by Walton himself on the mural tablet to Isaac Casaubon in the south transept of Westminster Abbey. Dean Stanley was very fond of pointing this out to his personal friends as he escorted them to the Poets' Corner; and it is the only desecration ever committed in the Abbey that he heartily forgave.

EDWARD WARD.

1667-1731.

NED WARD, the droll author of the 'London Spy,' is said by William Oldys to have lived for a while in Gray's Inn, and later to have kept a public house in Moorfields, afterwards in Clerkenwell, and lastly a punch-house in Fulwood's Rents. His Clerkenwell establishment he described 'as at the Great Gates in Red Bull Yard, between St. John Street and Clerkenwell Green;' and he claimed that on

'That ancient venerable ground,
 Where Shakspere in heroic buskin trod,
A good old fabric may be found,
 Celestial liquors fit to charm a god.'

This alludes to the unfounded tradition that Shakspere was a player in the Red Bull Theatre, in Red Bull Yard, which has since been called Woodbridge Street (see DAVENANT, p. 75, and SHAKSPERE, p. 264).

Fulwood's Rents, at No. 34 High Holborn, nearly opposite Chancery Lane, contained in 1885 a number of very old and dilapidated buildings, doubtless standing there in Ward's time. His house, according to Oldys, was 'within one door of Gray's Inn,' and here 'he would entertain any company that invited him, with many stories and adventures of the poets and authors he had acquaintance with.'

He died at this house, and was buried in Old St. Pancras Churchyard (see GODWIN, p. 118) in the most quiet manner, and in accordance with the directions of his poetic will:—

> 'No costly funeral prepare;
> 'Twixt Sun and Sun I only crave
> A hearse and one black coach to bear
> My wife and children to my grave.'

ISAAC WATTS.

1674–1748.

ISAAC WATTS came to London in 1690 to enter the College for Dissenters in Newington Green (see DE FOE, p. 76). In 1693 he 'was admitted to Mr. Rowe's Church,' which then worshipped at Girdlers' Hall, still standing in 1885, at Nos. 38 to 40 Basinghall Street. In 1698–99 'he preached as Dr. Chauncey's assistant in Ye Church in Mark Lane' (City). His connection with this congregation lasted until his death, fifty years later. In June, 1704, as is recorded in his Diary, 'we removed our meeting place to Pinner's Hall [Old Broad Street, see BAXTER, p. 18], and began exposition of Scripture.' In 1708 the congregation removed again to Duke's Place, Bury Street, St. Mary Axe; but there is now no trace left of either of these chapels.

Watts lived with 'Mr. Thomas Hollis in the Minories' in 1702, and here probably wrote the poems which, in his Diary, he says were published in 1705. In 1710 he 'removed from Mr. Hollis's and went to live with Mr. Bowes, December 30.' With this year his brief and unsatisfactory Diary ends; and his biographers have not cared to say more definitely where his homes in London were situated.

In the year 1713 or 1714 he became a guest in the house of Sir Thomas Abney, at Theobalds, Cheshunt, Herts, about fifteen miles from London. Subsequently he went with the Abneys to Stoke Newington; and in 1748 died in their house at the end of a somewhat protracted visit of thirty-five years.

Sir Thomas Abney's house at Stoke Newington was taken down in 1844, and its site is now occupied by Abney Park Cemetery, in which stands a statue of Watts.

Dr. Watts was buried in Bunhill Fields —

deep in the earth, among the relics of many of his pious fathers and brethren whom he had known in the flesh, and with whom he wished to be found in the resurrection. . . . In order that his grave might read a lecture of that moderation which his life had exemplified and his pen advocated, he desired that his funeral should be attended by two Independent ministers, two Presbyterian and two Baptist.

<small>Rev. Thomas Milner's Life of Watts, chap. xviii.</small>

An altar tomb covers his grave, in the northeastern corner of the ground, not far from the City Road entrance.

JOHN WESLEY.

1703–1791.

WESLEY was sent at an early age to the Charter House School (see ADDISON, p. 1), from which he went to Oxford in 1720. In after life he frequently asserted that much of his good health was due to the command of his father that he should run around the Charter House playground three times every morning, — a task which he conscientiously performed.

For some years Wesley was pastor of the congregation which worshipped in Pinner's Hall, Old Broad Street (see BAXTER, p. 18); and he preached at Bromley, and at the Foundry at Moorfields, which stood on the site of the Chapel subsequently erected in Tabernacle Row, Finsbury, near City Road.

In 1752 Wesley took possession of the New Wells, a place of popular amusement in Clerkenwell, which he opened as a tabernacle, and in which he preached. It stood on Lower Rosoman Street, on the site of the houses afterwards numbered 5, 6, 7, and 8, according to Pink in his 'History of Clerkenwell;' and it was taken down shortly after the expiration of Wesley's lease. Wesley preached Whitefield's funeral sermon (1770) in the Tottenham Court Road Chapel, in 1885 numbered 79 Tottenham Court Road; and in 1777 he laid the foundation stone of the Chapel, No. 48 City Road, opposite the Cemetery of Bunhill Fields, where, as Southey shows, great multitudes assembled to hear and see him, and assist at the ceremony.

Opposite the Eastern Gate of the Artillery Ground in the City Road is a handsome Chapel, built by the late Rev. John Wesley, for the Methodists of the Arminian persuasion. It is a plain structure of brick, the interior very neat; there is also a spacious Court behind the building, planted with some trees, and uniform houses on each side, the first of which on the right hand, entering from the City Road, was occupied by Mr. John Wesley when in town, and that also in which he died. *Brayley's London and Middlesex, vol. iii.*

'Wesley's House,' so marked, is in front of this chapel, and in 1885 was numbered 47 City Road.

During his last illness Wesley said: 'Let me be buried in nothing but what is woollen; and let my corpse be carried in my coffin into the chapel.' This was done according to the will, by six poor men, each of whom had 20/; 'for I particularly desire,' said he, 'that there may be no hearse, no coach, no escutcheon, no pomp, except the tears of them that love me, and are following me to Abraham's bosom.' *Southey's Life of Wesley, vol. ii.* On the day preceding the interment, Wesley's body lay in the chapel in a kind of state becoming the person, dressed in his clerical habit, with gown, cassock, and band, the old clerical cap on his head, a Bible in one hand, and a white handkerchief in the other. . . . The crowds who flocked to see him were so great that it was thought prudent, for fear of accident, to accelerate the funeral, and perform it between five and six in the morning. The intelligence, however, could not be kept entirely secret, and several hundred persons attended at that unusual hour.

As I was walking home one day from my father's bank, I observed a great crowd of people streaming into a chapel in the City Road. I followed them, and saw laid out upon a table the dead body of a clergyman in full canonicals. It was the corpse of John Wesley; and the crowd moved slowly and silently round the table to take a last look at that most venerable man. *Rogers's Table Talk.*

Wesley lies in the little burial-ground behind the City Road Chapel, under a monument erected to his memory by the members of the society to which he gave his name.

GEORGE WITHER.

1588-1667.

WITHER, whose famous shepherd refused to waste in despair and die because a certain fair woman was not fair to him, was a student of Lincoln's Inn, and wrote his best-known poem in the Marshalsea Prison. Later he was confined — always for political reasons — in Newgate and in the Tower. This was not the Marshalsea Prison of Dickens's youth. It stood on the east side of the Borough High Street, opposite Union Street and next to the Nag's Head, the modern Newcomen Street passing over its site. The Marshalsea Debtors' Prison was nearer St. George's Church (see DICKENS, p. 80).

Wither died, it was said, in the Savoy, and, according to Wood's 'Athenæ Oxonienses,' was buried 'between the east door and south end' of the Church of St. Mary-le-Savoy, known now as the Savoy Chapel, Savoy Street, Strand (see CHAUCER, p. 46). This church dates back to the very beginning of the sixteenth century, but has no memorial of Wither.

JOHN WOLCOT.

1738-1819.

'PETER PINDAR'S' first permanent home in London was at No. 1 Chapel Street, next to the corner of Great Portland Street, Portland Place, where he lodged about the year 1782. The Portland Hotel has since been erected on the site of this house. Later he occupied a garret room in No. 13 Tavistock Row, overlooking Covent Garden and near Southampton Street; and in 1807 he was lodging in Camden Town, then a suburban village, while he figured, not very creditably, in the law courts. He died twelve years later, near the nursery gardens which have since become Euston Square.

He always sat in a room facing the south. Behind the door stood a square piano-forte, on which there generally lay his favorite Cremona violin; on the left, a mahogany table with writing materials. Everything was in perfect order. . . . Facing him, over the mantelpiece, hung a fine landscape by Richard Wilson. . . . In writing, except a few lines hap-hazard, the Doctor was obliged to employ an amanuensis [he lost his eyesight a few years before his death]. Of all his acquisitions, music to him remained alone unaltered. . . . He even composed light airs for amusement. <small>Redding's Recollections of Fifty Years.</small>

Wolcot was buried in the Church of St. Paul, Covent Garden, at his own request that he might 'lie as near as possible to the bones of old Hudibras Butler.' His grave is believed to be under the floor of the vestry-room; but there is no tablet to his memory (see BUTLER, p. 29).

WILLIAM WORDSWORTH.

1770-1850.

WORDSWORTH made frequent visits to London, and we read of him here as the guest of Rogers, Lamb, Coleridge, Crabb Robinson, and others; but nowhere in his Diary, his Memoirs, his published letters, or in the works of his friends and contemporaries, is any hint given as to his abiding-places in town. While he was more closely identified with Yarrow or the Lake District than with the stream that flows through the vale of Cheapside, still he has left a thrush in the branches of the old tree on the corner of Wood Street, that will sing there as long as yellow primroses grow by rivers' brims.

WILLIAM WYCHERLEY.

Circa 1640-1715.

WYCHERLEY was entered as a student in the Middle Temple, but soon turned from the dry study of the law to lighter, looser, and more beloved pursuits. His only known residence in London was in Bow Street, Covent Garden, 'over against the Cock.' According to Peter Cunningham, it was on the west side of Bow Street, and 'three doors beyond Radcliffe,' whose house is known to have been on the site of Covent Garden Theatre. This Cock Tavern long since disappeared.

It was here that Charles II. called upon Wycherley while he was lying ill, — a very unusual compliment of royalty to a commoner; and the result of the visit was a gift of £500, out of the public purse, to enable the dramatist to seek rest and strength in France. Wycherley, however, soon incurred the displeasure of Charles by his marriage to a Court lady, the Countess of Drogheda, whom he visited in Hatton Garden, and carried, as his wife, to Bow Street. This unequal match brought as little happiness to either party as did that of Addison and his Countess; and Wycherley's contemporaries have put on record many entertaining stories of his married life, his wife being so jealous of him that he was rarely permitted to quit her side. It is said that when he visited the Cock he was ordered to leave open the windows of the room in which he sat, and to show himself from time to time, that the exacting lady over the way might be assured that all his companions were of his own sex.

Another and more serious result of this union was his confinement for several years in the Fleet Prison; his disputes concerning his marriage settlements with the Countess resulting in his financial ruin and in his committal to a debtors' gaol.

The Fleet Prison, destroyed in the Gordon Riots in 1780, but immediately rebuilt, stood on the east side of the present Farringdon Street until 1846. Its exact site may be described as upon the block of ground bounded on the west by Farringdon Street, on the east by Fleet Lane, on the north by Fleet Lane, and on the south by Fleet Lane. It was approached from the Old Bailey by Fleet Lane, an irregular street shaped like the letter Y.

Wycherley was married a second time in 1715, but died eleven days after the ceremony. He was buried in the vaults of the Church of St. Paul, Covent Garden. All traces of his grave were lost in the burning of the church in 1795 (see BUTLER, p. 29).

Favorite taverns of Wycherley, besides the Cock, were the Half Moon in Aldersgate Street, marked by Half Moon Passage, No. 158 Aldersgate Street (see GONGREVE, p. 64), and the Bear at the Bridge Foot (see PEPYS. p. 238).

EDWARD YOUNG.

1681-1765.

DR. YOUNG had almost no association with London except in his marriage at the Church of St. Mary-at-Hill, in Love Lane, Eastcheap, May 27, 1731. This church, one of Wren's, was still standing in 1885. The death of his wife in 1740 led to the writing of the famous 'Night Thoughts,' which established his reputation and is so rarely read. He lived and died in his country parish in Hertfordshire.

NOTES.

[1] Colonel F. Grant, in a letter to the London 'Athenæum,' Aug. 1, 1885, writes that a directory of London printed for Sam. Lee, 1677, is in the Bodleian, and that two other copies of the same work are known to exist.

[2] The 'Builder' (London), Sept. 19, 1885, says: 'The Royal Comedy Theatre in Panton Street should, we believe, be instanced as marking the situation of Addison's Haymarket lodging, which Pope showed to Harte as being the garret where Addison wrote "The Campaign."'

[3] The Chapter Coffee House, Paternoster Row, was torn down in 1887, but rebuilt upon the same site.

[4] The Rev. Robert Gwynne, in a private note dated Sept. 1, 1885, writes: 'In revising Baedeker's "London" I had a great deal of trouble in finding out that 24, not 16, Holles Street was the birthplace of Byron. I consulted Mr. Cordy Jeaffreson, author of "The Real Lord Byron;" Mr. Crace, the decorator in Wigmore Street, whose father collected the views, maps, etc., of London, now in the British Museum; Mr. Fry, the present owner of No. 24 Holles Street, and Mr. John Murray, Jr. . . . Mr. Fry informed me that 24 Holles Street is the only house in the street that has been rebuilt. The tablet in accordance with tradition is in front of this house. Peter Cunningham, in his "London," gives as his authority for naming No. 16 as the birthplace a paper in Mr. Murray's possession. Mr. John Murray, Jr., and I examined the paper, which is a tradesman's bill, and we were both convinced that the document does not bear out Mr. Cunningham's statement.'

[5] Long's Hotel, No. 16 New Bond Street, was taken down in 1887.

[6] The 'Baptist,' London, June 19, 1885, says that Cowper spent *one morning* in town when he 'breakfasted with his friend Rose in Chancery Lane in 1792, when returning from Eartham, the residence of Hayley, a brother poet.'

⁷ The extreme rear of the Marshalsea Prison which Dickens describes in the Preface to 'Little Dorrit' was transformed into a warehouse in 1887.

⁸ The old house No. 16 Fetter Lane was demolished in 1887.

⁹ A writer in the 'British Quarterly Review,' October, 1885, says that in the company of the late Mr. W. Smith Williams, he frequently saw Leigh Hunt in his house at Hammersmith, and 'admired the taste which he managed to communicate to his small rooms, and also the graceful garrulousness and suavity of the old man in his long black robe, and his long white hair.'

¹⁰ The British Hotel, Cockspur Street, was torn down in 1887; Stanford, the publisher of maps, building upon its site.

¹¹ The Cock Tavern, Fleet Street, was taken down in 1887, and a branch of the Bank of England was built upon its site.

¹² Subsequent research shows that the Margaret Jonson who was married in 1575, according to the register of St. Martins-in-the-Fields, died in 1590; while the mother of Ben Jonson is known to have been alive as late as 1604.

¹³ Mr. Sidney Colvin, in his 'Life of Keats' (English Men of Letters Series), says that Keats lived over the Queen's Head in the Poultry in 1816, and moved to No. 76 Cheapside during the next year. No. 76 Cheapside was rebuilt in 1868. It was in this house, according to Peter Cunningham, that Keats wrote his Sonnet on Chapman's 'Homer.'

¹⁴ Holly Lodge, named Airlie Lodge, when it was occupied by an Earl of Airlie, has since been given its old name, and was called Holly Lodge in 1887.

¹⁵ Edward Walford, in his 'Greater London,' vol. ii. p. 111, writes: 'Suffice it to say that, beyond his tomb at Twickenham, the only memorials of the poet [Pope] now visible are the gardens and the famous grove in which he took such great delight, and also the grotto, or rather the tunnel, for it has been despoiled of many of its rare marbles, spars, and ores, and is now a mere damp subway.'

¹⁶ The old house at No. 96 Piccadilly was torn down in 1887, and the Junior Travellers' Club was built upon its site.

¹⁷ Mr. Jeaffreson believes that this hotel in Dover Street was only an occasional resort of Shelley's, and that the fact of his writing there a letter announcing his child's birth is not sufficient evidence that the event occurred on the premises

INDEX OF PERSONS.

Abney, Sir Thomas, 317.
ADDISON, JOSEPH, 1-9; mentioned, v, ix, x, 175, 202, 204, 243, 287, 288, 302, 322; quoted, 96, 97.
Agnew, Thomas, 293.
Aikin, Lucy, quoted, 2, 288.
AKENSIDE, MARK, 10-11.
Albert, Prince Consort, 306.
Alcinoüs, 190.
Andersen, Hans Christian, quoted, 84.
Anne, Queen, 55, 155, 156, 243, 244.
Arbuthnot, Dr. John, 243.
Archer, Francis, 204.
Argyll, Duke of, 203.
Atterbury, Bishop Francis, 6.
Aubrey, John, mentioned, 171; quoted, 11, 13, 19, 29, 74, 91, 107, 172, 173, 199, 211, 212, 215, 216, 223, 225, 249, 295, 310.

BACON, FRANCIS, 11-14; mentioned, 202.
Baillie, Agnes, 15.
Baillie, Dr. Matthew, 14.
BAILLIE, JOANNA, 14-15.
Baker, David Erskine, 196.
Ballantyne, James, 261.
BARBAULD, ANNA LETITIA, 16; quoted, 253, 254.
Barbauld, Rev. Rochemont, 16, 256.
Barber, Francis, 90, 163.
Barclay and Perkins, 17, 18, 19, 70, 163, 174, 266, 268.
Barham, H. R., quoted, 142
Barrett, Elizabeth (Mrs. Browning), 151, 217.

Barton, Bernard, 185, 190.
Batten, Sir W., 236.
BAXTER, RICHARD, 16-19.
Baxter, Mrs. Richard, 16, 17, 18.
Beaconsfield, Countess of, 89.
BEACONSFIELD, EARL OF (see Disraeli).
Beattie, Dr. W., quoted, 37.
Beauclerc, Topham, 121, 159.
BEAUMONT, FRANCIS, 19-20; mentioned, 103, 107, 286.
Bentham, Jeremy, 213, 214.
Bentley, Dr. Richard, 71.
Berthelette, Thomas, quoted, 127.
Bevry, Adam de, 46.
Bickerstaff, Isaac, 121.
Birch, Thomas, quoted, 251.
Blackstone, Sir William, 121.
Blake, William, x.
Blanchard, Laman, 85.
Blanc, Louis, 305.
Blessington, Lady, 88, 90, 195, 278.
Blinde, Mathilde, quoted, 98.
BLOOMFIELD, ROBERT, 20-21.
Boccaccio, 257.
Bohn, Henry G., 79.
Bolingbroke, Viscount, 242, 247.
Boswell, Dr., 164.
BOSWELL, JAMES, 21-22; mentioned, x, 105, 122, 167; quoted, 120, 123, 156, 158, 159, 161, 162, 163, 164, 165, 166, 167, 168, 169, 170.
Boufflers, Madame de, 159-160.
Boyer, Jeremy, 56.
Bracegirdle, Mrs., 63.
Brawne, Fanny, 179, 181, 182.
Bray, Dr. Nicholas, 264.

INDEX OF PERSONS.

Braybrooke, Lord, 234.
Brayley, Edward Wedlake, quoted, 13, 250, 319.
Brewster, Sir David, quoted, 227, 228.
Brigham, Nicholas, 48.
Brigham, Rachel, 48.
Brontë, Anne, 22.
BRONTË, CHARLOTTE, 22–23; quoted, 305–306.
Brooks, Shirley, 305; quoted, 306.
Brougham, Lord, 201.
Brown, Charles, 180, 181, 182.
Browning, Elizabeth Barrett, 151, 217.
Browning, Robert, 305.
Brydges, Mr. Alderman, 254.
Buchanan, Robert, quoted, 39.
Bucke, C., quoted, 10.
Buckland, Dean William, 174.
Buller, Charles, 38.
Buller, Mr. Justice, 56
BULWER LYTTON, 23–24; mentioned, 194.
BUNYAN, JOHN, 25–26.
Burbage, Richard, 265.
Burdette, Robert J., quoted, 231.
BURKE, EDMUND, 27–28; mentioned, 68, 122, 123, 167.
Burne-Jones, Edward, 254.
Burney, Dr. Charles (Elder), 72, 73, 158.
Burney, Charles (Younger), quoted, 164, 165.
BURNEY, FANNY (see Madame D'Arblay).
Burns, Robert, x.
Busby, Dr. Richard, 91, 197, 246, 258.
BUTLER, SAMUEL, 28–29; mentioned, x, 321.
Byron, Augusta Ada, 32.
Byron, Lady, 32.
BYRON, LORD, 30–35; mentioned, 145, 220, 263; quoted, 257.
Byron, Mrs., 30.

Camden, William, 45.
CAMPBELL, THOMAS, 35–37; mentioned, 32.

Campbell, Mrs. Thomas, 35, 36.
CARLYLE, THOMAS, 38–40; mentioned, viii, 85; quoted, 147, 158.
CARTER, ELIZABETH, 40–41.
Cary, Henry Francis, 192.
Casaubon, Isaac, 315.
Cave, Edward, 157, 260.
CENTLIVRE, SUSANNA, 41; mentioned, x.
Cervantes, 106.
Chantrey, Sir Francis, 72.
Chapman, Dr. John, 97, 170.
Charles I., 174.
Charles II., 66, 96, 207, 214, 301, 322.
Charles X., of France, 134.
Charlton, Margaret (see Mrs. Richard Baxter).
CHATTERTON, THOMAS, 42–45; mentioned, v.
CHAUCER, GEOFFREY, 45–48; mentioned, 20, 66, 91, 94, 257, 259, 285, 286.
Chawcer, Richard, 45.
CHESTERFIELD, EARL OF, 49–50; mentioned, 112, 241.
Church, Mrs. Ross (Florence Marryat), quoted, 206.
CHURCHILL, CHARLES, 50–51; mentioned, 66, 70, 72.
Cibber, Caius Gabriel, 7, 54.
CIBBER, COLLEY, 52–55; mentioned, x, 195.
Cibber, Theophilus, quoted, 104, 264.
Clarke, Charles Cowden, quoted, 153, 177, 178, 179.
Clarke, John, 178.
Clarke, Mary Cowden, quoted, 153, 177, 178, 179.
Clive, Lord, 202.
COLERIDGE, SAMUEL TAYLOR, 56–60; mentioned, 148, 184, 186, 187, 285, 321.
Collier, John Payne, 204.
COLLINS, WILLIAM, 60–61.
COLMAN, GEORGE (Elder), 61–62; mentioned, 51, 70, 167.
COLMAN, GEORGE (Younger), 62–63.
CONGREVE, WILLIAM, 63–64; mentioned, 8, 9.

INDEX OF PERSONS. 329

Constable, Archibald, quoted, 35.
Cook, Eliza, 139.
Cooke, George Willis, quoted, 98, 99.
Corry, Montagu (Lord Rowton), 88.
Coventry, Baron Thomas, 18.
COWLEY, ABRAHAM, 64-66; mentioned, 94.
COWPER, WILLIAM, 66-67; mentioned, ix, 50, 71.
CRABBE, GEORGE, 68-69; mentioned, 28.
Craik, Henry, 299.
Croft, Sir Herbert, 42, 43.
Croker, John Wilson, quoted, 160.
Cromwell, Oliver, 37, 136, 207, 213.
Crosby, Sir John, 269.
Cross, John Walter, 99.
CRUDEN, ALEXANDER, 69-70.
Cruikshank, George, 305.
CUMBERLAND, RICHARD, 70-71; mentioned, 66.
CUNNINGHAM, ALLAN, 71-72.
Cunningham, Peter, quoted, 20, 44, 52, 92, 101, 105, 169, 175, 177, 178, 197, 244, 246, 263, 277, 283, 288, 295, 301, 313, 322.

Dallas, R. C., 31.
Danvers, Sir John, 223.
D'ARBLAY, MADAME, 72-73.
Davenant, Lady, 74.
DAVENANT, SIR WILLIAM, 74-75; mentioned, x, 6.
Davies, Tom, x, 21, 160, 161.
Davis, John, quoted, 42.
DAY, THOMAS, 75.
DE FOE, DANIEL, 76-78; mentioned, 256.
De Foe, Daniel, Jr., 77.
De Foe, Sophia, 77.
Delaney, Mrs. (Mary), 73.
Denham, Sir John, 74.
Dennis, John, mentioned, 196; quoted, 231.
DE QUINCEY, THOMAS, 78-79.
DICKENS, CHARLES, 79-86; mentioned, 217, 305, 306, 320; quoted, 305.

Dickens, Charles, Jr., vi.
Dickens, Mrs. Charles, 83.
DISRAELI, BENJAMIN, 86-89; mentioned, 89.
D'ISRAELI, ISAAC, 89-90; mentioned, 87, 88, 165, 256, 292; quoted, 2.
Dixon, Hepworth, 12.
Dobson, Austin, quoted, 105.
Dodsley, Robert, 11, 28, 251, 312.
Donnes, Dr. John, 173.
Doran, Dr. John, quoted, 53, 103, 231, 265, 283.
Downe, John, quoted, 230.
DRAYTON, MICHAEL, 90-91; mentioned, ix, 174.
Drogheda, Countess of, 322, 323.
Drummond, William, quoted, 286.
DRYDEN, JOHN, 91-96; mentioned, vii, x, 48, 175, 197, 230, 243; quoted, 196, 210.
Dryden, Lady Elizabeth, 92.
Dumergues, Charles, 261, 262.
D'URFEY, TOM, 96-97.
Dyce, Alexander, 85.
Dyer, George, 191.
Dyke, Bessy (Mrs. Thomas Moore), 220, 221.
Dyson, Jeremiah, 10.

Edward VI., 46, 57, 108.
Edwardes, Edward, quoted, 251.
ELIOT, GEORGE, 97-99; mentioned, 170.
Elizabeth, Queen, 12, 108, 249, 250.
Elmsley (the Publisher), 114.
Elwood, Mrs. A. K., quoted, 73, 150.
Erasmus, 224, 225.
Essex, Devereux, Earl of, 7, 286.
EVANS, MARY ANN (George Eliot), 97-99; mentioned, 170.
EVELYN, JOHN, 100-102; mentioned, x, 52; quoted, 66, 235.
Evelyn, William J., 101.

FARADAY, MICHAEL, 102-103.
FARQUHAR, GEORGE, 103-104.
Faulkner, Thomas, quoted, 106, 224, 290, 308, 310.

INDEX OF PERSONS.

Ferguson, Dr. Robert, 263.
FIELDING, HENRY, 104–106; mentioned, v, x.
Fields, James T., quoted, 85, 86, 149, 303.
Fitzgerald, Percy, quoted, 183.
Fitzherbert, William, 159.
Flaxman, John, 257.
FLETCHER, JOHN, 107–108; mentioned, 19, 20, 103, 286.
Foe, James, 76.
Foote, Samuel, 163.
Ford, Edward, quoted, 89.
Forman, H. Buxton, quoted, 181.
Forster, John, mentioned, 79, 83, 84; quoted, 77, 79, 85, 119, 123.
Fountaine, Sir Andrew, 297.
Fowler, Thomas, 172.
Fox, Charles James, 274.
FOX, JOHN, 108–109.
Fox, William Johnson, 85.
Francis, Lady, 109.
FRANCIS, SIR PHILIP, 109–110.
FRANKLIN, BENJAMIN, 110–112.
Froude, James Anthony, quoted, 38, 39, 40.
Fuller, Thomas, quoted, 171, 176, 222.

Garrick, David, x, 21, 86, 113, 123, 125, 156, 157, 167, 222.
Garrick, Mrs. David, 222.
Garrick, Peter, 170.
Garth, Dr. Samuel, 7, 8, 94, 259.
Gaskell, Mrs. Elizabeth Cleghorn, quoted, 22–23, 305–306.
GAY, JOHN, 112–113; mentioned, 243, 249.
George III., 156.
GEORGE ELIOT (see Eliot, George).
GIBBON, EDWARD, 113–115.
Gilchrist, Anne, quoted, 188.
Gilfillan, Rev. George, quoted, 50.
Gilman, John, 58, 59.
Gilpin, John, 67.
Glen, William, 158.
GLOVER, RICHARD, 115.
GODWIN, WILLIAM, 116–118; quoted, 272.

Godwin, Mrs. William (Mary Wollstonecraft), 116, 118, 256, 272.
Godwin, Mrs. William (second), 116, 117.
Godwin, Mary Wollstonecraft (Mrs. Shelley), 271, 272.
GOLDSMITH, OLIVER, 118–126; mentioned, v, 21, 91, 105, 162, 167, 169.
Goodwin, Dr. Thomas, 214.
Gosse, Edmund, quoted, 128.
GOWER, JOHN, 126–127; mentioned, 46.
Grant, Baron, 150.
GRAY, THOMAS, 127–129; mentioned, 71.
Greatorex, Rev. Dan., 54.
Greville, Charles C. F., quoted, 201, 274.
Grimshaw, Rev. T. S., quoted, 67.
GROTE, GEORGE, 129–130.
Gwynne, Nell, 208.

HALLAM, HENRY, 131.
Halliwell-Phillipps, 172.
Hall, S. C., quoted, 57, 88, 117, 148.
Hall, Susannah, 265.
Handel, 242, 243.
Hare, Augustus J. C., quoted, 169.
Harness, Rev. William, 185.
Harris, Joseph, 95.
Harte, Walter, 2.
Hastings, Warren, 51, 66, 70, 202.
Haweis, Rev. H. R., 242.
Hawkins, Sir John, mentioned, 165; quoted, 166, 169, 313.
Hawkins, Letitia Matilda, quoted, 224.
Haydon, Benjamin Robert, 189.
Hazlitt, John, 131.
HAZLITT, WILLIAM, 131–135; mentioned, 191, 213.
Hazlitt, Mrs. William (Sarah Stoddard), 131.
Henderson, John, 86.
Henry IV., 47.
Henry VIII., 108, 224, 256.
HERBERT, GEORGE, 136.
HERRICK, ROBERT, 136–137.

INDEX OF PERSONS. 331

Hoare, Henry, 9.
Hoare, Lemuel, 68.
Hobhouse, Thomas, 33.
Hodder, George, quoted, 59, 154, 304, 306.
Hogarth, William, 79, 189, 253.
Holbein (Younger), 224.
HOLCROFT, THOMAS, 137.
Holland, Lady, quoted, 93, 279.
Holland, Lord, 275.
Holland, Sir Henry, quoted, 204.
Holley, O. L., 111.
Homer, 172, 243.
HOOD, THOMAS, 137-139; mentioned, 79.
Hood, Thomas, Jr., quoted, 138, 139.
HOOK, THEODORE, 140-143.
Hoole, John, 167.
Horace, 94, 96, 97.
Horne, John, 309.
Hotten, J. C., quoted, 43.
Houghton, Lord, 139, 181.
Howitt, William, mentioned, 181, 182; quoted, 15, 43, 125, 180, 211, 213, 256, 289, 290.
HUME, DAVID, 143-144.
Humphrey, Ozias, quoted, 160.
HUNT, LEIGH, 144-149; mentioned, 57, 271; quoted, 4, 5, 95, 150, 158, 168, 169, 179, 180, 184, 199, 298.
Hunt, Mrs. Leigh, 147.
Hunter, Dr. John, 14.

INCHBALD, MRS., 149-151.
Ingleby, C. M., quoted, 215, 216, 297.
Ireland, William, 266.
Irving, Edward, 38.
Irving, Washington, quoted, 119, 121, 122, 124.

James I., 8, 13, 108, 172, 249, 250.
James II., 234.
JAMESON, ANNA, 151-152.
Jeaffreson, Dr. John B., 87.
Jeaffries, Lord, 94.
Jerrold, Blanchard, quoted, 117, 148, 152, 153, 154, 271.
JERROLD, DOUGLAS, 152-155; mentioned, 85, 117, 306.

Jesse, John H., quoted, 12, 28, 32, 241, 261, 276, 307.
JOHNSON, SAMUEL, 155-171; mentioned, v, ix, x, 3, 21, 49, 50, 60, 90, 98, 121, 122, 123, 125, 204, 222, 247, 253, 256, 260, 274; quoted, 4, 6, 64, 94, 105, 120, 122, 231, 240, 259, 260, 261, 288, 289, 292.
Johnson, Mrs. (mother of Samuel), 155.
Johnson, Mrs. (wife of Samuel), 158.
Jones, Inigo, 12, 51.
Jones, Owen, 98.
JONSON, BEN, 171-177; mentioned, 6, 11, 20, 74, 136, 270, 286.
Jonson, Mrs. Margaret, 172, 173.
Joyce, Dr. Thomas, 203.

Kat, Christopher, 8.
Kearsley, George, 164.
KEATS, JOHN, 177-182; mentioned, 27.
Keats, Thomas, 179, 181.
Kingsley, Charles, x.
Kingsley, Henry, x.
Kingston, Duke of, 218.
Knatchbull, Sir Edward, 34.
Kneller, Sir Godfrey, 9.
Knight, Charles, quoted, 163, 223, 266.
Knipp, Mrs., 238.

LAMB, CHARLES, 182-193; mentioned, v, ix, x, 57, 60, 79, 131, 132, 133, 138, 144, 146, 178, 273, 284, 285, 321; quoted, 56.
Lamb, Elizabeth, 183, 186, 273.
Lamb, John, 183, 186, 273.
Lamb, John, Jr., 184.
Lamb, Mary, 79, 131, 132, 144, 185, 186, 187, 190, 193.
LANDON, LETITIA E., 194.
LANDOR, WALTER SAVAGE, 194-195; mentioned, 217.
Landseer, Sir Edwin, 248.
Langbaine, Gerrard, 282.
Langton, Bennet, 123, 164.
LEE, NATHANIEL, 195-196.
Leech, John, 302, 305,

INDEX OF PERSONS.

Lemon, Mark, 305.
Lenox, Mrs. Charlotte, 169.
L'Estrange, Sir Roger, 208.
Lever, Charles, x.
Levett, Robert, 162.
Lewes, George Henry, 98, 99.
Lewis, Mrs. (Countess of Beaconsfield), 89.
Lewis, Samuel, quoted, 54, 249, 250, 257.
Linley, Miss (Mrs. Sheridan), 273.
Lintot, Bernard, 159.
LOCKE, JOHN, 197-198; mentioned, 227.
Lockhart, John Gibson, quoted, 33, 73, 262, 263.
Lockhart, Mrs. J. G., 262.
Loftie, Rev. W. J., quoted, 62, 66, 67, 225, 268, 292, 293.
Lovelace, Countess of (Augusta Ada Byron), 32.
LOVELACE, RICHARD, 198-199.
LOVER, SAMUEL, 199-200.
Lowell, James Russell, mentioned, 235; quoted, 252.
Lucas, John, 217.
Lysons, Samuel, quoted, 100.
LYTTON, LORD (see Bulwer Lytton).

MACAULAY, THOMAS BABINGTON, 200-204; quoted, 6, 22, 257.
Macaulay, Zachary, 201.
Macdonald, John, quoted, 292.
Mackintosh, Sir James, quoted, 224.
Maclise, Daniel, 85.
Maitland, William, quoted, 153.
Malone, Edmund, quoted, 5, 92, 172, 173, 196, 266.
Manning, Thomas, 188, 189.
Manningham, John, quoted, 269.
MARLOWE, CHRISTOPHER, 204-205.
Marryat, Florence (see Mrs. Ross Church).
MARRYAT, FREDERICK, 205-207.
Marryat, Joseph, 206.
Martin, Dr. B. E., quoted, 58, 59, 80, 84, 85, 87, 88.
Martin, Sir Theodore, 305.
MARVELL, ANDREW, 207-208.

Mary I., 108.
Maseres, Baron, 188.
MASSINGER, PHILIP, 209.
Masson, David, quoted, 212, 215.
Mathews, Charles, 34.
Mathews, Charles James, 305.
Matthews, Captain Thomas, 273.
Meteyard, Eliza, quoted, 14.
Milbanke, Miss (Lady Byron), 32.
Millais, John Everett, 305.
Miller, Joe, mentioned, 143; quoted, 291.
Milner-Gibson, Thomas, 85, 86.
Milner, Rev. Thomas, quoted, 317.
Milnes, Richard Monckton (see Lord Houghton).
MILTON, JOHN, 210-216; mentioned, 4, 132, 133, 146, 153, 201, 207.
Milton, Mrs. John (Mary Powell), 212.
Milton, John (father of poet), 210.
Mitford, Dr., 216.
MITFORD, MARY RUSSELL, 216-217.
Montagu, Basil, 248.
Montagu, Mrs. Basil, 248.
Montague, Charles, 94.
Montague, Mrs. (Elizabeth), 312.
MONTAGUE, MARY WORTLEY, 218-219.
Montgomery, Henry R., quoted, 287.
Moore, Anne Barbara, 221.
Moore, Peter, 274.
MOORE, THOMAS, 220-221; mentioned, 32, 33, 35, 36, 93, 262; quoted, 4, 30, 31, 32, 34, 145, 275.
Moore, Mrs. Thomas, 220, 221.
MORE, HANNAH, 222.
MORE, SIR THOMAS, 222-225.
More, Thomas, quoted, 225.
MURPHY, ARTHUR, 226-227; mentioned, 55; quoted, 159.
Murray, John, 33, 34, 68, 262, 285.

Napoleon I., 134.
Nelson, John, quoted, 69.
Nelson, Lord, 125.
Nettleton, Robert, 208.
Neve, Philip, 216.
Newland, Abraham, 221.

INDEX OF PERSONS.

Newton, Sir Isaac, 227-229; mentioned, 73.
Nichols, John Gough, 277.
Nicolas, Sir Harris, 313.
Noorthhouck, John, quoted, 78.

Oldfield, Mrs., 64, 103.
Oldys, William, quoted, 196, 282, 315, 316.
Otway, Thomas, 229-230; mentioned, 93.

Parkes, John James, quoted, 10, 109, 110, 157.
Parkes, Joseph, quoted, 109, 110.
Parnell, Thomas, 243.
Parr, Dr. Samuel, quoted, 165.
Patmore, P. G., quoted, 132, 133, 135.
Pembroke, William Herbert, Earl of, 269.
Pembroke, Countess of, 269, 276.
Penn, William, 231-232.
Pennant, Thomas, viii.
Pepys, Samuel, 232-239; mentioned, ix, x; quoted, 74, 95, 100, 111.
Pepys, Mrs. Samuel, 234, 235.
Percy, Bishop Thomas, quoted, 119, 121.
Peter the Great, 100, 234.
Philips, Robert, quoted, 25, 26.
Phillipps-Halliwell, 172.
Pink's History of Clerkenwell, quoted, 19, 26, 296, 318.
Piozzi, Mrs. (see Mrs. Thrale).
Pitt, William, 109.
Pope, Alexander, 240-244; mentioned, x, 2, 19, 41, 95, 112, 219, 245, 247, 257, 289.
Pope, Alexander (father of the poet), 240, 241.
Porson, Richard, 244-245.
Porter, Mrs. Lucy, 158.
Procter, Adelaide, 248.
Procter, B. W., 248; mentioned, 217; quoted, 133, 146, 257.

Quarles, Francis, 91.
Quiney, Richard, 270.

Radcliffe, Dr. John, 322.
Raleigh, Carew, 250, 252.
Raleigh, Lady, 250, 252.
Raleigh, Sir Walter, 249-252.
Ralph, James, 110.
Redding, Cyrus, quoted, 36, 321.
Reid, Stuart J., quoted, 280.
Reynolds, Sir Joshua, 21, 121, 122, 123, 153, 160, 161, 167, 168, 222.
Richard III., 269.
Richardson, Samuel, 252-255; mentioned, 16, 118; quoted, 215.
Richardson, Mrs. Samuel, 253, 255.
Riley, Henry Thomas, 46.
Ritchie, Mrs. R. (Anne Thackeray), 303.
Robinson, Henry C., mentioned, 321; quoted, 15, 56, 57, 193.
Robinson, Jacob, 27.
Robinson, William, quoted, 314.
Rochester, Earl of, 95.
Rogers, Dr. Joseph, 125.
Rogers, Samuel, 255-258; mentioned, 15, 22, 32, 36, 73, 93, 165, 221, 262, 284, 321; quoted, 33, 57, 58, 69, 309, 319.
Roper, Margaret, 225.
Roscoe, William, quoted, 243.
Roubilliac, S. F., 257.
Rousseau, J. J., 143, 144, 162.
Rowe, Nicholas, 258-259.
Rowton, Lord (see Montagu Corry).
Russell, Dr. William H., 305.

St. John, Henry (Bolingbroke), 242.
Salter, Mr. (Don Saltero), 291.
Savage, Richard, 259-261; mentioned, 157, 288.
Scott, Sir Walter, 261-263; mentioned, 73; quoted, 92, 93, 94, 175.
Severn, Joseph, 181.
Shadwell, Thomas, 264; mentioned, 92; quoted, 107.
Shakspere, Edmond, 267, 269.
Shakspere, 264-271; mentioned, 20, 71, 125, 146, 153, 154, 162, 172, 175, 176, 215, 216, 257, 286, 301, 306, 315, 316; quoted, 223,

SHELLEY, PERCY BYSSHE, 271-272.
Shelley, Mrs., 271.
Shelley, Sir Timothy, 272.
SHENSTONE, WILLIAM, 272.
Sheppard, Jack, 143.
SHERIDAN, RICHARD BRINSLEY, 273-275; mentioned, 86, 167.
Sheridan, Mrs. (Miss Linley), 273.
SHIRLEY, JAMES, 275-276.
Shirley, Mrs. James, 276.
Siddons, Mrs., 283.
SIDNEY, SIR PHILIP, 276-277.
Sloane, Sir Hans, 224.
Smith, Charles Roach, quoted, 9, 45, 246, 254.
Smith, George, 23.
SMITH, HORACE, 277-278.
SMITH, JAMES, 277-278.
Smith, James, quoted, 23.
Smith, Robert ('Bobus'), 170, 256, 280.
SMITH, SYDNEY, 278-280; mentioned, 93.
Smithwick, John, 91.
SMOLLETT, TOBIAS, 280-282.
Somerset, Protector, 311.
SOUTHERNE, THOMAS, 282-284.
SOUTHEY, ROBERT, 284-285; mentioned, 60, 132, 187; quoted, 318, 319.
Sparks, Jared, 111.
Speght, T., quoted, 46.
Spence, Joseph, 2, 6, 8, 63, 65, 231, 240.
SPENSER, EDMUND, 285-286; mentioned, 91, 146.
Spenser, Gabriel, 173.
Spiller, John, 54.
Sprat, Dean Thomas, 65.
Stanfield, Clarkson, 85, 217.
Stanhope, Sir William, 241.
Stanley, Dean Arthur Penrhyn, mentioned, 315; quoted, 47, 86, 91, 112, 174, 203, 204, 229, 286.
Staunton, Howard, quoted, 253.
STEELE, SIR RICHARD, 287-291; mentioned, v, x, 2, 4, 6, 8, 9, 97, 261.
Steele, Lady, 288, 289, 290.

Steele, Mrs. Richard, 288.
STERNE, LAURENCE, 292-294.
Stevens, George, 216.
Stoddard, Sarah (Mrs. Hazlitt), 131.
Stow, John, mentioned, viii; quoted, 48, 104, 127, 173, 195, 227, 235, 267, 269.
Strype, John, mentioned, viii; quoted, 18, 104, 170, 176, 237.
Stuart, Lady Louisa, 218.
Stukely, Dr. William, 228.
SUCKLING, SIR JOHN, 294-295.
Suckling, Rev. Alfred, 295.
SWEDENBORG, EMANUEL, 296-297.
SWIFT, JONATHAN, 297-300; mentioned, 3, 241, 243; quoted, 7, 247.
Symington, A. J., quoted, 221.

Talfourd, Thomas Noon, mentioned, 188, 191; quoted, 183, 185, 188, 190, 191.
Taylor, John, quoted, 53, 55, 110, 245.
TAYLOR, JOHN (Water Poet), 301-302.
Taylor, Rev. John, 165.
Taylor, Tom, mentioned, 302, 305; quoted, 228.
Terence, 97.
Thackeray, Anne (Mrs. Ritchie), 303.
THACKERAY, WILLIAM MAKEPEACE, 302-306; mentioned, ix, 3, 154, 203; quoted, 2, 105, 287.
Theodore, King of Corsica, 134.
Thirlwall, Bishop, 130.
Thompson, Edward, quoted, 208.
Thompson, Mrs. A. F., quoted, 72.
THOMSON, JAMES, 307-308.
Thorne, James, quoted, 14, 36, 65, 106, 129, 148, 180, 181, 182, 206, 219, 221, 241, 311, 312.
Thrale, Henry, 163, 168.
Thrale, Mrs. Henry, 156, 163; quoted, 307.
Throgmorton, Elizabeth (Lady Raleigh), 250, 252.
Thurlow, Lord Chancellor, 201.
Thynne, Charles, 251.
Tickell, Thomas, 5.

INDEX OF PERSONS.

Ticknor, George, quoted, 36.
Timbs, John, quoted, 24, 142, 143, 240.
Todd, H. J., quoted, 212, 214.
Tonson, Jacob, 8, 9.
TOOKE, JOHN HORNE, 309–310.
Traill, H. D., quoted, 293.
Trevelyan, G. O., quoted, 201, 202, 203.
Trevelyan, Lady, 203.
Trollope, Anthony, 302, 305.
Turner, J. M. W., 245.

Vanbrugh, Sir John, 8.
Vandyke, 295.
Vaughan, Sir John, 13.
Venables, George, 302.
Vernon and Hood, 137.
Verrio, Antonio, 144.
Vertue, George, 295.
Victoria, Queen, 39, 234, 306.
Voltaire, quoted, 63, 64.
Von Homrigh, Esther, 298, 299.

Walcott, M. E. C., quoted, 27, 47.
Walford, Edward, quoted, 49, 228, 230, 259.
WALLER, EDMUND, 310–311; mentioned, x.
WALPOLE, HORACE, 311–313; mentioned, 5, 53, 128, 222, 241; quoted, 219, 226.
Walpole, Sir Robert, 311.
Walter, James, quoted, 265.
WALTON, IZAAK, 313–315; mentioned, 64; quoted, 136, 173.
Ward, Edward, 315, 316.
Ward, E. M., R. A., 49.
Warwick, Countess of, 3, 4, 6, 322.
Warwick, Earl of, 3, 4, 5.

WATTS, ISAAC, 316–317.
Welwood, Dr., quoted, 259.
WESLEY, JOHN, 318–319.
Wheatley, B. W., quoted, 114.
White, Gilbert, quoted, 61.
White, William, quoted, 297.
Whitefield, Rev. George, 318.
Whittington, Richard, 145.
Wilde, John, 253.
Wilkes, John, 51.
Wilkes, Robert, 104.
Wilkie, David, 153.
William III., 264.
William IV., 125, 270.
William of Wickham, 126.
Williams, Anna, 158, 162, 163.
Williams, Dr. Charles J. B., 24.
Wilson, Richard, 321.
Wilson, Sir Robert, 174.
Winter, William, quoted, 59, 252.
Witherborne, Dr., 13.
WITHER, JOHN, 320.
WOLCOT, JOHN, 320–321; mentioned, x.
Wollstonecraft, Mary (Mrs. Godwin), 116, 118, 256, 272.
Wood, Anthony, mentioned, 107; quoted, 29, 198, 199, 209, 212, 275, 283, 313, 314.
Wordsworth, Dorothy, 190.
WORDSWORTH, WILLIAM, 321–322; mentioned, 15, 58, 185, 217.
Wren, Sir Christopher, 45, 92, 136, 199, 210, 265, 324.
WYCHERLEY, WILLIAM, 322–323; mentioned, x.

Yates, Edmund, quoted, 306.
YOUNG, EDWARD, 324; mentioned, ix, 5, 63.

INDEX OF PLACES.

ABBOTSFORD, 263.
Abchurch Lane, 102, 290, 300.
Aberdeen, 69.
Abingdon Buildings, Westminster, 71.
Abingdon Street, Westminster, 71.
Abney Park Cemetery, 317.
Acton, 17, 106.
Adam and Eve Tavern, Kensington Road, 275.
Adam Street, Adelphi, 139.
Addlestone, Surrey, 75.
Adelaide Road, 289.
Adelphi, The, 87, 138, 139.
Adelphi Club, Maiden Lane, Covent Garden, 245.
Adelphi Terrace, Adelphi, 139, 222, 249.
African Tavern, St. Michael's Alley, Cornhill, 245.
Airlie Lodge, Campden Hill, 202, 203.
Albany, The, Piccadilly, 23, 32, 202.
Albemarle Street, Piccadilly, 32, 33, 34, 35, 53, 68, 102, 115, 263, 284.
Albert Hall, Kensington, 195.
Albion Street, Oxford Street, 293, 303.
Albion Tavern, Aldersgate Street, 130.
Albion Tavern, Russell Street, Covent Garden, 154–155.
Albyn House, Parson's Green, 255.
Aldersgate Street, 64, 75, 108, 130, 170, 211, 212, 213, 301, 322.
Aldgate, 46–47.

Alexandra Palace, 221.
Alfred Club, Albemarle Street, 34–35.
All Hallows Church, Bread Street, 210.
All Hallows Lane, Upper Thames Street, 239.
All Saints Church, Fulham, 142.
Almack's, 305.
Alma Terrace, Fulham Road, Hammersmith, 206.
Almonry Office, Middle Scotland Yard, 37.
Alpha Road, St. John's Wood, 193.
Amen Corner, Paternoster Row, 279.
Amen Court, Paternoster Row, 279.
Amesbury, 112.
Angel Court, High Street, Borough, 80.
Apothecaries' Hall, 265.
Apsley House, 261, 273.
Argyll Lodge, Campden Hill, 203.
Argyll Road, Kensington Road, 275.
Argyll Rooms, 295.
Arlington Street, Piccadilly, 218, 311.
Arthur Street, Fulham Road, 221.
Artillery Ground, Bunhill Row, 318.
Artillery Place, Bunhill Row, 215.
Artillery Walk, Bunhill Row, 214–215.
Arundel Hotel, Norfolk Street, Strand, 232.
Arundel House, Highgate Hill, 13–14.
Arundel House, Strand, 235.
Arundel Street, Strand, 117, 155, 170, 235, 258.

INDEX OF PLACES.

Athenæum Club, 24, 103, 142–143, 204, 221, 258, 278, 306.
Augustus Square, Regent's Park, 153.
Augustus Street, Regent's Park, 153.
Austin Friars, 277.
Axe Yard (Fluyder Street), 75, 233.

BACK LANE, Twickenham, 105.
Back Road, Islington, 250.
Baker Street, Enfield, 205.
Baker Street, Portman Square, 23.
Ball's Pond, Newington Green, 256.
Bankend, Bankside, 266.
Bankside, 19, 20, 107, 118, 174, 176, 209, 266, 270.
Barbican, Aldersgate Street, 212, 213, 301.
Barn-Elms, 9, 65.
Barnes, 200.
Barnes Common, 106.
Barnsbury Road, Penton Street, 126.
Bartholomew Close, Little Britain, 110, 111, 214.
Bartholomew Lane, City, 130.
Bartlett's Buildings, Fetter Lane, 183.
Bartlett's Passage, Fetter Lane, 183.
Basinghall Street, 235, 237.
Bateman's Buildings, Soho Square, 61.
Battersea, 65, 242.
Battersea Bridge, 224.
Bay Cottage, Edmonton, 192.
Bayham Street, Camden Town, 79, 81.
Bayswater, 299.
Beaconsfield, Bucks, 28, 310.
Bear and Harrow, Butcher Row, 196.
Bear-at-the-Bridge-Foot, 295, 323.
Bear Gardens, 174, 266, 267, 268.
Bear Inn, Southwark, 238.
Beauchamp Tower, Tower of London, 251.
Beaufort Buildings, Strand, 106.
Beaufort House, Chelsea, 224.
Beaufort Row, Chelsea, 224.
Beaufort Street, Chelsea, 224.
Beaumont Street, Marylebone, 195, 248.
Beckenham, Kent, 129.

Bedfordbury, 274.
Bedford Coffee House, Covent Garden, 51, 61, 106, 226, 242, 274, 312.
Bedford Gardens (Bedford Square), 128.
Bedford Head Tavern, Maiden Lane, Covent Garden, 207.
Bedford Hotel, Covent Garden, 5, 303.
Bedford House (Southampton House), Bloomsbury Square, 52.
Bedford Place, Russell Square, 71, 156, 217.
Bedford Square, 140.
Bedford Street, Covent Garden, 49, 245, 259.
Bedford Tavern, Maiden Lane, Covent Garden, 207.
Beefsteak Club, 51, 62, 63, 226.
Belgrave Place, Belgrave Square, 130.
Belgrave Square, 130.
Bell Inn, Aldersgate, 301.
Bell Inn, Carter Lane, 270, 271.
Bell Inn, Fore Street, Edmonton, ix, 192.
Bell Inn, King Street, Westminster, 236, 244, 300.
Bennet's Hill, City, 105.
Bennett Street, St. James's Street, 31, 115.
Bentinck Street, Manchester Square, 114.
Berkeley House, Piccadilly, 310.
Berkeley Square, 53, 71, 219, 311, 312.
Berkeley Street, Piccadilly, 240, 241, 310.
Berners Street, Oxford Street, 140–141, 199.
Bethlehem Hospital, 175–176.
Bethnal Green, 69.
Bevis Marks, 86.
Birchin Lane, Cornhill, 44, 128, 200, 300.
Bird-in-Hand-Court, Cheapside, 179.
Bishop of London's Meadows, Fulham, 24, 143.
Bishopsgate Street, 185, 195, 268, 276, 295.

INDEX OF PLACES.

Blackfriars, 112.
Blackfriars Bridge, 216, 268.
Blackfriars Road, 141.
Blackfriars Theatre, 265, 269.
Black Jack Tavern, 143.
Blackman's Street, Southwark, 17.
Black-Spread-Eagle-Court, Bread Street, Cheapside, 210.
Blandford Square, 98.
Blandford Street, Portman Square, 102.
Bloody Tower, Tower of London, 251.
Bloomfield Street, Finsbury, 196.
Bloomsbury Square, 10, 17, 52, 87, 88, 90, 128, 131, 288.
Bloomsbury Street, 140.
Blue Bells Tavern, Lincoln's Inn Fields, 238.
Blue Coat School (*see* Christ-Hospital).
Blue Hart Court, Coleman Street, 20.
Blue Stocking Club, 312.
Boar's Head Tavern, Eastcheap, 125, 270.
Bodleian Library, Oxford, 9, 234.
Bolingbroke House, Battersea, 242.
Bolt Court, Fleet Street, 90, 158, 163, 164, 165, 222, 256.
Bolton House, Hampstead, 14.
Bolton Street, Piccadilly, 34, 73.
Bond Street, 114, 307.
Boodle's Club House, 115.
Borough High Street, 10, 17, 48, 80, 163, 320.
Borough Market, Southwark, 70.
Borough Road, Southwark, 17.
Boswell Court, Carey Street, 195.
Boulogne, France, 37.
Bournemouth, 118.
Bouverie Street, Fleet Street, 133.
Bow Church, 210.
Bow Lane, Cheapside, 45.
Bow Street, Covent Garden, x, 105–106, 152, 155, 170, 189, 190, 237, 243, 299, 307, 310.
Bradenham House, Buckinghamshire, 90.

Brandenburg House, Hammersmith, 206.
Bread Street, Cheapside, 176, 210, 270, 271.
Breakneck Stairs, 119, 120.
Brentford, 177, 309.
Brew House, Axe Yard, 75.
Brick Court, Middle Temple Lane, 105, 121, 123.
Bridge Street, Westminster, 57.
Bridgewater House, St. James's Street, 240.
British Coffee House, 170, 282.
British Institution, Pall Mall, 144.
British Museum, 25, 53, 89, 128, 140, 152, 178, 201, 270, 271.
Broad Court, Bow Street, Long Acre, 118, 152, 155.
Broad Sanctuary, Westminster, 227.
Bromley, 318.
Brompton, Kensington, 194.
Brompton, near Huntingdon, 232.
Brompton Road, 153, 226.
Brompton Square, 63.
Brooke Street, Holborn, 42, 43, 44, 260.
Brooks's Club, St. James's Street, 28, 110, 115, 144, 221, 274, 312.
Brothers' Club, 247, 300.
Brunswick Square, 248.
Bruton Street, Berkeley Square, 53, 151.
Brydges Street, Drury Lane, 113, 189, 237.
Buckingham Court, Strand, 41, 246.
Buckingham Gate, 115.
Buckingham House (Buckingham Palace), 156, 298.
Buckingham House, Chelsea, 224.
Buckingham Palace, 95, 102, 156, 298.
Buckingham Palace Road, 37, 71.
Buckingham Street, Strand, 12, 104, 234, 282.
Bucklersbury, 223, 224.
Bull and Bush Tavern, Hammersmith, 8.
Bullingham House, Campden Hill, 228.
Bull Inn Court, Strand, 238.

Bull Inn, Shoreditch, 227.
Bull Inn, Tower Hill, 231.
Bull's Head Tavern, Clare Market, 290.
Bull's Head Tavern, Spring Gardens, 52, 53, 213.
Bunhill Fields, 25, 26, 78, 214, 215, 317, 318.
Bunhill Row, 215.
Burford Bridge, 180.
Burlington Arcade, 140.
Burlington Gardens, 10, 30, 32, 112, 273, 279.
Burlington Street, Strand, 113.
Burnham, 130.
Burnham Beeches, 128.
Bury Street, St. James's Street, 30, 68, 220, 263, 271, 288, 297, 298.
Bury Street, St. Mary Axe, 317.
Butcher Row, 170, 196, 272.
Button's Coffee House, x, 6, 149, 175, 260, 291, 300.

CADOGAN PLACE, Sloane Street, 201.
Cambridge, 19, 65, 70, 91, 136, 171, 175, 195, 205, 211, 227, 244, 245, 293.
Camden Passage, Islington, 69, 70.
Camden Town, 321.
Campden Grove, Kensington, 228.
Campden Hill, Kensington, 202, 228, 299.
Cannon Row, Westminster, 197.
Cannon Street, 92, 115, 125, 239, 268, 271.
Cannon Street Station, 239.
Cannons, Edgeware, 243.
Canon Alley, St. Paul's Churchyard, 109, 167.
Canonbury Fields, Islington, 87.
Canonbury House, Islington, 122.
Canonbury Place, Islington, 122.
Canonbury Square, Islington, 122.
Canonbury Tower, Islington, 87, 122.
Canon Row, Westminster, 239.
Canterbury, 48, 225.
Capel Court, Bartholomew Lane, 130.
Carey House (Tavern), Strand, 238.

Carey Street, Lincoln's Inn Fields, 74, 198.
Carlisle Street, Soho, 61.
Carlton House, 18, 258.
Carmarthen, Wales, 290.
Carter Lane, Doctors' Commons, 265, 270.
Castle Street, Cavendish Square, 157.
Castle Street, Holborn, 74.
Castle Tavern, Henrietta Street, Covent Garden, 273.
Castle Tavern, Islington, 54.
Castle Tavern, Savoy, 238.
Castle Yard, Holborn, 74.
Cat and Fiddle Inn, 8, 218.
Catherine Street, Strand, 156, 237.
Cavendish Square, 30, 36, 109, 151, 219.
Cavendish Street, Cavendish Square, 151.
Chalfont, Bucks, 232.
Chalton Street, Euston Road, 116.
Chancery Lane, 64, 133, 135, 172, 173, 188, 191, 238, 239, 274, 313, 316.
Chandos Street, Covent Garden, 142, 239, 274.
Change Alley, Cornhill, 300.
Channel Row, Westminster, 197.
Chantry House, 72.
Chapel Place, Poultry, 137.
Chapel Royal, St. James's, 141.
Chapel Street, Mayfair, 40, 41, 271.
Chapel Street, Pentonville, 187–188.
Chapel Street, Portland Place, 320.
Chapel Street, Somers Town, 116.
Chapter Coffee House, Paternoster Row, 22, 44, 124.
Chapter House Court, Paternoster Row, 44.
Charing Cross, 41, 53, 171, 176, 213, 233, 236, 238, 239, 244, 246, 260, 268, 307.
Charing Cross Station, 12, 81.
Charles Street, Berkeley Square, 23–24, 280.
Charles Street, Berners Street, 199.
Charles Street, Manchester Square, 102.
Charles Street, Portland Square, 102.

INDEX OF PLACES. 341

Charles Street, St. James's Square, 26, 28, 68, 104.
Charles Street, Westminster, 75, 247.
Charlotte Street, Bedford Square, 140.
Charter House, 108, 222, 275.
Charter House Lane, 19.
Charter House School, 1, 2, 75, 129, 198, 287, 302, 318.
Charter House Square, v, 1, 19, 75.
Charter House Street, 19.
Charter House Yard, 18.
Chase Side, Enfield, 191.
Chatelain's Coffee House, 238.
Cheapside, 77, 136, 175–176, 179, 211, 236, 239, 270, 322.
Chelsea, viii, 1, 3, 38, 63, 99, 112, 146, 153, 197, 223, 224, 264, 281–282, 288, 291, 298, 311.
Chelsea Church, 63, 225, 264, 290, 298.
Chelsea Hospital, 311.
Chelsea Workhouse, Fulham Road, 197.
Chenies Street, Tottenham Court Road, 151.
Chertsey, 65–66.
Cheshire Cheese Tavern, 120, 170.
Cheshunt, Herts, 317.
Chesterfield House, 49, 50.
Cheyne Row, Chelsea, 99.
Cheyne Walk, Chelsea, 112, 282.
Chigwell, 232.
Chigwell Grammar School, 232.
Child's Bank, Fleet Street, 6, 175.
Child's Coffee House, 7.
Chiswell Street, Finsbury Square, 108, 215.
Chiswick, 241.
Chiswick Church, 241.
Chiswick Lane, 241.
Christ Church, Enfield, 191.
Christ Church, Newgate Street, 18.
Christ Church, Oxford, 232.
Christ-Hospital, 56–57, 60, 144, 183, 184, 253.
Churches: All Hallows, Bread Street, 210; All Saints, Fulham, 142; Bow, 210; Chapel Royal, St. James's, 141; Chelsea, 63, 225, 264, 290, 298;

Chiswick, 241; Christ, Enfield, 191; Christ, Newgate Street, 18; Christ, Oxford, 232; Danish, Wellclose Square, 54; Edmonton, 192–193; Grosvenor Chapel, South Audley Street, 41, 50, 219; Hackney, 77; Hampstead, 15; Holy Trinity, Little Queen Street, Holborn, 187; Kensington (see St. Mary, Kensington); Lady Chapel, Westminster Abbey, 47; Marylebone, 146; Orange Chapel, St. Martin's Street, Leicester Square, 227; St. Andrew's, Holborn, 87, 131–132, 259; St. Andrews-by-the-Wardrobe, 265; St. Ann's, Carter Lane, 265; St. Ann's, Soho, 134; St. Bartholomew the Great, 214; St. Benedict's Chapel, Westminster Abbey, 20, 48; St. Benet's, Paul's Wharf, 105; St. Bennet Fink, 16, 240; St. Botolph's, Aldgate, 47; St. Bride's, Fleet Street, 92, 199, 211, 212, 255; St. Clement Danes, 92, 117, 165–166, 170, 195, 196, 231; St. Dunstan's, Canterbury, 225; St. Dunstan's, Fleet Street, 6, 17, 91, 198, 257; St. Faith's, 211; St. George's, Hanover Square, 4, 99, 293; St. George's, Southwark, 80, 81, 320; St. Giles's, Cripplegate, 76, 77, 108, 215, 216; St. Giles's-in-the-Fields, 208, 276; St. Helen's, Bishopsgate, 268; St. James's, Clerkenwell, 314; St. James's, Garlickhithe, 45; St. John's Chapel, Hampstead, 182; St. John the Evangelist, Smith Square, 50–51; St. Katherine Cree, 47; St. Lawrence's, Brentford, 309; St. Luke's, Chelsea, 63, 225, 264, 290, 298; St. Margaret's, Westminster, 35, 66–67, 233, 252, 310; St. Martin's-in-the-Fields, 11, 41, 92, 104, 171, 172, 173, 220, 245, 278, 301, 302; St. Mary-Aldermary, 45; St. Mary-at-Hill, 324; St. Mary Axe, 87, 317; St. Marylebone, 12, 30; St. Mary-le-Bow, 210; St. Mary-le-Savoy, 320; St. Mary-le-Strand, 116; St. Mary-Magdalen, Milk Street, 17; St. Mary-Magdalen, Richmond, 308; St. Mary-Overy, 107, 108, 126, 127, 209, 266, 267, 269; St. Mary's Chapel, Westminster Abbey, 47; St. Mary's, Ealing, 309; St. Mary's, Kensington, 62, 63, 151, 203; St. Mary's, Putney, 113; St. Mary's, Wyndham Place, Bryanston Square, 194; St. Mary-Woolchurch, 275; St. Michael's, Cornhill, 128; St. Michael's, Highgate, 58; St. Michael's, Old Verulam, 13; St. Mildred's, Bread Street, 271; St. Nicholas's, Deptford, 204-205; St. Olive's, Hart Street, 233, 234, 235, 238; St. Pancras-in-the-Fields, 116, 118, 271, 273, 316; St. Paul's Cathedral, 39, 109, 276-277, 279; St. Paul's, Covent Garden, x, 29, 41, 218, 283, 284, 302, 321, 323; St. Paul's, Dock Street, 54; St. Paul's, Hammersmith, 226; St. Peter's, Southwark, 268; St. Saviour's, Southwark, 107, 108, 126, 127, 209, 266, 267, 269; St. Sepulchre's, Holborn, 26, 116, 117; St. Swithin's, London Stone, 92; St. Vedast's, Foster Lane, 136; Savoy Chapel, 46, 320; Stepney, 250; Stoke Newington, 16; Stoke Pogis, 129; Swedish, Ratcliffe Highway, 296; Temple, 123; Tower Chapel, 225; Twickenham, 242; Westminster Abbey, 5, 20, 24, 37, 39, 47, 51, 53, 66, 74, 91, 94, 101, 112, 130, 164-165, 172, 173, 174, 203-204, 214, 227, 229, 259, 264, 274, 285, 286, 288, 315; Zoar Chapel, Southwark, 25.

Church Entry, Carter Lane, 265.
Church Lane, Chelsea, 298.
Church Road, Battersea, 242.
Church Row, Islington, 250.
Church Street, Chelsea, 264, 298.
Church Street, Edmonton, 178, 192.
Church Street, Fulham Road, 221.
Church Street, Greenwich, 157.
Church Street, Kensington, 228.
Church Street, Stoke Newington, 16, 77.
Cider Cellar, Maiden Lane, Covent Garden, 245.
Circus Road, St. John's Wood, 154.
City Road, viii, 26, 126, 146, 317, 318, 319.
City Road Chapel, 319.
Clapham, 138, 200, 201, 234, 253.
Clapham Common, 201.
Clare Market, Lincoln's Inn Fields, 54, 55, 196, 290.
Clarence Gate, Regent's Park, 262.
Clarendon Hotel, New Bond Street, 167.
Clarendon Square, Somers Town, 116.
Clarges Street, Piccadilly, 40, 202.
Clement's Inn, 222.
Clerkenwell, 157, 172, 314, 315, 318.
Clerkenwell Green, 315.
Cleveland Court, St. James's Street, 240.
Cleveland Row, St. James's Street, 141.
Clifford Street, New Bond Street, 32.
Clifton's Tavern, Butcher Row, 170.
Clink Street, Southwark, 266.
Clock House, Hampstead, 15.
Cloth Fair, City, 214.
Clothworkers' Hall, Mincing Lane, 235.
Club, The, x, 21, 22, 28, 115, 123, 131, 167, 204, 274, 280.
Clubs: Adelphi, Maiden Lane, Covent Garden, 245; Alfred, Albemarle Street, 34-35; Athenæum, 24, 103, 142, 143, 204, 221, 258, 278, 306; Beefsteak, 51, 62, 63, 226; Blue Stocking, 312; Boodle's, 115; Brooks's, 28, 110, 115, 144, 221, 274, 312; Brothers', 247, 300; Club, The, x, 21, 22, 28, 115, 123, 131, 167, 204, 274, 280; Cocoa Tree, 8, 35, 115; Conservative, 114, 204; Crockford's, 142; Devonshire, 142; Dilettanti Society, 62; East India Service, 110; Eccentric 274; Gar-

INDEX OF PLACES. 343

rick, 200, 278, 306, 307; Gratis, 155; Hook and Eye, 154; Ivy Lane, 166, 169; King of Clubs, 170, 258, 288; King's Head, 166, 167; Kit Kat, 8, 64, 218, 289, 290; Literary (see The Club); Mulberry, 118; Museum, 155; October, 243, 244, 300; Our Club, 154; Reform, 154, 306; Rota, 208, 238; Saville, 274; Scriblereus, 113, 243, 244, 300; Spiller's Head, 54; The Club (see Club, The); Union, 278; United Service, 207; Watier's, 34; White's, 54; Whittington, 153, 170, 258.
Clunn's Tavern, Covent Garden, 154.
Cockpit Alley, Drury Lane, 75.
Cockpit Place, Drury Lane, 75.
Cockpit Theatre, 75.
Cockspur Street, 170, 282.
Cock Tavern, Bow Street, Covent Garden, 322, 323.
Cock Tavern, Fleet Street, 170, 238.
Cock Tavern, Suffolk Street, Haymarket, 238.
Cock Tavern, Tothill Street, 284.
Cocoa Tree Club, 8, 35, 115.
Cocoa Tree Tavern, 7-8, 247, 259.
Coffee Houses (see Taverns).
Coldbath Fields, 296.
Coldbath Square, 296.
Colebrook Cottage, Islington, 190, 284.
Colebrook Row, Islington, 54, 88, 190, 191.
Colebrook Terrace, Islington, 190.
College of Surgeons, Lincoln's Inn Fields, 74.
College Street, Camden Town, 82.
College Street, Westminster, 70, 114, 179.
Combe-Florey, 280.
Compton Road, Islington, 122.
Compton Street, Clerkenwell, 75.
Compton Street, Soho, 123, 167.
Conduit, Cheapside, 77.
Conduit Street, Regent Street, 21, 81, 152.
Coney Court, Gray's Inn, 12.
Connaught Square, 194.

Conservative Club, 114, 204.
Consolidated Bank, Threadneedle Street, 222.
Copt Hall, Twickenham, 105.
Cornhill, 77, 127-128, 200, 239, 245, 300.
Cousin Lane, Upper Thames Street, 239.
Covent Garden, v, 51, 95, 128, 154, 155, 190, 219, 226, 237, 238, 239, 242, 273, 283, 321.
Covent Garden Theatre, 51, 62, 226, 322.
Coventry Street, Haymarket, 242, 295.
Cowley House, Chertsey, 65.
Cowper's Court, Birchin Lane, 45.
Cox's Hotel, Jermyn Street, 30.
Cragg's Court, Charing Cross, 307.
Cranbourn Street, Leicester Square, 61.
Crane Court, Fleet Street, 229.
Craven Cottage, Fulham, 24.
Craven Street, Strand, 10, 111, 278.
Crockford's Club House, 142.
Cromwell House, Highgate Hill, 207.
Cromwell Lane, Brompton, 146.
Cromwell Lodge, Parson's Green, 255.
Cromwell Road, South Kensington, 112.
Crooked Billet Tavern, Wimbledon, 309.
Crosby Hall, Bishopsgate Street, 223, 268, 269, 276.
Crosby Place, 223, 268, 269, 276.
Cross Court, Bow Street, Covent Garden, 118, 155.
Cross Keys Inn, St. John Street, Clerkenwell, 260.
Crown and Anchor Tavern, Arundel Street, Strand, 155, 170, 258, 280.
Crown and Horse-Shoes, Enfield, 191.
Crown Court, Chancery Lane, 313.
Crown Office Row, Temple, 182, 183, 303.
Crown Tavern, Hercules' Pillars Alley, 237.
Crown Tavern, King Street, Cheapside, 260.

INDEX OF PLACES.

Crown Tavern, King Street, Westminster, 244.
Crown Tavern, Vinegar Yard, 274.
Crutched Friars, Mark Lane, 234, 235.
Cursitor Street, 173, 274.
Curtain Court, Shoreditch, 172.
Curtain Theatre (Green Curtain), Shoreditch, 172, 173, 204.
Curzon Street, Mayfair, 89, 280.
Cut-throat Lane, Stoke Newington, 77.
Czar Street, Evelyn Street, Deptford, 101.

DALSTON, 184.
Danish Church, Wellclose Square, 54.
Dartmouth Street, Westminster, 283–284.
Dawley Court, Harrington, Middlesex, 242.
Deacon Street, Walworth Road, 284.
Deadman's Place, Southwark, 70, 266.
Dean Street, Borough, 178, 179.
Dean Street, Soho, 61, 78, 124, 125, 134.
Dean's Yard, Westminster, 27, 114.
De Foe Street, Stoke Newington, 77.
Delahay Street, Westminster, 246.
Denman Street, Southwark, 10.
Deptford, 100, 101, 204–205.
Deptford Dockyard, 205.
Deptford Green, 205.
Derby Street, Westminster, 81.
Devereux Court, Strand, 7, 10, 124, 168, 229, 247, 285, 291.
Devil Tavern, Fleet Street, 6, 7, 124, 169, 175, 238, 290, 300.
Devonshire Club, 142.
Devonshire House, Piccadilly, 240, 310.
Devonshire Terrace, Regent's Park, 83.
Dick's Coffee House, Fleet Street, 8, 67, 290.
Dilettanti Society, 62.

Dock Street, Royal Mint Street, 54.
Dolphin Tavern, Seething Lane, 236.
Don Saltero's, Chelsea, 112, 282, 291.
Dorant's Hotel, Jermyn Street, 30.
Dorset Buildings, Salisbury Square, 229.
Dorset Court, Salisbury Square, 197–198.
Dorset Court, Cannon Row, Westminster, 197.
Dorset Garden Theatre, 229.
Dorset Street, Baker Street, 23.
Dorset Street, Salisbury Square, 229.
Doughty Street, Mecklenburgh Square, 82, 83, 278–279.
Dover Street, Piccadilly, 101, 271.
Dove's Tavern, Upper Mall, Hammersmith, 227, 308.
Downing Street, 21, 71, 75, 280, 311.
Downshire Hill, Hampstead, 181, 182.
Down Street, Piccadilly, 133.
Drapers' Garden, 130, 200.
Drapers' Hall, 200.
Drummond's Bank, 246.
Drury Lane, 75, 152, 189, 274.
Drury Lane Theatre, 52, 103, 113, 239.
Dryden Press, viii, 92.
Duke of York's Tavern, Shire Lane, 8.
Duke's Head Tavern, Parson's Green, 255.
Duke's Place, Bury Street, St. Mary Axe, 317.
Duke Street, City, 47, 214.
Duke Street, Lincoln's Inn Fields, 110, 111, 196.
Duke Street, St. James's Street, 28, 37, 205, 220, 263.
Duke Street, Strand, 12.
Duke Street, Westminster, 246, 247.
Duke's Theatre, Lincoln's Inn Fields, 74, 75, 195.
Dulwich, 130.
Dulwich College, 130.
Durham House, 249.

INDEX OF PLACES.

EALING, 106, 200, 309.
Earl's Court Road, 150.
Earl's Terrace, Kensington Road, 150.
East Barnet, 194.
Eastcheap, 125, 270, 324.
East Heath Road, Hampstead, 9.
East India House, 185, 186.
East India Service Club, 110.
Eaton Street, Pimlico, 37.
Eccentric Club, 274.
Eccleston Street, Pimlico, 72, 130.
Edgeware Road, viii, 122, 146.
Edinburgh, 287.
Edith Villas, Hammersmith, 254.
Edmonton, 144, 178, 192, 193.
Edmonton Church, 192, 193.
Edwardes Square, Kensington, 58, 148.
Edward Street, Soho, 275.
Eldon Chambers, 7, 229.
Elia Cottage, Colebrook Row, Islington, 191.
Elm Tree Road, St. John's Wood, 138.
Emerson Street, Southwark, 266.
Enfield, 89, 178, 191, 192, 193, 205.
Essex Court, Middle Temple, 100, 244.
Essex Court, Strand, 7.
Essex Hall, Higham Hill, Walthamstow, 88-89.
Essex Head Tavern, 168.
Essex House, Essex Street, Strand, 197, 285.
Essex Road, Islington, 250.
Essex Street, Strand, 28, 168, 197, 227, 272, 285, 291.
Eton, 309.
Eton College, 128.
Euston Road, viii, 146.
Euston Square, 321.
Evelyn Street, Deptford, 101.
Eversham Buildings, Somers Town, 116.
Exeter Change, 112, 113.
Exeter House, Essex Street, Strand, 197, 238, 285.
Exeter Street, Strand, 106, 156.

FALCON DOCK, Bankside, 176, 268, 270.
Falcon Inn, Bankside, 25, 176, 268, 270.
Falcon Wharf, Bankside, 176, 270.
Farrar's Buildings, Inner Temple, 21.
Farringdon Market, 44.
Farringdon Street, 301, 323.
Feathers Tavern, 187.
Featherstone Buildings, Holborn, 273.
Fenchurch Street, 235, 236, 239.
Fetter Lane, 17, 92, 93, 183, 230, 238.
Finch Lane, Cornhill, 16.
Finchley, 248.
Finchley Road, 138.
Finsbury Circus, 78, 177, 178, 196.
Finsbury Pavement, 78, 196.
Fischer's Hotel (Stevens's), New Bond Street, 31.
Fish Street, City, 118.
Fish Street Hill, 239.
Fleece Tavern, Covent Garden, 237.
Fleet Lane, 323.
Fleet Market, 119.
Fleet Prison, 232, 323.
Fleet River, 301.
Fleet Street, v, ix, 6, 8, 17, 27, 46, 64, 67, 91, 92, 118, 119, 120, 124, 164, 165, 168, 169, 170, 175, 183, 197, 199, 211, 236, 237, 238, 253, 255, 275, 276, 290, 300, 313, 314.
Fleur-de-lys Court, Fetter Lane, 93.
Fluyder Street, Westminster, 75, 223.
Foley Place, Regent Street, 37.
Fordhook, 106.
Fore Street, Cripplegate, 108.
Fore Street, Edmonton, 192.
Fortis Green, 130.
Foster Lane, Cheapside, 136.
Foundling Hospital, 279, 303.
Foundry, Moorfields, 318.
Fountain Court, Middle Temple, 121.
Fountain Court, Strand, 170, 290.
Fountaine Tavern, Strand, 170, 290, 300.
Fox Court, Holborn, 259, 260.

INDEX OF PLACES.

Francis Street, Gower Street, 79.
Freeman's Court, Cornhill, 76.
Friday Street, Cheapside, 176, 270.
Frith Street, Soho, 133-134, 149, 217.
Frognal, Hampstead, 157.
Fulham, 1, 2, 3, 10, 13, 23, 24, 131, 141, 194, 254, 255.
Fulham Road, 131, 153, 197, 206, 221, 298.
Fulwood's Rents, Holborn, 8, 315-316.
Furnival's Inn, 74, 82, 223.

Gad's Hill, 84, 86.
Garden Court, Middle Temple, 121.
Garden House Tower, 251.
Garlickhithe, 45.
Garraway's Coffee House, 300.
Garrick Club, 200, 278, 306-307.
Garrick Street, Covent Garden, 29, 96, 278, 307.
Gate House, Highgate, 59.
Gate House, Westminster, 27, 198, 236, 251, 261.
Gate Street, Lincoln's Inn Fields, 187.
General Post Office, 97.
George Court, Strand, 12.
George's Row, Hyde Park, 149.
George Street, Hanover Square, 219.
George Street, Manchester Square, 102.
George Street, Portland Square, 220.
George Tavern, Church Street, Kensington, 228.
George Tavern, Pall Mall, 300.
George Tavern, Strand, 226, 227, 272.
Gerard Street, Soho, x, 28, 93, 94, 167, 222.
Germain Street (*see* Jermyn Street).
Gilpin Grove, Edmonton, 192.
Giltspur Street, 144.
Girdlers' Hall, Basinghall Street, 316.
Globe Alley, Bankside, 266.
Globe Tavern, Bankside, 266.
Globe Tavern, Fleet Street, 124, 300.
Globe Theatre, Bankside, 19, 174, 266, 267, 268, 269.
Gloucester Place, Enfield, 191.

Gloucester Place, Marylebone Road, 146.
Gloucester Row, Shoreditch, 172.
Gloucester Street, Shoreditch, 172.
Goat Tavern, Charing Cross, 238.
Golden Eagle Tavern, New Street, 238.
Golden Fleece Tavern, Edmonton, 192.
Golden Hart Tavern, Greenwich, 157.
Golden Lion Tavern, Charing Cross, 238.
Golder's Hill, North End, Fulham, 10.
Goldsmith House, Peckham, 119.
Gordon's Hotel, Albemarle Street, 32.
Gore House, Kensington, 195, 220.
Gothic House, Wimbledon Common, 207.
Gough Square, Fleet Street, 89, 141, 158.
Gower Place, Euston Square, 117.
Gower Street, Bedford Square, 79, 80, 151.
Grace Church Street, City, 125.
Grafton Street, New Bond Street, 32, 167.
Grammar School, Highgate, 59, 60.
Granby Street, Hampstead Road, 82.
Grand Junction Canal, 242.
Grange, North End, Hammersmith, 254.
Gratis Club, 155.
Gravel Lane, Southwark, 25.
Gravel Pits, Kensington, 299.
Gray's Inn, 12, 28, 121, 159, 202, 226, 275, 276, 284, 315, 316.
Gray's Inn Gardens, 88.
Gray's Inn Lane, 275, 281.
Gray's Inn Road, 88, 260.
Gray's Inn Square, 12, 13.
Great Bath Street, Coldbath Square, 296.
Great Bell Alley, Coleman Street, 20.
Great Bell Yard, Coleman Street, 20.
Great Chapel Street, Soho, 61.
Great Cheyne Row, Chelsea, viii, 38, 147.

INDEX OF PLACES. 347

Great College Street, Westminster, 70, 71, 179.
Great Coram Street, 303.
Great George Street, Westminster, 34, 202, 274.
Great Newport Street, Long Acre, 309.
Great Ormond Street, 201.
Great Peter Street, Westminster, 137.
Great Portland Street, Oxford Street, 21, 320.
Great Queen Street, Lincoln's Inn Fields, 61, 111, 217, 273.
Great Russell Street, Bloomsbury Square, 131, 140, 271.
Great Sanctuary, Westminster, 239.
Great Scotland Yard, 307.
Great Smith Street, Westminster, 179.
Great Tower Hill, 231.
Great Tower Street, 234.
Great Turnstile, Holborn, 213, 273.
Great Wild Street, Drury Lane, 75, 111.
Great Winchester Street, City, 18.
Great Windmill Street, Piccadilly, 14, 295.
Grecian Chambers, Devereux Court, Strand, 7.
Grecian Coffee House, Devereux Court, Strand, 7, 10, 124, 168, 229, 291.
Greek Street, Soho, 78, 123, 152, 167.
Green Arbor Court, Old Bailey, 119-120.
Green Curtain Theatre (*see* Curtain Theatre).
Green Street, Grosvenor Square, 280.
Greenwich, 157.
Gresham College, Gresham Street, 235.
Gresham College, Old Broad Street, 235.
Gresham House, Old Broad Street, 235.
Gresham Street, 235, 236.
Grey Friars Monastery, Newgate Street, 57.
Grocers' Hall, 277.
Grocers' Hall Court, Poultry, 137, 277.
Grosvenor Chapel, South Audley Street, 41, 50, 219.
Grosvenor Place, Pimlico, 37.
Grosvenor Square, 24.
Grove End Road, St. John's Wood, 248.
Grove, Highgate, 58-59.
Grove Terrace, Hammersmith, 254.
Grub Street, St. Giles's, 78, 108.
Guildford Street, Chertsey, 65.
Guildhall, 265.
Gunpowder Alley, Shoe Lane, 199.
Guy's Hospital, 81.

HACKNEY, 77, 86.
Hackney Church, 77.
Half Moon Passage, Aldersgate Street, 64, 176, 323.
Half Moon Street, Piccadilly, 21, 73, 133.
Half Moon Tavern, Aldersgate Street, 64, 176, 323.
Hall Court, Middle Temple, 100.
Hamilton Place, Hyde Park Corner, 261.
Hammersmith, 8, 148-149, 206, 226, 227, 254, 308.
Hammersmith Bridge, 227, 308.
Hammersmith Road, 58, 194, 211, 254.
Hammersmith Terrace, 226.
Hampstead, 112, 128, 157, 179, 180, 181, 289.
Hampstead Church, 15.
Hampstead Heath, 9, 68, 148, 179, 180, 242, 271.
Hampstead Hill, 12.
Hampstead Lane, Highgate, 59.
Hampstead Road, 82.
Hampton Court, 289.
Hampton Court Green, 102-103.
Hand Court, Holborn, 187.
Hand-in-Hand Tavern, Wimbledon, 309.
Hanover Court, Long Acre, 302.
Hanover Gate, Regent's Park, 202.

INDEX OF PLACES.

Hanover Square, 41, 99, 219.
Hanwell, 151.
Harcourt Buildings, Middle Temple Lane, 183.
Hare Court, Temple, 8, 189.
Hurley Street, Cavendish Square, 109, 248.
Harp Alley, Shoe Lane, 314.
Harrington, Middlesex, 242.
Harrington Road, South Kensington, 146.
Harris Place, Sloane Street, 194, 216, 217, 271.
Harrow Tavern, Fleet Street, 313.
Hartshorne Lane (Northumberland Street, Strand), 171-172.
Hart Street, Bloomsbury Square, 88.
Hart Street, Covent Garden, 302.
Hart Street, Crutched Friars, 233, 234, 235, 238.
Hastings Street, Burton Crescent, 271.
Hatton Garden, 322.
Haycock's Ordinary, 208.
Hayes Station, 242.
Haymarket, 1, 2, 9, 18, 104, 128, 274.
Haymarket Theatre, 104.
Hay's Lane, Tooley Street, Southwark, 179.
Hayward's Place, St. John's Gate, Clerkenwell, 75.
Heath Road, Twickenham, 219.
Heaven Tavern, Lindsay Lane, 238.
Hellespont, 56.
Hell Tavern, Westminster, 238.
Hendon Road, Hampstead Heath, 68.
Henrietta Street, Covent Garden, 222, 273.
Henry VII.'s Chapel, Westminster Abbey, 5-6, 47.
Hercules' Pillars Alley, Fleet Street, 237.
Hercules' Pillars Tavern, Hyde Park, 273, 291.
Hertford Street, Mayfair, 23, 273, 279.
Hertingfordbury, 9.
Higham Hill, Walthamstow, 89.
Highgate, 13, 58-59, 60, 128, 148.

Highgate Cemetery, 99, 103, 130.
Highgate Churchyard, 59-60.
Highgate Grammar School, 258.
Highgate Hill, 13, 58, 207.
High Holborn, 316.
High Laver, Essex, 198.
High Road, Tottenham, 314.
High Street, Borough, 10, 17, 48, 80, 163, 320.
High Street, Clapham, 200.
High Street, Hampstead, 16.
High Street, Islington, 70, 126.
High Street, Kensington, 62, 150, 305.
High Street, Marylebone, 12, 80, 83.
High Street, Putney, 149.
Hill Street, Berkeley Square, 312.
Hill, The, Hampstead Heath, 68.
Holborn, 44, 116-117, 133, 183, 187, 212, 213, 214, 260, 273, 313.
Holborn Bridge, 26.
Holborn Hill, 301.
Holborn Viaduct, 26, 117, 120, 131, 301.
Holland Arms Inn, Kensington, 4.
Holland House, 1, 3, 4, 68, 202, 220, 258, 275, 279, 299.
Holland Lane, 4.
Holland Park, 150.
Holland Street, Southwark, 270.
Holles Street, Cavendish Square, 30.
Holly Bush Inn, Hampstead, 14.
Holly Hill, Hampstead, 14.
Holly Lodge, Campden Hill, 202-203.
Holy Trinity Church, Little Queen Street, Holborn, 187.
Holywell Lane, Shoreditch, 172, 204.
Holywell Street, Strand, 196.
Hook and Eye Club, 154.
Hope Theatre, Bankside, 268.
Hornsey Churchyard, 258.
Horse and Groom Tavern, Edmonton, 192.
Horsemonger Lane, 145, 146.
Horsemonger Lane Gaol, 145-146.
Hotels (see Taverns).
Houndsditch, 47.
House of Commons, 27, 76, 207, 238.

INDEX OF PLACES.

House of Lords, 31.
Houses of Parliament, 71, 118.
Howard Street, Strand, 63.
Hoxton Fields, Shoreditch, 173.
Hoxton Square, Shoreditch, 173.
Hull, 207.
Hummums Hotel, Covent Garden, 68, 69.
Hungerford Market, Strand, 80–81.
Hungerford Stairs, Strand, 80–81.
Huntington, 232, 233.
Hutton Street, Salisbury Square, 220.
Hyde Park, 149, 273, 293, 303.
Hyde Park Corner, 240, 242, 261, 309.
Hyde Park Place, 85.

INNER TEMPLE, 19, 21, 46, 62, 67, 309.
Inner Temple Gateway, 27, 160, 275.
Inner Temple Lane, 21, 159, 160, 161, 189.
Inns (see Taverns).
Institution of Civil Engineers, Great George Street, Westminster, 34.
Ireland Yard, Doctors' Commons, 265, 266.
Ironmongers' Lane, 179.
Islington, 53, 54, 60, 69–70, 86–87, 122, 126, 249, 308.
Islington Green, 69.
Ivy Lane, Newgate Street, 44, 166, 167, 187.
Ivy Lane Club, 166, 169.

JACK'S COFFEE HOUSE (Walker's Hotel), 124–125.
Jacob's Wells Mews, George Street, Manchester Square, 102.
James Street, York Street, Buckingham Gate, 115.
Jeffreys Street, Camden Town, 82.
Jermyn Street, St. James's Street, 18, 104, 128, 227, 263, 272, 274, 288.
Jerusalem Chamber, Westminster Abbey, 5, 64, 229.
Jerusalem Tavern, St. John's Gate, 157.

Jewin Street, Cripplegate, 214.
Jewry Street, City, 47.
Johnson's Buildings, Inner Temple, 21, 159, 189.
Johnson's Court, Fleet Street, 158, 162, 163.
John Street, Bedford Row, 87.
John Street, Hampstead, 180, 181, 182.
John Street, Mecklenburgh Square, 82–83.
John Street, Pall Mall, 262.
Joiner Street, Southwark, 10.
Jolly Farmer Tavern, Church Street, Edmonton, 192.
Jump Tavern, 143.

KEATS'S BENCH, Well Walk, Hampstead, 180.
Keats's Corner, Well Road, Hampstead, 180.
Keats's Cottage, John Street, Hampstead, 182.
Keats's Villa, Well Road, Hampstead, 180.
Kensal Green Cemetery, 72, 139, 149, 152, 280, 305.
Kensington, 1, 3, 4, 9, 62, 63, 111, 202, 228, 229, 299, 303, 304, 305.
Kensington Church (see St. Mary the Virgin).
Kensington College, 228.
Kensington Gore, 195.
Kensington House, 150.
Kensington Palace, 299.
Kensington Palace Gardens, 305, 306.
Kensington Road, 3, 4, 150, 275.
Kensington Square, 1, 3, 289.
Kentish Town, 179.
Kerion Lane, City, 45.
Kew Foot Lane, Richmond, 308.
Kew Green, 38.
Kilburn Priory, St. John's Wood, 154.
King of Clubs, 170, 258, 280.
King's Arms Tavern, Pall Mall, 9.
King's Bench Prison, Southwark, 17, 141.

INDEX OF PLACES.

King's Bench Walk, Inner Temple, 62, 188.
King's Head Club, 166–167.
King's Head Tavern, Fleet Street, 238.
King's Head Tavern, Islington, 239.
King's Head Tavern, Ivy Lane, 167.
King's Head Tavern, Pall Mall, 290.
King's Head Tavern, Tower Street, 239.
King's Place, Pall Mall, 11.
King's Road, Camden Town, 82.
King's Road, Fulham, 3.
King's Road (Theobald's Road), Bedford Row, 87, 88.
King's Square (Soho Square), 61, 101.
King's Square Court, Soho, 61.
Kingston, 207.
Kingston-upon-Hull, 208.
Kingston-on-Thames, 113.
King Street, Cheapside, 56, 260.
King Street, Covent Garden, 57, 96, 156, 258, 278, 307.
King Street, Grosvenor Square, 90.
King Street, St. James's Street, 11, 305.
King Street, Westminster, 75, 233, 239, 285, 286, 297, 300.
King William Street, City, 125.
King William Street, Strand, 282.
Kit Kat Club, 8, 64, 218, 289, 290.
Knightsbridge, 239.

LADY CHAPEL, Westminster Abbey, 47.
Lalla Rookh Cottage, Muswell Hill, 221.
Lamb's Cottage, Edmonton, 192.
Lancaster Court, Strand, 244.
Langham, Norfolk, 207.
Langham Street, Marylebone, 21, 37.
Lansdowne House, Berkeley Square, 220.
Lant Street, Borough, 81.
Lauderdale House, Highgate Hill, 207, 208.
Lawn Bank, John Street, Hampstead, 180, 181, 182.

Lawn Cottage, John Street, Hampstead, 181.
Lawrence Manor House, Chelsea, 281.
Lawrence Street, Chelsea, 281.
Leadenhall Market, 185.
Leg Tavern, King Street, Westminster, 236.
Leicester Court, Leicester Fields, 149.
Leicester Fields (*see* Leicester Square).
Leicester House, Leicester Fields, 93, 285.
Leicester Square, 61, 137, 149, 288, 297, 299.
Leonard Place, Kensington, 150.
Lewis Place, Great Ormond Street, 201.
Lewis Place, Hammersmith Road, Fulham, 194.
Lichfield, 1.
Lime Grove, Putney Hill, 113.
Lincoln's Inn, 61, 62, 223, 226, 232, 320.
Lincoln's Inn Fields, 8, 37, 54, 74, 84, 110, 195, 198, 217, 238.
Lincoln's Inn Gateway, 171, 172, 173.
Lindsay Lane, Westminster, 238.
Lion and Sun Hotel, Highgate, 59.
Lisbon, Spain, 106.
Lisle Street, Leicester Square, 87, 143, 285.
Litchfield Street, Soho, 309.
Literary Club (*see* The Club).
Little Britain, 110, 111, 144, 155.
Little College Street, Camden Town, 82.
Little Dean's Yard, Westminster, 51.
Little Newport Street, Long Acre, 93.
Little Queen Street, Holborn, 186, 187.
Little Ryder Street, 297.
Little Tower Street, 307.
Little Turnstile, Holborn, 213.
Liverpool Road, 188.
Lloyd's, Abchurch Lane, 290.
Load of Hay Tavern, Haverstock Hill, 289, 290.

Lockitt's Ordinary, Charing Cross, 246.
Lombard Street, 152, 197, 239, 240, 290, 300.
London Bridge, 25, 199, 209, 225, 238, 266, 295.
London Institution, Finsbury Circus, 78, 245.
London Wall, 177, 195, 196, 200, 231.
Long Acre, viii, x, 29, 61, 92, 96, 247, 301, 302.
Long's Hotel, New Bond Street, 32, 34, 263.
Lordship's Lane (or Road), Stoke Newington, 77.
Lothbury, 138.
Lovell's Court, Paternoster Row, 253, 254.
Lower Belgrave Place (Buckingham Palace Road), 71–72.
Lower Grosvenor Street, New Bond Street, 73, 273.
Lower Heath Road, Hampstead, 180.
Lower Richmond Road, 154.
Lower Rosoman Street, Clerkenwell, 318.
Lower Serles Place, Fleet Street, 8.
Luke Street, Westminster, 71.
Lyceum Theatre, 113.

Maida Vale, 154.
Maid Lane, Bankside, 266.
Maidenhead Court, St. Martin's-le-Grand, 212.
Maiden Lane, Covent Garden, 207, 245.
Maiden Lane, Upper Thames Street, 45.
Mall, The, 41, 213.
Manchester Square, 102, 114.
Manor House, Chiswick, 241.
Mansion House, City, 275.
Marble Arch, viii, 86, 293.
Marbledown Place, Burton Crescent, 271.
Margaret Street, Cavendish Square, 36.
Market Lane, Pall Mall, 298.
Mark Lane, City, 316.

Marshalsea Place, Southwark, 80.
Marshalsea Prison, 79–80, 81, 82, 320.
Marylebone Church, 146.
Marylebone High Street, 12.
Marylebone Lane, 114.
Marylebone Road, viii, 12, 30, 83, 146.
Marylebone Street, 21.
Mawson Lane, Chiswick, 241.
Mawson Row, Chiswick, 241.
Maynard Street, Muswell Hill, 221.
May's Buildings, St. Martin's Lane, 274.
Mecklenburgh Square, 82.
Mercers' Hall, 179.
Merchant Taylors' School, 1, 275, 285.
Mermaid Tavern, Cheapside, 20, 175–176, 270.
Metropolitan Meat Market, Charter House Street, 19.
Michael's Grove, Brompton Road, 153.
Middle Heath Road, Hampstead, 180.
Middle Scotland Yard, 37.
Middlesex Hospital, Mortimer Street, 140, 199.
Middle Temple, 27, 63, 67, 75, 78, 100, 104, 121, 126, 220, 249, 258, 264, 273, 284, 322.
Middle Temple Gate, 27.
Middle Temple Hall, 269.
Middleton Buildings, Regent Street, 37.
Milbourne House, Barnes Common, 106.
Mile End, 250.
Milk Street, Cheapside, 17, 170, 222, 236.
Mill Walk, Battersea, 242.
Milton Street, Cripplegate, 78, 108.
Mincing Lane, 235.
Minories, 47, 276, 317.
Missolonghi, Greece, 34.
Mitford Lane, Strand, 170, 258.
Mitre Chambers, Fenchurch Street, 236.
Mitre Court Buildings, Temple, 188.
Mitre Court, Fleet Street, 169.
Mitre Court, Wood Street, Cheapside, 236.

INDEX OF PLACES.

Mitre Tavern, Fenchurch Street, 236.
Mitre Tavern, Fleet Street, 168, 169, 236.
Mitre Tavern, St. James's Market, 103–104.
Mitre Tavern, Wood Street, Cheapside, 236.
Monmouth House, Lawrence Street, Chelsea, 281.
Montague Square, 23.
Monument Yard, City, 118.
Moorfields, 195, 196, 315, 318.
Mortimer Street, Cavendish Square, 140, 151, 199.
Mortlake, 9.
Mount Street, Berkeley Square, 71.
Mulberry Club, 118.
Mulberry Gardens, 95, 101–102.
Museum Club, 155.
Muswell Hill, 221.
Muswell Hill Road, 221.

Nag's Head Tavern, High Street, Borough, 320.
National Deposit Bank, Russell Street, Covent Garden, 55.
National Portrait Gallery, 9, 146.
Navy Office, Seething Lane, 233–234.
Neville Court, Fetter Lane, 17.
New Bond Street, 31, 33, 167, 263.
New Buildings, Chiswick, 241.
Newcomen Street, Southwark, 320.
New Court, Temple, 7.
New Court, Throgmorton Street, 130.
New Finchley Road, 139.
New Fish Street, City, 239.
Newgate Prison, 232, 261, 320.
Newgate Street, 18, 26, 57, 97, 117, 146, 167, 168, 187, 285.
Newington Causeway, 146.
Newington Green, 16, 76, 256, 316.
New Inn, Wych Street, 222.
New Law Courts, 170, 195, 196, 198.
New Oxford Street, viii.
New Palace Yard, 117–118, 208, 238.
New Park Street, Southwark, 266.
Newport Market, 309.

Newport Street, St. Martin's Lane, 61, 242, 309.
New Queen Street, Upper Thames Street, 176.
New River, 190, 191.
New Road (Marylebone Road), viii, 146.
New Square, Lincoln's Inn, 226.
Newstead Abbey, 34.
New Street, Covent Garden, 156.
Newton House, Campden Hill, 228.
New Wells, Clerkenwell, 318.
Nightingale Lane, Highgate, 58.
Norfolk Street, Strand, 58, 217, 232.
North Bank, St. John's Wood, 98–99.
North End, Fulham, 10, 68, 254, 255.
North End Road, 8.
North Gower Street, Bedford Square, 79, 80.
North Road, Highgate, 59.
Northumberland Street, Marylebone, 78.
Northumberland Street, Strand, 152, 155, 172.
Nottingham Place, Marylebone, 23.
Notting Hill, 299.

October Club, 243, 244, 300.
Old Bailey, 120, 261, 323.
Old Baptist Head Tavern, 126, 170.
Old Bond Street, 21, 292, 293.
Old Broad Street, 18, 235, 240, 317, 318.
Old Brompton Road, 146.
Old Burlington Street, 10, 112.
Old Cavendish Street, Oxford Street, 37.
Old Fish Street, City, 239.
Old Jewry, 89, 245.
Old Kensington Square (see Kensington Square).
Old Palace Yard, 251.
Old Red Lion Inn, 126, 170, 308.
Old St. Pancras Road, 118, 271.
One Tun Tavern, St. James's Market, 274.
Onslow Square, 303–304.
Orange Chapel, St. Martin's Street, 227.

INDEX OF PLACES. 353

Orange Street, Leicester Square, 89, 137.
Orbell's Buildings, Kensington, 228.
Orchard Street, Portman Square, 273, 279.
Orchard Street, Westminster, 137.
Our Club, 154.
Oxendon Street, Haymarket, 18.
Oxford, 2, 9, 60, 114, 195, 197, 198, 232, 234, 287, 318.
Oxford Circus, 18.
Oxford Street, viii, 18, 78, 140, 293.
Ozinda's Coffee House, 300.

PADDINGTON, 147.
Palace Chambers, St. James's Street, 303.
Palace Gardens, Kensington, 202.
Palace Gate, Kensington, 150.
Palace Green, Kensington, 304.
Palace Yard, Lambeth, 25.
Palace Yard, Westminster, 76.
Pall Mall, 7, 9, 11, 24, 28, 57, 58, 114, 144, 151, 154, 204, 206, 207, 221, 244, 247, 251, 258, 262, 278, 290, 292, 297, 298, 300, 306, 308, 312.
Pall Mall Place, Pall Mall, 11.
Palsgrave's Head Inn, Strand, 247.
Palsgrave's Place, Strand, 247.
Palsgrave Restaurant, Strand, 208.
Pantheon, Oxford Street, 78.
Paper Buildings, Temple, 183.
Paradise Tavern, 238.
Park Lane, 24, 32, 89.
Park Place, St. James's Street, 144, 288.
Park Street, Grosvenor Square, 90.
Park Street, Southwark, 17, 18, 70, 163, 174, 266.
Park Village, Regent's Park, 153.
Paris, France, 295.
Paris Garden, Bankside, 268.
Parliament Street, Westminster, 81, 244.
Parsloe's Coffee House, St. James's Street, 62.
Parson's Green, Fulham, 13, 254, 255.
Parson's Green Lane, 131.

Paternoster Row, 22, 23, 44, 94, 166, 253.
Paul's Cross, 108–109.
Paul's School, 109, 211, 233.
Paul's Wharf, 105.
Pavement, High Street, Clapham, 200.
Pavement, Moorfields, 177-178.
Peabody Buildings, Drury Lane, 75.
Peak Hill Avenue, Sydenham, 36.
Peak Hill Road, Sydenham, 36.
Peak Hill, Sydenham, 36.
Peckham, 119.
Peerless Pool, Old Street Road, 215.
Pembridge Villas, Bayswater, 203.
Penton Street, Pentonville, 126.
Pentonville Road, viii, 126, 146.
Peterborough House, Parson's Green, 255.
Petersham, 112.
Peter Street, Westminster, 70.
Petty France, Westminster, 213, 214.
Phœnix Alley, Long Acre, 301-302.
Phœnix Street, Somers Town, 116.
Physicians' Hall, Warwick Lane, Paternoster Row, 94.
Piazza, Covent Garden, 51, 154, 155, 219, 274, 312.
Piccadillo Hall, 295.
Piccadilly, 10, 30, 32, 34, 37, 53, 73, 242, 261, 262.
Piccadilly Circus, 30.
Piccadilly Terrace, 32.
Pickett Street, St. Clement Danes, 196.
Pied Bull Inn, Islington, 249-250.
Pillars of Hercules Tavern, 261.
Pimlico, 37.
Pineapple Inn, New Street, 156.
Pinner's Court, Old Broad Street, 18.
Pinner's Hall, 17, 18, 317, 318.
Pitcher's Court, Great Bell Alley, Coleman Street, City, 20.
Pitt's Buildings, Kensington, 228.
Pitt's Place, Parson's Green, 254.
Pitt Street, Kensington, 228.
Playhouse Yard, Ludgate Hill, 265.
Plough Court, Carey Street, 198.
Plough Court, Lombard Street, 240.

INDEX OF PLACES.

Plough Inn, High Street, Clapham, 201.
Plough Inn, Plough Court, Carey Street, 198.
Poets' Corner, Westminster Abbey, 5, 37, 47, 71, 79, 130, 274, 285, 286, 288, 315.
Poet's Head, Phœnix Alley, 301.
Poland Street, Oxford Street, 72.
Polygon, Somers Town, 116.
Pompeii, 24.
Pontack's Ordinary, 102, 299, 300.
Pope's Head Alley, Cornhill, 239.
Pope's Head Inn, Chancery Lane, 239.
Pope's Head Inn, Pope's Head Alley, 239.
Pope's Villa, Twickenham, 241-242.
Portland Hotel, Portland Place, Oxford Street, 320.
Portland Place, Hammersmith, 58.
Portland Place, Oxford Street, 320.
Portman Square, 36, 102, 312.
Portsea, 79.
Portsmouth, 125.
Portsmouth Street, Lincoln's Inn Fields, 143.
Portugal Row, Lincoln's Inn Fields, 74.
Portugal Street, Lincoln's Inn Fields, 8, 10, 74, 143.
Poultney Hill, 115.
Poultry, 77, 137, 179, 223, 277.
Princes Square, Ratcliffe Highway, 296, 297.
Princes Street, Hanover Square, 256.
Priory, St. John's Wood, 98-99.
Prospect Place, Newington Butts, 284.
Puddle Wharf, Blackfriars, 265.
Pump Court, 104.
Putney, 9, 141, 149.
Putney Bridge, 142, 154.
Putney Common, 153, 154.
Putney Hill, 113.

QUAKER TAVERN, Westminster, 239.
Queen Anne Mansions, Westminster, 132, 214.

Queen Anne Street, Cavendish Square, 21, 27, 71, 131.
Queen's Arms Tavern, Cheapside, 179.
Queen's Arms Tavern, Newgate Street, 97, 168.
Queen's Arms Tavern, St. Paul's Churchyard, 167-168.
Queensbury House, 112.
Queen's College, Cambridge, 19.
Queen's College, Oxford, 2.
Queen's Gate, South Kensington, 146.
Queen's Head Alley, Newgate Street, 167:
Queen's Head Lane, Islington, 249.
Queen's Head Street, Islington, 250.
Queen's Head Tavern, Cheapside, 179.
Queen's Head Tavern, Islington, 249, 250.
Queen's Hotel, Queen Street, Soho, 125.
Queen's Road, Finchley Road, 139.
Queen's Row, Knightsbridge, 226.
Queen Square, Bloomsbury, 51, 72, 73.
Queen Street, Berkeley Square, 273, 280.
Queen Street, Hammersmith, 226.
Queen Street, Soho, 124, 125.
Queen Street, Upper Thames Street, 176, 237.
Queen Victoria Street, 223, 265.

RAINBOW TAVERN, 27.
Ranelagh, 60.
Ratcliffe Highway. 54, 296.
Rathbone Place, Oxford Street, 131.
Rational Club, 155.
Reading, 217.
Red Bull Theatre, Clerkenwell, 75, 264, 316.
Red Bull Yard, Clerkenwell, 75, 264, 315, 316.
Red Lion and Sun Hotel, Highgate, 59.
Red Lion Fields, Holborn, 214.
Red Lion Hill, Hampstead, 14.
Red Lion Inn, Parliament Street, 81.

INDEX OF PLACES. 355

Red Lion Square, 214, 248.
Reform Club, 154, 300.
Regent's Park, 18, 98, 138, 199, 262.
Rhenish Wine Inn, Canon Row, Westminster, 239.
Rhenish Wine Inn, Steel Yard, Upper Thames Street, 239.
Richard's Coffee House (Dick's), 67.
Richmond, 62, 308.
Richmond Bridge, 62.
Rising Sun Tavern, Enfield, 191.
Robert Street, Adelphi, 138.
Robin Hood Tavern, Essex Street, Strand, 28.
Robinson's Coffee House, Charing Cross, 260.
Rogue's Lane, Fleet Street, 8.
Rope Makers' Alley, Moorfields, 77–78.
Rope Makers' Street, Moorfields, 78.
Rosamond's Pond, St. James's Park, 61.
Rose Street, Bankside, 174.
Rose Street, Covent Garden, viii, 29, 95–96.
Rose Street, Newgate Street, 60.
Rose Tavern, Brydges Street, 113.
Rose Tavern, Holborn Hill, 301.
Rose Tavern, Russell Street, Covent Garden, 239.
Rose Theatre, Bankside, 174, 268.
Rosslyn Hill, Hampstead, 16.
Rota Club, 208, 238.
Round Court, Strand, 282.
Royal Academy of Arts, 32.
Royal Albert Hall, 195.
Royal Exchange, 63, 69, 76, 77, 92, 239, 313.
Royal Institution, Albemarle Street, 102.
Royal Society, 229, 235.
Rummer Court, Spring Gardens, 246.
Rummer Tavern, Spring Gardens, 246.
Running Footman Tavern, Charles Street, Berkeley Square, 24.
Russell Square, 217.
Russell Street, Covent Garden, x, 6, 7, 21, 55, 62, 71, 101, 149, 154, 155, 170, 189, 226, 237, 239, 243, 291, 300.
Rutland House, Aldersgate Street, 75.
Ryder Street, 297.

SADLERS WELLS THEATRE, 190.
St. Albans, 67.
St. Alban's Place, Haymarket, 298.
St. Alban's Street, Haymarket, 298.
St. Andrew's Church, Holborn, 87, 131–132, 259.
St. Andrew's Hill, 265.
St. Andrew's-by-the-Wardrobe, 265.
St. Anne's Church, Carter Lane, 265.
St. Anne's Church, Soho, 134.
St. Anne's Hill, Chelsea, 65.
St. Anne's Lane (St. Anne's Street), Westminster, 136–137.
St. Anne's Street, Westminster, 137.
St. Anthony's Free School, Threadneedle Street, 222.
St. Bartholomew-the-Great, 214.
St. Benedict's Chapel, Westminster Abbey, 20, 48.
St. Benet's Church, Paul's Wharf, 105.
St. Bennet Fink, 16, 240.
St. Botolph's Church, Aldgate, 47.
St. Bride's Church, Fleet Street, 92, 199, 255.
St. Bride's Churchyard, Fleet Street, 211, 212.
St. Clement Danes' Church, 92, 117, 165–166, 170, 195, 196, 231.
St. Dunstan's Church, Canterbury, 225.
St. Dunstan's Church, Fleet Street, 6, 17, 91, 198, 257.
St. Dunstan's Churchyard, 314.
St. Faith's Church, 211.
St. George's Church, Hanover Square, 4, 99, 293.
St. George's Church, Southwark, 80, 81, 320.
St. George's Hospital, Hyde Park, 149.
St. George's Place, Hyde Park, 149.
St. George Street, Shadwell, 54, 296.

INDEX OF PLACES.

St. Giles's Church, Cripplegate, 76, 77, 108, 215, 216.
St. Giles's-in-the-Fields, 208, 276.
St. Helen's, Bishopsgate, 268.
St. James's Church, Clerkenwell, 314.
St. James's Church, Garlickhithe, 45.
St. James's Coffee House, St. James's Street, 7, 89, 290, 299.
St. James's Hotel, Jermyn Street, 263.
St. James's Market, 103, 104, 274, 298.
St. James's Market Place, 17, 18.
St. James's Park, 41, 61, 101, 115, 213, 214, 238, 246.
St. James's Place, 1, 6, 32, 73, 90, 205, 257–258, 262, 285, 297, 303.
St. James's Square, 28, 49, 109–110, 297.
St. James's Street, 7, 8, 31, 33, 35, 37, 54, 62, 89, 110, 114, 115, 142, 167, 204, 221, 240, 244, 247, 259, 274, 291, 310, 312.
St. John's Chapel, John Street, Hampstead, 152.
St. John's College, Cambridge, 171.
St. John's Gate, Clerkenwell, 40, 157, 260.
St. John's Lane, Clerkenwell, 126, 170, 260.
St. John's Road, Islington, 308.
St. John's Street, Clerkenwell, 19, 75, 260, 264, 315.
St. John's Street Road, Islington, 126, 170.
St. John's Wood, 138, 154, 193.
St. John-the-Evangelist, Smith Square, 50–51.
St. Katherine-Cree, 47.
St. Lawrence's Church, Brentford, 309.
St. Luke's Church, Chelsea, 63, 225, 264, 290, 298.
St. Luke's Hospital, Old Street, 215.
St. Margaret's Church, Westminster, 35, 66–67, 233, 252, 310.
St. Margaret's Hill, Southwark, 48.
St. Martin's-in-the-Fields, 11, 41, 92, 104, 171, 172, 173, 220, 245, 278, 301, 302.
St. Martin's Lane, 61, 156, 176, 242, 274, 295.
St. Martin's-le-Grand, 97, 168, 212.
St. Martin's Street, Leicester Square, 72–73, 227, 228, 299.
St. Mary Aldermary, Watling Street, 45.
St. Mary-at-Hill, 324.
St. Mary Axe, 87, 317.
St. Marylebone Church, 12, 30.
St. Mary-le-Bow Church, 210.
St. Mary-le-Savoy, 320.
St. Mary-le-Strand, 116.
St. Mary Magdalen, Milk Street, 17.
St. Mary Magdalen, Richmond, 308.
St. Mary Overy, 107, 108, 126, 127, 209, 266, 267, 269.
St. Mary's Chapel, Westminster Abbey, 47.
St. Mary's Church, Ealing, 309.
St. Mary's Church, Kensington, 62, 63, 151, 203.
St. Mary's Church, Putney, 113.
St. Mary's Church, Wyndham Place, Bryanston Square, 194.
St. Mary Woolchurch, 275.
St. Michael's Alley, Cornhill, 245.
St. Michael's Church, Cornhill, 128.
St. Michael's Church, Highgate, 58.
St. Michael's Church, Old Verulam, 13.
St. Michael's Court, Cornhill, 245.
St. Mildred's Church, Bread Street, 271.
St. Mildred's Court, Poultry, 137.
St. Nicholas's Church, Deptford, 204–205.
St. Olave's Church, Hart Street, 233, 234, 235, 238.
St. Pancras Gardens, 118, 271, 272.
St. Pancras-in-the-Fields (Old St. Pancras Church), 116, 118, 271, 273, 316.
St. Paul's Cathedral, 39, 109, 276–277, 279.
St. Paul's Church, Covent Garden, x, 29, 41, 218, 283, 284, 302, 321, 323.

INDEX OF PLACES.

St. Paul's Church, Dock Street, 54.
St. Paul's Church, Hammersmith, 226.
St. Paul's Churchyard, 7, 109, 137, 167–168, 211, 236, 271.
St. Paul's School (*see* Paul's School).
St. Paul's School, Shadwell, 54.
St. Peter's Church, Sumner Street, Southwark Bridge Road, 268.
St. Peter's College (*see* Westminster School).
St. Peter's Street, St. Albans, 67.
St. Saviour's Church, Southwark, 107, 108, 126, 127, 209, 266, 267, 269.
St. Sepulchre's Church, Holborn, 26, 116, 117.
St. Swithin's Church, London Stone, 92.
St. Thomas's Hospital, 10, 173.
St. Vedast's Church, Foster Lane, 136.
Salisbury, 1.
Salisbury Court, Fleet Street (*see* Salisbury Square).
Salisbury Square, 92, 113, 198, 229, 253, 264.
Salutation and Cat Inn, Newgate Street, 60, 187, 285.
Salutation Inn, Newgate Street, 60.
Samson's Ordinary, St. Paul's Churchyard, 236.
Sandford, Manor House, Chelsea, 3.
Sandy End, Fulham, 2.
Sardinia Place, Lincoln's Inn Fields, 111.
Sargent's Inn, 64.
Savile Club, 274.
Savile House, Twickenham, 219.
Savile Row, Burlington Gardens, 112, 130, 274, 279.
Savoy, The, 69, 238.
Savoy Buildings, Strand, 170, 290, 300.
Savoy Chapel, 46, 320.
Savoy Hill, 46.
Savoy Palace, 46.
Savoy Street, 46, 320.
Sayes Court, Deptford, 100, 101.

Sayes Court Street, 101.
Schomberg House, 300.
Scotland Yard, 207, 213.
Scriblerus Club, 113, 243, 244, 300.
Seething Lane, 233, 234, 235, 236.
Selby House, North End, Hammersmith, 254.
Serle's Coffee House, 8, 10.
Serle Street, Lincoln's Inn Fields, 8, 10, 198.
Sessions House, Westminster, 239.
Sevenoaks, 129, 200.
Seymour Place, Connaught Square, 194.
Seymour Street, Portman Square, 23, 36.
Shacklewell, 184.
Shadwell, 75.
Shaftesbury House, Kensington Road, 275.
Shanet Place, Strand, 247.
Sheffield Street, Clare Market, 290.
Ship Tavern, Charing Cross, 246.
Ship Tavern, Little Tower Street, 307.
Ship Yard, Strand, 196.
Shire Lane, Fleet Street, 8, 141, 218, 291.
Shoe Lane, v, 42, 43, 44, 124, 199, 238, 314.
Shooter's Court, Throgmorton Street, 130.
Shoreditch, 42, 172, 227.
Simpson's Tavern, 170.
Sir Richard Steele's Tavern, Haverstock Hill, 290.
Skinner Street, Holborn, 26, 116–117.
Slaughter's Coffee House, 61, 242.
Sloane Street, Knightsbridge, 30, 150, 194.
Sloane Terrace, Sloane Street, 30.
Smith Square, Westminster, 50.
Smith Street, Westminster, 284, 288.
Smyrna Coffee House, Pall Mall, 247, 299, 300, 308.
Snow Hill, 25–26, 117.
Society of Arts, v, 28, 30, 90, 102, 111, 112, 222, 227, 273, 311.
Soho Square, 60, 61, 63, 78, 101, 124–125, 140.

Somerset House, 46, 68, 310, 311.
Somerset Place, Portman Square, 273.
Somers Town, 116, 141.
Southampton Buildings, Holborn, 133, 135, 188, 191.
Southampton Coffee House, Southampton Buildings, 135.
Southampton House, Bloomsbury Square, 52.
Southampton House, Holborn, 52.
Southampton Row, Bloomsbury Square, 128, 217, 248.
Southampton Square, 17.
Southampton Street, Bloomsbury Square, 52.
Southampton Street, Strand, 52, 63, 321.
South Audley Street, 41, 49, 50, 89, 137, 219.
Southgate, 144.
South Kensington (see Kensington).
South Kensington Museum, 83, 85, 111.
South Sea House, 184-185.
South Square, Gray's Inn, 202.
Southwark, 10, 48, 70, 107, 141, 163, 174, 178, 209, 238, 295.
Southwark Bridge Crossing, 266.
Southwark Bridge Road, 19, 174, 176, 266.
Spanish Place, Manchester Square, 102, 206.
Spiller's Head Club, 54.
Spring Gardens, 41, 52, 53, 213, 246, 282.
Squire's Coffee House, 8.
Stafford, 314.
Stanhope Place, Oxford Street, 293.
Staple Inn, 159.
Star and Garter Tavern, Pall Mall, 247, 300.
Star Tavern, Cheapside, 239.
Steele's Cottage, Haverstock Hill, 289-290.
Steele's Studios, Haverstock Hill, 290.
Steel Yard, Upper Thames Street, 239.
Stepney Church, 250.

Stevens's Hotel, New Bond Street, 31.
Stockbridge Terrace, Pimlico, 37.
Stock Exchange, 130.
Stoke Court, Stoke Pogis, 128-129.
Stoke Newington, 16, 75, 77, 130, 256, 317.
Stoke Newington Church, 16.
Stoke Pogis, 128-129.
Stoke Pogis Church, 129.
Strand, 8, 56, 97, 106, 112, 113, 116, 117, 176, 183, 197, 208, 227, 235, 238, 247, 249, 256, 258, 272, 280, 282, 290, 300, 310.
Stratford-on-Avon, 264, 270.
Stratford Place, Oxford Street, 279.
Stratton Street, Piccadilly, 310.
Strawberry Hill, 53, 311, 312.
Streatham, Surrey, 162-163.
Stretford, Nottinghamshire, 50.
Suffolk Lane, Upper Thames Street, 275, 285.
Suffolk Street, Haymarket, 298.
Sumner Place, Onslow Square, 304.
Sumner Street, Southwark, 266.
Sun-behind-the-Exchange Inn, 239.
Sunbury, Middlesex, 23.
Sun Tavern, Chancery Lane, 239.
Sun Tavern, King Street, Westminster, 239.
Sun Tavern, New Fish Street, 239.
Surrey Street, Strand, 63, 64.
Surrey Theatre, Southwark, 141.
Sussex Chambers, Duke's Street, St. James's Street, 37.
Sussex House, Hammersmith, 206.
Sussex Place, Regent's Park, 262.
Swallowfield, 217.
Swallow Place, Oxford Street, 18.
Swallow Street, Piccadilly, 17, 18.
Swan Inn, Fenchurch Street, 239.
Swan Inn, Old Fish Street, 239.
Swan Inn, Tottenham, 314-315.
Swedish Church, Ratcliffe Highway, 296.
Sydenham, 30, 35, 36.

TABARD INN, Southwark, 48.
Tabernacle Row, Finsbury, 318.
Talbot Inn, Southwark, 48.

INDEX OF PLACES.

Talbot Inn Yard, 48.
Taverns: Adam and Eve, Kensington Road, 275; African, St. Michael's Alley, Cornhill, 245; Albion, Aldersgate Street, 130; Albion, Russell Street, Covent Garden, 154–155; Argyll Rooms, 295; Arundel Hotel, Norfolk Street, Strand, 232; Bear and Harrow, Butcher Row, 196; Bear-at-the-Bridge-Foot, 295, 323; Bear Inn, Southwark, 238; Bedford Coffee House, Covent Garden, 51, 61, 106, 226, 242, 274, 312; Bedford Head Tavern, Maiden Lane, Covent Garden, 207; Bedford Hotel, Covent Garden, 5, 303; Bedford Tavern, Maiden Lane, Covent Garden, 207; Bell Inn, Aldersgate, 301; Bell Inn, Carter Lane, 270-271; Bell Inn, Edmonton, ix, 192; Bell Inn, King Street, Westminster, 236, 244, 300; Black Jack, 143; Blue Bells, Lincoln's Inn Fields, 238; Boar's Head, Eastcheap, 125, 270; Brew House, Axe Yard, 75; British Coffee House, 170, 282; Bull and Bush, Hammersmith, 8; Bull, Shoreditch, 227; Bull, Tower Hill, 231; Bull's Head, Clare Market, 290; Bull's Head, Spring Gardens, 52, 53, 213; Button's, x. 6, 149, 175, 260, 291, 300; Carey House, Strand, 238; Castle, Henrietta Street, Covent Garden, 273; Castle, Islington, 54; Castle, Savoy, 238; Cat and Fiddle, 218; Chapter Coffee House, 22, 44, 124; Chatelain's, 238; Cheshire Cheese, 120, 170; Child's, 7; Cider Cellar, Maiden Lane, Covent Garden, 245; Clarendon Hotel, New Bond Street, 167; Clifton's, Butcher Row, 170; Clunn's, Covent Garden, 154; Cock, Bow Street, 322, 323; Cock, Fleet Street, 170, 238; Cock, Suffolk Street, 238; Cock, Tothill Street, 234; Cocoa Tree, 7, 8, 247, 259; Cox's Hotel, Jermyn Street, 30; Crooked Billet, Wimbledon, 309; Cross Keys, St. John's Street, Clerkenwell, 260; Crown and Anchor, Arundel Street, Strand, 155, 170, 258, 280; Crown and Horse-Shoes, Enfield, 191; Crown, Hercules Pillars' Alley, 237; Crown, King Street, Cheapside, 260; Crown, King Street, Westminster, 244; Crown, Vinegar Yard, 274; Devil, Fleet Street, 6, 7, 124, 169, 175, 238, 290, 300; Dick's, 8, 67, 290; Dolphin, Seething Lane, 236; Don Saltero's, Chelsea, 112, 282, 291; Dorant's Hotel, Jermyn Street, 30; Doves, Hammersmith, 227, 308; Duke of York's, Shire Lane, 8; Duke's Head, Parson's Green, 255; Essex Head, 168; Falcon, Bankside, 25, 176, 268, 270; Feathers, 187; Fischer's Hotel, New Bond Street, 31; Fleece, Covent Garden, 237; Fountaine, Strand, 170, 290, 300; Garaway's, 300; George, Church Street, Kensington, 228; George, Pall Mall, 300; George, Strand, 226, 227, 272; Globe, Bankside, 266; Globe, Fleet Street, 124, 300; Goat, Charing Cross, 238; Golden Eagle, New Street, 238; Golden Fleece, Edmonton, 192; Golden Hart, Greenwich, 157; Golden Lion, Charing Cross, 238; Gordon's Hotel, Albemarle Street, 32; Grecian, Devereux Court, Strand, 7, 10, 124, 168, 229, 291; Half Moon, Aldersgate Street, 64, 176, 323; Hand-in-Hand, Wimbledon, 309; Harrow, Fleet Street, 313; Haycock's, 208; Heaven, 238; Hell, 238; Hercules Pillars', 273, 291; Holland Arms, Kensington, 4; Holly Bush, Hampstead, 14; Horse and Groom, Edmonton, 192; Hummums, Covent Garden, 68–69; Jack's (Walker's Hotel), Queen Street, Soho, 124–125; Jerusalem, St. John's Gate, 157; Jolly Farmer,

INDEX OF PLACES.

Edmonton, 192; Jump (Black Jack), 143; King's Arms, Pall Mall, 9; King's Head, Fleet Street, 238; King's Head, Islington, 239; King's Head, Ivy Lane, 167; King's Head, Pall Mall, 290; King's Head, Tower Street, 239; Leg, King Street, Westminster, 236; Lion and Sun Hotel, Highgate, 59; Load of Hay, Haverstock Hill, 289–290; Lockitt's Ordinary, Charing Cross, 246; Long's Hotel, 32, 34, 263; Mermaid, Cheapside, 20, 175–176, 270; Mitre, Fenchurch Street, 236; Mitre, Fleet Street, 168, 169, 236; Mitre, St. James's Market, 103–104; Mitre, Wood Street Cheapside, 236; Mulberry Gardens, 95, 101–102; Nag's Head, Southwark, 320; Old Baptist Head, 126, 170; One Tun, 274; Ozinda's, 300; Palsgrave's Head, Strand, 247; Palsgrave Restaurant, 208; Paradise, 238; Parsloe's, St. James's Street, 62; Piccadillo Hall, 295; Pied Bull, Islington, 249, 250; Pillars of Hercules, 261; Pineapple, New Street, 156; Plough, Clapham, 201; Plough, Plough Court, Carey Street, 198; Poet's Head, 301; Pontack's, 102, 299, 300; Pope's Head, Chancery Lane, 239; Pope's Head, Pope's Head Alley, 239; Portland Hotel, Portland Place, 320; Quaker, Westminster, 239; Queen's Arms, Cheapside, 179; Queen's Arms, Newgate Street, 97, 168; Queen's Arms, St. Paul's Churchyard, 167, 168; Queen's Head, Cheapside, 179; Queen's Head, Islington, 249, 250; Queen's Hotel, Queen Street, Soho, 125; Rainbow, 27; Red Lion and Sun, Highgate, 59; Red Lion, Parliament Street, 81; Rhenish Wine, Canon Row, Westminster, 239; Rhenish Wine, Steel Yard, Upper Thames Street, 239; Richard's, 67; Rising Sun, Enfield, 191; Robin Hood, Essex Street, Strand, 28; Robinson's, Charing Cross, 260; Rose, Brydges Street, 113; Rose, Holborn Hill, 301; Rose, Russell Street, Covent Garden, 239; Rummer, Spring Gardens, 246; Running Footman, Charles Street, Berkeley Square, 24; St. James's Coffee House, St. James's Street, 7, 89, 290, 299; St. James's Hotel, Jermyn Street, 263; Salutation, Newgate Street, 60; Salutation and Cat, Newgate Street, 60, 187, 285; Samson's, St. Paul's Churchyard, 236; Serle's, 8, 10; Ship, Charing Cross, 246; Ship, Little Tower Street, 307; Simpson's, Strand, 170; Sir Richard Steele's, Haverstock Hill, 290; Slaughter's, 61, 242; Smyrna, 247, 299, 300, 308; Southampton Coffee House, Southampton Buildings, 135; Squire's, 8; Star and Garter, Pall Mall, 247, 300; Star, Cheapside, 239; Sun-behind-the-Exchange, 239; Sun, Chancery Lane, 233; Sun, King Street, Westminster, 239; Sun, New Fish Street, 239; Swan, Fenchurch Street, 239; Swan, Old Fish Street, 239; Swan, Tottenham, 314–315; Tabard, Southwark, 48; Talbot, Southwark, 48; Thatched House, St. James's Street, 204, 291; Three-Cranes-in-the-Vintry, 176, 237; Three Feathers, Russell Street, Covent Garden, 101; Three Pigeons, Brentford, 177; Three Tuns, Charing Cross, 239; Tom's, Birchin Lane, 44–45; Tom's, Devereux Court, Strand, 10; Tom's, Russell Street, Covent Garden, x, 55, 62, 170, 226, 282; Triumphant Chariot, Hyde Park Corner, 261, 291; Trumpet, Shire Lane, 8, 291; Turk's Head, Gerard Street, Soho, 123, 167; Turk's Head, New Palace Yard, 208, 238; Turk's Head, Strand, 98, 170

INDEX OF PLACES.

245; Upper Flask, Hampstead, 9, 242, 289; Vauxhall, 61; Victoria, Muswell Hill, 221; Walker's Hotel, Queen Street, Soho, 124–125; Waterloo Hotel, Jermyn Street, 263; West Indian, St. Michael's Alley, Cornhill, 245; White Bear, Southwark, 267; White Conduit Tavern, Islington, 126; White Conduit Tea Gardens, Islington, 126; White Hart, High Street Borough, 270; White Horse, Chelsea, 291; White Horse, Kensington, 4; White Horse, Lombard Street, 239; White Rose, Westminster, 47; White Swan, Tottenham, 314–315; Will's, v, x, 7, 95, 113, 170, 175, 189, 234, 243, 282, 291, 299; World's End, Knightsbridge, 239; Wrekin, 118, 154–155.

Tavistock House, Bloomsbury Square, 131.
Tavistock House, Tavistock Square, 84, 217.
Tavistock Row, Covent Garden, 321.
Tavistock Square, 84, 217.
Teddington, 232.
Telegraph Street, Coleman Street, City, 20, 21.
Temple (see Inner Temple, and Middle Temple).
Temple Bar, 7, 8, 17, 67, 169, 172, 173, 175, 208, 236, 238, 272, 300, 313.
Temple Church, 123.
Temple Gardens. 104–105, 121.
Temple Gate, 169, 175.
Temple Place, Blackfriars Row, 141.
Thames Street, 47, 197.
Thatched House Tavern, St. James's Street, 204, 291.
Thayer Street, Manchester Square, 102.
The Club (see Club, The).
Theobalds, Cheshunt, Herts, 317.
Thistle Grove, Fulham Road, Chelsea, 153.
Thomas Street, Southwark, 10.

Threadneedle Street, 130, 185, 200, 222, 223, 235, 276.
Three-Cranes-in-the-Vintry, 176, 237.
Three Cranes Lane, Upper Thames Street, 176.
Three Feathers Inn, Russell Street, Covent Garden, 101.
Three Pigeons Inn, Brentford, 177.
Three Tuns Inn, Charing Cross, 239.
Throgmorton Avenue, 200.
Throgmorton Street, 130, 200.
Thurloe Place, South Kensington, 112.
Tilbury, 76.
Titchfield Street, Soho, 78.
Tokenhouse Yard, Lothbury, 138.
Tom's Coffee House, Birchin Lane, 44–45.
Tom's Coffee House, Devereux Court, Strand, 10.
Tom's Coffee House, Russell Street, Covent Garden, x, 55, 62, 170, 226, 282.
Took's Court, Cursitor Street, Chancery Lane, 274.
Tooley Street, Southwark, 179, 238.
Torquay, 24.
Tothil Fields, Westminster, 283.
Tothill Street, Westminster, 27, 283, 284.
Tottenham, 314–315.
Tottenham Court Road, viii, 318.
Tottenham Court Road Chapel, 318.
Tottenham Cross, 214.
Tower Chapel, 225.
Tower Hill, 225, 231, 232, 285.
Tower of London, 47, 225, 232, 235, 249, 250, 251, 301, 309, 320.
Tower Street, 239.
Trafalgar Bay, 125.
Trafalgar Square, 41, 206, 213, 278.
Trinity College, Cambridge, 70, 91, 172, 195.
Trinity Row (Upper Street), Islington, 87.
Trinity Square, Newington Causeway, 146.
Triumphant Chariot Tavern, Hyde Park Corner, 261, 291.

Trumpet Inn, Shire Lane, 8, 291.
Tufton Street, Westminster, 179.
Tully's Head, Pall Mall, 11, 28, 257, 312.
Tunbridge Wells, 71, 278.
Turk's Head Coffee House, Strand, 98, 170, 245.
Turk's Head Tavern, New Palace Yard, 208, 238.
Turk's Head Tavern, Soho, 123, 167.
Twickenham, 12, 105, 219, 232, 241, 242.
Twickenham Church, 242.
Twickenham Park, 12.
Tyburn, 293.

UNION CLUB, 278.
Union Road, Newington Causeway, 146.
Union Street, Borough, 320.
United Service Club, 207.
University Street, Tottenham Court Road, 79.
Upper Berkeley Street, Portman Square, 194.
Upper Cheyne Row, Chelsea, 146–147, 281.
Upper Flask Tavern, Hampstead, 9, 242, 289.
Upper Grosvenor Street, 89.
Upper Harley Street, Cavendish Square, 248.
Upper Mall, Hammersmith, 227, 308.
Upper Seymour Street, Portman Square, 23, 39.
Upper Street, Islington, 69, 87.
Upper Thames Street, 45, 105, 176, 239, 285.
Upton Road, 154.
Uxbridge House, 112.
Uxbridge Road, 17, 106, 151.

VALE OF HEALTH, Hampstead Heath, 148, 179.
Vauxhall, 61.
Vere Street, Clare Market, 290.
Verulam, 13.
Vesuvius, 24.

Victoria Inn, Muswell Hill, 221.
Victoria Street, Buckingham Palace Road, 37.
Villiers Street, Strand, 12, 81, 101, 290.
Vinegar Yard, Drury Lane, 274.
Vine Street, Westminster, 50.

WALKER'S HOTEL, Queen Street, Soho, 124, 125.
Wallingford House, Whitehall, 66.
Walthamstow, Essex, 89.
Walworth Road, 284.
Wardour Street, Soho, 134, 275.
Wardrobe Place, Doctors' Commons, 265.
Wardrobe Terrace, St. Andrew's Hill, 265.
Warner Street, Clerkenwell, 296.
Warwick Lane, Paternoster Row, 94.
Warwick Street, Charing Cross, 282.
Waterloo Bridge, 46.
Waterloo Hotel, Jermyn Street, 263.
Waterloo Place, Pall Mall, 24, 206, 221, 258, 262, 298.
Water Oakley, 9.
Watier's Club, 34.
Watling Street, City, 45, 210–211.
Welbeck Street, Cavendish Square, 114.
Wellclose Square, Shadwell, 54, 75.
Wellington Barracks, St. James's Park, 115.
Well Road, Hampstead, 180.
Well Walk, Hampstead, 16, 179, 180.
Wells Lane, Sydenham, 30.
Wentworth House, John Street, Hampstead, 180–181, 182.
Wentworth Place, Downshire Hill, Hampstead, 180–181, 182.
Westbourne Grove, 148.
West Horsley, Surrey, 252.
West Indian Tavern, St. Michael's Alley, Cornhill, 245.
West Kensington Road, Hammersmith, 254.
Westminster Abbey, 5, 20, 24, 37, 39, 47, 51, 53, 66, 74, 91, 94, 101, 112, 130, 164–165, 172, 173, 174,

INDEX OF PLACES.

203-204, 214, 227, 229, 259, 264, 274, 285, 286, 288, 315.
Westminster Bridge, 163.
Westminster Hall, 225.
Westminster Hospital, 28.
Westminster School, 50, 51, 61, 62, 64, 65, 66-67, 70, 91, 114, 136, 171, 173, 195, 197, 246, 258, 284, 309.
West Street, Finsbury Circus, 178.
Weymouth Street, Portland Place, 248, 279.
White Bear Inn, Bear Gardens, Southwalk, 267.
White Conduit Tavern, 126.
White Conduit Tea Gardens, 126.
Whitefriars, 275.
Whitehall, v, 41, 101, 112, 207, 213, 233, 236, 244, 246, 299.
Whitehall Gardens, 89.
White Hart Inn, High Street, Borough, 270.
White Horse Inn, Chelsea, 291.
White Horse Inn, Kensington, 4.
White Horse Inn, Lombard Street, 239.
Whitehorse Street, Piccadilly, 262.
White Rose Tavern, Westminster, 47.
White's Club, 54.
White Swan Inn, Tottenham, 314-315.
Whittington Club, 153, 170, 258.
Whitton, 294.
Wigmore Street, Cavendish Square, 220.
Wild Court, Great Wild Street, 111.
Wilderness Lane, 229.
Willis's Rooms, King Street, St. James's Street, 305.
Will's Coffee House, v, x, 7, 95, 113, 170, 175, 189, 237, 243, 282, 291, 299.
Wimbledon, 309, 310.
Wimbledon Common, 206-207, 309.
Wimbledon House, Wimbledon Common, 206.
Wimbledon Park, 206.

Wimpole Street, Cavendish Square, 27, 71, 131, 151.
Winchester Park, Bankside, 266.
Winchester Street, Bankside, 266.
Winchester Yard, Bankside, 266.
Windmill Hill, Hampstead, 14-15.
Windmill Street, Piccadilly, 295.
Wine Office Court, 120, 170.
Woodbridge Street, Clerkenwell, 75, 264, 316.
Woodford, Essex, 278.
Woodstock Street, Oxford Street, 157.
Wood Street, Cheapside, 136, 176, 236, 322.
World's End Tavern, Knightsbridge, 239.
Wormwood Street, Old Broad Street, 235.
Wrekin Tavern, 118, 154-155.
Wych Street, Drury Lane, 222.
Wyndham Place, Bryanston Square, 194.

YARROW, 322.
York Buildings, New Road, 146.
York Buildings, Villiers Street, Strand, 290.
York Chambers, St. James's Street, 37.
York Gate, Buckingham Street, Strand, 12, 230.
York House, 11-12, 290.
York Mews, Fulham Road, 221.
York Place, Marylebone Road, 146.
York Place, Queen's Elms, Brompton, 221.
York Street, Buckingham Gate, 115.
York Street, Covent Garden, 79, 84, 237.
York Street, Westminster, 132-133, 214.
Young Street, Kensington, 303, 305.

ZOAR CHAPEL, Southwark, 25.
Zoar Street, Southwark, 25.
Zutphen, 276.

NOTICES OF THE PRESS.

In "Literary Landmarks of London," Mr. Laurence Hutton has worked out a felicitous idea with industry, skill, and success. For the first time, so far as we are aware, we have within the pages of a moderate-sized volume all that is known or can be discovered of the streets, houses, apartments, chambers, single rooms, and even garrets, in which have resided, at one time or other of their lives, the men and women who were famous in English letters. . . . It is a volume that every one should possess who takes an interest in the local associations which London is so full of, unknown though they be to the vast majority of its inhabitants. With this compendium in one's hand there is hardly a walk that one can take in London in which some fresh feature of interest would not be disclosed for all persons who have any taste for, and knowledge of, literature and letters. — *The Standard, London, June 5, 1887.*

Mr. Hutton's unpretending volume makes no show of learning or originality. . . . The great value of the book is that it sets forth plainly and succinctly what the condition of these historic monuments, these earthly abodes of the immortals, actually is in this year 1885. A century hence the information will be greedily sought after by chroniclers and commentators of all sorts. At the present moment it is well worth having; and Mr. Hutton deserves the gratitude of the public for supplying it. — *The Daily News, London, June 5, 1885.*

In his entertaining work, "Literary Landmarks of London," Mr. Laurence Hutton, who deserves to be remembered as a most accomplished gossip, reminds us that our vast metropolis "has no associations so interesting as those connected with its literary men." Convinced of the truth of this, he has perambulated the town and suburbs with an unwearying enthusiasm worthy of Old Mortality himself, to detect footprints as well as to recover facts and legends before it is actually too late to do such work at all. — *The Baptist, London, June* 19, 1885.

Mr. Hutton has compiled a book which is so obviously what we all constantly want that it seems odd and hard to believe that it has not been forestalled long ago. True, places of literary association are noted incidentally in ordinary handbooks, but this is the first work in which a systematic attempt has been made to trace the residences of literary worthies in London. Mr. Hutton has attained a great measure of completeness in his task, and it would be difficult to name any author of importance he has omitted. . . . Traditional evidence is proverbially bad, yet in many cases Mr. Hutton has had little else to go by. And we can only congratulate him on the moderate and undogmatic manner in which he has stated doubtful conclusions.

There is hardly anything more interesting in its way than to go through the London streets and try to realize their appearance at the time of any particular eminent inhabitant. Sometimes the task is too difficult, as, for example, when we remember that John Bunyan lived for a time and died on Snow Hill, at the house of his friend Mr. Strudwick, the grocer. The house was probably removed when Skinner Street was built in 1802, and Mr. Hutton is no doubt right in supposing that it was directly under the eastern pier of Holborn Viaduct. . . .

The book is admirably arranged, the authors' names being placed in alphabetical order. It commences with Joseph Addison, and ends with Edward Young. Of Young, by the way, there is not much to record. He "had almost no association with London, except in his marriage at the church of St. Mary-at-Hill, in Love Lane, East Cheap, May 27, 1731." It is said that the death of Mrs. Young, nine years later, was the proximate cause of the composition of the famous "Night Thoughts." Mr. Hutton has had many difficulties to contend with. We have noticed the confusion caused by renumbering and renaming. Besides this, in many instances entire streets have been swept away. It is easier to-day, as Mr. Hutton observes, to discover the house of a man who died two hundred years ago, before streets were numbered at all, than to identify the houses of men who have died within a few years. Dryden, for instance, was living in 1686 on the north side of Long Acre, over against Rose Street. The house is easily found; but the house in which Carlyle died has already, most needlessly and stupidly, had its number altered, and is now 24 Great Cheyne Row. It often happens, also, by some strange fatality, that an interesting house has been removed or "restored" out of knowledge, while adjacent old buildings about which no tradition or association lingers are left intact. Thus Drayton's house in Fleet Street, near St. Dunstan's Church, has been altered beyond recognition, while the two houses next door remain as they were in his day. So, too, among a multitude of old-fashioned inns which stand in Edmonton, as they stood long before Lamb and Cowper, the "Bell" which they immortalized has been rebuilt again and again. Among the more absurd changes is that which has befallen the once famous Grub Street. Here, it is said, John Fox, or Foxe, the martyrologist, was living when he published the "Acts and Monuments." "It lies between Fore Street and Chiswell Street, and has now been called Milton Street, in honor of the author who emphatically had no connection or association with the original Grub Street or its literature." The house in which Hood was born in the Poultry has been taken down; and so has No. 7 Little Queen Street, where, in 1796, was enacted the awful tragedy which clouded and saddened the lives of Charles and Mary Lamb. A church is on the site, but Mr. Hutton notices that behind it a tree is still standing in what had once been the back garden. It would be easy to prolong these notes and extracts. To any one who is interested in the history of literature, to any one who is interested in old London, — and the two classes comprise almost all the reading public, — Mr. Hutton's book will be a delightful boon. There are two indexes : the first of persons, in which not only the celebrities noticed but the authors quoted are named; and the second of places. Altogether, this is a book of which literary America may be proud, and literary London ashamed. Mr. Hutton has done for us what we have never done for ourselves. — *The Saturday Review, London, July 4,* 1885.

Mr. Laurence Hutton, a well-known American writer, has done excellent work in "Literary Landmarks of London." With extraordinary patience he has consulted old maps, directories, chronicles, parish surveys, records of estates, to discover the exact houses inhabited in London at various times by literary celebrities. The result is a volume of extraordinary accuracy and deep interest. Never before has anything of the kind approaching this in thoroughness been attempted; and it will long remain the standard work on the subject. — *The Graphic, London, July* 11, 1885.

The author who devises a new and appropriate treatment of an old subject deserves much praise, and to this praise Mr. Hutton is strictly entitled. The many hunters after the haunts of great men must so often have found the need of such a book as this that we cannot but express surprise that the want has not been supplied before the year 1885. That it should now be supplied by an American is most natural, for doubtless our cousins over the water make pilgrimages to shrines that are quite neglected by ourselves.

The plan laid down by the author is admirably carried out, and the main object is distinctly kept in view from beginning to end. There is no attempt to write lives of the persons chronicled, but all the facts connected with the London residences of those authors included in the book are marshalled with care, and the result is a most readable volume.

Mr. Hutton has not been content to gather his materials from the various sources available, but he has taken care to verify the different statements on the spot; and we may here note one very useful feature, which is, that whenever the somewhat vague word "now" is used the actual date is always added in parentheses. The gain to precision here is great. . . . .

As we turn over the pages of this handy volume and follow the alphabet from Addison to Young, we cannot but feel how much our authors have done to throw a charm over the bricks and mortar of our great city. The men who make history are as a rule excluded, but those who keep that history from being forgotten are here in full force. Who shall say that the surroundings of a great town are uncongenial to the poetic spirit, when we remember that our greatest poets — Chaucer, Shakspere, and Milton — spent their busy lives in the streets of London ? Even Wordsworth, who naturally has but few lines devoted to him, expressed in his majestic sonnet his sense of the beauty of the sleeping city as he looked at it from Westminster Bridge. It is strange to find how few of our famous authors have been entirely unconnected with London.

Every page contains several facts, — facts that have to be verified, — and it is great praise to be able to say that these are generally accurate. An index of persons and another of places complete the book. — *The Athenæum, London, July* 18, 1885.

London to the literary man — and especially the literary man who has reached middle age without the conventional surrender of sentiment — is a land of shadows. Hardly a nook of this huge city — "opulent, enlarged, and still increasing" — but is hallowed by some unsubstantial shade, which, like the picture to the Spanish monk, is more real to him than the palpable and demonstrative persons who "scrowdge" and jostle him in its crowded streets. It is Gray picking his way back from Covent Garden with his dearly loved pinks and scarlet Martogon lilies; it is Fielding at tea in the upper room at Bow Street, reading the case of Elizabeth Canning; it is Steele making fun in the circle at Will's over the last utterance of Blackmore; or perhaps it is Lamb rejoicing that he can see both theatres from the windows of his lodgings; or Ben Jonson baptizing his sons in the "Apollo;" or Newton going in his chair to visit the Princess Caroline. It is a hundred and one incidents of the past that seem to be a part of his own past, and to strive for existence with his personal recollections. To those who admit these visionary antecedents, who delight in these appropriated memories, there can be no more delightful companion than the modest volume, "plain in its neatness," to which its writer, Mr. Laurence Hutton, has given the name of "Literary Landmarks of London." It is one of those books of which one may say emphatically that they have been labors of love. The writer — an American well known for his frequent visits to this country — has not only accumulated with exemplary patience all the written information that he could discover about the homes and haunts of London *littérateurs*, but he has visited those haunts and homes himself wherever possible, and makes fit record of their sites or aspect. It is this, perhaps, which gives its greatest value to the book, that, wherever at all practicable, its facts have been verified *de visu*, — an advantage which in these days, when annihilation flourishes under the name of improvement, and the renumbering of streets is fast producing chaos, can scarcely be overestimated. Mr. Hutton's plan has been to trace the various dwellings of his subjects from their cradles to their graves, illustrating each ascertained stage by some apposite quotation, and faithfully giving his authorities. The result is a book which it is delightful either to read through or to glance at for ten minutes, with this advantage, that when it has served its turn of amusement it takes its position on the shelves as a trustworthy book of reference, for which its admirable double index of names and places more than sufficiently equips it. Its author, we gather, intends to follow it by a volume dealing with the dwellings of artists and actors, which do not form part of his present enterprise. We can only say that we trust he will lose no time in giving us this indispensable complement to what he has already done so conscientiously and successfully. — *Notes and Queries, London, July* 18, 1885.

Volumes which at once combine the merits of a work of reference and of a work that affords delightful entertainment by continuous perusal are not common; but Mr. Laurence Hutton has succeeded in producing one of them. His "Literary Landmarks of London" really contains a series of short biographical sketches of almost all the famous men and women of English literature. It is brief and to the point, yet is enriched with many a quaint story and many a pleasing reminiscence. It is a model of industry. The author has done his best to find out every house in London that was ever associated with a literary man, and every literary man that ever made his residence in a London house. Commencing with Addison, and finishing with Young, he goes through the alphabet. It has been no easy task, as his preface tells us. The constant change in London, the pulling down of old houses, the cutting of new thoroughfares, and the renumbering of streets, have necessitated the exercise of great patience in fixing the sites. . . .

These samples of Mr. Hutton's work must suffice. In his volume we come across a London, not of fog and dirt and trade and turmoil, but of great minds and immortal names; a London of learning and poetry, of philosophy and science. Henceforth it ought to be deemed as akin to Athens as it is generally said to be to Babylon. — *The Literary World, London, July 26, 1885.*

Mr. Laurence Hutton's "Literary Landmarks of London" is an attempt to identify the houses in London where famous literary men have lived, or lounged, or worked. This is a much more difficult task than might be expected, because streets have been again and again renamed and renumbered; but Mr. Hutton has been very careful and painstaking, and has succeeded in making his rather novel kind of guide-book surprisingly full and complete. As far as we have tested it, it seems also to be accurate. — *The Contemporary Review, London, August,* 1885.

Mr. Hutton gives the information which he has here collected in alphabetical order, and without much effort to invest it with literary attraction. This, perhaps, is quite right, considering the plan of the book. If the writer had dealt at all fully with either the character or the biography of the hundreds of literary persons whom he mentions, his very reasonable limits would soon have been exceeded. It is much to his credit that he resists the temptation. His object is to give topographical details, when these details connect the subjects of his brief notices with London; and he very wisely does not go beyond this purpose. The work is of limited extent; but it could not be done without a very considerable amount of research, and Mr. Hutton must be allowed the credit of having done it in a complete fashion. An instance of his manner of treatment may be given. He comes in the course of his work to the name of Laurence Sterne. Now, it would have been easy to say a great deal about Sterne, but Mr. Hutton keeps strictly to his subject. "Sterne," he says, "saw but little of London." In 1760 he lodged in Pall Mall for about three months. He occupied in subsequent seasons various lodgings which cannot be identified. In 1768 he died at 41 Old Bond Street, "over the silk-bag shop." Whether the house now thus numbered is the real No. 41 seems doubtful. He was buried in "the new burying-ground in Tyburn," from which, it is said, his body was stolen and sold to the professor of anatomy at Cambridge, in whose dissecting-room it was recognized by a friend. Would it not be well, by the way, to throw this disused burial-ground open? — *The Spectator, London, Aug. 1, 1885.*

It would be difficult to praise Mr. Hutton too highly for the spirit in which he has conceived his design, and for the thoroughness with which he has carried it out. Not content with collecting the occasional references of his predecessors, he has cheerfully undertaken the double drudgery of verifying their statements (wherever possible), by means of contemporary documents, and by tracing the succession of bricks and mortar down to the year 1885. He has thus written not only for the present but also for the future. . . . Our children will therefore be grateful to Mr. Hutton for commemorating in each case the result of his own inspection of every historic house, its condition, and its present name and number. And we ourselves thank him for having incalculably augmented the value of his book for use by two exhaustive indexes, — tho one of names, the other of places. — *The Academy, London, Aug. 8, 1885.*

www.ingramcontent.com/pod-product-compliance
Lightning Source LLC
Chambersburg PA
CBHW030400230426
43664CB00007BB/676